ALSO BY HAROLD SCHECHTER

NONFICTION

The A to Z Encyclopedia of Serial Killers (with David Everitt)

Bestial: The Savage Trail of a True American Monster

Depraved: The Shocking True Story of America's First Serial Killer

Deranged: The Shocking True Story of America's Most Fiendish Killer

Deviant: The Shocking True Story of Ed Gein, the Original "Psycho"

Fatal: The Poisonous Life of a Female Serial Killer

Fiend: The Shocking True Story of America's Youngest Serial Killer

Savage Pastimes: A Cultural History of Violent Entertainment

*The Serial Killer Files: The Who, What, Where, How, and Why
of the World's Most Terrifying Murderers*

The Whole Death Catalog: A Lively Guide to the Bitter End

NARRATIVE NONFICTION

Killer Colt: Murder, Disgrace, and the Making of an American Legend

*The Devil's Gentleman: Privilege, Poison, and the Trial That
Ushered in the Twentieth Century*

FICTION

Nevermore

Outcry

The Hum Bug

The Mask of Red Death

The Tell-Tale Corpse

PSYCHO USA

PSYCHO
USA

FAMOUS AMERICAN KILLERS
YOU NEVER HEARD OF

Harold
Schechter

BALLANTINE BOOKS TRADE PAPERBACKS
NEW YORK

A Ballantine Books Trade Paperback Original

Copyright © 2012 by Harold Schechter

Published in the United States by Ballantine Books,
an imprint of The Random House Publishing Group,
a division of Random House, Inc., New York.

Library of Congress Cataloging-in-Publication Data
Schechter, Harold.
Psycho USA : famous american killers you never heard of / Harold Schechter.
p. cm.
Includes bibliographical references and index.
ISBN 978-0-345-52447-8 (pb. : alk. paper)—ISBN 978-0-345-52448-5 (ebook : alk. paper)
1. Murderers—United States—Biography. 2. Murder—United States—Case Studies. I. Title.
HV6785.S345 2012
364.152'3092273—dc23   2012004990

Printed in the United States of America

www.ballantinebooks.com

2 4 6 8 9 7 5 3 1

Book design by Susan Turner

In memory of David Everitt

CONTENTS

III
POST—CIVIL WAR MONSTERS
1866–1880

IV
TURN-OF-THE-CENTURY PSYCHOS
1892–1896

PSYCHO USA

INTRODUCTION

DURING THE LATE SUMMER AND EARLY FALL OF 2010—WHILE THIS BOOK WAS still in progress—the country was riveted by the trial of Steven J. Hayes, accused of one of the most monstrous crimes in recent memory. Three years earlier, on the night of July 23, 2007, Hayes and an accomplice, Joshua Komisarjevsky—a pair of small-time hoodlums who had bonded at a halfway house for parolees—invaded the home of Dr. William A. Petit in the bucolic community of Cheshire, Connecticut. After savagely beating and binding the fifty-year-old endocrinologist, they proceeded to terrorize and torture his family, raping his wife, Jennifer Hawke-Petit, and at least one of the couple's two daughters. In the morning, they forced Hawke-Petit to go to the local bank and withdraw $15,000, after which they brought her back home, strangled her to death, doused the children—Hayley, seventeen, and Michaela, eleven—with gasoline and set the house on fire. Only Dr. Petit managed to survive.

The horror visited upon the Petit family was so appalling that even passionate opponents of the death penalty were willing to make an exception in this case. Indeed, among the mild-mannered citizenry of Cheshire, there were many who felt that lethal injection was far too mild a punishment for the perpetrators of such an atrocity. Hayes and Komisarjevsky were the objects of universal detestation, their names synonymous with incomprehensible evil.

Yet for all the attention the case received, including major coverage on network TV news, if you were to mention those names today, few people would be able to identify them. In contrast to, say, the Fall River murders of 1892 or the double slaying of Nicole Brown Simpson and Ron Goldman a century later, the Cheshire tragedy seems unlikely to become one of those landmark crimes that exert a strange, enduring grip on the communal imagination.

As a student of American serial murder, I've often wondered why certain psychopaths have achieved near-mythic status, while other once-notorious killers, guilty of equally heinous crimes, have been completely forgotten. There's a centuries-old phrase, dating at least as far back as Shakespeare's time, for something that generates widespread, often frenzied interest for a few fleeting days and then fades into total oblivion: a nine-day wonder. Our voracious celebrity culture is full of these diversions: a homeless man with the golden voice of a radio announcer, for example, who achieves dizzying TV stardom for a week before subsiding again into obscurity, or a chorus line of bridesmaids and their escorts whose dancing entrance down the wedding aisle makes them a momentary media sensation. Enormities such as the slaughter of the Petit family, which transfix the nation for a little while and then vanish from memory, seem like the nightmarish equivalent of such phenomena: nine-day horrors, as it were.

To the public, the press, and even the perpetrators themselves, these sensationally shocking homicides often seem, at the time of their commission, to be crimes of historic proportion. Immediately after the 1866 execution of Martha Grinder, one of the most notorious serial murderers of her day, the *Chicago Tribune* proclaimed that the world "will never forget or cease to shudder at her monstrous deeds"—a prediction that has proved to be completely mistaken. Her contemporary Lydia Sherman, an even more prolific serial poisoner, was so infamous in her lifetime that children sang ditties about her: "Lydia Sherman is plagued with rats / Lydia has no faith in cats / So Lydia buys some arsenic / And then her husband gets sick / And then her husband he does die / And Lydia's neighbors wonder why." Today—when people can still recite the nursery rhyme about Lizzie Borden's forty whacks—Sherman is remembered, if at all, only by the most devoted students of American crime.

In his own time, the psychopathic scholar Edward Ruloff was enough of a criminal celebrity to attract the fascinated interest of Mark Twain, who described him in print as "one of the most marvelous intellects of this or any other age." Lizzie Halliday, another late nineteenth-century psycho killer, was not only compared to Jack the Ripper; some people believed that she actually *was* Jack the Ripper. The Gilded Age sociopath Harry Hayward—trumpeted in the press as "the most depraved, the most cold-blooded murderer ever to walk" the earth—achieved such notoriety that early marketers of Edison's phonograph rushed out a wax-cylinder recording of his confession to feed the morbid appetites of the public.

Hayward, who fancied himself the "Napoleon of crime," believed that his name would go down in the annals of infamy alongside those of Dr. H. H. Holmes and the San Francisco sex killer Theo Durrant (aka "The Demon of the Belfry"). Other once-notorious American psychos shared the same grandiose conviction. William Edward Hickman, guilty of one of the most grisly child abductions in American history, believed that he would become as famous as Leopold and Loeb—a reasonable expectation, given the widespread shock and horror provoked by his enormity. Apart from hard-core true crime aficionados, however, no one remembers his name today, while the two Jazz Age "thrill killers" continue to be the subjects of movies, plays, and bestselling books.

Hickman's case reveals an interesting point. While inordinately gruesome or macabre crimes might appeal to a primal human need for morbid excitement, they are not necessarily the ones that exert the deepest fascination on the public. The crimes that come to define an era tend to be those that reflect its most pressing anxieties. To grown-ups of the 1920s, for example, the pampered, joyriding, college-age hedonists Leopold and Loeb were the living embodiments of the out-of-control "Flaming Youth" of the period—just as, forty years later, Charles Manson and his depraved followers seemed like the realization of every parent's worst nightmares about sex- and drug-crazed hippies.

Conversely, there are sensational crimes that quickly fade from the front pages because they don't speak to prevailing societal fears. If a domestic terrorist blew up a schoolhouse full of children today, then killed himself and a bunch of onlookers by detonating a car bomb, the atrocity would certainly be remembered as one of the most infamous of our age, certainly on a par with, say, the Columbine massacre. In 1927, however, when Americans didn't live with the pervasive dread of terrorism, that very crime—committed by a madman named Andrew Kehoe—disappeared from the public consciousness in a shockingly short time.

That our nation experienced a horrendous act of terrorist mass murder just days before Charles Lindbergh's epochal flight will, no doubt, come as a great surprise to most readers of this book—as it did to me when I first learned about the Kehoe case. Indeed, in researching and writing this book, I was amazed at the number of once-famous homicides I was only dimly aware of, or had never heard about at all—crimes that once held the whole country rapt with horror, committed by some of the most atrocious killers in the annals of American murder.

There was Peter Robinson, perpetrator of a murder so appalling that it inspired Edgar Allan Poe's "The Tell-Tale Heart." Anton Probst, whose systematic slaughter of all eight members of a Pennsylvania farm family matched the savagery of the Manson murders a century later. Franklin Evans, a nineteenth-century sex killer whose hideous assaults on children foreshadowed the atrocities of the 1930s pedophiliac monster Albert Fish. Charles Freeman, the Cape Cod fanatic, driven to slaughter his own child in a deranged act of religious sacrifice. Elsie Whipple and Jesse Strang, the 1820s counterparts of Ruth Snyder and Judd Gray, the infamous "Double Indemnity" killers of the Roaring Twenties. Harry Powers, the Depression-era Bluebeard who kept his victims in a torture bunker on his West Virginian "murder farm" and whose crimes inspired the cinematic classic *The Night of the Hunter*.

Readers will meet them all and many others in the pages of *Psycho USA*, which presents their cases in chronological order. Insofar as their dreadful deeds have become shrouded in obscurity, this book, which delves into the darkness of the forgotten past, can be considered a shadow history of American crime.

I

FIENDS OF
THE EARLY
REPUBLIC

1782–1826

WILLIAM BEADLE, FAMILY ANNIHILATOR

THE DIFFERENT ERAS IN OUR NATION'S SOCIAL HISTORY HAVE BEEN DISTINGUISHED not only by their specific fads and fashions—the kinds of clothes people wore, food they ate, music they listened to, slang they spoke, and so on— but also by the particular criminal types that captured the public imagination: the tommy-gun-toting gangsters of the 1920s, the switchblade-wielding juvenile delinquents of the 1950s, the sex-crazed psycho killers of the 1970s, and—in our own post-9/11 age—the suicidal mass murderers, whether school and workplace shooters or apocalyptic terrorists.

During the early years of the Republic, for reasons that historians and sociologists have been at pains to understand, America was gripped by fears of a new kind of killer: the so-called family annihilator, the formerly loving father and husband who, in a sudden fit of homicidal frenzy, hideously slaughtered his children and wife. And of these nightmarish figures, perhaps the most infamous was William Beadle, perpetrator of what one contemporary described as "a crime more atrocious and horrible" than any ever committed in New England "and scarcely exceeded in the history of man."

*　*　*

BORN IN ENGLAND in 1730, Beadle emigrated to America at the age of thirty-two and eventually settled in the village of Wethersfield, Connecticut, where he operated a country store stocked with an unusually "handsome assortment of goods." Surviving documents show him to have been possessed by the sort of overweening egotism typical of family annihilators. Though acknowledging his unprepossessing looks, he regarded himself as far superior to the run of humanity. "My person is small and mean to look on," he wrote in one journal entry, "and my circumstances were always rather narrow, which were great disadvantages in the world. But I have great reason to think that my soul is above the common mould." In his self-conceit, he likened himself to "a diamond among millions of pebbles."

For several years his business thrived. Fiercely proud of his success, he maintained a handsome residence and entertained guests in grand style. He was held in high esteem by his neighbors, who saw him as an honorable tradesman, generous host, loving husband, and doting father.

In the aftermath of the Revolutionary War, however, Beadle suffered reversals that left him in dire financial straits. Unable to "bear the mortification of being thought poor and dependent," he struggled to keep "up the outward appearance of his former affluence." Eventually, however, he succumbed to despair. The thought of being perceived as a failure by his townsmen was more than he could tolerate. "If a man, who has once lived well, meant well, and done well, falls by unavoidable accident into poverty and submits to be laughed at, despised, and trampled on by a set of mean wretches as far below him as the moon is below the sun; I say, if such a man submits, he must become meaner than meanness itself."

Concluding that suicide was less shameful than poverty, he decided to kill himself and his family. Like other killers of his psychopathic breed, he justified his intended atrocity as an act of kindness, even love. "I mean to close the eyes of six persons through perfect humanity and the most endearing fondness and friendship; for mortal father never felt more of these tender ties than myself." Initially, he thought he might spare his wife. After much deliberation, however, he concluded that it would be cruel "to leave her behind to languish out a life in misery and wretchedness." With her entire family suddenly gone, death would be a mercy for her.

As he began to mull over his plan, he "kept hoping that Providence would turn up something to prevent it, if the intent were wrong." Instead, "every circumstance, from the greatest to the smallest trifle," only served to convince him that destroying his family was the only sensible course. For a while, he prayed that his twelve-year-old son and three little daughters might perish accidentally, thus sparing him the necessity of killing them. To facilitate that end, he removed the protective wooden cover from the backyard well. He also encouraged them to swim in the deepest and most treacherous parts of the nearby river. When the children stubbornly survived these perils, he resolved to take more direct action.

Though uncertain at first as to when and how he would accomplish his "great affair" (as he described the intended massacre), he had no doubt that he would not quail when the time came. "How I shall really perform the task I have undertaken I know not till the moment arrives," he wrote in his journal. "But I believe I shall perform it as deliberately and as steadily as I would go to supper, or to bed."

He eventually fixed on the eighteenth of November for the execution of his plan. He first "procured a noble supper of oysters, that my family and I may eat and drink together, thank God, and then die." He was forced to abandon his plan, however, when the maid—who had been sent off on an errand—returned unexpectedly and "prevented him for that time."

A few weeks later, he made another aborted attempt that he described in his journal:

> On the morning of the sixth of December, I rose before the sun, felt calm, and left my wife between sleep and wake, went into the room where my infants lay, found them all sound asleep; the means of death were with me, but I had not before determined whether to strike or not, but yet thought it a good opportunity. I stood over them, and asked my God whether it was right or not now to strike; but no answer came: nor I believe ever does to man while on earth. I then examined myself, there was neither fear, trembling, nor horror about me. I then went into a chamber next to that to look at myself in the glass; but I could discover no alteration in my countenanced of feelings: this is true as God reigns, but for further trial I yet postponed it.

Five days later, in the early morning hours of December 11, 1782, Beadle finally carried out his atrocity. Tiptoeing into the second-floor bedchamber shared by his four children and the housemaid, he shook the latter awake, then "ordered her to rise gently without disturbing the children" and meet him downstairs. When she appeared several minutes later, he handed her a note for the family physician, Dr. Farnsworth, who lived about a quarter-mile away. His wife, Beadle explained, had been "ill all night." The housemaid was to proceed to Farnsworth's home at once, give him the note, and remain there until he "should come with her."

No sooner had she left on this errand than Beadle hurried into his bedroom, where he had stashed a newly sharpened axe and carving knife. After crushing his sleeping wife's skull with the axe, he slit her throat with the knife, taking care to drain the blood into a vessel so as not to stain the bedsheets. After covering her face with a handkerchief, he proceeded to the children's room, where he committed the same butchery upon them. He left the little boy lying in bed. The slaughtered girls were placed side by side on the floor, "like three lambs," and covered with a blanket.

Leaving a trail of bloody footprints on the stairs, Beadle then descended to the kitchen, placed the axe and knife—"reeking with the blood of his family"—on a table, and seated himself in a Windsor chair by the fireplace. Several weeks earlier, in preparation for this moment, he had brought his two flintlock pistols to the village gunsmith for repair. He now took a pistol in each hand and, supporting his elbows on the arms of the chair, pressed the muzzles against his ears and pulled both triggers simultaneously, "splattering his brains against the walls and wainscoting."

By then, Dr. Farnsworth had been roused from his bed by the maid and handed the note, which "announced the diabolical purpose of the writer." Though Farnsworth "thought it impossible that a sober man could adopt so horrible a design," he immediately alerted his neighbor, the Hon. Stephen Mix Mitchell, later chief justice of the state. The two men then rushed to the Beadles' house, where they were greeted by the "tragical scene."

Before long, news of the atrocity had spread throughout the village. "Multitudes of all ages and sexes" overran the house for a firsthand look at the carnage. The scene was described by Judge Mitchell, whose narrative account of the "horrid massacre" became one of the best-selling true crime pamphlets of its day:

> The very inmost souls of the beholders were wounded at the sight and torn by contending passions. Silent grief, with marks of astonishment, were succeeded by furious indignation against the author of the affecting spectacle, which vented itself in incoherent exclamations. Some old sol-

diers, accidentally passing through the town that morning on their way from camp to visit their friends, led by curiosity, turned in to view the sad remains. On sight of the woman and her tender offspring, notwithstanding all their firmness, the tender sympathetic tear stealing gently down their furrowed cheeks betrayed the anguish of their hearts. On being showed the body of the sacrificer, they paused for a moment, then muttering forth an oath or two of execration, with their eyes fixed on the ground in silent sorrow, they slowly went their way. So awful and terrible a disaster wrought wonderfully on the minds of the neighborhood. Nature itself seemed ruffled and refused the kindly aid of balmly sleep for a time.

"Frantic with indignation and horror at a crime so unnatural and monstrous," the inhabitants of Wethersfield refused to allow its perpetrator a Christian burial. Tying the bloody carving knife to his breast, they dragged him on a small sled to the riverbank, dug a grave in the unconsecrated ground, and tossed his uncoffined body into the hole "like the carcass of a beast." A few days later, after deciding that the site was too close to the ferry landing, "sundry persons" dug up the corpse and transferred it "with utmost secrecy" to an "obscure spot." Despite this precaution, "some children accidentally discovered the place." The body was exhumed again and removed to yet another place "where it is hoped mankind will have no further vexation with it."

In stark contrast to the contemptuous treatment of Beadle's corpse, his victims' funeral was a ceremonious affair. "The remains of the children were borne by a suitable number of equal age, attended with a sad procession of youths of the town, all bathed in tears," wrote one observer. "Side by side the hapless woman's corpse was carried in solemn procession to the parish churchyard, followed by a great concourse who, with affectionate concern and every token of respect, were anxious to express their heartfelt sorrow in performing the last mournful duties."

Though subjected to an ignominious burial, William Beadle was granted a kind of immortality in the form of a widely circulated broadside ballad, illustrated with a woodcut showing a knife-wielding Beadle attacking his children:

> A bloody scene I'll now relate,
> Which lately happen'd in a neighboring state

A murder of the deepest dye, I say,
O be amaz'd for surely well you may.
A man (unworthy of the name) who slew
Himself, his consort, and his offspring, too;
An amiable wife with four children dear,
Into one grave was put—Oh drop a tear!

Soon in the morning of the fatal day,
Beadle, the murd'rer sent his maid away,
To tell the awful deed he had in view;
To their assistance the kind neighbors flew.

It truly gives me pain for to pen down,
A deed so black, and yet his mind was sound.
Says he, "I mean to close six persons' eyes,
Through perfect fondness and the tend'rest ties."

Detest the errors to this deed him drew,
And mourn the hapless victims whom he slew;
And pray to God that Satan may be bound,
Since to deceive so many he is found.

Fly swiftly round, ye circling years,
Hail the auspicious day,
When love shall dwell in every heart—
Nor men their offspring slay!

[*Sources:* S. M. Mitchell, *A Narrative of the Life of William Beadle*
(Greenfield, CT, 1805); John Marsh, *The Great Sin and Danger of
Striving with God. A Sermon Preached at Wethersfield, December
13th, 1782. At the Funeral of Mrs. Lydia Beadle, Wife of the Late
William Beadle, and Their Four Children, Who Were All Murdered
by His Own Hands on the Morning of the 11th Instant* (Middlebor-
ough, MA: N. Coverly, 1783).]

Domestic Slaughter Then And Now

"Something strange and horrible happened in a number of American households of the early republic," writes scholar Daniel Cohen in a groundbreaking study of family annihilators such as William Beadle. "In a series of curiously clustered incidents, a handful of men, loving husbands and affectionate fathers, took axes from under their beds, or off their mantelpiece, and slaughtered their wife and children."

To be sure, though the public was transfixed by reports of these atrocities, the crimes themselves were actually quite rare during the first quarter century of our nation's existence. Cohen himself cites just five instances of familicide—"the slaughter of an entire family by its patriarchal head"—between 1781 and 1806. Uxoricide—the murder of a wife by her husband—was only slightly more common. According to recent research by historian Randolph Roth, "In all of New England, only about 35 spouses . . . were murdered before 1800."

For complex social and cultural reasons, the situation began to change in the early decades of the nineteenth century, when "the rate of wife murder increased fivefold" throughout the north. At the same time (as crime historian Karen Halttunen shows in her classic book *Murder Most Foul*), printed accounts of familicide began to appear with increasing frequency, offering detailed descriptions of domestic butchery that sometimes bordered on the pornographic. Moralists who believe that today's popular culture is unusually graphic in its depiction of violence might consider this passage from an 1857 crime pamphlet called *The Triple Murderer,* recounting the enormities of a midwestern family annihilator named Reuben Ward. After killing his wife Olive, Ward proceeded to dispose of the corpse in the most grisly way imaginable:

> *I tore the clothes open from the throat down. I then took a small pocket knife and opened the body, took the bowels out first, and then put them in the stove upon the wood; they being filled with air would make a noise in exploding, so I took my knife and pricked holes through them to prevent the noise; then took out the liver and heart . . . I then took out the blood remaining in the cavity of the body by placing a copper kettle close to the same and cupping it out with my hands . . . I broke off the ribs and took out the breast bone, and threw it into a large boiler; unjointed the arms at the shoulders, doubled them up and placed them in the boiler; then severed the remaining portions of the body by placing a stick of wood under her back and breaking the back bone over the same, cutting away the flesh and ligaments with a knife.*

According to Roth, men who committed family homicide during this period were generally driven by the same intolerable sense of mortification that had overwhelmed William Beadle: "the feeling that they had failed in society's eyes." As Roth explains, circumstances in the early to mid-1800s placed increasingly high expectations on married men:

Having a house was no longer enough: it had to be a nice house. Having a job was no longer enough: a man had to have a career that followed an upward trajectory. Husbands were also expected to be more than just good providers; they had to be sober, amiable, and respectable. . . . When men could not meet society's expectations or fulfill their own hopes in what was, after all, the land of opportunity, they often turned on their wives, who were a persistent reminder of failure.

For a growing number of husbands, this societal pressure "to be sober, industrious, and successful only intensified their sense of themselves as failures" and bred an unbearable shame that climaxed in the destruction of their families and—more often than not—themselves.

The latest research into familicide confirms that modern-day perpetrators fit the same psychological profile as their early American counterparts. In his landmark study, *Familicidal Hearts: The Emotional Styles of 211 Killers,* criminologist Neil Websdale demonstrates that today's "typical family killer is a man who, in his own eyes, is, or is about to become, a failure" and that "the presence of intense shame," brought about by "social and economic pressures," is "the single most important and consistent theme among familicide cases."

Professor Jack Levin of Northeastern University, one of the country's leading experts on mass murder, offers a similar view, describing the typical familicide as "a middle-aged man, a good provider who would appear to neighbors to be a dedicated husband and a devoted father. He will have suffered some prolonged frustration and feelings of inadequacy, but then suffers some catastrophic loss. It is usually financial. . . . He doesn't hate his children but he often hates his wife and blames her for his miserable life. He feels an overwhelming sense of his own powerlessness."

Typical of this breed was forty-eight-year-old businessman Russell Gilman of Scottsdale, Arizona, a seemingly solid citizen and family man who suffered devastating financial reversals when his marketing company went bankrupt. In the first week of August 2009, Gilman sat down at his dining room table and calmly wrote a note, explaining that "the money is gone, the bills keep coming, and the job I was offered fell through. There is no other solution but the one you find today." He then methodically shot his forty-five-year-old wife, Stacey, and their two sons, Trevor and Liam, ages seven and three, before turning the 9-millimeter handgun on himself.

[*Sources:* Daniel Cohen, "Homicidal Compulsion and the Condition of Freedom: The Social and Psychological Origins of Familicide in America's Early Republic," *Journal of Social History* (Summer 1995); Karen Halttunen, *Murder Most Foul: The Killer and the American Gothic Imagination* (Cambridge, MA: Harvard University Press, 1998); Randolph Roth, *American Homicide* (Cambridge, MA: Harvard University Press/Belknap, 2009); Neil Websdale, *Familicidal Hearts: The Emotional Styles of 211 Killers* (New York: Oxford University Press, 2010.]

SAMUEL GREEN:
PRODIGY OF CRIME

NEAR THE START OF CALEB CARR'S 1994 BESTSELLER *THE ALIENIST*, THE NARrator, John Moore—a reporter for the *New York Times*—visits the residence of the book's titular hero, a psychologist named Laszlo Kreizler. A kind of nineteenth-century criminal profiler, the enlightened Kreizler holds to the theory, scandalous for its time, that psychopathic killers (as we'd now call them) are the product of severely abusive upbringings.

Finding Kreizler absorbed in some writing, Moore passes the time by perusing a book:

> Waiting for him to look up, I approached a small bookshelf near the secretary and took down one of my favorite volumes: *The Career and Death of the Mad Thief and Murderer, Samuel Green.* The case, dating from 1822, was one that Laszlo often cited to the parents of his "students," for the infamous Green had been, in Kreizler's words, "a product of the whip"— beaten throughout his childhood—and at the time of his capture had openly acknowledged that his crimes against society were a form of revenge. My own attraction to the book was prompted by its frontispiece, which depicted "The Madman Green's End" on a Boston gallows. I always enjoyed Green's crazed stare in the picture. . . .

Carr, exercising the prerogative of a novelist, invents the name of Moore's "favorite volume"; no book with that title is known to exist. Its subject, however, is no fiction. Indeed, Samuel Green, though long forgotten, was one of the most infamous American criminals of his time. His appalling career confirms the belief that today's forensic psychiatrists share with Carr's fictitious "alienist": that, almost without exception, psychopathic killers are subjected to extreme and unrelenting cruelty as children.

IN HIS OWN time, when New England was still permeated by the grim spirit of Puritanism, Green's lawless behavior was set down to "innate depravity." Despite the best efforts of his "poor, honest parents" to "give him some education," Green—born in Stafford County, New Hampshire, in 1797—was trouble from the start. "From his earliest childhood," writes one nineteenth-century chronicler, "mischief was his whole study."

It is clear from this account, however, that, in seeking to curb the boy's unruly conduct, Green's parents, along with other adult caretakers in his life, took the old adage "Spare the rod and spoil the child" to extremes. He was whipped for playing hooky and whipped for misbehaving at school. Apprenticed at eight years old to a blacksmith, he committed a petty theft, "for which he received a sound flagellation."

He was later sent back to school, "but usually played the truant and was as constantly whipped." On one occasion, he skipped school and went to the general store, where he shoplifted a mouth harp. "Returning home, his master whipped him for running away, and on the morrow discovered the theft; for which he whipped the boy again and sent him to restore his booty, with a promise that unless he returned in due time, he should be flogged once more. Green again transgressed, and his master kept his word." The boy escaped "back home to his parents, who made him taste of the rod afresh and sent him back to his master, who applied the whip to his back once more."

Nowadays, we have come to understand that brutalizing a child is a surefire way to turn him or her into a sociopath. If a person is hideously maltreated from the earliest years, it is almost guaranteed that he or she will grow up with a malignant view of existence. To such a person, the world is a hateful place where all human relationships are based not on love and respect but on power and domination. Having been tortured by his primary caretakers, he will, in later life, seek to inflict torture on others, partly as a way of taking revenge—of making other people suffer the way he has suffered—and partly because he has been so psychologically warped by his experiences that he can feel pleasure only by inflicting pain.

Some inkling of this truth appears to have entered the minds of Green's contemporaries. "Perhaps, had mild measures been taken," writes James Faxon, his first biographer, "reform might have been the result; but the scourge confirmed him in obstinacy and awakened a spirit of revenge in his bosom." Even Faxon, however, concludes that the real problem was not the draconian discipline to which the boy was subjected but his own inborn character, his "stubborn and ugly disposition."

Unsurprisingly, after years of relentless punishment and humiliation, young Green began displaying the symptomatic behavior of budding serial killers: juvenile sadism and precocious pyromania. On one occasion, he "drowned a dog in the family well." On another, he "stabbed a swine." He also tried to burn down his master's house, "but the fire was discovered in time and the dwelling was saved." For each of these acts, young Green was horsewhipped to within an inch of his life.

His already vicious behavior took its inevitable turn toward the homicidal when, in a fit of vengeful fury, he attempted to murder his master. The latter, we are told, "had a workshop, the door of which opened outward. Against this, the young desperado laid a heavy stick of timber on the inside, and on the top a broad axe, in the hopes that when his master opened the door, they would fall upon and destroy him." As a backup, Green also "prepared the barn door in the same fashion, poising a pitchfork on the top, with the points downward."

By good luck, Green's intended victim escaped both of these booby traps alive, if not entirely unscathed. "The fall of the timber bruised his shoulder," Faxon informs us, "and at the barn the pitchfork wounded his foot." Neither injury proved sufficiently disabling to prevent Green's master from administering a savage flogging to his young would-be murderer.

HAVING NARROWLY AVOIDED death at the hands of his incorrigible apprentice, Green's master lost no time in ridding himself of the boy, who returned to the home of his now aged parents. Before long, Green fell in with a local crook who became his mentor in vice, "showing him how to break open shops and window shutters." The older man "also gave him counterfeit money to pass, promising him half the profits." The wily Green proved an apt pupil, quickly disposing of forty-seven counterfeit dollars and—with the aid of a fellow delinquent named Ash—burglarizing a neighborhood shop of "merchandise to the value of an hundred dollars."

From the scant historical record, it's difficult to determine exactly how old Green was at this time. Evidence suggests, however, that—though already embarked on a career as a professional thief—he was still a preadolescent.

Along with their new criminal pursuits, Green and his accomplice, Ash, found plenty of time to perpetrate various acts of juvenile mayhem. On one occasion, while attempting to steal a rowboat, they were set upon by the owner, who "succeeded in laying his hands upon Ash." Snatching up a large rock, Green struck the boat's owner on the head, then broke his arm with the stone "as he lay on the ground."

Some months afterward, when winter had set in, the two young reprobates came upon a group of children sledding down a hill "with great velocity" and threw a piece of timber under its runners, causing it to crash. "One boy had his arm and another his thigh broken," reports Faxon. When the children's schoolmaster, "a large man," learned of the deed, he tracked down the perpetrators and "beat them severely." In retaliation, Green and Ash armed themselves with clubs and waylaid the teacher as he made his way home one evening. After "felling him to the earth," they "bound him, beat him, stripped him naked, and tore his clothes to pieces before his face. It was a very cold night but, notwithstanding, they left him thus with his hands tied behind his back." Ash—described by Faxon as even more vicious than Green—wanted to slice off the man's nose but, in a rare moment of compunction, "Green would not consent."

Having roused the fury of the law with their savage attack on the schoolmaster, the two hooligans fled town and took to the road. With their pockets full of "bad money," they caroused through the New England countryside, bankrolling their debaucheries with the counterfeit bills, supplemented with the proceeds from countless burglaries and armed robberies. When Green wasn't cheating at cards, drinking himself into a stupor, consorting with "abandoned women," or breaking into houses to steal silverware and jewelry, he was busily seducing young girls, including one "daughter of a poor widow" he ruined after arranging to rendezvous with her at church. "Thus," intones Faxon, "even in the temple of the Almighty, his depravity was proved."

His sole redeeming feature was a small soft spot he harbored in his heart for his mother. After one particularly successful burglary—a break-in at a "wholesale store" that netted him enough money to treat himself to a fancy new set of clothes along with a "fine horse"—he displayed his filial devotion in the single act of generosity he is known to have performed. During a brief visit home to his mother, reports Faxon, "he gave her a cow."

Though "chiefly a burglar," Green found ample opportunity to indulge his appetite for sociopathic violence. On one occasion, when a tavernkeeper caught Green and Ash trying to pass a bad five-dollar bill at his establishment and threatened to alert the authorities, they overpowered the man and attempted to throw him alive into the roaring fireplace. Only the timely "interference of his wife and servant maid," who heard the commotion and raised the alarm, saved the man's life. Not long afterward, the pair waylaid and robbed a traveling peddler, then—acting on Ash's philosophy that "a dead cock never crows"—beat the man to death, "tied some large stones to the corpse and sunk it in a pond."

Over the next few years—sometimes assisted by Ash but more often operating on his own—Green terrorized the Northeast, becoming in the process what crime historian Jay Robert Nash calls "America's first Public Enemy Number One":

> He was arrested and jailed several times on suspicion, but evidence was lacking to indict him and he was routinely released. After looting a jewelry store in Montreal, Canada, Green was pursued by a posse. He fought his way out of a trap, shooting several men, but he was later apprehended and jailed. He was tried, convicted and sentenced to death, but his friend Ash helped him to escape. Returning to the remote mountains of New Hampshire, Green hid for some months. He then went on another crime spree, burglarizing stores and homes in Albany, New York and New York City. In Middlebury, Vermont, he robbed and shot to death a French traveler. By this time, nothing was beyond the ambitions of Samuel Green. He left a trail of burglary, rape, horse-stealing, counterfeiting, and murder from Montpelier, Vermont to Schenectady, New York; from Saco, Maine to Barre, Vermont. Half the country was looking for him; the bounties to be paid for his capture were enormous.

Exactly how many homicides Green committed during this period is unclear, though certainly enough to qualify him as one of our country's earliest serial killers.

There was one especially savage killing still to come. It would prove to be Green's last.

WHILE PASSING THROUGH the town of Danvers, Massachusetts—the site, a century earlier, of New England's infamous witch hysteria—Green got drunk, broke into a general store, and stole $30 in cash, along with "goods of all description." Pursued by a posse, he was apprehended soon afterward, promptly tried, and sentenced to thirty days in solitary confinement in the state prison followed by four years of hard labor. Like all new inmates, Green was scrubbed, shaved bald, and clothed in coarse prison garb upon admission. He was then tossed into a dark, cramped cell furnished with a narrow cot, two threadbare blankets, and a bucket. Three times a day, attendants came around to feed him his meals of bread and water.

Emerging after thirty days, he was put to work breaking rocks in the prison yard. Before long, he made a failed escape attempt. For his trouble, he was outfitted with a heavy wooden clog shackled to his leg—a crude precursor of the ball and chain. He was forced to wear this torturous appurtenance for nine months. Several years were also added to his sentence.

Three years later, Green and several cohorts plotted to break out of jail. Their plan was foiled, however, when another prisoner, an African American named Billy Williams, got wind of it and informed the keeper. Vowing revenge, Green cornered Williams in a prison workshop and attacked him with an iron bar, shattering his arms, legs, and rib cage and breaking open his skull. Somehow, Williams managed to cling to life for a week.

At his trial for murder, Green insisted that he merely meant to beat the informer, not kill him—a claim clearly belied by the sheer ferocity of the assault. He was convicted and sentenced to die on the gallows—"a fate," observes Faxon, "he had a thousand times merited."

The execution took place on Boston Common on the morning of April 25, 1822. On the day of his death, Samuel Green was just twenty-five years old. For his contemporaries, the young malefactor was a kind of prodigy, whose energies, had they been put to better use, would have singled him out for high distinction. "The records of America—we may say, indeed, of the world—do not furnish the name of an individual who crowded so many crimes into so short a life," concludes Faxon. "Nor have we ever seen a more utter perversion of abilities which, properly directed, might have served and adorned the name of humanity."

[*Sources:* James Faxon, *The Record of Crimes in the United States; Containing a Brief Sketch of the Prominent Traits in the Characters and Conduct of Many of the Most Notorious Malefactors, Who Have Been Guilty of Capital Offences; and Who Have Been Detected and Convicted* (Buffalo: H. Faxon & Co., 1834); George N. Thomson, *Confessions, Trials, and Biographical Sketches of the Most Cold-Blooded Murderers, Who Have Been Executed in This Country from Its First Settlement Down to the Present Time—Compiled Entirely from the Most Authentic Sources; Containing Also, Accounts of Various Other Daring Outrages Committed in This and Other Countries* (Hartford, CT: S. Andrus and Sons, 1837); Jay Robert Nash, *The Great Pictorial History of World Crime*, vol. I (Wilmette, IL: History, Inc., 2004).]

JESSE STRANG AND THE CHERRY HILL MURDER

GIVEN THE MORE OR LESS IMMUTABLE TRAITS OF HUMAN NATURE, INCLUDING OUR innate potential for violently antisocial behavior, it's no surprise that certain kinds of crimes recur over the centuries. During the 1920s, America was transfixed by the case of the brassy Queens housewife Ruth Snyder, who persuaded her lover, a mousy corset salesman named Judd Gray, to help murder her unwanted husband. At the time, the case (which inspired the classic noir novel and film *Double Indemnity*) was seen as emblematic of the age, a symptom of the "anything goes" ethos and breakdown of traditional moral values that characterized the Roaring Twenties. As it happened, however, a crime almost identical to the Snyder-Judd case occurred in America a full century earlier. Its perpetrators were a pair of illicit lovers, a flighty young female named Elsie Whipple and her lovesick patsy, Jesse Strang.

BORN IN POVERTY and raised "to hard labor," Strang was a thirty-year-old drifter who—after deserting a wife and two children in Dutchess County, New York—led a footloose life out west before making his way to Albany in 1826. By then, he was going under the name Joseph Orton. Severely nearsighted, he wore bifocal eyeglasses that endowed him with a learned appearance wildly at variance with his actual intelligence. Acquaintances called him "Doctor."

It was in the early part of August 1826, just weeks after showing up in Albany, that he first set his myopic eyes on Elsie Whipple, disporting herself in a barroom. At his initial glimpse of the vivacious, golden-haired beauty, "the flame of lawless love" (as an early chronicler put it) was kindled in Jesse's bosom. Assuming from her free-and-easy behavior that she was "a young, sprightly girl," he remarked to a companion: "I would not mind passing a night in her chamber." He was surprised to learn that Elsie was in fact a married woman, wed to one John D. Whipple, a well-to-do canal engineer nine years her senior. Still, his companion assured him, "he need not despair." After all, many another wife married to an older husband had taken a young lover.

A few weeks later, by either chance or design, Jesse took a live-in job for $13 a month at the very place where Elsie and her husband boarded: Cherry Hill, the mansion owned by the Albany blueblood Philip Van Rensselaer, Elsie's uncle by marriage. For a time, "no particular intimacy took place" between the two future conspirators. Eventually, however, Elsie—undoubtedly perceiving Jesse's barely suppressed hunger for her and his susceptibility to sexual manipulation—declared her passion for him, her unhappiness in her marriage, and her willingness to run off with him. She had never believed that "there was such a thing" as true love, she informed him, "until it was awakened by the beauty of his eyes"—a quality evidently magnified by Jesse's thick-lensed spectacles.

Elated, Jesse proposed that they elope at once and resettle in Ohio, where they could live under assumed names. He "would be as a husband to her," he declared, "and take the best care of her that was in his power." Elsie consented, though she insisted that they would need at least $1,200 (roughly $26,000 in today's money) to establish a new life together.

She first suggested that Jesse "forge a check on the bank in Whipple's name" for the requisite sum, a plan that Strang quickly vetoed since he could barely write. She then came up with another proposal. If her husband died, she stood to inherit more than enough money to make their dream come true. Unfortunately, John Whipple was in excellent health. The obvious solution, Elsie explained, was for Jesse to do away with her husband.

Though Jesse was not overburdened with moral scruples, he was shocked by the suggestion and adamantly refused. Elsie responded in the time-honored way of her ilk—by casting aspersions on his manhood. Clearly, Jesse was not as "bold" as another of her suitors, a fellow who had offered to dispose of John Whipple "if she would consent to have him." With his paramour threatening to withhold her favors from him and bestow them on another man, it wasn't long before the weak-willed Jesse relented.

Repairing to the nearest apothecary shop, Jesse purchased an ounce of powdered arsenic, explaining to the druggist that his house was overrun with rats. He then brought the poison home to Elsie, who stirred a heaping teaspoon into a steaming cup of tea. Before proceeding further, the "abominable pair" swore a solemn oath, pledging that, even if subjected to the most extreme forms of duress, they would never, under any circumstances, betray each other. Elsie then brought the poisoned tea out to her husband, who drained the cup. For some reason, however—either because the arsenic was defective or because John Whipple's "constitution was uncommonly strong"—the dose had no effect.

Strang tried again, this time buying arsenic from a different druggist. Again, however, Whipple, who seemed weirdly immune to the poison, imbibed a dose with no ill effects.

Apparently assuming that someone else might have better luck, Jesse next approached the family cook, a female slave named Dinah Jackson, and offered her $500 to poison Whipple. In stark contrast to Strang—regarded by dint of his color as her social and moral superior—Washington stoutly refused. "I won't sell my soul to hell for all the world," she declared. Several other efforts to hire paid assassins came to nothing.

In the meantime, Jesse and Elsie continued their adulterous affair, sometimes slipping off to an inn in a neighboring town and putting up for the night under the guise of husband and wife. It was during one of these assignations that Elsie proposed a new plan. Her husband was about to undertake a trip to Vermont and had to be at the stagecoach depot early Monday morning. Her idea was that Jesse waylay Whipple on his way into town and "shoot him or take an axe or club and knock out his brains."

When Jesse convinced her that such an ambush was too risky, Elsie came up with yet another scheme: that Strang steal one of Mr. Whipple's pistols and, from a vantage point outside the house, shoot her husband through his bedroom window as he sat at his table.

Jesse objected that he had never fired a pistol in his life and was "as likely to kill another member of the family as the one intended." He thought, however, he might be able to do the job with a "two-barreled rifle." With $20 provided by Elsie, he embarked on a shopping trip to Albany. Finding that a double-barreled weapon was beyond his means, however, he purchased a rifle instead.

Back home, Jesse spent some time perfecting his marksmanship in the woods. Elsie—worried that her husband's window might deflect the bullet—provided him with several panes of glass for his target practice. She promised to leave her husband's window curtains open on the fateful night, so that Jesse would have an unobstructed shot. On the day before the planned assassination, they sealed their unholy compact with a final bout of adulterous sex in a hayloft.

The following evening, Monday, May 7, 1826, at around 9:00 p.m., Jesse climbed to a spot atop a shed not far from John Whipple's second-floor bedroom. Through the window, he could see his target seated at his desk. Carefully aiming at a spot just under Whipple's arm, he pulled the trigger, firing the rifle—as he later confessed— "with as much composure as if I had shot at a deer."

"Oh Lord!" cried Whipple, and tumbled from the chair, dead.

After disposing of his rifle deep in the woods and "readjusting his clothes," Jesse strode to the main road and returned to his lodging, pretending that he had just gotten back from a trip to Albany. Informed that Mr. Whipple had been shot, he hurried up to the room where his victim was lying. At his first glimpse of the blood-soaked corpse, he turned so deathly pale that his reaction would later be taken as "the first symptom of guilt."

As he and Elsie had prearranged, Jesse informed the authorities that he had recently seen a pair of canal workers prowling near the house and believed that these roughnecks--supposedly disgruntled employees of Whipple's—might be the culprits. It wasn't long, however, before Jesse's alibi fell apart and his affair with Elsie was uncovered. Both were promptly arrested.

For a while, Jesse stoutly maintained his innocence. Confronted with overwhelming evidence, however—including the testimony of the gunsmith who had sold him the murder weapon—he finally broke down and confessed. Despite their solemn pledge of mutual loyalty, Jesse immediately tried to pin the blame on Elsie, insisting that she had masterminded the crime and offering to testify against her in exchange for a pardon. Rebuffed by the district attorney, Jesse stood trial in July 1847. The jury took fifteen minutes to find him guilty and sentence him to hang.

Three days later, Elsie went on trial. In an age that perceived women as the "tender sex," incapable of cold-blooded murder, Elsie, for all her "weak, frivolous, and wanton" behavior, was widely and sympathetically viewed as a susceptible young female who had been led astray by an "artful and designing villain." The jury acquitted her without leaving their seats.

A FESTIVE CROWD of more than thirty thousand spectators—"persons of every age and description"—showed up to watch Jesse Strang hang on Friday, August 24, 1827. While most came from "adjacent towns," many had traveled "from places of even one hundred miles distance." Of this "vast multitude," "fully one third were females."

To maintain order, "at least one thousand soldiers, including several uniformed companies from distant parts of the county of Albany, attended." Despite this heavy military presence, the scene was so raucous that public executions were thereafter banned in Albany.

The scaffold had been erected in a little valley called Beaver Hill Hollow, situated "a short distance south of the Capitol." It was, wrote one observer, an ideal site for such a spectacle: "surrounded by a number of hills capable of affording to each spectator a perfect view of the gallows; and they were crowded to their summits, strangers continuing to flock to the spot from all quarters."

At precisely one o'clock, Strang emerged from the jailhouse, attended by his spiritual advisor, the Rev. Mr. Lacey. He was "dressed in a long, white robe, trimmed with black, black gloves and shoes, and wearing on his head a white cap, also trimmed with black. Preceding him in a wagon, drawn by black horses, was his coffin."

Ascending the scaffold with "firm and undaunted steps," he made a brief address to the spectators, "expressing his contrition for having committed the awful crime for which he was about to suffer the just sentence of the law. He hoped the unsuspecting and the guilty would take warning by him and shun all evil ways, unnatural passions, and sinful lust which had proved his ruin and caused his disgraceful death. He hoped that his death might be received as an atonement for his sins and that the spectators would return peaceably to their homes with their hearts softened by what they had witnessed and dedicated to virtue and truth."

After a final, fervent prayer, Strang bid a tearful farewell to the Rev. Mr. Lacey, who "commended him to his Maker." The sheriff, a fellow with the curious name of Ten Eyck, then stepped forward and adjusted the noose around Strang's neck. In a final display of fortitude that won the admiration of the crowd, Jesse "himself drew the cap over his face." Unfortunately, Sheriff Eyck botched his job. When the trap was sprung, the knot, which should have been positioned beneath Jesse's left ear, slipped to the back of his neck. As a result, Strang's "neck did not break and his sufferings were apparently long and painful."

He hung for a full twenty minutes before he was cut down and placed in the waiting coffin. For the sake of his siblings and "poor afflicted father," who had attracted much public sympathy, Jesse's cadaver was spared the usual postmortem fate of executed criminals: public dissection in an anatomy school. Instead, his remains were loaded aboard a steamboat and conveyed to his family home in Dutchess County, "there to receive the usual rites of Christian burial."

Two years after Jesse Strang's abject, agonizing death, Elsie Whipple—then living in New Brunswick, New Jersey—remarried.

[*Sources: The Authentic Confession of Jesse Strang, Executed at Albany, Friday, August 24, 1827, for the Murder of John Whipple; as Made to the Rev. Mr. Lacey, Rector of St. Peter's Church, Albany; From the Time of Strang's Imprisonment down to the Hour of His Execution. Published to the World at Strang's Dying Request! Together with the Account of His Execution and Conduct Under the Gallows.* (New York: E. M. Burden & A. Ming Jr., 1827); Louis C. Jones, *Murder at Cherry Hill: The Strang-Whipple Case, 1827* (Historic Cherry Hill, NY: A Cherry Hill Publication, 1982).]

Hawthorne and Strang

Though the murder at Cherry Hill didn't inspire any famous works of fiction or film, it made a deep impression on one of our greatest authors, Nathaniel Hawthorne.

Given his sense of "Puritanic gloom" (as his friend Herman Melville called it)—his obsession with sin, guilt, and the darker urges of the human heart—it is unsurprising that Hawthorne was addicted to murder pamphlets and trial reports throughout his life. One of his favorite childhood books was the seventeenth-century crime collection *The Triumphe of God's Revenge Against the Crying and Execrable Sin of Murther,* a volume he reread so compulsively that he completely wrecked its binding. His craving for such prurient fare was so intense that during his stint as American consul to Liverpool during the mid-1850s, he had a friend ship him regular batches of penny papers so that he could keep up with the grisly goings-on back home. One of the last memories Hawthorne's son Julian had of his father was of the aged man "sedulously leafing through an enormous volume of trial reports."

Hawthorne was a particular fan of James Faxon's 1833 volume, *The Record of Crime in the United States,* an early true crime anthology containing (as the subtitle put it) sketches of "the most notorious malefactors who have been guilty of capital offenses and who have been detected and convicted." Among the cases detailed in the book was that of Jesse Strang.

In July 1838, Hawthorne, according to his journal, made a special trip to Boston to view a "show of wax-figures, consisting almost wholly of murderers and their victims." Among the most lifelike of the statues were, in Hawthorne's words, those of "Strang and Mrs. Whipple who together murdered the husband of the latter." To judge by the entry, Hawthorne considered writing a "satire" based on the exhibit, but evidently abandoned the idea.

II

ANTEBELLUM MANIACS

1840–1860

ROBERT McCONAGHY,
"THE INHUMAN BUTCHER"

A VETERAN OF THE WAR OF 1812 KNOWN FOR HIS GRUFF MANNER AND QUICK temper, William Brown had just turned thirty-seven when he married his first wife, Rosanna, in 1817. Eleven years later, the couple settled in Huntingdon County, Pennsylvania, purchasing a 126-acre farm on the east slope of Jack's Mountain. By then, they were the parents of two girls and four boys, the whole family sharing a crude one-story log house built by Brown.

In the spring of 1840, only four of the children still lived at home: seventeen-year-old Betsy and the three youngest boys, David, Jacob, and George, whose ages ranged from ten to sixteen. Their big brother, twenty-one-year-old John—after years of increasingly violent quarrels with his father—had moved four miles away to Shirleysburg, where he worked for a farmer named Samuel Carothers. The oldest of the Brown siblings, twenty-two-year-old Peggy, lived in a small cabin on her father's land with her husband, Robert McConaghy, and their three small children.

Apart from his age—thirty-one at the time he perpetrated what his contemporaries called "the most awful atrocity in the annals of crime"—little information has come down to us about Robert McConaghy. We know that he could barely read, occasionally drank to excess, and was much given to coarse language. He was also filled with a seething resentment toward his father-in-law. Though hardly rich, William Brown was a man of substance in his little community. His farm—including house, barn, and outbuildings—was valued at roughly $4,000, more than $100,000 in to-day's dollars. McConaghy not only coveted his father-in-law's property but felt enti-tled to it. "I thought I had as good a right to it as any of them," he would later confess. He knew it would never be his, however, unless his wife inherited it.

For that to happen, the rest of her family would have to die.

BY THE MIDDLE of May 1840, McConaghy had concocted a plan to wipe out his wife's entire family at a single awful stroke. The first step was to lure young John Brown back home.

Among the Browns' livestock was a handsome year-old colt. From the time it was foaled, John had been eager to own it. Owing to the bad blood between them, how-ever, his father had refused to sell it to him.

Late Friday afternoon, May 29, John was out plowing corn for his employer, Samuel Carothers, when his brother-in-law suddenly appeared. To the young man's surprise, McConaghy announced that he had been sent there with a message from John's father. The old man had decided to let John have the colt for $15. Though the price was slightly higher than John expected, he quickly agreed to the terms and said he would come fetch the animal in a few days, when he was done with the plowing. McConaghy persuaded him, however, that he had better get there sooner, before the old man had a change of heart. John promised he would come the next day.

BY THE FOURTH decade of the nineteenth century there were more than one hundred iron furnaces operating throughout Pennsylvania. One of these was the Matilda Fur-nace, located in Mount Union about ten miles from William Brown's farm. To sup-plement his income, Brown worked regularly at the furnace, often remaining in Mount Union for days at a stretch. Early in the afternoon of Saturday, May 30, hav-ing been away from his farm nearly a week, he packed his few belongings and started for home by foot.

He took his time, stopping along the way to shoot the breeze with some acquain-tances. It was close to 5:00 p.m. when he approached his farm. As he crossed the boundary line separating his land from his nearest neighbor's, he heard his "dog bark and howl." The dog kept up the noise as Brown continued toward the house. "I was surprised to hear it," he later testified.

He got another surprise when he stepped onto the log stoop and reached to open the front door. The handle was missing. Puzzled, he turned to look around. As he glanced toward the barn, he saw a flash from the hayloft, heard the crack of a rifle, and felt a bullet whistle by his head. An instant later, a second shot rang out. This time, the bullet grazed his jaw and sheared off part of his ear.

Leaping from the stoop, Brown ran toward the barn. As he did, a bareheaded man in dark clothes jumped down from the hayloft and bolted for the woods. "You damned infernal rascal," Brown screamed after him. "What are you doing there?" By then, the man had vanished.

Inside the barn, Brown found the missing front-door handle lying beside his own two flintlock rifles, normally kept in his house. Grabbing the firearms, he ran back to the house for his shot pouch, intending to reload the guns and take off after his would-be assassin. When he burst into his front room, however, he saw a body lying facedown on the floor. "It was my son John," Brown said later. "I put my hand to him and turned him round on his back. He was all stiff. His face was black, and blood was running out of each side of his mouth." He had been shot through the chest.

Leaving the rifles, Brown ran up the road, where he found two of his neighbors, William Atherton and John Taylor, chopping wood in an orchard. "My God, what's happened to you?" cried Atherton, seeing Brown's frantic look and mangled ear. Brown told them he'd been shot and his son John killed. While Atherton hurried off to raise the alarm, Taylor and Brown returned to the latter's farmhouse. It was Taylor who first spotted the bulky form beneath the quilt in the bedroom. "Brown, you had better look in that bed," he said grimly. Stepping to the bedside, Brown pulled the quilt down, uncovering (as he put it) "my old lady's head laying on the pillow." Her skull had been crushed and her throat slit with an axe blade.

The four youngest children weren't located until the following day when neighbors scouring the property found their corpses, partly covered by old leaves and sticks, in different places on the farm. Fourteen-year-old Jacob had been shot through the back of the head. Sixteen-year-old George had been savagely bludgeoned with a blunt instrument, then strangled. Betsy, eighteen, had had her skull crushed with stones. Eleven-year-old David had died of strangulation, though a bullet passing through his pants between his legs had also (according to the testimony of the physician who conducted the postmortem) "circumcised him, as it were."

Surrounded by his neighbors, Brown wept openly. "I don't know what injury I ever done to the man that he should kill off my family so," he said through his tears. As for the man's identity, Brown had no doubts at all. He had gotten a clear look at the killer "from his breast to the top of his head" before the man leapt down from the hayloft and fled. It was his son-in-law, Robert McConaghy.

THE DRIED BLOOD of his victims was still caked beneath his fingernails when McConaghy was arrested the following day. Locked up in the county jail, he tearfully protested his innocence but could give no convincing account of his whereabouts at the time of the slaughter. He was convicted after a brief trial in mid-November 1840 and sentenced to die in November. "Your case is without parallel in criminal jurisprudence," the judged intoned on delivering the dread sentence. "For barbarity, treachery and depravity, your cruelty and wickedness have not been surpassed by the pirates of the West Indies or the savages of the wilderness!"

He continued to maintain his innocence right up to the day of his execution, having somehow gotten it into his head that "he would not be hung unless he confessed to the murder." The exhortations of his spiritual advisors, the Revs. George L. Brown and John Peebles—who assured him that God would have no mercy on his soul unless he made a clean breast of his sins—were unavailing. "He denied it again and again," Rev. Brown wrote later.

On the morning of Friday, November 16, 1840, after a sleepless night spent in agonized prayer, McConaghy, dressed in his grave clothes, was led to the scaffold. His legs were so unsteady that he had to be supported by Sheriff Joseph Shannon and a deputy. Taking him by the hand, Rev. Brown made one last attempt to elicit a confession. "Oh, do not bother me," McConaghy cried. "I can tell no more!" A moment later, the hangman released the drop.

Then something happened that, in the view of astonished observers, seemed like an act of God—a "Providential occurrence," in the words of Rev. Brown.

As the condemned man's bound and hooded body plunged through the air, the rope snapped. McConaghy hit the ground on his feet, then toppled onto his back.

Stunned but still very much alive, McConaghy was infused with sudden hope. "They ought now to let me go clear," he exclaimed to the clergymen. It was not until he was informed that "he must try it again" that he finally accepted the inevitable. While another noose was made ready, he asked the Revs. Brown and Peebles to "stoop low, put your faces close to mine." Then, speaking in a tremulous voice, he offered a brief, chilling account of his methodical slaughter of his father-in-law's wife and five children:

> I was not long in making up my mind to commit this murder—about a week as near as I can recollect. I killed George first. I beat him with the supple of a flail and left him wounded. I thought he was dead but I found he was not. I then choked him to death.
>
> I then took little Dave out into the woods. I knocked him down with a little stick and choked him to death. I then went back to the house and took Jacob and told him the boys were gunning back there. I then shot him as he was going on before me. I killed him dead. I went back to see if the two boys, George and Dave, were dead. I found them dead. After I had killed George, I would not have gone any further if little Dave had not come out to me.
>
> I then went to the house and took Elizabeth and led her out to gather strawberries; she had a little bucket and me a pan. I beat her on the head with stones and then put my foot upon her neck and choked her to death. I then went back to the barn and sat there a spell, waiting for the old woman to come out. She came near the door and I shot at her and hit her in the arm, and she ran about the house holding her arm. I then ran to the house and asked her if she knew who done it. She said she did not know. I told her to go into the room and go to bed. I said this for fear she would faint. I then brought her a drink of water. God bless her, but I have pitied her since. I thought a heap of her. I don't know whether I can be forgiven for being so wicked. I then got the axe and hit her above the right eye with the pole or the right side of the axe, I am not certain which. She then fell over on the bed on which she was sitting. I then cut her throat with the axe to put her out of her misery. I then threw a quilt over her.
>
> I then went to Brown's chest and took from between seven and eight dollars from it—this was all I could find. I also took some tobacco, a box of percussion caps, and some lead. I then took them to the barn and hid them. I then washed the blood off the axe. I then fastened the window down, shut the door, took the handle off and went to the barn.
>
> I then went up to my house, got some water to drink and also some water and soap to wash my clothes. I then took my shirt, pantaloons and

vest off; they were spotted with blood. I washed them and hung them up in the sun to dry. I put on an old shirt and pantaloons which I brought from my house while the others were drying. I sat there until John came home. When he came, he got off and hitched his beast in the lane. He then went to the door but as I had the handle, he could not get it open. He turned around with his face toward the barn. I shot and hit him in the breast. He started to run, and climbed over the fence and hallowed and made a great noise. He ran up the hill about twenty-five or thirty yards and laid down. I went to him with the gun in my hand, intending to shoot him again if he was not dead. I found him dead. I took hold of him to drag him to the house. I had a hard siege in getting him in. I dragged him across the floor into the little back room and pushed him under the bed. I found eleven dollars on him, some in his pocket loose and the rest in his pocket book.

I then went to the barn and waited for Brown. After a while the old man came home. I shot at him and missed him, and then I shot again. He then ran towards me. I then jumped down and ran away.

I did not like Brown and murdered them for their little bit of property. I thought I had as good a right to it as any of them. If I had killed Brown, I intended to put him in the house and burn them all up. I was near making a confession three or four times before but didn't like to do it because it would be a disgrace to my family.

Having finally unburdened himself, McConaghy fixed the two clergymen with a desperate look. "Oh, can I be saved?" he cried. They "directed him to Christ, the Savior of Sinners." McConaghy then reascended the scaffold. Before the black hood was drawn over his head, he called William Brown to his side and begged his forgiveness. A moment later, the drop fell again. This time, the rope held.

[*Sources:* Anon., *Trial and Confession of Robt. McConaghy, the Inhuman Butcher of Mr. Brown's Family, on Saturday, May 30, 1840, in Huntingdon County. Six of His Own Relatives: The Mother of His Own Wife, Her Four Brothers and Sisters to Which Is Added the Judge's Charge and Sentence and the Eloquent Argument of George Taylor, Esq.* (Huntingdon County, PA, 1840); John D. Lawson, *American State Trials,* vol. X (St. Louis: F. H. Thomas Law Book Co., 1918); Jon Baughman, *More Strange and Amazing Stories of Raystown County* (Saxton, PA: Broad Top Bulletin, 2003).]

The Mohawk Massacre

Four years after the presiding judge condemned Robert McConaghy for committing a crime more atrocious than the cruelties of any pirate or Indian, another shockingly similar massacre occurred in Pennsylvania. This time, the perpetrator actually was a Native American.

A thirty-five-year-old inhabitant of the Seneca Reservation in Cattaraugus County, New York, Samuel Mohawk worked sporadically as a lumber raftsman, transporting logs to Pittsburgh from the upper Allegheny Valley. In late June 1843, he was making his way home by stage from one such voyage when he stopped for the night at the Stone House Tavern in Butler County, Pennsylvania. At around 1:00 a.m., after having imbibed one too many whiskeys, he got into a violent argument with the proprietor, John Sill, who ended up breaking a chair over Mohawk's head and shoulders and forcibly ejecting him from the tavern.

The following morning, June 30, Mohawk was seen wandering up the road in the direction of the Wigton farm, situated about two miles north of the tavern.

Several hours earlier, at daybreak, the farm's owner, James Wigton, had gone off on an errand, leaving behind his thirty-five-year-old wife, Peggy, and their five children, ranging in age from one to eight years old. He had been gone for about an hour when his nearest neighbor, Lemuel Davis, arrived at the farm to borrow a wagon. Inside the house, he found Wigton's wife, Peggy, sprawled in a puddle of gore, her skull having been shattered with a fireplace stone, which now lay bloody beside her. Nearby was the cradle of her year-old infant, John Wallace. At first Davis thought the child was sleeping. When he went to lift him up, however, "the brains fell out in the cradle" (as he later testified). He discovered the other four children upstairs, the three girls on their shared mattress, the boy alone in his trundle bed. All had had their brains beaten out with such force that the ceiling was splattered with blood.

It was around 8:00 a.m. when James Wigton—who had hiked to his father's farm a few miles away to borrow a horse for plowing—came riding back on the beast. He was startled to see a crowd of his neighbors gathered around the entrance to his house. As he dismounted, Lemuel Davis' wife, Margaret, came running over to him. "James, you mustn't go in," she said, seizing him by the arm. "Your family are all murdered." Wigton, it is said, never entered his house again.

By then, Sam Mohawk had made his way across Slippery Rock Creek to the farm of Philip Keister. Spotting a little boy playing in the yard, Mohawk threw a rock at the child's head, knocking him senseless. Then, grabbing up a large stone in each hand, he fled into Keister's house. At that moment, a crowd of about sixty enraged farmers, who had followed Mohawk's trail from Wigton's farm, rushed up and began pouring into the house. Mohawk, who had retreated to the top of the stairs, hurled one of his stones at the first man through the door, Thomas Blair, who dropped heavily to the floor, blood gushing from his forehead. Charles McQuiston, a brother of the slain Peggy Wigton, was next up the stairs. Mohawk flung his second rock, but McQuiston dodged it and leapt at the killer. The two grappled desperately until another man, Joseph Donegy, ran up the stairs and knocked Mohawk out with a club.

He was bound with ropes and dragged outside, where James Wigton and several others were bent on lynching him from an oak tree in Keister's backyard. Mohawk begged them to shoot him instead. In the end, cooler heads prevailed. At the coroner's inquest, held at the scene of the massacre, he confessed to the murders, expressing his remorse and explaining that he had gone on his rampage because he had "been mad at white folks" because "they treated him so bad." At his four-day trial in mid-December, his lawyers pleaded insanity, claiming that he had committed the crime while suffering from alcohol-induced delirium tremens. The jury took less than an hour to convict him. He was hanged on March 22, 1844. Though he was baptized while awaiting execution, no cemetery in Butler County would permit him a Christian burial. His body was interred in the woods.

[*Source: Case of Samuel Mohawk, an Indian of the Seneca Tribe, Charged with the Murder of the Wigton Family, in Butler County, Penna. with the Charge of the Court, as Reported for* The Spirit of the Age (Pittsburgh: Foster, McMillan & Gamble, 1843).]

PETER ROBINSON,
THE "TELL-TALE HEART" KILLER

IN DECEMBER 1840, MR. ABRAHAM SUYDAM, RESIDENT OF NEW BRUNSWICK, NEW Jersey, was one of the city's most prominent men. A well-to-do dry-goods merchant, forty-five years of age, he had recently been named president of the Farmers' and Mechanics' Bank. To bolster his already substantial income, he had also taken to speculating in land.

Eighteen months earlier, he had sold a building lot to a carpenter named Peter Robinson, who took a mortgage from Suydam amounting to $780. A few years younger than Suydam, Robinson had led a knockabout life. Born and raised in poverty, the son of an abusive drunk who abandoned his family when Peter was still a boy, he had grown up—as he put it—"wild and unmanageable." Unable to deal with her wayward son, his mother shipped him off at twelve to a family in Parsippany, New Jersey, where he apprenticed to a chairmaker named Quinn, a harsh taskmaster of "low moral character." Eventually Robinson and Quinn came to blows. When, shortly thereafter, Quinn's barn burned down under mysterious circumstances, young Robinson was accused of arson.

Fleeing to New York City, he found work with a cabinetmaker named Barnes. For the next several years, he spent his days practicing his craft and his nights—as he later confessed—"learning all kinds of wickedness" in the company of "rowdy young men and young women." At eighteen, his imagination fired by tales of high-seas adventure, he shipped out to Florida, where he ended up working on a plantation, constructing cotton gins. Returning to New York City a year later, he made his way to New Brunswick, where he married, started a family, and found regular work as a carpenter. In 1839, he purchased the lot from Suydam and, with borrowed money, put up a simple frame house.

At that time—twenty-three years before Abraham Lincoln declared it a national holiday—Thanksgiving Day was celebrated in New Jersey on December 3. Shortly after he breakfasted that Thursday morning, Abraham Suydam informed his wife that he had an appointment at ten o'clock but would be back in time to accompany her to church at eleven. Then—after removing some papers from his bureau drawer and checking the time on his gold pocket watch—he left his house.

He never returned.

Within twenty-four hours, news of the banker's mysterious disappearance had spread through the city, generating what newspapers described as "a terrible excitement" among the populace. Suydam's wife posted a large reward for any information about her missing husband. Though certain rumormongers claimed he had absconded to Europe, the general consensus was that he had met with foul play. No one, however, could come up with a likely suspect.

A few days later, however, Peter Robinson showed up at the lumberyard of a neighbor named James Edmonds, flaunting a fancy gold watch. When Edmonds expressed surprise that the carpenter owned such a costly timepiece, Robinson replied that he had recently come into a substantial sum of money—enough to pay off his mortgage to Abraham Suydam. Later that day, Edmonds relayed this conversation to his father, Jacob. His suspicions aroused, the elder Edmonds lost no time in conveying them to the mayor of New Brunswick, David W. Vail.

Accompanied by two constables, Vail proceeded directly to Robinson's house and asked to see the mortgage document. When Robinson produced it, Vail saw at once that there was no receipt attached to it—"nothing," as he later testified, "to show that the payment was made." When Vail asked the perennially cash-strapped carpenter where he'd gotten the money to settle the loan, Robinson grew flustered and stammered an obviously far-fetched explanation. Taken before a magistrate for further questioning, Robinson offered up such flagrant falsehoods that he was immediately arrested on suspicion of murder.

In the meantime, three deputies, Charles Smith, Elias Thompson, and Joseph Dansberry, had begun a thorough search of Robinson's house. Noticing a section of newly laid flooring in the front part of the basement, they tore up the planks. Underneath, they discovered "a soft spot of dirt," as if the ground had recently been turned up. Fetching spades, they began to dig by candlelight. They had gotten to a depth of about two feet when Smith cried out that his blade had hit "something spongy." Stripping off his coat, he knelt by the hole and stuck his hand into the muck. In an instant, he was back on his feet.

"I'd take my oath there's a man down there," he said.

Quickly the three men began to shovel away the remaining layer of dirt. As they did, a sickening stench wafted out of the hole. A moment later, a man's corpse, lying facedown in the muck, came into view. Throwing down their spades, the three men carefully removed the body from its makeshift grave and placed it on one of the floorboards. When they turned it over and wiped the clotted mud from the face, they recognized him at once as Abraham Suydam.

Confronted with this overwhelming evidence of his crime, Peter Robinson blithely denied his guilt. The real murderer, he claimed, was a mysterious stranger who had come to his house on Thanksgiving Day to meet with Abraham Suydam. Leaving the two to discuss business matters in the kitchen, Robinson had gone down into the basement to fetch some firewood. When he came back upstairs a few moments later, he found the stranger standing over Suydam's dead body. While Robinson stood paralyzed by shock, "the other man took the body down to the front basement and buried it where it was found."

Robinson stuck to this outrageous story throughout the course of his sensational trial in March 1841. For the eight days of its duration, he observed the proceedings with an air of supreme indifference, broken only by occasional outbursts of wildly inappropriate laughter. He remained unmoved even when the inevitable guilty verdict was handed down and the presiding judge, Chief Justice Hornblower, imposed the dread sentence.

"The outraged majesty of the law demands your life, and nothing else will satisfy it," the judge intoned. "You cannot intend to assume an idle indifference to your fate, to the solemn death that awaits you, or to the scenes of everlasting life you have to pass through. You may indeed affect an indifference to all this; you may deceive men and die as the foolish dieth. But that is the most you can do—you cannot deceive God.

His eye is upon you, as it was at that moment when you struck the fatal blow—and as it will be until the moment when the breath ceases to animate your body—and it will follow you to another world; and his wrath will rage against you through the unwasting age of eternity if his justice is not satisfied by the atoning blood of his redeeming Son."

By the time the judge was finished, wrote the reporter for the *New York Herald*, "there was scarcely a dry eye in the court. Some spectators sobbed audibly, and all were deeply affected." All, that is, except Peter Robinson, who appeared amused by the sentence. "Since I'm a carpenter," he joked as the sheriff led him away, "I think I ought to be employed to build my own gallows and make my own coffin and give my wife the money."

Forty-eight hours before his scheduled hanging in April, however, Robinson finally broke down and made a full confession to his spiritual advisor, Rev. H. J. Leacock, officiating minister of the Presbyterian Episcopal Church. The truth turned out to be even more awful than anyone had suspected—so shocking that Edgar Allan Poe incorporated elements of it into his classic horror story "The Tell-Tale Heart."

ACCORDING TO HIS confession, Robinson, who was in dire financial straits and unable to meet his obligation to Suydam, had decided that the only way to escape his predicament was by eliminating his creditor. Calling on Suydam on the evening of December 2, he claimed to have come into a large sum of money. If Suydam came to his house the next morning with the mortgage document, Robinson would settle the debt.

When Suydam arrived on schedule, he was admitted by Robinson, who invited him to warm himself by the kitchen fire. As Suydam stepped inside and seated himself by the hearth, Robinson quietly "locked the door again without him noticing it."

Robinson repeated that he was prepared to repay the loan but would require a written receipt. His wife, he explained, had gone out to the stationer's for pen, ink, and paper and would return momentarily. In the meantime, he wondered if Suydam would like to see his newly dug basement. Rising, Suydam proceeded to the gloomy stairwell and began to descend, unaware that, directly behind him, Robinson had picked up a mallet.

"My intention," Robinson said in his written confession, "was to murder him in the basement." At the last moment, however, his "heart failed" him. After a few minutes, the two men returned upstairs.

Finding that Robinson's wife had still not come back, Suydam said "that he would go out and take a walk and return again." As he stepped to the doorway, Robinson, suddenly infused with a fierce resolve, raised the mallet and delivered a savage blow to the back of the older man's head, driving the banker to his knees. "He undertook to rise, when I struck him again on the head, and he fell over and laid still and senseless," wrote Robinson.

Certain that Suydam was dead, Robinson hurried down into the basement and began to dig a hole. He had not gotten far, however, when it occurred to him that he ought "not leave the body upstairs." Throwing down his spade, he returned to the kitchen, only to see Suydam "on his hands and knees, with his face and hands all bloody."

"Oh, Peter," moaned the banker.

Seizing the mallet, Robinson struck him another vicious blow on the head. This time, the carpenter was sure that his creditor was "perfectly dead."

After dragging the limp body into the cellar, Robinson rifled through Suydam's pockets and helped himself to the contents: a penknife, a wallet containing $10, coins amounting to two shillings, and a gold pocket watch. He then grabbed his spade and began to dig again, tossing the excavated dirt up over his shoulder, where much of it landed on Suydam's body, which lay face-up on the ground beside the deepening hole.

In the dark, icy cellar, the only sounds were the rhythmic *chunk* of the spade as Robinson drove it again and again into the frozen, hard-packed earth and his own increasingly labored breathing.

Then he heard a muffled groan.

At the realization that Suydam was still alive beneath the blanket of dirt that now covered his face and body, Robinson was seized with horror. "I shuddered to hear him," he wrote. Leaping from the makeshift grave, he "tied and bound" the banker, who continue to "groan so horribly" that Robinson "could not bear to hear him." Gagging Suydam's mouth with a balled-up rag, Robinson fled the house.

He did not return to the icy cellar until Saturday morning, three full days later. To his horror, Suydam was still breathing. Grabbing his shovel, he finished digging the grave, then rolled his victim into it alive. "I then stood upon his head to smother him," wrote Robinson. "He groaned so hard that I got off of him and struck him with the edge of the spade upon the head, which sank completely to the brain."

After assuring himself that the banker was now truly dead, Robinson covered him over with dirt. Two days later, he purchased a wagonload of boards and laid a new wood floor over the grave.

When this confession appeared in the papers, Peter Robinson—already regarded as a monster—became, in the words of one observer, "more execrated" than any criminal in living memory. Attended by thousands of raucous spectators, his public hanging on Friday, April 16, 1841, was "a gala event" in New Brunswick.

[*Source:* William Attree, *The Trial of Peter Robinson for the Murder of Abraham Suydam, Esq., President of the Farmers' and Mechanics' Bank of New Brunswick* (New York: New York Herald, 1841).]

Another Tell-Tale Murder

Though certain aspects of the Robinson-Suydam case clearly found their way into Poe's "The Tell-Tale Heart"—in which the cold-blooded killer conceals his victim's corpse beneath the floorboards of his home—another earlier crime also influenced the tale.

It took place in Salem, Massachusetts, in 1830. On the morning of April 7, Captain Joseph White, an eighty-two-year-old widower who had made a fortune as a shipmaster, merchant, and slave trader, was found murdered in bed, his skull crushed and his body perforated with more than a dozen dagger wounds. The killer had entered from the backyard by leaning a wooden plank against the house and climbing in through an open ground-floor window. Though White kept a stash of gold doubloons in an iron chest in his bedroom, the coins hadn't been touched. Nor were any other valuables missing.

There were no obvious suspects. White's live-in help—his maidservant, Lydia Kimball, and handyman, Benjamin White (a distant relation)—were old and trusted employees with no motive for murder. Bootprints left by the intruder in the muddy backyard, moreover, "in no manner resembled the prints made by either servant." The only other inhabitant of White's magnificent Essex Street "mansion-house" was his forty-five-year-old niece, Mary Beckford, who served as his housekeeper and who, at the time of the murder, was seven miles away on a visit to her grown daughter, wife of a young farmer named Joseph Knapp Jr.

"The perpetration of such an atrocious crime," writes a nineteenth-century chronicler, "deeply agitated and aroused the whole community." Fearing for their own security, the citizens of Salem outfitted their houses with extra window bolts and door locks and "furnished themselves with cutlasses, fire-arms, and watch-dogs." Despite the offer of a large reward and the tireless exertions of a twenty-seven-member Vigilance Committee, the investigation went nowhere.

The case broke open a month after the murder when Joseph Knapp Sr.—father of the young man who had married Captain White's grandniece—received a mysterious letter, threatening to disclose young Knapp's role in the crime unless the sender received a payoff of $350. A trap was laid for the blackmailer, who turned out to be an ex-convict named John C. R. Palmer. Taken into custody and promised immunity, Palmer revealed that a criminal cohort of his named Richard Crowninshield had been offered $1,000 to kill Captain White by Joseph Knapp Jr. and his brother John, who (so they believed) stood to profit from a large inheritance upon White's demise. On the evening of April 2, Joseph Knapp snuck into White's house and made sure that the rear ground-floor window was "unbarred and unscrewed." A few nights later, armed with a hand-crafted club and a dagger with a five-inch blade, Richard Crowninshield snuck in through the unlocked window and savagely dispatched the sleeping old man.

All three conspirators—the two Knapp brothers and Crowninshield—were promptly taken into custody. Three days after their arrest, Joseph Knapp dictated a nine-page confession that fingered Crowninshield as the principal perpetrator. Before he could be brought to trial, Crowninshield hanged himself with a handkerchief tied to the bars of his cell.

The two Knapps were subsequently convicted in separate, highly publicized trials and hanged three months apart. Joseph's trial was particularly notable for the opening address by the legendary orator Daniel Webster, who had been brought in to assist the prosecution and who, as crime historian E. J. Wagner observes, "captivated the courtroom with a dramatic re-creation of the crime."

"The deed," intoned Webster,

was executed with a degree of self-possession and steadiness equal to the wickedness with which it was planned . . . Deep sleep had fallen on the destined victim, and on all beneath his roof. A healthful old man, to whom sleep was sweet, the first sound of slumbers of the night held him in their soft but strong embrace. The assassin enters. . . . With noiseless foot he paces the lonely hall, half lighted by the moon; he winds up the ascent of the stairs and reaches the door of the chamber. Of this, he moves the lock, by soft and continuous pressure, till it turns on its hinges without noise; and he enters and beholds his victim before him . . . The face of the innocent sleeper is turned from the murderer, and the beams of the moon, resting on the gray locks of the aged temple, show him where to strike. The fatal blow is given, and the victim passes without a struggle or a motion from the repose of sleep to the repose of death!

According to literary scholars, Webster's speech, reported in papers throughout the country, left a deep impression on the imagination of Edgar Allan Poe. Thirteen years after the Salem case, Poe published "The Tell-Tale Heart," which centers on a strikingly similar crime: the brutal murder of a sleeping old man by a killer who sneaks into the victim's bedroom at night and commits the atrocity with (in Webster's words) "a degree of self-possession and steadiness equal to the wickedness with which it was planned."

POLLY BODINE,
"THE WITCH OF STATEN ISLAND"

GIVEN OUR NOTORIOUSLY SHORT HISTORICAL MEMORY, IT'S NO SURPRISE that we Americans have completely forgotten Polly Bodine. In her own time, however, she was a figure of nationwide notoriety—the Lizzie Borden of her day. Like Lizzie, she was accused of hacking two family members to death. Like Lizzie, she was ultimately exonerated. Despite the judgment of the courts, however, most people, then and afterward, firmly believed that she was guilty. Indeed, there seems little doubt that Polly Bodine, like her 1890s counterpart, got away with double murder.

For all their similarities, however, there were significant differences between the two women. At the time of the Fall River horror, its alleged perpetrator was a prim and proper spinster. Polly

N ᴇ_____ ___ __

Bodine was a different breed of woman. Born in 1809 on Staten Island—then "a rural seafaring community of 10,000 people living in hamlets"—she was married at fifteen to an oysterman named Andrew Bodine and bore him a daughter and son in rapid succession. Five years after the wedding, owing to some unspecified "misconduct on the part of the wife," the couple separated and the children were taken into the home of their maternal grandparents.

Soon afterward, Polly ran off to Washington, D.C., with a Frenchman and reportedly gave birth to another baby, who was evidently abandoned by the wayward young mother. Following the sudden death of her foreign-born paramour, she adopted the name Mary Ann Houston and took up with a series of men before becoming the mistress of a married Buffalo merchant. She was eventually abandoned by her lover, though not before wrecking his marriage.

She next showed up in New York City, where, rumor had it, she ran a high-class bordello. Sometime in 1835, she took up with an apothecary named George Waite, proprietor of a drugstore on Canal Street. During the course of their eight-year affair she underwent eight pregnancies. Seven were terminated by abortions performed by Waite himself.

In the meantime, Polly's husband, Andrew—to whom she was still legally wed—had descended into a life of drunken debauchery, supposedly as a result of his wife's flagrant infidelities. Sometime around 1841, without bothering with the formality of a divorce, he married "a disreputable character by the name of Simpson." Two years later, the second Mrs. Bodine was found dead in bed, and Andrew was arrested for her murder. He was acquitted for lack of evidence but promptly indicted for bigamy, found guilty, and sentenced to two years in Sing Sing. By the time he emerged, his first wife, Polly, had become the central figure in the country's most sensational crime.

SITUATED ON THE North Shore of Staten Island, Granite Village (later rechristened Graniteville) derived its name from the extensive rock quarry that operated nearby. In 1843, the entire community consisted of "one church, a tavern, several stores of various kinds, and about forty or fifty private dwellings." One of the latter was home to Polly Bodine's parents, Abraham and Mary Houseman. Another—"a pretty cottage scarcely more than a stone's throw away"—belonged to her brother, George.

A "big, bluff, good-natured" schooner captain, George had a pretty young wife, the former Emeline Van Pelt, who had borne him a daughter within a year of their marriage. Partly because Emeline's health had been fragile since the baby's arrival—and partly because he distrusted banks and kept all his savings in his house—George was reluctant to leave his wife alone when he was away at sea. To keep her company during his absences, he often relied on his sister Polly. During the winter months, the three females—Polly, Emeline, and baby Eliza—slept in a corner of the kitchen near the stove.

On the afternoon of Sunday, December 24, 1843—while George was heading home from a month-long voyage to Virginia—a young neighbor of the Houseman's, fourteen-year-old Matilda O'Rourke, paid a Christmas Eve visit to Emeline. She had been there only a short time when Polly arrived to spend the night with her sister-in-law. Before Matilda left—as she would later testify—she saw Emeline place her silver teaspoons, dessert spoons, and sugar tongs in a cabinet and "twice take her gold watch out of a drawer to learn the time." Matilda also observed that the baby, then twenty months old, "had on the string of coral beads and gold locket which it usually wore upon its neck."

AT AROUND SIX o'clock the next morning, Christmas Day, Polly returned to her parents' home from her overnight stay with Emeline. Though her voluminous clothes kept her condition concealed from the world, she was eight months pregnant at the time and possessed of a ravenous appetite.

She devoured a substantial breakfast. Then—telling her mother that she was off to spend the holiday with George Waite at his apothecary shop in lower Manhattan—she put on her cloak and bonnet, loaded a large wicker basket with some pies, and headed outside again.

As she emerged from the house, she spotted a neighbor boy named John Thompson pounding on the kitchen door of Emeline's house. "If you knock much harder, you'll knock that door down," Polly called to him. The boy explained that he had been sent by his ailing grandmother to borrow some liver pills from Emeline. Polly told him that Emeline had gone to spend Christmas with her parents, the Van Pelts, and would not be home all day. As John turned to leave, he saw Polly walk to the corner and board the stagecoach to the ferry.

＊   ＊   ＊

A FEW HOURS later, at roughly 9:00 a.m., the ferry docked in Manhattan, where Polly was met by her sixteen-year-old son, Albert, who worked as a live-in apprentice at George Waite's pharmacy. Albert took the wicker basket from his mother and the two proceeded toward the store. On their way, they stopped at a milliner's, where, for 50¢, Polly purchased a hood and a green veil.

When they arrived at Waite's place on Canal Street, Albert immediately went to the basement to finish stacking some boxes, leaving Polly and her lover alone in the store. A while later, the boy came back upstairs and found the two adults deep in conversation. Handing Albert some money, Waite told him to go out and buy a leg of mutton for Christmas dinner. Albert expressed surprise. Waite—as the boy later testified—"had never spoke of getting a leg of mutton before." Besides, "there was a-plenty in the house to eat." And in any case, the market was bound to be "closed up for the holiday."

Waite, however, was insistent. If the local market was closed, there was another one about three-quarters of a mile away. And if *that* was closed, too, Albert could always try the meat stands on Washington and Greenwich streets.

It took Albert about an hour and a half to complete the errand. When he returned with the mutton at 2:30 p.m., his mother wasn't there. When Albert asked about her, Waite only said she "was gone out, but he did not know where."

AT AROUND 1:30 p.m., while Albert was off in search of the mutton, a woman dressed in a cloak and veiled hood entered the pawnshop of Aaron Adolphus at 332 William Street, where she accepted an offer of $35 for a gold watch engraved with the initials "EH." At another shop on East Broadway, she pawned the gold chain belonging to the watch for $25. She then made her way to two more pawnbrokers, both on Chatham Street, where she pawned a set of silver teaspoons, dessert spoons, and sugar tongs, all engraved with the initials "EH." Her final stop was the jewelry store of Thomson & Fisher at 331 Broadway, where she traded a child's necklace—a little gold locket attached to a string of coral beads—for a woven hair bracelet and 50¢ in coin.

Not long after Albert returned from his errand, his mother reappeared at the store with her wicker basket looped over one arm. Inside were some additional holiday treats: a New Year's cake and some donuts for her son. Oddly, given all the food that she and Waite had brought in, she did not stay for dinner. She left at around 3:30 p.m., telling her son that she planned to spend the night at the nearby home of a friend, a Mrs. Strong.

Albert, as he later testified, "did not see her again that day."

BACK ON STATEN Island, the trim little cottage of Captain George Houseman stood quiet all day. Sometime toward dusk, a neighbor named Richardson, who lived about a half mile away, was riding his horse past the shuttered house when he spotted a woman standing in the front yard. As he rode past, she turned and entered the front door. Richardson didn't recognize the woman, whose face was obscured by a hood and green veil. He was certain, however, that she was not Emeline Houseman.

A FEW HOURS later, at around 9:30 p.m., two boys returning from a skating party saw smoke billowing from George Housman's residence. Their shouts brought the neighbors running. Armed with water pails, several of the men broke in through the back door and quickly extinguished the fire, which was confined to the northwest corner of the kitchen, near the stove.

No one appeared to be home. Abraham and Mary Houseman, who had been first on the scene, explained to the others that, according to their daughter Polly, Emeline had taken the baby to her parents' home for Christmas—a fortunate circumstance, since her bed, set up close to the stove, had been incinerated by the flames.

Lifting up the smoldering mass of feathers and straw, one of the rescuers, Andrew Miller, discovered a charred object with a vaguely human shape. His first thought was that it was a ship's wooden figurehead, perhaps belonging to Captain George's schooner. Only when he peered more closely did he realize, to his horror, that it was the body of Emeline Houseman.

Throwing a blanket over the corpse, Miller grabbed it under the arms while another man, Daniel Cocheron, took hold of the legs. As they carried the body outside, Emeline's roasted right arm became detached from the shoulder and fell to the ground.

Setting the remains on the stone walkway, the men returned to the kitchen, where they found what was left of the baby. Wrapping it in a calico spread, Miller carried it outside and laid it beside its mother.

A postmortem conducted later that day by Dr. William G. Eadie revealed that both mother and child had been slaughtered hours before the fire was set. Emeline's throat had been gashed and her skull broken open so savagely that the exposed remnants of her brain had been baked in the fire. An axe blow to her left forearm had shattered the bones, whose blackened ends protruded from the roasted flesh. Most of the baby's skull was missing—fragments would later be found in the wreckage—as was its right leg, burned off below the knee. Both victims, in the words of one contemporary chronicler, "could scarcely be said to bear any resemblance to the human species." Indeed, positive identification of Emeline was possible only because of "the peculiarity of her teeth."

Robbery appeared to be the primary motive for the atrocity. Family members inspecting the house determined that it had been ransacked of its valuables, including Emeline's engraved silver spoons, sugar tongs, and gold watch. Missing, too, were a pair of household items that—despite an extensive search of the premises—would never be found: a hatchet and a carving knife.

AT APPROXIMATELY 7:30 a.m. on December 26, the morning after the fire, a witness saw Polly Bodine trudging toward the ferry landing in Tompkinsville, having evidently made the six-mile trip from Granite Village on foot. He recognized her, so he later testified, by her most distinctive feature, the "long, hooked nose" that would help inspire her future nickname: "The Witch of Staten Island."

Boarding the little steam vessel, she sank into a chair in a darkened corner of the cabin and summoned the ship's chambermaid, Catherine Jane Hawkins. Explaining that she was "fatigued from having walked a long way," she asked if there was any food and gin aboard. Marveling that anyone, let alone a woman, would crave a drink of gin at that hour of the day, Catherine nevertheless hustled off, returning a few minutes later with a big slice of pie and a glass of the liquor, which Polly lost no time in consuming.

* * *

SOMETIME BEFORE 10:00 a.m, Freeman Smith, a cousin of the Housemans, arrived at George Waite's drugstore on Canal Street to inform Polly of the terrible developments back home. He found her son Albert behind the counter. Telling Smith that his mother had spent the night at the house of a friend named Strong, Albert pulled on his cap and hurried off to notify Polly. When he arrived at Mrs. Strong's residence, however, he was told, to his great surprise, that his mother had not been there at all.

Moments after he returned to the store, Polly showed up. Hearing Smith's report, she burst into a storm of grief. Then, accompanied by Smith, she made her way to the ferry that would carry her back home.

By a bizarre coincidence, Emeline's husband, George, had docked his schooner at a Hudson River pier that same morning and—happily anticipating a reunion with his wife and baby daughter—was striding toward the ferry landing at the same time. He and Polly met on the boat, and it was she who broke the awful news to him. "With convulsive sobs she spoke of the melancholy fate of his dear little child," writes one nineteenth-century chronicler, "also of his beloved Emeline, whom she had ever prized as dearly as one of her own sisters." Rendered dumbstruck by the news, Captain Houseman made the trip in a stunned silence.

On Wednesday, December 27, while the coroner's inquest was still under way, funeral services were held at the village church, where Polly put on another ostentatious show of grief. By the next day, however, suspicion had already begun to fall on her. Writing a desperate letter to Waite, she told him that, if asked by police, he must swear that she had spent all of Christmas Day at his store. Unfortunately for Polly, detectives found the deeply incriminating letter in Waite's pocket when he was taken into custody for questioning. In the meantime, other officers, scouring the pawnshops in lower Manhattan, located the brokers, who positively identified Polly as the woman who had pawned Emeline Houseman's spoons and other articles the day after the murder.

By New Year's day, Polly was under arrest for murder and incarcerated in the Richmond County Jail. A few nights later, while she was alone in her cell, she gave birth to a baby girl. It was found dead the next morning. Officially the child was declared stillborn, though there were many who believed that Polly—whose previous seven pregnancies by Waite had not resulted in a single live delivery—had strangled the child at birth.

* * *

IN THE THIRD week of June 1844, six months after the murders, Polly was brought to trial. Crowds of New Yorkers, some traveling by chartered boats, swarmed to Staten Island, while the penny papers ran special editions carrying the latest updates on the proceedings. Though the press was unanimous in condemning Polly— "There cannot be a doubt as to the guilt of this wretched woman," declared the *Evening Post*—at least one journalist predicted that she would be acquitted. In a brief dispatch on the eve of the trial, Edgar Allan Poe, then a correspondent for a Philadelphia newspaper, wrote: "This woman may possibly escape, for they manage these things wretchedly in New York."

Poe was right. Though eleven jurors voted to convict, the twelfth refused to render a verdict upon circumstantial evidence.

Her second trial, held in Manhattan in March 1845, generated even more feverish excitement than the first, thanks partly to P. T. Barnum, whose American Museum was located only a few blocks from the courtroom. Looking to cash in on the public's fascination with the case, the great showman installed a waxwork figure of Polly—depicted as a toothless, eighty-year-old hag—hacking away at her victims. To advertise this attraction, he papered the city with flyers featuring a woodcut illustration of the grisly scene.

After a three-week trial, Polly was found guilty. The verdict was overturned on appeal, however, and a third trial ordered. Feelings about Polly ran so high among New Yorkers that it proved impossible to seat an impartial jury. A change of venue was granted and, in March 1846, the case was removed to Newburgh in Orange County. This time, the jury voted to acquit. When the verdict was announced, Polly "dropped into her seat as if she had been shot" and wept with relief. Then, turning to her lawyer, she said through her tears: "Now I can sue Barnum, can't I?"

POLLY MOVED BACK to Staten Island, where she purchased a small cottage on Lafayette Avenue in Port Richmond and set up housekeeping with her two grown children, Albert and his sister, Eliza. An object of intense curiosity, she shielded her face with a veil on those rare occasions when she ventured outside. At the age of seventy-five, she was partially paralyzed by a stroke. She survived for another nine years, dying at the age of eighty-four on July 27, 1892—one week before Lizzie Borden hacked her way into American legend.

[*Sources:* Anon., *The Early Life of Polly Bodine, Together with the Complete Testimony Given in at Port Richmond on the Preliminary Examinations, Much of Which Was Taken with "Closed Doors," Consequently Never Before Published* (New York, 1846); Henry Lauren Clinton, *Extraordinary Cases* (New York: Harper & Brothers, 1896); Will M. Clemens, "The Staten Island Mystery of 1843," *The Era Magazine*, vol. XIV, no. 4 (October 1904): 324–333.]

"The Worst Woman on Earth"

Polly Bodine wasn't the only female criminal comparable to Lizzie Borden. In September 1893—just a few months after the Borden trial ended—another Lizzie was arrested for multiple murder. Her full name was Lizzie Halliday, and her crimes were so appalling that newspapers branded her "The Worst Woman on Earth" and "The Female Jack the Ripper." Her notoriety, however, was extremely short-lived. Within a few years, she had been mostly forgotten, while her Fall River namesake became part of American folklore.

Born Eliza McNally in 1859, she emigrated from Ireland with her parents at the age of eight. At fifteen she married her first husband, a farmer named Ketspool Brown. Five more marriages—several of them bigamous—followed. Most of her husbands were much older men with army pensions. The first two died under highly suspicious circumstances. The fourth barely escaped with his life after she served him a cup of arsenic-spiked tea.

Her sixth and final husband would not be as lucky.

She was arrested for the first time in her mid-twenties. Living in Philadelphia, she opened a small shop, then promptly torched it for the insurance money. Convicted of arson, she did two years in Eastern State Penitentiary. In 1889, shortly after her release, she was hired as a housekeeper by Paul Halliday, resident of a small village in upstate New York. A twice-widowed farmer just shy of his seventieth birthday, Halliday had a substantial spread, a military pension, and a severely disabled son. Not long after Lizzie went to work for him, the old man proposed marriage, apparently as a way to avoid paying her wages. Lizzie, forty years his junior, accepted.

Not long after their wedding in May 1890, Lizzie—according to a report in the *New York Times*—"eloped with a neighbor, stealing a team of horses in order to accelerate their flight. In Newburg[h] her companion deserted her and she was arrested. Her counsel entered a plea of insanity, and she was sent to an asylum." Discharged as cured in May 1893, she was returned to the care of her husband. A few weeks later, Halliday's house burned down. His disabled son, home alone at the time, died in the conflagration.

Beyond her acute mental derangement, it's impossible to know what drove Lizzie Halliday to perpetrate the crimes that secured her reputation as a female Jack the Ripper. Early on the morning of Wednesday, August 30, 1893, she hitched her horse to an old buckboard and drove twenty-three miles to the home of a poor farmer named Thomas McQuillan, whose wife, Margaret, and nineteen-year-old daughter, Sarah Jane, hired themselves out as menials. Representing herself as a boardinghouse keeper named Smith who required a live-in house cleaner, she proposed paying Mrs. McQuillan the "princely sum" of $2 a day plus board for her services. Mrs. McQuillan jumped at the offer. Packing a few belongings, she accompanied Lizzie back to the

Halliday farm. That same night, after Margaret went to bed, Lizzie snuck into her room, chloroformed her, shot her through the heart with her husband's revolver, dragged her body into the barn, and concealed it in a pile of hay.

Whether Paul Halliday was already dead by then is unknown. At some point during that evening, Lizzie shot him while he dozed on a couch, then crushed his skull with an axe. As the *New York Times* reported, she then "drew the couch away from the wall, lifted the planks, dug a shallow hole, tied the old man's face in a wet cloth and rolled him off the couch into the grave beside it. Having filled up the grave and restored the boards to the floor, she then wheeled the couch back to its place against the wall and went to sleep on the blood-soaked couch with the seeming peacefulness of a child."

After awakening in the late morning, she climbed back into her wagon, drove back out to the McQuillan farm, and persuaded nineteen-year-old Sally "to return with her on the pretext that Mrs. McQuillan had met with a disabling accident. Sometime between Thursday at midnight and sunset on Friday, this poor girl was shot full of bullets while sleeping and, with her hands and legs bound as her mother's were, dragged to the barn and laid beside her mother's body."

A few days later, on Monday, September 4, neighbors, suspicious about Paul Halliday's whereabouts, searched the barn, where they discovered the decomposing corpses of the two McQuillan females covered with hay. Two more days would pass before Paul Halliday's remains were unearthed from beneath the kitchen floorboards. Following her arrest for these butcheries, Lizzie was not merely likened to Jack the Ripper; some observers proposed that she actually *was* the Ripper. "Recent investigation shows that Mrs. Halliday is in all probability connected to the Whitechapel murders," claimed one widely circulated newspaper story, "for it has been proved she was in Europe at the time of the murders and often refers to the murders when she is in possession of her mental faculties."

Found guilty of murdering her husband, she was condemned to the electric chair, but the sentence was later commuted and she was sent back to her former institution, the Matteawan State Hospital for the Criminally Insane. Several years later, when her favorite nurse, a young woman named Nellie Wickes, informed her that she had gotten engaged and was resigning, Lizzie threw herself at Wickes' feet and begged her to stay. When the young nurse repeated her intention to leave, Lizzie sprang to her feet, seized a pair of scissors attached to a chain at Wickes' waist, and stabbed her more than two hundred times in the neck and face. The young woman died a few minutes later, just as her fiancé arrived at the hospital to help her pack her belongings.

Lizzie Halliday was still immured in Matteawan when she died of natural causes on June 18, 1918, at the age of fifty-eight.

DR. VALOROUS P. COOLIDGE, THE WATERVILLE POISONER

ONE OF THE MOST INFAMOUS OF ALL BRITISH CRIMINALS WAS THE NINETEENTH-century serial poisoner Dr. William Palmer. A womanizing rogue whose addiction to horse racing, expensive wine, and fine cigars kept him constantly in debt, he supplemented his medical income by dispatching assorted family members—including his wife and brother—after taking out hefty insurance policies on their lives. Other victims he appears to have murdered for pure pleasure, including several of his own children, whom he reportedly killed "by getting them to lick a mixture of honey and arsenic from his fingers." In late 1855, after his close friend John Parsons Cook won £3,000 at the racetrack, Palmer poisoned him with strychnine, then attempted to collect the money for himself. When a postmortem was conducted on Cook's body, Palmer took part in the procedure, doing his best to sabotage the examination. As a result, he has gone down in history not only as Victorian England's "Prince of Poisoners" but also as one of only two medical murderers known to have conducted autopsies on their own victims.

The other was an American physician with the imposing name of Valorous P. Coolidge. In contrast to Palmer—believed to have killed as many as fourteen victims—Coolidge committed only a single homicide. But the details of the case were so bizarre that it became one of the greatest crime sensations of the day.

*   *   *

VALOROUS COOLIDGE MAY not have been a psychopath, but he did share another personality trait with William Palmer. He was a profligate spender, perpetually in dire need of cash to support his extravagant ways and ruinous addiction to land speculation. By the time he had reached his mid-twenties, the young physician—widely admired by the citizens of Waterville, Maine, who had no inkling of his financial fecklessness— was smothering under a mountain of debt. For years, he had been borrowing money from one creditor after another, swearing each to secrecy so that the rest would remain unaware of his desperate condition. The public would not learn the sordid truth until his trial, when a parade of witnesses testified to the many loans he had never repaid: $100 each from William Tobey, Warren K. Doe, Robert Drummond, and Daniel Moors; $200 from David Smilie, Augustine Perkins, Isaac Britton, and John R. Philbrick; $500 from Job Richards, Jones A. Goodwin, and Franklin N. Dunbar; and smaller sums from numerous individuals, totaling more than $3,000 in 1840s dollars—equivalent to over $80,000 today.

Eventually, no one in town would risk lending him money, not even on terms that a Mafia loan shark would consider usurious. In the summer of 1847, he approached an acquaintance named George Gilman, proposing to pay him $500 for a three-month loan of $2,000. Gilman refused. A few weeks later, he offered the same exorbitant interest to James F. Gray for a six-month loan of $1,000. Gray also turned him down.

It was then that a sudden opportunity presented itself. Among Coolidge's patients were the three Matthews brothers, the oldest of whom, Edward, was a successful dealer in cattle. In early September, Coolidge learned that Matthews expected to realize $1,800 from the sale of a small herd of cattle he was planning to drive to the village of Brighton, forty miles away. Inviting Matthews over to his office, Coolidge made the drover an offer he couldn't refuse: $400 in interest for a ten-day loan of $1,500. The two men sealed the deal with a handshake and a glass of the brandy Coolidge kept on the shelf for medicinal uses.

ON THURSDAY, SEPTEMBER 16, Matthews set off with his drove for Brighton. The following day, Coolidge sent a letter to Joseph Burnett, a Boston apothecary, putting in an order for various items. Along with an "abdominal supporter," one pound of "Zinc

Muriate Iron," two ounces of "Sulphate Quinine," and "any new preparation that will be worthy of trial," he requested one ounce of hydrocyanic acid, "as strong as it can be."

A colorless, transparent liquid with a pungent, acrid taste that (in the words of one standard chemistry manual) "is easily concealed in medicine or alcoholic beverages," hydrocyanic acid (also known as prussic acid) is an exceptionally deadly and fast-acting poison. In the Victorian era, when medications contained everything from strychnine to arsenic, it was used in extremely diluted form for the treatment of stomach cramps, heart palpitations, and "nervous irritation," among other ailments. A lethal dose was known to cause almost instantaneous death. Tests on dogs and other small animals that evidently died in great distress when poisoned with the substance had led to the belief that "death from prussic acid is always preceded by a shriek." Observation of human victims, however, had shown that "death comes in a placid manner, the patient passing away without a struggle."

Two days after mailing his order to Joseph Burnett, Dr. Coolidge sent a letter to another apothecary, Benjamin Wales of Hallowell, Maine. "Dear Sir," he wrote. "Will you send me one ounce of the strong Hydrocyanic acid as strong as it is made? If have not the strongest, send as strong as you have."

On Thursday, September 23, Coolidge showed up at the Parker House—the hotel where Edward Matthews boarded when he was in town—and asked the bartender, George Robinson, to notify him as soon as the drover got back from Brighton. Matthews returned to Waterville on Saturday the twenty-fifth but, despite the barkeep's promise, a few days went by before he got a message to Coolidge. By then, the drover had deposited the full proceeds from his cattle sale—$1,800—in the Taconic Bank.

On Wednesday afternoon, September 29, Mr. Elbridge Getchell was strolling along the main street of Waterville when he encountered Edward Matthews outside Phillips' General Store. The two men had been conversing for a few minutes when Dr. Coolidge strode up and told Matthews that he wished to see him. Excusing himself, Matthews turned and (as Getchell later testified) "went in the direction of Dr. Coolidge's office, in which direction also the doctor had gone a few minutes before."

Not long afterward, Benjamin Ayer arrived at Coolidge's office for a consultation.

As he sat in the waiting room, the door to the rear office opened and out stepped the physician and Edward Matthews. Coolidge escorted Matthews to the front door, where the two men paused to converse in hushed tones. As Matthews opened the door to leave, Ayer heard Coolidge say something like "keep dark." Though he couldn't quite make out the words, he had the distinct impression that, as he later put it, the doctor was "enjoining Matthews to secrecy."

SOMETIME IN THE middle of Thursday afternoon, September 30, Charles Matthews was behind the counter of his bookstore when he received a visit from his brother Edward. Moments later, a messenger boy arrived with a note for Edward. As Edward extracted it from the envelope and began to read, Charles glanced over his shoulder. "Come to the office this evening and arrange that business, but reveal it not for your life," it said. Though the note was unsigned, Charles had no trouble recognizing the handwriting, having seen it many times before on prescriptions written for him by Dr. Coolidge.

No sooner had Edward finished the letter than he excused himself and proceeded to the Taconic Bank, where he withdrew $1,500 from his account.

CHARLES MATTHEWS WAS with his brother again that evening at the Parker House. "We were together at a small party there," he later testified. At around 8:00 p.m., Edward, after checking the time on his gold pocket watch, "said he supposed it was time for him to be going to Dr. Coolidge's office." He then rose from the table and left.

"And that," Charles Matthews said afterward, "was the last I ever saw of him."

A FEW HOURS earlier, at around 6:00 p.m., Timothy Flint, a twenty-four-year-old student of Coolidge's, entered the doctor's office and found him in a "nervous state." Coolidge explained that a fellow named Stackpole—a shady individual who, among other questionable enterprises, supplied contraband cadavers to anatomy schools—had promised him a fresh "subject" for dissection. He planned to deliver it at around eight o'clock. Because Stackpole was naturally skittish about his dealings, Coolidge wanted Flint to leave before he showed up.

Sure enough, at a few minutes past eight, someone knocked on the front door. As-

suming it was the corpse dealer, Flint exited through the rear of the office and returned to his boardinghouse, where he sat down in the parlor and invited the
proprietor's comely daughter, Emily Williams, to join him in a game of backgammon.

About an hour later, Flint bid Miss Williams good night, took a lamp, and headed
for his room. As he made his way along the shadowy hallway, he was startled to see a
figure lurking outside his door. Coming closer, he saw that it was Dr. Coolidge, who
immediately grabbed him by the arm and commanded the young medical student to
accompany him to his office at once.

As soon as they entered, Coolidge locked the door behind them and, speaking in
a low, urgent voice, said: "Charles, I am going to reveal to you a secret which involves
my life." He then proceeded to explain that, a short time earlier, "that cursed little
Edward Matthews came in here and wanted a brandy and fell down dead. He now lies
in the other room." Not wishing to be held responsible for the drover's death, Coolidge
had "thumped him on the head" to make it appear that Matthews had fallen victim to
"the hand of violence on the street."

As Flint struggled to absorb this dumbfounding news, Coolidge asked, "What do
you think we should do with him?"

"I don't know," Flint stammered in reply.

"We must get him out of the office," Coolidge said firmly. "I wish we could throw
him in the river."

Flint—who by that point had regained a measure of self-possession—pointed out
that, given the brightness of the moonlight and the distance to the river, they would
surely be spotted. He raised the same objection when Coolidge proposed depositing
the body in "a place back of the building."

"We cannot safely carry the body farther than the cellar," Flint declared. "That's
as far as I will go."

Though Coolidge protested that sticking the body in the cellar guaranteed that it
"would be found by seven o'clock the next morning" when the janitor arrived, Flint
was adamant. Oil lamp in hand, Coolidge led the way into the rear office. There on
the floor between a counter and a back window lay Edward Matthews' corpse, blood
pooling from three ghastly wounds on its head, evidently made by a hatchet.

The sight seemed to unnerve Coolidge. "I think it's best to put something around
the head," he said. Kneeling, he retrieved Matthews' hat, which lay a few feet away,
and jammed it over the mutilated head, so far down that it almost covered the dead

man's eyes. Then, with Flint grasping the corpse under its stiffening arms and Coolidge holding it by the ankles, they wrestled it down the stairs and deposited it next to a woodpile near the outside cellar door.

Back upstairs in the office, Coolidge used a towel to wipe up the blood from the floor. When he was satisfied, he turned to Flint and asked "what it was best to do."

"Just go on with your business," said the medical student, who suddenly found himself playing counselor to his shaken master. "Let the matter come out as it will."

Promising to return first thing in the morning, Flint then turned to leave. As he did, Coolidge barked out a semihysterical laugh. "They can't suspect me, can they?" he cried. "No, it's impossible. My popularity is too great!"

As COOLIDGE EXPECTED, the murder was discovered early the next morning when the building janitor, Joseph Hasty, arrived at seven o'clock and found the "body resting on a pile of wood, its head bearing marks of repeated violent blows and pockets rifled of money and gold watch." A coroner's jury was immediately summoned and an autopsy performed by the killer himself, assisted by two other local physicians, Drs. Thayer and Plaisted.

Removing the stomach, Coolidge emptied its contents into a washbasin, which immediately gave off a strong stink of brandy. Turning to a witness, Cyrus Williams, Coolidge—clearly hoping to get rid of any incriminating evidence—told him to take the basin outside and throw the contents away "as they might smell up the room." Dr. Thayer, however, intervened. Insisting that the stomach matter would require further analysis, he instructed Williams to lock up the basin in an icehouse for preservation. As Williams carried the bowl out of the room, Coolidge, seemingly by accident, jostled him. Williams, however, managed to keep hold of the receptacle and deposit it in the icehouse, where it remained overnight. Early the following morning, Saturday, October 2, it was conveyed to the offices of a chemistry professor named Loomis.

Though Loomis, as he would later testify, had never attended medical school, he "had considerable experience in morbid anatomy" and knew something about the effects of prussic acid, having conducted a recent experiment in which he took a 50 percent solution of the poison and "put a drop into the eye of a cat, producing death in ten seconds." Analyzing the half-digested matter removed from Edward Matthews' stomach, Loomis found that it "exhibited the unmistakable presence of prussic acid."

Further tests on the liver, lungs, spleen and brain similarly "indicated the action of prussic acid."

In spite of his confident prediction to Flint, Coolidge immediately fell under suspicion. He was arrested on Monday, October 4, when Matthews' gold watch was found concealed in the physician's sleigh, wrapped in white paper matching the kind Coolidge used for his correspondence. He was promptly arrested and indicted on four counts of first-degree murder.

So many people showed up for the opening of his trial on March 14, 1848, that the county courthouse in Augusta could not accommodate the crowds. The proceedings were immediately adjourned to South Congregational Church, capable of seating fifteen hundred people. As soon as the doors were thrown open, it was filled within minutes, "the galleries principally with ladies."

After a week of testimony—highlighted by Flint's devastating revelations—the jury took less than a day to return a guilty verdict. The prisoner was sentenced, as per Maine law, "to be hanged after the expiration of a year spent in hard labor." Confined in an unheated, windowless cell measuring eight by four feet in the Thomaston State Prison, Coolidge cheated the hangman by committing suicide on May 18, 1849.

[*Sources:* The Trial of Valorous P. Coolidge: For the Murder of Edward Matthews, at Waterville, Maine (Boston: *Boston Daily Times*, 1848); Jay Robert Nash, *Murder, America* (Simon & Schuster, 1982).]

"The Ballad of Edward Matthews"

According to the signature on this printed broadside ballad, its author was V. P. Coolidge himself. However—as folklore scholar Olive Wooley Burt observes in her book, *American Murder Ballads and Their Stories*—"whether he actually composed the verses or this was a wily trick of one who wished to profit by the event is impossible to say."

Poor Edward Matthews, where is he?
Sent headlong to eternity,
The mortal debt by him is paid,
And in his narrow bed he's laid.

No more will anguish seize his soul;
No more will poison fill his bowl;
No more will fiendship clutch his throat,
Or o'er his mangled body gloat.

O, V. P. Coolidge, how could you
So black a deed of murder do?
You on your honor did pretend
To be his nearest earthly friend.

You knew to Brighton he had gone,
And watched each hour for his return,
The hay for cattle which he drove
You swore within your heart to have.

You failed in that but did succeed,
By promising a mortgage deed,
Of all on earth that you possessed
So that he could safely rest.

The money from the bank he drew
And brought with faithfulness to you,
Not dreaming of your vile intent,
Alone into your office went.

You said, "Dear Matthews, worthy friend.
Our friendship here shall never end.
A glass of brandy you must drink;
'Twill do you good, I surely think."

He drank the liquor you had fixed,
With Prussic acid amply mixed.
Then cried, "O Lord! What can it be?
What poison have you given me?"

You seized his throat and stopp'd his breath,
Until your friend lay still in death.
Then with your hatchet bruised his head
After he was entirely dead.

His money then you took away,
And his watch out in your sleigh;
Then called to your confederate
And all your doings did relate.

I have a secret, Flint, you said,
And if by you I am betrayed
The state will me for murder try
And on the gallows I must die.

That cursed Matthews, don't you think?
Came here and did some brandy drink,
Then instantly he fell down dead,
And I have thumped him on the head.

Where can we now his body thrust,
So that no one can us mistrust,
In yonder room his corpse is laid,
I wish the river were its bed.

The murder we have done this night,
Tomorrow will be brought to light,
But my character and name
Will shield me from all harm and blame.

We dragged his lifeless form away,
Into a cellar there to lay,
Until someone by chance did see
His mangled, bruised and dead body.

O, Edward Matthews, could you know
The scathing pangs I undergo,
You surely would look down from Heaven,
And say, "Let Coolidge be forgiven."

HENRIETTA ROBINSON,
"THE VEILED MURDERESS"

O N MONDAY MORNING, MAY 15, 1905, PAPERS FROM COAST TO COAST RAN ARTI-cles about the death, by natural causes, of an elderly woman whose age was variously reported as seventy-eight and eighty-nine. The story was news-worthy for several reasons. For one thing, the woman in question had spent the last fifty-two years in confinement for a double murder she committed in 1853. For another, though she went by the assumed name of Henrietta Robinson, no one in all that time ever learned her real identity.

There were, in lieu of facts, various fanciful rumors about her origins. According to one, she was the illegitimate child of an Irish lord named Pagnum. Born and raised in the ancestral castle, she was seduced at an early age by a scoundrel named Robin-son, son of her father's steward, who carried her off to New York City, then deserted her, "taking with him every penny she had in the world." Moving upstate to Troy, she became the mistress "of a certain well known gentleman of that city," who also cast her off after a few years, plunging her into a life of "reckless dissipation."

Another version claimed that she was born in Quebec, the daughter of one of the city's oldest and most eminent families. Sent to an exclusive female seminary in Troy at the age of sixteen, she fell passionately in love with a young man who, though of "estimable character," came from a much less exalted social class. Fearing that their

Henrietta Robinson

daughter might marry beneath her station, her parents removed her from the school, brought her back to Canada, and married her off to a British aristocrat, who took her to England. Though their marriage produced two children, it was a cold and loveless union. After a few years, her aversion to her husband had grown so extreme that she ran away and returned to her family home in Quebec.

Far from receiving a sympathetic welcome, however, she was spurned by her outraged father, who denounced her for bringing disgrace upon the family and "drove her from the house with an admonition never to return." Eventually she made her way back to Troy, where, for a while, she lived as the kept woman of a prominent local politician. When that relationship ended, her behavior grew increasingly erratic. "Addicted to the use of intoxicating liquors" (as one early biographer puts it), she began to show signs of what a later age would diagnose as paranoia. Rambling aimlessly through the streets, she would

stop casual passers-by to tell them that her neighbors were a band of burglars who were plotting to pillage her house. She continually imagined that she was surrounded by a mob. She armed herself with pistols and openly threatened "to wash her hands in the blood of her enemies." On one occasion, she entered the house of a neighboring woman, inquired for her son, and very deliberately remarked that she desired to shoot him. She was found groping in the dark, through the halls of public buildings, inquiring for the police office and demanding of the authorities assistance to protect her house.

Though the truth about her background would never be established, no doubts exist about the events that earned her nationwide notoriety in the spring of 1853. At the time, Mrs. Robinson, as she called herself, was renting a small cottage in a largely Irish neighborhood at the north end of Troy. Directly across the street stood a low wooden building occupied by Timothy Lanagan, a thirty-seven-year-old Irish immigrant, his wife, and their four small children. The building was divided in two, one half serving as the family dwelling, the other as a small grocery and liquor store and a popular hangout for his countrymen. Occasionally Lanagan supplemented his income by holding dances there on a Saturday night.

From the time Lanagan opened his business in October 1852, Mrs. Robinson had been one of his regulars, coming in nearly every day to purchase her household provisions, along with a steady supply of beer and brandy. She paid her bills promptly and was on good enough terms with the Lanagans to borrow small sums of money from them when she ran low on funds. Despite her eccentricities, the Lanagans regarded her as a friend.

Then came the trouble at the dance.

It happened in early March 1853. Mrs. Robinson was attending one of the Saturday night socials held by Lanagan when a young man approached her and asked her to dance. Precisely how he phrased the request is unknown, but Mrs. Robinson became violently incensed. Drawing the pistol she kept concealed in her bosom, she aimed it at the young man and threatened to "blow his brains out." Seeing the disturbance, Lanagan hurried over, told her that he would not tolerate "such a noise, and that she must leave." When she resisted, he took her firmly by the arm and escorted her across the street to her own door.

Two mornings later, Mrs. Robinson showed up at the Lanagans' front door and began to berate the proprietor's wife, telling her that she was a "mean woman" who invited "rowdies to her house to insult me." She threatened to get the family evicted and have their grocer's license revoked. Roused from his bed by the uproar, Lanagan ordered Mrs. Robinson to leave at once.

"Do you mean to throw out so good a customer?" cried Mrs. Robinson.

Lanagan replied that he "did not want her custom" anymore and repeated his demand.

Mrs. Robinson refused. If he wanted her to leave, "he would have to get a constable to do it."

Eventually Lanagan managed to get her out of there. For several weeks, the grocer and his wife saw nothing of Mrs. Robinson. Gradually, however, she resumed her visits to the store, and by the middle of May their relationship had returned to its former cordial status. Or so it seemed.

SHORTLY AFTER DAYBREAK on Wednesday, May 25, Mrs. Robinson appeared at the Lanagans' store, where she purchased a quart of beer and a pound of soda crackers. She returned a few hours later to ask for a loan of $2. When Mrs. Lanagan replied that she did not have the money on hand, Mrs. Robinson left in a huff.

She was back before noon, in a state of extreme agitation. She had just received a dreadful telegram, she exclaimed. Her husband, "a very prominent citizen" who was traveling out west, had been killed in a railway accident. This was a wild tale that Mrs. Robinson's neighbors had heard before. Several of Lanagan's chums were hanging around the store, and one of them joked that he didn't see what Mrs. Robinson was so upset about. "I have a wife out West," he said, "and if she was dead, I wouldn't fret about it." The remark brought a burst of laughter from the others. Turning on the men, Mrs. Robinson began to rant at them. The scene became so ugly that she was finally shown the door.

She wasn't gone long. Less than two hours later, Timothy Lanagan, his wife, and a visiting relation, twenty-five-year-old Catherine Lubee, were finishing their midday meal at the kitchen table when she reappeared. Inviting herself to join them, Mrs. Robinson pointed to an uneaten hard-boiled egg and asked, "Whose is that?"

"Yours if you want it," said Lanagan, then rose from his chair and disappeared into his store.

Mrs. Robinson seated herself at the table, while her good-natured hostess peeled a potato and set it before her. As she did, she noticed a piece of white paper, folded into a small packet, clutched in one of Mrs. Robinson's hands. Later she would realize what the little packet contained. At the time, however, Mrs. Lanagan thought nothing of it.

After polishing off her simple repast, Mrs. Robinson asked for a glass of beer and invited the other two women to join her. Both declined.

As Mrs. Lanagan rose to fetch beer for her idiosyncratic guest, Mrs. Robinson asked if she had any sugar. Mrs. Lanagan was surprised. Why did Mrs. Robinson need sugar? She had already bought several pounds during the past week.

No, no, Mrs. Robinson replied. She didn't want to buy any. She only wanted a little to mix in her beer to cut the bitterness.

Stepping into the store, Mrs. Lanagan returned a few moments later with a quart measure of beer and a saucer heaped with powdered sugar. Having decided to join her neighbor in a drink after all, she poured the beer into two tumblers. As she did, Mrs. Robinson rose and stepped away from the table, her back toward Mrs. Lanagan. In one hand she held the saucer full of sugar; in the other, the folded packet of paper.

When she stepped back to the table a moment later, Mrs. Robinson complained that the glasses were not full. Indulgent as ever of her neighbor's whims, Mrs. Lanagan went back into the store for more beer. When she returned, Mrs. Robinson was stirring sugar into the tumblers.

After filling the glasses to the brim, Mrs. Lanagan reseated herself and took hold of her tumbler. As she lifted it to her lips, however, she noticed a powdery film on the surface. Thinking, as she later testified, that "it was some dust from the sugar," she picked up a spoon to skim it off. Immediately, Mrs. Robinson, who was observing her closely, snatched the spoon from her hand and exclaimed, "Don't do that! That's the best part."

At that very moment, Timothy Lanagan called to his wife. Placing the untouched glass back on the table, she crossed into the grocery, where her husband asked her to mind the store while he ran an errand downtown. On his way out, he passed through the kitchen, spotted the untasted beer, and paused to drink it. No sooner had he drained the glass and departed than Mrs. Robinson—who had not so much as sipped her own beer—rose and hurried from the house without a word.

Left alone at the table, Catherine Lubee, who had initially turned down the offer of a drink, evidently decided not to let Mrs. Robinson's beer go to waste. Though it tasted slightly peculiar, she finished it off. Within minutes, she began to feel unwell.

Not long afterward, Henrietta Robinson returned and found Mrs. Lanagan tending to Catherine, who lay groaning on a bed in the back room. Stepping to the bedside, Mrs. Robinson asked the young woman "how she felt."

"Very poorly," moaned Catherine, who accused Mrs. Robinson of putting "something in the beer that sickened her."

Mrs. Robinson denied the charge with one of her preposterous lies. She "had put nothing in it," she told the stricken young woman, "but what would do you good." She had indeed spiked the victim's drink, but only (so she implied) with something medicinal—a dose of vegetable bitters, perhaps, or one of the countless other nostrums peddled in those days under names like Professor Mintie's Dyspepsia Powder or Acker's Cathartic Extract.

Timothy Lanagan, his normally ruddy face drained of color, showed up a short time later. Staggering across the room, he collapsed on a sofa, convulsed with nausea.

"Run for the doctor," he gasped to his horrified wife. "I am done for."

Turning on Henrietta Robinson, who stood watching with detached interest, Mrs. Lanagan shrieked: "What have you done? You have killed the father of my children!"

"I have done no such thing," Mrs. Robinson sniffed. She then stepped toward the sofa, as if to speak to the agonized grocer, who raised his hands and cried, "Go, woman! Go!"

Dr. Henry Adams, the Lanagans' family physician, arrived moments later. By then, Lanagan was racked with excruciating abdominal pain and vomiting uncontrollably. Dr. Adams, recognizing at once that his patient had been poisoned, did what he could to relieve his sufferings and bolster his spirits. But Lanagan was under no illusions about his condition. "The villain has destroyed me," he told the doctor, "and I shall not recover."

A few hours later, with his mother kneeling at his bedside in prayer, he died in the arms of his sobbing wife. His last words to her were: "Do not grieve. You must make the best of it."

Catherine Lubee clung to life until five o'clock the next morning. Her final hours, like those of Timothy Lanagan, were an unremitting torment.

BY THE TIME death came to Catherine Lubee, Henrietta Robinson was in custody. She had been arrested the previous evening at around seven o'clock. On her way to jail, she had laughed and joked with the police officers—a harbinger of the increasingly bizarre behavior she would display throughout her long confinement.

That same evening, an autopsy on Timothy Lanagan's corpse revealed that he had ingested enough arsenic to kill ten men. Searching Henrietta Robinson's house, the police found a packet of the poison hidden under a carpet in her back parlor. Within twenty-four hours, they had traced it to a local druggist named William Ostrom, who confirmed that, a few weeks earlier, Mrs. Robinson had purchased four ounces of arsenic from him, ostensibly to deal with an infestation of rats from a nearby flour mill.

By the second day of her incarceration, Mrs. Robinson's mania was already at full boil. She was possessed by paranoid delusions: a mob of two or three hundred people had broken into the jail and tried to kill her; a couple in the adjoining cell had heated a cauldron of water and threatened to boil her alive. In the ensuing months, she would fly into uncontrolled rages, demolishing the furnishings in her cell—her washstand and wardrobe, a table, several chairs, and a looking glass. These outbursts alternated with bouts of deep melancholia, and at one point she attempted suicide by swallowing sulfuric acid. Only the quick action of her jailers, who immediately summoned two physicians to her cell, saved her.

After a year-long delay, her trial finally opened in May 1854. Hordes of curiosity seekers showed up, eager to glimpse the notorious madwoman and hoping for a display of her notoriously bizarre behavior. They were not disappointed.

She arrived at the courthouse "magnificently attired in an elegant black dress, a white shirred bonnet ornamented with artificial flowers, white kid gloves, and a rich black mantilla lined with white satin." The most striking feature of her apparel, however, was the heavy blue veil that shrouded her face and which she steadfastly refused to remove throughout the six days of the proceedings. At one point, when the exasperated judge ordered her to unveil herself, she haughtily replied, "I am here, your Honor, to undergo a most painful trial—not to be gazed at." The sensational papers of the time quickly dubbed her with the catchy nickname by which she would thenceforth be known: "The Veiled Murderess."

Despite abundant testimony to her mental derangement, the jury rejected the defense of insanity and returned a guilty verdict. At her sentencing, after Judge Ira Harris decreed that she be "hanged by the neck until dead," she drew herself up, pointed a finger at him, and cried out: "Judge Harris, may the judge of judges be *your* judge!"

On July 27, 1855, a week before the day of her scheduled execution, her sentence was commuted to life imprisonment in Sing Sing. Eventually she was transferred to the Matteawan State Hospital for the Criminally Insane, where she passed the last fifteen years of her life. Toward the end, when it was clear she was dying, she was urged to reveal her true identity. She answered that she had "kept the secret for half a century" and intended to "die with it." No one came forth to claim her body, and she was buried in the hospital cemetery, veiled in mystery to the end.

[*Sources:* John D. Lawson, *American State Trials*, vol. XI (St. Louis: F. H. Thomas Law Book Co., 1919); David Wilson, *Henrietta Robinson* (New York: Miller, Orton & Mulligan, 1855); Hollis A. Palmer, *Curse of the Veiled Murderess* (Saratoga Springs, NY: Deep Roots Press, 2004).]

The Age of Arsenic

Exactly why there were so many female serial poisoners in nineteenth-century America is a matter of debate. In her classic 1981 study *Women Who Kill,* for example, scholar Ann Jones takes a feminist view of the phenomenon. In her analysis, such "domestic fiends" (as they were portrayed in the press) were the product of patriarchal oppression, of the stifled, tyrannized lives to which married women were subjected in those benighted times. Some wives resorted to poison to escape brutal husbands. Others—crushed by poverty and deprived of career opportunities because of their gender—disposed of insured family members for financial reasons.

Whatever the sociopolitical roots of the phenomenon, one factor certainly contributed to the prevalence of poison murders in the 1800s. Back then, arsenic was everywhere, as readily available to aspiring Borgias as aspirin is today.

The preferred pesticide of its era, powdered arsenic was sold freely to anyone—man, woman, or child—not only by druggists but also by grocers. It was cheap as well. Half an ounce—enough to inflict an agonizing death on fifty people—cost just a penny. In his eye-opening book *The Arsenic Century* (Oxford University Press, 2010), Professor James C. Whorton relates the story of a little girl coming into a "rural grocery" in 1851 to purchase sugar, flour, currants, and other ingredients for a pudding, along with two ounces of white powdered arsenic "for the rats." The various purchases were then wrapped in paper and tossed together into a single bundle. Another customer, observing the transaction, was taken aback. "What if the paper holding the arsenic were to tear?" he asked the grocer. "Might not the girl's whole family be poisoned?" The grocer was unfazed. "They should mind what they're at," he answered with a shrug.

Ninteenth-century advertisement for arsenic soap

Needless to say, such cavalier handling of the poison did in fact result in countless fatal accidents. Transferred into unmarked jars and stored on household shelves—"as much a part of the farmer's, shepherd's or cottager's cupboard as the family's food," in the words of one nineteenth-century commentator—it was easily mistaken for everything from sugar to flour to baking powder.

Even more extraordinary was arsenic's bizarre popularity as a Victorian beauty product. Thanks to unsubstantiated reports emanating from Styria—a remote, mountainous area of Austria whose inhabitants supposedly used it to promote health and vigor—arsenic quickly gained a reputation both in America and in Britain as a cosmetic wonder drug. In that pre-regulation era, when the marketplace was flooded with snake oil, quack physicians began peddling dozens of products with names such as "Bellavita Arsenic Beauty Tablets" and "Dr. Campbell's Medicated Arsenic Soap." As late as 1902, the Sears Roebuck catalog featured an ad for something called "Dr. Rose's Arsenic Complexion Wafers," touted as a "sure cure for freckles, moles, blackheads, pimples, rough or muddy skin. . . . Even the coarsest and most repulsive skin and complexion, marred by freckles and other disfigure-ments, slowly changes into an unrivaled purity of texture, free from any spot or blemish whatever," the ad trumpeted. "The pinched features become agreeable, the angular form gradually transforms itself into the perfection of womanly grace and beauty."

In addition to its supposedly beautifying properties, arsenic was widely believed to be beneficial for a host of ills. Not only charlatans but legitimate physicians as well dispensed it for everything from insomnia to impotence, rheumatism to morning sickness. As Whorton documents, arsenic was also a common ingredient in paints, clothing fabrics, toys, wallpa-per, candles, and countless other commercial items. In short—for all the infamous Borgias that the Victorian era produced—the average person was far more likely to suffer arsenic poisoning from a household product than from a homicidal maniac.

RETURN J.M. WARD, "THE TRIPLE MURDERER"

IN THE VIEW OF MANY HISTORIANS, THE SINGLE MOST SENSATIONAL CRIME OF ANTE-bellum America was the murder of Dr. George Parkman by Harvard chemistry professor John White Webster. A member of Boston's social elite and one of the city's wealthiest men, the sixty-year-old Parkman—who had long since abandoned his medical practice to devote himself to his real estate business—left his Beacon Hill home at around noon on Friday, November 23, 1849. He was last seen alive at roughly 2:00 p.m. in the vicinity of the Harvard medical college.

After a week of frantic citywide searching, suspicion alighted on Professor Webster, a distinguished member of the Harvard faculty who was hopelessly in debt to Parkman. Though initial searches of Webster's lab turned up nothing, the school janitor, an inveterate snoop named Ephraim Littlefield, took it upon himself to burrow through the basement wall at night. Breaking into a vault beneath the professor's privy with a crowbar and chisel, he discovered a human pelvis and a dismembered leg. Others chunks of the butchered Dr. Parkman were stuffed inside a tea chest in Webster's rooms, while fragments of the skull and his charred but unmistakable false teeth were found among the ashes from the lab oven.

Webster's twelve-day trial in March 1850 was a bona fide media circus, covered by journalists from as far away as Paris and Berlin and attended by an estimated sixty thousand spectators. It also proved to be a forensic milestone, the first time that dental evidence was allowed in a courtroom. The devastating testimony of Dr. Nathan Keep—who positively identified the cremated dentures as Parkman's—was key to securing Webster's conviction.

Shortly before his execution date, Webster made a full confession, claiming that on the fatal Friday, Parkman—who had been hounding him to make good on his long-overdue debt—showed up at the lab and threatened to ruin him. Tempers flared, angry words were exchanged, and—in a frenzy of passion—the volatile Webster snatched up a heavy piece of wood and bludgeoned his nemesis to death. He paid for his crime on August 30, 1850, when he was publicly hanged in Boston's Leverett Square.

EIGHT YEARS AFTER fire-blackened fragments of George Parkman's skull were pulled from John Webster's lab oven, newspapers carried stories of another, similarly grisly discovery: the butchered, charred body parts of an incinerated murder victim, found in a stove in a small midwestern town. These pitiful remains were all that was left of Mrs. Olive Ward, wife of a notorious reprobate with the peculiar first name of Return, who—as one paper reported—"seems to have copied the example of Webster in the murder of Parkman."

He was born in 1815, the son of Col. Jared Ward, a native Vermonter who had migrated westward and settled in the lush, rolling countryside of northwestern Ohio. When his mother, Huldah, died two years later, the infant—christened Return Jonathan Meigs Ward—was "put out among strangers and reared without parental care," in the words of his earliest biographer. Exactly what hardships he suffered in his childhood will never be known. It seems fair to assume, however, that—like virtually all sociopaths—he must have been subjected to serious abuse. Even his contemporaries, who knew little about the causes of criminal psychopathology, recognized that Ward's grim, loveless upbringing had, as one of them put it, "probably laid the foundation for that hardness of character which so marked his subsequent career."

After a stint as a cabin boy on a Great Lakes schooner inauspiciously named *Dread*, he found himself stranded in Erie, Pennsylvania, "without home and friends." Making his way back to Ohio, he apprenticed with a blacksmith for six or seven months until he was stricken with "a severe case of rheumatism," which left him "a cripple for life by the permanent distortion of his feet." He was thirteen years old.

After a knockabout adolescence, he found a new vocation as a tailor. He had his first run-in with the law at the age of twenty-six while plying his trade at a shop in Milan, Ohio. When a fellow journeyman named Adams complained that the shop was too stuffy and threw open the windows over Ward's objections, the latter, flying into a rage, sprang from his workbench and, with a heavy wooden board, "aimed a furious blow" at Adams, breaking his shoulder. Adams swore out a warrant against his assailant but was persuaded to drop the charges for a $5 payoff.

Not long afterward, Ward committed another assault, hurling a rock at a young man named Myers who had provoked him with an unspecified "practical joke." The rock, writes Ward's first chronicler, "struck Myers in the face and knocked him senseless, so that for a time it was feared he was dead." This time, Ward was arrested, "convicted of assault and battery, and sentenced to a diet of bread and water during several days in the county jail."

Despite an unprepossessing appearance and a personality to match—he is typically described as bald, squat, and bull-necked with a foul mouth, violent temper, and "sinister countenance"—Ward seems to have had no difficulty attracting the opposite sex. Around the time of his trouble with Adams, he won the heart of a young woman and, after promising marriage, promptly seduced her—"obtained such ascendancy over her that she yielded her person to his wishes," in the quaint words of his chronicler. Having "gratified his illicit passions," he then broke the engagement and discarded the poor, ruined maid.

Soon after "this base and dishonorable abandonment," he "bestowed his attentions" on a woman named Sarah Lamson, daughter of a prosperous farmer. Despite the objections of her father—who conveyed his displeasure by effectively writing her out of his will—Sarah eloped with Ward.

Domestic life did nothing to soften his brutal character. Quite the contrary. Not long after the nuptials, he set fire to the house of a business rival and found himself on trial for arson. Though ultimately acquitted, he remained under such a thick cloud of suspicion that he found it necessary to relocate to a different part of the state, where he took up a new vocation: tavern keeper. His nineteenth-century biographer, reflecting the intense anti-saloon sentiments of the age, argues that this new business was guaranteed "to smother what little of humanity remained" in Ward. Be that as it may, there is no question that, during this period, his crimes, formerly limited to assault and arson, escalated to murder.

* * *

In 1847, Ward became proprietor of a little tavern called the Eagle House, situated at the northeast corner of Wooster and Norwalk streets in Planktown, Ohio. One of his regulars was a merchant named Noah Hall, owner of the town general store. Owing to what one local historian describes as "some difference with his wife," the fifty-year-old Hall spent as little time as possible at home, sleeping on a cot in the rear of his store and taking most of his meals at Ward's tavern.

In those days, before there were such things as traveling salesmen, shopkeepers such as Hall had to make periodic trips to large urban centers to stock up on merchandise. One day in March 1850, while taking his dinner at Ward's tavern, Hall let it be known that he "was about to start for New York to purchase goods" with "a considerable sum of money." He planned to leave, he said, the day after next.

The following evening, while Hall was over at the Eagle House eating dinner, Ward snuck into his store and unfastened the back door. He then waited until midnight and, armed with a heavy iron poker, let himself in. As expected, he found Hall sleeping soundly in the rear. Then, as he describes in his confession, he proceeded to murder his friend with cool deliberation:

> Having carefully ascertained his position, I struck the rounded point through his skull on the left side above the ear, and then gave him a violent blow with the heavy end of the poker on the top of his head. He then began to struggle, and I seized his pillow and held it tightly over his mouth to prevent any sound from escaping and, with the other hand, grasped his windpipe strongly and held him thus till he ceased to struggle and life was evidently extinct. It was a fearful struggle, and I felt a sad relief when it was over.

Ransacking the store, he found Hall's stash of nearly $800 (around $22,000 in today's money). Before leaving, he arranged the crime scene "so as to create the impression that the business had been done by regular burglars." Ultimately Ward not only managed to direct suspicion onto two local ne'er-do-wells, Daniel Myers and Thomas McGarvy, but also served as the main prosecution witness at their trial.

* * *

SINCE THE HISTORICAL record tells us virtually nothing about Ward's wife, Sarah, it is impossible to know exactly why she suffered a severe psychological breakdown in the months following Noah Hall's murder. It is conceivable that she was not a very stable person to begin with. Certainly life with the psychopathic Ward—who, despite the sizable sum he had realized from the crime, seemed to grow more and more "irritable, restless and wretched" by the day—could not have benefited her mental health.

Ward himself eventually put forth his own theory: that, while he had succeeded in duping the rest of the town, Sarah "from the first suspected that her husband was the real murderer," and that her "insanity was caused by constantly dwelling on his guilt and by the dread of exposure."

Whatever the case, records clearly indicate that within a year of the crime, Sarah Ward had become "entirely deranged" and was committed to the State Lunatic Asylum at Columbus.

WHILE THE SLAYING of Noah Hall was impelled at least partly by greed, Ward's second murder seemed motivated simply by his newfound taste for blood. Certainly, he had no mercenary reasons for committing the crime. As his biographer observes, "his circumstances were now easy." The cash he had stolen from Hall had left him "in no pressing want of money," while his wife's incarceration in the insane asylum meant "he had no family to care for." In attempting to account for this seemingly gratuitous atrocity, Ward's contemporaries could only conclude that he was a "monster" who "evinced a coolness, a hardness and an insensibility which are very rare in the history of the greatest criminals." A later age would have a different name for such a being: serial killer.

The victim was a peddler named Lovejoy, who showed up at the Eagle House one evening about a year after Hall's murder, looking for supper and a bed for the night. After passing a congenial couple of hours conversing with Ward in the barroom, "he complained of being very tired and feeling very much in the need of sleep," according to Ward's later confession. Ward showed him to his room "on the second floor in the corner of the house," then retired to his own chamber. "At that time," said Ward, "I had no idea of killing him."

A few hours later, however, he "awoke about midnight, and the thought struck me that the peddler might have money." Knowing that "there was no lock on the door," he "got up, went to his room, opened the door softly and found him asleep. The moon was shining in at the window, making the room almost as light as day. I knew that he was very tired and that a slight noise would not disturb him. Everything was so favorable that the temptation to kill him seemed irresistible."

Descending to the barroom, Ward "got an old axe and returned upstairs to the peddler's room. I found him still sound asleep and lying in a favorable position; so I took hold of the axe with both hands and dealt him a tremendous blow on the top of his head. I struck him only once. He scarcely struggled and in a few moments was dead. He made no noise whatever."

How to dispose of the peddler's corpse was a question that, as Ward put it, he "had not sufficiently considered beforehand." A solution quickly suggested itself. Fetching a "dry goods box" from downstairs, he dismembered the corpse with his axe—"unjointed the legs at the thighs and knees," as he recounts in his confession. Then, after "wrapping the various parts in sheets and blankets so as to prevent the blood from oozing out," he packed the butchered remains "all safely in the box, put on the cover, and took the box to my bedroom."

The following morning, he "placed the box with its gruesome contents in his wagon and, under the pretext of going to his father's at Milan, traveled through the whole day" until, at around ten o'clock that night, he reached "the neighborhood of the Huron River. About a mile and a half above Abbott's Bridge," he "tumbled the box, heavily weighted with various irons, into the river," where it sank to the bottom and was never found. From this "startling and revolting crime" (as one observer characterized it) Ward realized the sum of $50.

NOT LONG AFTERWARD, Ward moved again, this time to the town of Shelby, where he took up his former occupation as a tailor. He hadn't been there long when he met, wooed, and—without bothering to obtain a divorce—bigamously wed a woman named Susan Reese.

In 1854, the couple relocated to Sylvania in northwestern Ohio, renting a small wooden one-story building that served as both dwelling and tailor shop. Shortly after their arrival, Susan gave birth to a girl who died at the age of two months. The child was buried on the Reese family farm.

In January 1856, Susan followed her infant to the grave. At the time, there was no suspicion of foul play; the official cause of her death was given as "bilious typhoid fever." In light of later events, however, that diagnosis would be called into serious question.

WARD, WHO HAD long since squandered his ill-gotten gains from his two murder-robberies, was now living alone in his little house in Sylvania's "downtown" area—a single street lined with simple wooden dwellings like his own, along with the usual businesses: grocery, livery stable, blacksmith, saloon, and the like. He did not remain single for long, however. Within eight months of Susan's death, he had made the acquaintance of a widow named Olive Davis, a Michigan native with two young children of her own. Three days after they met, in the fall of 1856, they got married.

Their union was a nightmare from the start. Ward not only treated his new wife with unrelenting cruelty but was so vicious to her children that, for their own well-being, she shipped them off to live with relatives. Left by themselves in the cramped, sixteen-by-twenty-foot house, the couple were constantly at each other's throats. Before long, Olive was confiding to friends that she feared for her life. Ward, she said, had brandished a dagger and "told her if she did not look out, it would be the death of her."

In early January 1857—just a few months after their wedding—Olive fled Sylvania and went to stay with some friends in her hometown of Adrian, Michigan. Ward did not take kindly to the desertion. Following her to Adrian, he demanded that she come back to him. Olive refused, informing him that "she did not like him well enough to live with him."

Returning to Sylvania, Ward dispatched an emissary, an acquaintance named William Warren, instructing him to tell Olive that "if she would only come back and live with him," he would mend his ways—"do differently by her and let her have more liberty and not always accuse her of improper conduct." Warren came home with happy news: Olive had consented to return if Ward sent her $10 for train fare. The money was forthcoming, and at around midnight on Saturday, January 31, Olive arrived back at Sylvania. The next morning, however, Olive began packing up all her clothing. When Ward confronted her, she told him "plainly that she intended to leave him for good." She had only come back to collect her possessions. Her declaration, Ward later confessed, "aroused all the vile passions of my nature. From the moment she uttered it, I was fully resolved that she should never leave my house alive."

OLIVE MADE NO secret of her intentions. Early Tuesday evening, February 3, she went to the home of her neighbor Mrs. Harriet Nathans, who kept a henhouse in her backyard and made a little extra money selling eggs. Olive purchased a dozen, explaining that she planned to "make some custard pies." When asked about her recent absence, Olive informed Mrs. Nathans of her unhappiness and said "that she was going to leave Ward again soon." At around 6:00 p.m., Olive bid her neighbor good night and, carrying the eggs in a wicker basket she had brought along, headed back to her own house. Mrs. Nathans never saw her again.

LIBA ALLEN, THE Wards' next-door neighbor and proprietor of a little general store, had just opened her shop for business on the morning of Wednesday, February 4, when Ward came in to purchase a pound of sugar. In the course of their conversation, Ward mentioned that he and his wife were "going away early today and will be gone overnight." Allen was therefore surprised when, late that afternoon, he noticed smoke rising from the chimney of the Wards' little house.

At around 6:00 p.m., Ward dropped by the home of his niece, Mrs. Caroline Lewis. He stayed only long enough to tell her "that his wife had gone to the State of New York."

Several hours later, at approximately 10:00 p.m., Liba Allen's wife, Laura, was roused from her sleep by "unusual noises" coming from Ward's house next door. She would hear them again at around eleven and one. They sounded, she would subsequently testify, "like someone chopping up meat with an axe."

WARD WAS BACK in Liba Allen's store the next morning. When the shopkeeper inquired about Olive, Ward, sounding deeply aggrieved, said that she had left him again—this time for good, to "join another man in California." She had taken the train on Tuesday night, he said—a flat contradiction of what he had told Allen the previous day.

Allen was sufficiently perplexed that later that morning he strolled over to the depot to talk to the stationmaster, who told him that "no one had got on the train from there on Tuesday night."

Allen next headed over to the little tavern owned by Stephen Porter, situated directly across the street from Ward's house. Porter himself had noticed some strange goings-on at the Wards'. Though the curtains had been drawn since the previous day, they blocked only the lower half of the windows, and Porter had been able to see "someone moving inside." It looked, he later explained, "as if the person was scrubbing."

Even as Porter and Allen spoke, they noticed, through the tavern window, Ward's back door open and the tailor himself emerge onto the rear step. He was holding a big metal tub that he proceeded to empty into the back yard. The liquid, as Porter afterward described it, looked "like bloody water."

That same afternoon, Porter saw "large volumes of thick, black smoke issuing from Ward's chimney." Over the next few days, other residents of the town, as well as a number of travelers, would see—and smell—it, too. Passing through Sylvania on his way to Toledo, a fellow named Norman Tripp was struck by the "disagreeable smell" of the "heavy, dark smoke" issuing from Ward's chimney. His wife, Julia, "noticed the same smell. I asked my husband what it was that smelled so. I never smelled anything like it before." For another witness, Alden Roberts, the stench was easier to describe. "It smelled like meat cooking," he would explain, "only quite strong."

By Friday, February 6, rumors had spread throughout town that Olive had met with foul play. Determined to confront Ward, Liba Allen, William Warren, and a third neighbor, Anthony Burdo, showed up at his house and managed to talk their way inside. When they asked after Olive, Ward grew immediately flustered. She had left him on Monday night, he replied, then quickly corrected himself and said she had taken the train on Wednesday. "No, wait," he stammered, turning to Liba Allen. "What did I tell you, Mr. Allen?" When the latter said, "Tuesday," Ward replied, "Oh yes, that was it. She left on Tuesday." Before leaving, Allen took a good look at the floor of Ward's shop. Though the boards had clearly been "scrubbed hard" in recent days, he noticed a spot that bore the unmistakable appearance of dried blood.

More convinced than ever that Ward had done away with his wife, the men shared their suspicions with Constable Elijah Green, who, accompanied by a deputy named Printup, visited Ward on Friday and conducted a cursory search of the house. Green would later testify that he looked under Ward and Olive's bed, though—in light of later revelations—it would appear that he did not look very hard. Finding nothing incriminating, the two officers left.

On Monday, February 7, a resident of Adrian, Michigan, named Charles Dolph arrived in Sylvania with a story that put a temporary halt to the nascent investigation. According to Dolph, he had seen Ward's wife alive and well in Adrian. Five more days would pass before two of Olive's friends, B. M. Phillips and William Chapman, traveled down from Adrian to report that, contrary to Dolph's claim, "she was not there and had not been there since she was first missed."

At the urging of Phillips, Constable Green immediately assembled a group of men and proceeded to Ward's home, where they conducted a much more thorough search of the premises. This time, the worst fears of Olive's friends and neighbors were confirmed.

It was Jason Lowden, a boarder at Porter's tavern, who made the first grisly find—a charred section of human jawbone in an ash pile about six feet from Ward's back door. He shouted for Green. Hurrying to Lowden's side, the constable began sifting through the ashes and immediately turned up other anatomical remains, including fragments of a skull, several finger bones, a number of teeth, and "human entrails containing excrements" (as one Toledo paper reported). There were also remnants of Olive's belongings: the melted lock and hinges of her trunk, parts of her parasol, two finger rings, the metal hooks and eyes of her dresses, and various buttons. More human bones were found inside the kitchen stove, while the bedroom mattress was badly stained with dried blood—as if (in the words of one of the searchers) butchered "meat had been placed on it."

In custody, Ward stoutly "denied all knowledge of the murder." His trial opened on March 16, exactly one month after his arrest. Nine days later, he was convicted and condemned to death.

In early April, against the advice of his attorneys, Ward—convinced that his sentence would be commuted to life imprisonment if he acknowledged his guilt—issued a full confession that was widely published in regional newspapers and reprinted in a pamphlet titled *The Triple Murderer*. It quickly became clear to Ward that, as he put it, he "had committed a fatal error." If anything, his graphic account of the murder—"the most brutal, horrid, and disgusting in all the annals of crime," in the overheated words of one contemporary—destroyed whatever dim prospects he had for a commutation and sealed his doom.

Though Ward had arrived at the decision to kill Olive as early as Monday, February 1, it wasn't until Wednesday morning that he "determined to put my resolve into execution." As she stooped over to put on her shoes after rising from bed, he snuck up behind her with a clothes iron and "struck her a blow on the right side of the head, near the top, which broke in her skull and felled her to the floor. The blood flowed considerably from the wound and from her mouth and nose, and I took a couple of quilts and placed them under her to prevent it from oozing out on the floor. She struggled but little and did not speak after I struck her, and died in about fifteen minutes."

After rolling "up the body in two quilts" and shoving "it under the bed," he "stepped over to Liba Allen's store and purchased a pound of sugar, saying to him that we were going away and should be gone all day." Having "thus secured myself against interruption," he then returned to his house and, after drawing the curtains and locking the doors, sat down to "reflect on what I should do with the body. To take it out and bury it was impossible." With the "example of Professor Webster in mind," it "occurred to me that perhaps I might burn it. Something must be done; no time was to be lost."

He went about the gruesome task with chilling deliberation:

> I went to the bed and dragged out the body to a position near the stove and began to tear off her clothes. Having completely disrobed her, I cut open the abdomen and, taking out the bowels, crowded them into the stove, where I had an extra fire for the occasion. As they got hot, they appeared to fill with wind and explode, making so much noise in their confined situation that I feared the neighbors would hear what was going on and I should be exposed. But by pricking holes in the portions which seemed to be the most inflated, I succeeded in obviating this difficulty, and in a couple of hours the bowels were wholly consumed. I next proceeded, in the same way, with the lungs, heart, liver, etc., and by night had

made considerable progress in my disgusting work. The blood I had bailed out with my hands and put in a kettle, soaking up what I could not otherwise dispose of, by means of her skirts and undergarments and then burning it in the stove.

Having disposed of the lighter parts of the body, I next undertook to unjoint the legs at the hips, in doing which I had great difficulty. When I finally succeeded, I took the legs and divided them at the knees and put them in the large wash boiler attached to the stove. I then unjointed the arms in the same way, and after cutting them in two at the elbows, packed them in the boiler. Then I cut out the collar bone, the breast bone, and portions of the ribs and packed them in the boiler, burning up only such small portions as the fire would readily consume. Finally, I took the head off and put it in the boiler and, by the time night came on, I had reduced the body to such small pieces as to crowd it all in the boiler. I then covered the boiler over with a cloth and shoved it under the bed and, being exhausted by over-excitement and labor, I threw myself on the work table and slept till morning.

Over the course of the next week, Ward incinerated the remains bit by bit. He was inadvertently aided by the never-explained report from Charles Dolph—which, by temporarily allaying community suspicion, afforded Ward extra time to dispose of the corpse—and by the slipshod search conducted by Constable Green, who failed to notice the wash boiler full of chopped-up body parts stored under Ward's bed. By Sunday morning, February 14, after throwing the few remaining "slices of her flesh" into the stove and burning up "every article of clothing that had belonged to my wife, along with her trunk, her parasol, her rings, etc.," he "had, as I supposed, completely obliterated all the evidence of her previous existence."

Only fifty witnesses were invited to attend Ward's execution inside Lucas County Prison on Friday, June 12, 1857. Throughout the grim proceedings, they maintained a suitably solemn demeanor, "very similar to a gathering at a funeral." Outside the prison walls, however—where thousands of curiosity seekers had gathered—the mood was so festive that one reporter described the affair as a "hanging bee," complete with young boys "engaged in pitching pennies and in racing from point to point, as if to make the most of a holiday occasion."

Like so many psychopaths who are capable of feeling pity only for themselves, Ward spent his final minutes babbling in terror and insisting that he was a decent "hard working man" who had "always kept genteel company and never stole any money at all." His final words before the trap was sprung at five minutes before noon were: "Oh my God, I am thine! Thou art mine!"

[*Sources:* Anonymous, *The Triple Murderer: Life and Confessions of Return J. M. Ward, Who Killed and Burned the Body of his Wife at Sylvania, Lucas Co., O., Feb., 1857; Embracing a Full Confession of Three Murders Committed by Him* (Toledo, OH: Hawes & Co., 1857); Gaye E. Gindy, *Murder in Sylvania, Ohio as Told in 1857: The First Case of Capital Execution in Lucas County, Ohio. Presumed to be the First Serial Killer Crime in the State of Ohio* (Bloomington, IN: Author House, 2007); A. J. Baughman, *History of Richland County Ohio from 1808 to 1908*, vol. I (Chicago: S. J. Clarke Publishing Co., 1908).]

Burned Alive

Not every killer has been as methodical as John White Webster and Return J. M. Ward when it comes to cremating a victim. A particularly horrific example was the young Depression-era madman Lawrence Clinton Stone.

The black sheep of an old and distinguished New England family that traced its American roots back to the *Mayflower* pilgrims, the troubled, somewhat feeble-minded Stone did several stints in reformatories during his adolescence. By his early twenties, he was estranged from most of his family, longtime residents of the town of Litchfield, Connecticut.

On Sunday afternoon, October 14, 1934, Stone, then twenty-four-years old, was loitering on East Third Street in Mount Vernon, New York, where he had once been employed as a worker on a street-widening project. Across from where he stood, a five-year-old girl named Nancy Jean Costigan was happily playing with a small rubber ball on the terrace of the Pelhutchinson Apartments, one of the most exclusive apartment buildings in Mount Vernon. Nancy Jean's parents, Mr. and Mrs. Richard Costigan of Forest Hills, New York, were upstairs visiting friends.

At around 5:00 p.m., the building hallman, Carl Hutchinson, decided to go down to the basement to adjust the oil-burning furnace. Walking around to the basement entrance, which opened onto a side street called Warwick Avenue, Hutchinson was surprised to discover that the door was locked. He returned to the lobby and rode the elevator down to the basement, a dimly lit labyrinth of corridors, storage rooms, and locker space.

As he proceeded toward the steep metal staircase that descended into the subbasement, where the furnace was located, he noticed an erratic trail of red splotches that led from the Warwick Avenue entranceway across the basement floor, through the ping-pong room, and toward the subbasement.

Later, Nancy Jean's little rubber ball would be found in the ping-pong room, where it had rolled into a corner.

As soon as Hutchinson stepped inside the subbasement, he saw a puddle of blood on the cement floor directly beneath the white-hot firebox of the furnace. He turned and ran to call the police. As he rushed for the stairway, he thought he glimpsed the shadowy figure of a thickset young man crouched in a dark corner of the basement.

A short time later, Detective Frank Springer arrived. The two men returned to the subbasement. Springer opened the furnace door. Inside were the charred remains of a young child.

Springer immediately telephoned police headquarters, and a patrol wagon, carrying two more detectives and a patrolman, was dispatched to the scene. As the wagon neared the apartment house, however, it collided with an automobile. The three police officers were slightly injured. It took only a few minutes for an ambulance to arrive from Mount Vernon Hospital. As the attendants were seeing to the injured officers, a powerfully built young man in blood-spattered clothing stumbled up to the ambulance and clambered inside, insisting that he was badly hurt. He was driven to the hospital along with the officers. When physicians examined him, however, they discovered that he had sustained no injuries at all. At that point, the doctors couldn't say where all the blood on his clothing had come from. But it certainly wasn't his own.

The young man—Lawrence Clinton Stone—was taken to police headquarters for questioning. That night he confessed to the murder of Nancy Jean Costigan, though the story he stuck to at first was that the little girl's death had been accidental. According to Stone, he had taken the child down to the basement to play catch with her. At one point, he had carelessly tossed the small rubber ball too hard and hit her on the brow. The child "toppled to

The Stone atrocity hits the headlines. (*Courtesy of* The Times-Tribune, *Scranton, PA.*)

the floor," struck her head on the cement, and began bleeding from her mouth. Stone took her limp body into his arms, began carrying her upstairs, and then—believing she was dead—panicked and decided to dispose of her body in the fire.

Eventually Stone admitted that he had deliberately strangled the child. Investigators later ascertained that Stone had sexually assaulted the girl before he killed her, and that she had probably still been alive when he threw her into the furnace.

For all the front-page coverage it received—"Man Confesses He Cremated Girl, 5, in Furnace" was a typical banner headline—Stone's atrocity would have received even more tabloid attention had it not been overshadowed by the even more monstrous crimes of the notorious Albert Fish, arguably the most insanely depraved serial killer in the annals of American homicide, who was arrested shortly afterward for the dismemberment murder of a ten-year-old Manhattan girl, Grace Budd, whose body he subsequently cannibalized. Locked in adjoining cells in Westchester County's Eastview Prison while awaiting the start of their respective trials, the two pedophiliac sex-killers developed a mutual distaste for each other.

Fish, a religious fanatic who found justification for his outrages in scripture, complained to jailers that Stone's incessant ranting made it impossible for him to concentrate on his Bible studies. "The cell I am in now is nice and light," he wrote the warden, "but I can't stand Stone. I can't read my Bible with a mad man raving—cursing—snarling. Can't you put him down at the other end?" For his part, Stone, when informed of the crime for which Fish had been arrested, declared that he found it "disgusting."

FRANCIS GOULDY,
PRE—CIVIL WAR MASS MURDERER

PEOPLE WHO BELIEVE THAT WE LIVE IN A UNIQUELY VIOLENT AGE CLEARLY HAVEN'T been paying much attention to the past 250,000 years or so of human history. Our species has been committing appalling acts of savagery—rape, mutilation, torture, cannibalism, et cetera—since the days we dwelt in caves. While it's true that the term "serial murder" only dates back to the 1960s, the phenomenon itself—the successive slaughter of multiple victims over an extended period of time by a sadistic sexual psychopath—has existed from time immemorial, albeit under different names (lust murder, homicidal sex mania, etc.).

The same is true for the related crime we now call mass murder, in which a lone individual goes berserk and kills a bunch of people in a burst of apocalyptic violence that generally ends with his or her suicide. To be sure, the Columbine-style shootings that have become all too common in recent decades really do represent something new in the world, since they depend on modern weaponry. It's hard, after all, to massacre thirty-two people within a short span of time (as student Seung-Hui Cho did at Virginia Tech University in April 2007) without a rapid-fire gun.

Most studies of American mass murder begin with the case of Howard Unruh, a twenty-eight-year-old World War II veteran who, armed with a 9-millimeter Luger pistol, fatally shot thirteen of his neighbors in East Camden, New Jersey, during a twelve-minute rampage in September 1949. But though Unruh's killing spree may have foreshadowed the Columbine era, there were plenty of mass murders before him. Since their perpetrators lacked the advantage of semiautomatic firearms, they were unable to rack up double-digit body counts. Still, they were extremely shocking for their time. A particularly notorious example occurred in New York City a full ninety years before Unruh made criminal history.

Little is known about its perpetrator, eighteen-year-old Francis A. Gouldy Jr. From reports that surfaced in the wake of his atrocity, he appears to have been troubled since early childhood. Family acquaintances described him as "utterly devoid of self-restraint," "someone without a clear perception of moral duty," a "very hard boy." After flunking out of public school, he was shipped off to a boarding school in Delaware County but proved "so intractable and vicious" that he was expelled after a single term. A year at sea on board a merchant vessel failed to instill any discipline in him.

Moving back into his family home on West Thirtieth Street in Manhattan, he remained idle for months until forced to find a job. He tried his hand at clerical work but was fired from one position after another. Desperate to see his son established in life, his father—a successful lumber dealer, described as a stern but affectionate parent who "tried every way to make the boy steady"—took him on as a business partner. He also opened a sizable bank account in his son's name. Francis would be permitted to draw on the money when he came of age, provided that he demonstrated a capacity for mature and responsible behavior.

Despite this inducement, Francis continued to act erratically. Though affectionate at times to his younger siblings, he was often "morose and revengeful, and exhibited an uncontrollable temper." He went through a brief religious phase, joining his parents' church on probation, but was "finally dropped on account of his irregular habits." To his father's dismay, he began hanging around with a crowd of neighborhood loafers, spending his spare hours in a billiard hall and frequenting a beer and oyster saloon called Showler's. On more than one occasion, he stayed out drinking all night, staggering home late the following morning. Increasingly incensed at his son's wayward conduct, his father confiscated his night key. Their arguments grew uglier by the day.

At around eight o'clock on Tuesday evening, October 28, 1858, Francis was seen in Showler's, dining on oyster stew with one of his teenage cohorts. Several other patrons overheard him say that he and his father had recently gotten into a nasty "dispute about money." Other witnesses reported that he "drank no intoxicating liquor" with his meal and was "perfectly sober" when he left the eatery at approximately nine-thirty.

Ten minutes later, he showed up at the doorstep of his family's handsome residence and rang the bell. Normally the door would have been answered by one of the two servant girls. This time, it was opened by Francis senior, who had been waiting for his son's arrival. Several hours earlier, Mr. Gouldy had discovered that a bankbook had been removed from his desk. Now he demanded to know if Frank had taken it. "Yes," Frank said coolly, declaring that "as the money was placed in the bank in his name, he had a right to take it and do as he pleased with it." Infuriated by the boy's insolence, his father reprimanded him sharply. Francis answered with a contemptuous laugh, then turned his back on his father and headed upstairs to his third-floor room at the rear of the house.

It was a spacious and comfortable room, "well and tastefully furnished," according to newspaper accounts. On a table sat a pile of books, including Eugène Sue's *The Mysteries of Paris*, the complete works of Shakespeare, and a New Testament with commentary by Dr. Adam Clarke. Displayed on the fireplace mantle were some bronze and china knickknacks, along with several daguerreotypes of Frank and a young male friend. The walls were hung with engraved pictures and a map of the Holy Land. A trunk at the foot of his bed was "filled with wearing apparel, school books, fishing tackle, ice skates, and boys' playthings."

Precisely what happened next is a matter of some speculation, though physical evidence made it possible to reconstruct many of the details. "It would seem," the *New York Times* subsequently reported, "that he proceeded to his room and in a cool and collected manner, changed his dress, removing his coat, vest, and cravat, hanging his watch on a nail by the side of the mirror, taking off his boots, and even removing the sleeve-links of his shirt." He then rummaged in one of the trunks and came up with an object he had hidden away there several months earlier: a hatchet he had brought home from Sullivan & Wyatt's hardware store on Platt Street, where he had been briefly employed as a clerk the previous July.

Then, clutching the hatchet in one hand, he stole back downstairs in his stockinged feet and snuck into the sitting room, where his father was just turning off the gas. As his father, sensing someone behind him, turned his head, Francis brought the blade down on his right temple. So savage was the blow that a chunk of bone, three inches long by two and a half inches wide, flew from the older man's skull. With a fearful moan, Mr. Gouldy collapsed onto the carpeted floor, blood gushing from the wound.

Hearing a heavy fall in the adjacent room, Mrs. Jane Gouldy, who had just retired for the night, sat up in bed. Married to her husband for nine years, she was his second wife and the stepmother of his children. Contrary to the stereotype of the wicked stepmother, Jane was, by all accounts, a tender and warmhearted parent. "In her family," wrote the *New York Times*, "she was greatly beloved, and no one among her children manifested more affection for her than did Francis." Perhaps for this reason, there was genuine anguish in his voice when, seconds after murdering his father, he burst into Jane's bedroom and cried out, "Mother—oh, Mother!" Then, seizing the startled woman's hand, he delivered a vicious blow to her head with the hatchet. As she screamed and struggled to free herself from his grip, he struck her again and again until she collapsed to the floor, her face slathered with blood.

Making his way across the hallway, he entered the chamber where his two younger brothers, thirteen-year-old Nathaniel and six-year-old Charles, were sharing the same bed. He struck at them repeatedly as they slept, fracturing their skulls and chopping off chunks of bone later found amid the gore-caked bedclothes.

Next he climbed to the third floor, where the two servant girls, Johanna Murphy and Elizabeth Carr, shared a small room. Roused from their beds by the strange noises below, they had stepped out into the hallway in their nightclothes. Without speaking a word, Francis strode up to them and began hacking away at their heads. Though desperately wounded, Elizabeth—who had come to work for the Gouldy family only a few weeks earlier—grappled with her attacker and managed to wrest the weapon from his grasp.

"Give me that, Lizzie," Francis said calmly. "I won't kill you. I only want to get away."

Dazed from her wound, blood pouring into her eyes, the young woman loosened her hold on the hatchet. Snatching it from her hand, Francis delivered three more savage blows to her head.

Hearing her screams, Francis' fifteen-year-old sister, Mary, came to her door and peered into the dimly lit hallway, where a thickset figure loomed over the sprawled bodies of the two servant girls. In the darkness and confusion, she did not recognize her brother. Assuming that a burglar had broken into the house, she slammed and locked her door, threw open a window, and began shouting for help.

By then, Francis had returned to his own room. Kneeling by his trunk, he pulled out a pistol he had stashed among the jumble, pressed the muzzle to his skull just behind his right ear, and pulled the trigger.

Moments later, three police officers from the Twentieth Ward, responding to Mary's cries, broke open the front door. As they moved through the house, they encountered (as the *New York Times* put it) "a scene of horror such as they never before witnessed. The father lay upon the floor, his face and head covered with blood. The mother was insensible in the next room, and also deluged in blood. In the hall-bedroom, the little boys were in a similar condition. Ascending the stairs, they found the servant-girls lying in a pool of gore."

The killer himself, his skull "greatly shattered," lay sprawled on his back in a spreading pool of blood. Brain matter and bone fragments were scattered on the floor. His right hand clenched the pistol so tightly that one of the officers, Andrew Clow, had to yank it from his grip.

The story was front-page news the following morning. "Shocking Butchery!" blared the *New York Times*, which described the massacre as "a more horrible crime . . . than any we have ever before had occasion to record." Within twenty-four hours, a printed ballad, "The Thirtieth Street Murder. A Horrible Tragedy," was being peddled on the streets:

> A tragic scene transpired of late,
> The truth of which I will narrate,
> Ye muses touch your mournful lyres,
> The awful theme, a Bard inspires.
>
> The silver moon rolls bright and clear,
> But dreadful sounds salute my ear,
> In the lonely hour of solemn night,
> We are call'd to view a horrid sight.
>
> A youth has gone, his spirit's fled,
> And he is numbered with the dead,

A blooming son, his father's joy,
Did wickedly himself destroy.

But first his father, wounded sore,
Then left him bleeding in his gore,
Ah, pause and drop a silent tear,
For he would kill his mother dear.

Two brothers young, two servant girls,
With brutal hands he at them hurls
A hatchet keen, to take their lives
To kill them all the wretch contrives.

But wounded linger on the shore,
Yet soon alas may be no more,
Heart rending tale indeed to tell,
Horrific as the gates of hell.

With pistol his own brains blow'd out,
'Tis done, alas, beyond a doubt,
No more, poor youth, you'll join the glee
Of your youthful company.

But in the pit of dark despair
For ever groan in Tophet there,
A solemn warning to us all,
To watch, lest we like Gouldy fall.

The crime scene became an instant attraction. Such huge crowds flocked to the Gouldys' residence that a detachment of police officers from the Twentieth Ward was stationed outside around the clock to keep the curious from sneaking inside and making off with morbid souvenirs.

Sought out by reporters, family acquaintances offered harsh assessments of the killer. According to the Rev. Mr. Crawford of Trinity Methodist Episcopal Church, where the elder Gouldys worshipped, young Francis "was a coward. He never looked anyone straight in the face but always dropped his eyes while speaking or being spoken to. He was revengeful, obstinate, and morose. In intellectual qualities he was below mediocrity. The secretiveness of his disposition was eminently noticeable to all his friends. He was slow and heavy in his movements, and as a boy took very little part in the sports of his companions." A phrenologist, examining a daguerreotype portrait of Francis, pronounced his head "not good," with a "forehead that retreated like the plaster cast foreheads of idiots."

As is the case today—when mass homicides perpetrated by juvenile misfits provoke public outcries for gun control—there were those who, in the wake of the tragedy, called for laws to keep dangerous weapons out of the hands of teenage boys. According to one letter writer to the *Times*, Gouldy's crime exemplified "a startling evil" that was "becoming far more common than the public is aware of," namely, "the practice of our young men keeping in their rooms and carrying about their persons weapons of death, intending them merely as weapons of self-defense, but which in a sudden gust of passion, or to revenge a fancied wrong, or to defend themselves from a slight assault, they are tempted to use in such a way as to bring ruin upon themselves or upon others. I hope the Press will avail itself of this dreadful tragedy as to impress upon the minds of this community the enormity of this evil and be the means of producing a salutary reform."

Elizabeth Carr, the servant who had recently gone to work for the Gouldys, lingered for several days. Her last recorded words were: "Oh, that I should have gone there to be murdered by that bad boy, Frank."

[*Source:* "Shocking Butchery," *New York Times*, October 28, 1858, 1, and "The Thirtieth-Street Tragedy," *New York Times*, October 29, 1858, 8.]

The Saugerties Bard, Minstrel of Mayhem

In the centuries before the advent of tabloid journalism, accounts of sensational homicides were often transmitted through "murder ballads"—crudely written poems dashed off in the immediate aftermath of some grisly killing, printed on page-long sheets known as broadsides, and sold for a few pennies. Since most of the people who composed and peddled these verses were talentless hacks—interested only in turning a quick profit by pandering to the public's prurient interest in violent crime—they rarely signed their compositions. One exception was the author of "The Thirtieth Street Tragedy," who proudly identified himself at the bottom of his broadside as "The Saugerties Bard."

Thanks to folklore scholar John Thorn, we know a fair amount about this prolific balladeer, whose actual name was Henry Sherman Backus. Born in upstate New York in 1798, Backus came from a military background—his father was a major who died in battle during the War of 1812—and developed an early love of martial music, becoming an accomplished player of the fife, drum, and bugle. After teaching school for a number of years, he moved to Saugerties, married a local woman, and fathered five daughters. A series of personal tragedies, including the death of his wife and one infant daughter, apparently precipitated a breakdown that led to his confinement in a lunatic asylum and the dispersal of his remaining children to various foster homes. Upon his release, he embarked on the life of a traveling minstrel. Roaming from town to town, he would perform his self-composed ballads in taverns and roadhouses, then peddle cheaply printed copies of the lyrics to his audience. Eventually he made his way to New York City, where he continued to produce, publish, and distribute his song sheets.

Exactly how many pieces Backus composed is unknown, though scholars have attributed nearly three dozen extant broadsides to the Saugerties Bard. While he wrote on a range of subjects—prizefights, riots, Bowery gangs, steamship explosions, and other assorted disasters—he is best known for his murder ballads. Besides "The Thirtieth Street Murder," his known works include "Dunbar, the Murderer," "The Murdered Pedlar," "Dr. Burdell, or the Bond Street Murder," "The Murdered Policeman," and "Hicks the Pirate" (see p. 113).

Even his most ardent admirers concede that Backus' poetry rarely rose above the level of doggerel. Still, he possessed a narrative gift that distinguishes his lyrics from those of lesser balladeers. As Thorn says, "He was a master of brevity, able to tell a story that would go straight to the heart in a way that myriad columns of newspapers could not." Still, his talent failed to translate into financial success. He died homeless and broke in Saugerties at the age of sixty-three and was buried in a pauper's grave.

ALBERT HICKS,
"THE WORST MAN WHO EVER LIVED"

LITTLE IS KNOWN ABOUT ALBERT Hicks' family. His father, owner of a hard-scrabble farm in Gloucester, Rhode Island, "had the reputation of being an honest man." The same could not be said for Albert's older brother, Simon, a dull-witted lout with a nasty temper. Late one night in the mid-1850s—the exact date is difficult to ascertain—Simon snuck into the home of an acquaintance, an elderly bachelor named Crossman, and beat the sleeping old man to death with a club. He then stole several hundred dollars and absconded to Providence, where he proceeded to lavish gifts—a gold watch and "other articles of finery"—on his prostitute girlfriend. This spending spree

Albert Hicks

aroused suspicion and Simon was soon under arrest. Tried, convicted, and sentenced to be hanged, he was locked up in state prison but escaped during a riot and was never heard from again.

Brutish as he was, however, Simon was a solid citizen compared to his younger brother. Born in 1820, Albert ran away from home at an early age and launched into a lifelong career of crime, eventually progressing from petty crook to hired killer. A habitué of the infamous Five Points district of lower Manhattan, he allied himself with various Bowery gangs: sometimes with the Daybreak Boys, at others with the notorious Dead Rabbits. He liked to say that he was "the worst man who ever lived." After the events of March 21, 1860, there were few who disagreed with him.

AT ABOUT HALF past six that Thursday morning, the crew of the schooner *Telegraph*, commanded by Captain H. Listare, encountered a strange apparition on the lower bay of New York harbor between Sandy Hook and Coney Island Point: a sloop, the *E. A. Johnson*, drifting aimlessly over the misty waters, its sails down, its bowsprit broken off, and its rigging trailing in the water. No one could be seen on deck.

Maneuvering alongside the seemingly derelict vessel, Listare boarded it and was immediately startled (in the words of one contemporary news account) "by the presence of blood in large quantities upon the deck." Descending into the cabin, the captain discovered even more shocking signs of carnage, "the floor and all the furniture being covered or spotted with blood." Even at a glance, it was appallingly clear "that the sloop had been the scene of some dreadful and bloody tragedy."

Towed into port by the steam tug *Ceres*, the ship was tied up at the Fulton Market Slip. Shortly thereafter—the police having been notified of the discovery—the coroner and his deputies arrived. Their report, summed up in the daily press, offered a vivid picture of the butchery that had occurred on board the doomed vessel:

> A coffeepot, covered with blood and human hair, was found in a corner near the stove. A broom, which had apparently been used in sweeping the blood from the floor, and a hammer, also smeared with blood, were found near the companionway. Marks of blood were found on the ladder leading up to the deck, upon the lockers, upon the sides of the cabin, and upon the ceiling. There were found fresh and distinct marks, as if made with the blade of a

knife or sharp hatchet, upon the beams and ceiling. And one of the indentations was stained with blood. The runs were, upon examination, found to be filled with blood, which had leaked down from the floor and been allowed to remain there in the clotted state in which it was discovered. All the lockers and drawers were stained with blood—probably by the assassin in search of plunder—as also the stove and cooking utensils.

THE BLOOD-STAINED CABIN OF THE OYSTER SLOOP "E. A. JOHNSON"

From the cabin, the blood was traced up the companionway to the deck, where marks as if produced by the dragging of some bloody substance were observable all along from the cabin door to the side of the vessel. The rail, too, was smeared with blood, and also the side of the sloop, showing that the assassin concluded his work by throwing the evidence of his guilt into the sea. The finger marks of blood on the rail and the indentation of a knife leads to the belief that the murderer was compelled to sever the hand of his victim as he clung to the frail support before he could throw him overboard.

Even as the coroner's men continued to poke through the shambles, police officers from the Second Precinct were tracking down information about the ship. They quickly discovered that, a week earlier, it had left from the Catherine Market Slip, bound for Deep Creek, Virginia, to pick up a cargo of oysters. In addition to its usual crew—Captain George H. Burr and two young sailors, Smith Watts and his brother Oliver—the sloop carried a fourth man, a hulking fellow named William Johnson who had signed on as first mate for the voyage.

The news spread quickly. Before the day was out, accounts of the apparent massacre had already appeared in the late editions. On the following morning, every daily in the city ran some variation of the same headline: "Dreadful Murder in an Oyster-Boat in New York Bay!"

When Patrick Burke, proprietor of a shabby rooming house at 129 Cedar Street, read about the tragedy in the morning papers, he hurried to the nearest police station. Boarding at his place, he explained, was a man named William Johnson, who lived there with a wife and infant son. The previous day, Johnson, who had been away at sea for about a week, returned home unexpectedly, flaunting a large wad of banknotes that he claimed to have received as a reward for "rescuing a sloop in the bay." Johnson had spent the next few hours packing up his belongings and, after settling his bill, vacated his room, telling Burke that he was taking his family to Fall River, Massachusetts.

Before the day was over, other witnesses had come forward with stories that bolstered the landlord's suspicions. A man matching Johnson's description—tall, powerfully built, wearing a monkey coat and slouch hat, his jawline fringed with thick black whiskers—had been spotted the previous day rowing to shore on Staten Island in the yawl belonging to the doomed sloop. After landing a little below Fort Richmond, he had removed a large canvas bag from the boat, slung it over his shoulder, and proceeded by foot to Vanderbilt's Landing, where he stopped at a tavern for breakfast, offering a gold ten-dollar piece in payment (the equivalent of more than $250 today), which the proprietor could not change. A few hours later, after taking the ferry to Manhattan, he appeared at the South Street office of a broker named Albert S. James, where he exchanged $130 worth of gold and silver coins for small-denomination bills issued by the Farmers' and Citizens' Bank of Brooklyn.

Convinced that Johnson was their man, police detectives tracked him to Fall River and from there to Providence, Rhode Island, where they found him in a rooming house, slumbering soundly beside his wife. Shaken awake, Johnson bolted upright, breaking into a profuse sweat at the sight of the officers. Though a search of his possessions turned up a silver pocket watch belonging to the slaughtered Captain Burr along with $121 in small-denomination bills from the Farmers' and Citizens' Bank of Brooklyn, Johnson stoutly maintained his innocence. He was taken into custody and brought to the local jailhouse, where Elias Smith, a reporter for the *New York Times* who had accompanied the detectives on their mission, confronted him.

"You are charged with imbruing your hands in the blood of three of your fellow men for money," Smith declared.

"I don't know anything about it," Johnson replied, insisting "upon his soul" that he had never been on board the oyster sloop.

Agreeing to accompany the arresting officers back to New York City, he behaved "so coolly and indifferently" throughout the trip that George Nivens, the officer in charge, was "almost convinced that we had mistaken our man." At every railway stop along the way, enormous crowds gathered to glimpse the prisoner. Some cried out for a lynching. At the New London depot, the mob was so ugly that as Nivens escorted Johnson to a different train, he found it necessary to draw his pistol and warn that "he would shoot the first man who touched" the prisoner.

No sooner were they back in the city than police learned that Johnson was really Albert W. Hicks, known to his acquaintances as "Hicksey." A parade of witnesses were brought to his cell to identify him as the man who had shipped out aboard the *E. A. Johnson.* A more thorough search of his belongings turned up deeply incriminating evidence, including a daguerreotype of Oliver Watts' seventeen-year-old girlfriend, Catherine Dickenson.

Hicks, however, continued to profess his innocence and did so throughout his sensational five-day trial, which opened on May 14, 1860. Despite the butchery he had perpetrated, he was tried not for murder but for piracy, defined by Congress as "robbery committed upon the high seas, or in any basin or bay within the admiralty maritime jurisdiction of the United States." Given the wealth of stolen property found in his possession—and the fact that no corpses had ever been found—this was an easier charge to prove against Hicks and, very important, one that carried a far more severe penalty than robbery committed upon land. As the prosecuting attorney James F. Dwight explained to the jurors in his opening statement, robbery committed upon the high seas was "punishable with death," a sentence "designed to protect more effectually and punish more thoroughly offenses committed upon vessels upon the high seas, where the protection for person and property is not so great as it can be on land, where individuals are so much surrounded by the police regulations to protect them and their property."

Throughout the proceedings, Hicks remained utterly unmoved, even during the most heart-wrenching moments of the trial. These occurred on the third day, when Smith and Oliver Watts' mother tearfully identified various articles of her sons' clothing, and Catherine Dickerson, Oliver's lovely seventeen-year-old girlfriend, was asked to compare a lock of his hair she kept as a love token with some blood-clotted strands found on the deck of the doomed sloop. Even when the jury returned its inevitable guilty verdict and he was sentenced to be hanged, Hicks "maintained a show of cold indifference."

WITH DEATH LOOMING, Hicks—out of either genuine remorse or financial calculation—agreed to publish a detailed confession, all proceeds to go to his otherwise penniless wife. With the aid of an anonymous ghostwriter, he churned out a memoir whose title accurately reflects both its prurient tone and extravagantly lurid contents: *The Life, Trial, Confession and Execution of Albert W. Hicks, the Pirate and Murderer, Containing the History of His Life (Written by Himself) from Childhood up to the Time of His Arrest. With a Full Account of His Piracies, Murders, Mutinies, High-Way Robberies, Etc. Comprising the Particulars of Nearly* ONE HUNDRED MURDERS! Describing himself as a person whose sole ambition, from earliest youth, was to get rich without working "and then give free rein to the passions and desires which governed me," Hicks recounts an adolescence spent in and out of prison for a variety of crimes. Following a stint in solitary confinement—during which he "swore vengeance against the whole human race"—he embarked on a career of seafaring villainy. During the next few years, he and his fellow brigands roamed the seas from the Marquesas to Cape St. Lucas, robbing and butchering natives, instigating mutinies, and in general "living a wild, guerilla life, plundering all who promised anything like booty and never hesitating to take the lives of such as resisted us or were likely to betray us. We spared neither age nor sex. How many times during this period I dyed my hands in human blood, I do not know. No prayers, no entreaties moved us; it seemed as if my heart was dead to every human feeling and was a stranger to pity and every soft emotion."

Hicks' life of unbridled lawlessness took him from the California gold fields—where he squandered his ill-gotten gains in barrooms, brothels, and gambling dens—to Rio de Janeiro, "where we robbed all worth robbing and murdered all who resisted us." Making his way to New York City, he married in 1857, though his new life of domesticity did nothing to curtail his criminal activities. Shipping out on various commercial vessels, he managed to commit a string of onboard robberies, always keeping "a sharp lookout" for particularly vulnerable vessels.

Hearing of the *E. A. Johnson* and its impending voyage, Hicks saw at once that it was "easy prey." The ship was reportedly carrying "something over a thousand dollars" in cash to exchange for a cargo of oysters, and "the entire crew consisted of but two boys," along with Captain Burr. So amiable a fellow was Burr that even the stony-hearted Hicks could not help but like him. His "kindly feelings" toward the man, however, did not alter his savage resolve. "I engaged myself to him solely for the cruel purpose of taking his life, the lives of the two young men, and making myself master of the money I supposed he had on board."

In graphic detail, Hicks proceeds to describe the massacre he perpetrated on his three unsuspecting victims. Oliver Watts, the younger of the two brothers, was first. The eighteen-year-old was on nighttime lookout at the bow when Hicks, concealing an axe behind his back, approached him. "Look," said Hicks, pointing into the darkness. "Ain't that Barnegat Lighthouse over there?" When Watts turned to look, Hicks split the back of his skull with the axe blade. The boy dropped heavily to the deck.

At the sound, Oliver's brother, who had been resting below, emerged from the companionway.

"What's the matter?" Smith asked.

"Nothing," said Hicks, then brought the axe down on Smith's neck. "It was like chopping a small tree," he later confessed. "His whole head came off. The rest of him took a few steps, spouting like a fountain. Then it sagged down as the head rolled along the deck."

Hurrying down into the darkened cabin, Hicks set upon Captain Burr, who lay resting on his bunk. Grappling desperately with his assailant, Burr managed to knock him to the floor and get his hands around his throat, but Hicks was too strong for him. Throwing Burr off with a savage shove, Hicks leapt to his feet and brought the axe down on the captain's skull. "The blow took away half of his head," Hicks wrote. "Half of his eye was on the blade, a piece of his nose, some beard."

Exhausted from the struggle, Hicks made his way up on deck for some air. He was startled to see Oliver Watts—fearfully wounded but still alive—staggering to his feet. Rushing at the boy, Hicks bludgeoned him with the blunt end of the axe, then dragged him to the rail and heaved him over the side. Reflexively, the dying boy grabbed on to the rail and held on so fiercely that Hicks was unable to pry his fingers free. With a vicious curse, Hicks chopped off Watts' hand at the wrist, sending him tumbling into the water.

Retreating to the cabin, Hicks refreshed himself with several tankards of ale before disposing of the other two corpses. In the darkness, he had some trouble locating the decapitated head of Smith Watts, which had rolled into the shadows. At length, he found it and tossed it overboard, along with the murder weapon. By then, dawn was approaching and, through the fog, Hicks could make out the coastline of Staten Island. Collecting his booty in a large canvas sack, he lowered the small lifeboat and rowed for shore.

HICKS' OPEN-AIR HANGING on Friday, July 13, 1860, was a gala event, generating nearly as much excitement as the big Independence Day celebrations nine days earlier. All that was missing were the fireworks.

As the perpetrator of a federal crime, Hicks had to be executed on federal property. Bedloe's Island, future site of the Statue of Liberty, was the logical choice. The gallows was erected atop a grassy terrace on the northeast side of the little island—"a place," as the *New York Times* reported, "which was selected for the purpose of giving as many persons as possible an opportunity to witness the spectacle." A week before the designated day, ads began to appear in the city papers, offering holiday excursions to the hanging:

> HO! FOR THE EXECUTION.—THE BEAUTIFUL AND COMMODIOUS STEAMboat CHICOPEE will leave this city on Friday morning for the purpose of affording all on board an opportunity of witnessing the execution of Albert Hicks, the Pirate. The boat will lay near the island until the ceremonies are over. This will be a fine chance for sea captains and sea-faring men generally to view the exit of one of the most atrocious of these scourges of their profession. The boat will leave the foot of Spring St. at 8 o'clock a.m. Refreshments on board. Tickets, $1 each.

Between the sightseeing vessels, steamships, barges, oyster sloops, shallops, and pleasure craft, a virtual armada turned out for the grand occasion. According to the reporter from the *Times*, "not less than 10,000 persons" showed up "in costumes almost as variegated as a carnival. White shirts, red shirts, blue shirts, blue jackets, red jackets, green jackets, and every steamer, vessel, and yacht decorated with lively colored flags, while the uproar was incessant—cries of, 'Down in front!' 'Get out of the way!' rising from hundreds of throats at the same time." Fashionably dressed women, perched on cushioned rowboat seats, shielded "their complexions from the sun with their parasols, while from beneath the fringes and tassels" they strained for a better look at the gallows.

Hicks, having been awakened from an untroubled sleep at around 4:00 a.m., devoured a last meal of bacon, eggs, bread, and tea before dressing himself in the handsome new garb that had been provided for the occasion: a blue cottonade coat ornamented with gilt buttons and needlework anchors, blue pants, white shirt, and a pair of light pumps. The outfit was a considerable improvement over the threadbare suit he had been arrested in and had worn throughout most of his imprisonment. That suit, however, was no longer in his possession. It had been purchased by P. T. Barnum.

Eager to cash in on the public's fevered fascination with the mass murderer, Barnum—in his cheerfully shameless way—showed up at the Tombs not long before Hicks' execution and, for $25 in cash, two boxes of fine Havanas, and a new suit of clothes, purchased Hicks' apparel. Though Hicks was pleased with the cigars, he complained that the suit was "shoddy" and persuaded his jailer to supply him with a spiffier set of duds for the big day. "I feel like an admiral," Hicks said, beaming, when he put on the blue cottonade suit on the morning of his hanging.

Escorted to a waiting carriage, Hicks was driven to the pier at the foot of Canal Street, where an estimated one thousand men, women, and children besieged the vehicle, breaking the windows and tearing away the curtains for a glimpse of the killer, who, unfazed by the commotion, gazed out at the mob with a "derisive smile." Hustled aboard a chartered steamboat, he was sequestered in the ladies' cabin, while the other passengers crowded into the refreshment saloon. "The day was warm," wrote the correspondent for the *Times*, "and lager beer proved an excellent and cooling beverage."

Arrived at the island, Hicks was marched to the scaffold, which was surrounded by two hundred U.S. marines assigned to hold back the crowd. Wearing a look of utter indifference, he stood calmly while the hangman adjusted the noose around his neck. Asked if he had any last words, he shook his head and said, "Hang me quick—make haste." An instant later, the trap was sprung. "He died very easily," the *Times* reported the following day, "the third cervical vertebra being at once broken." He was allowed to dangle for thirty minutes, affording the flotilla of boisterous, beer-fueled spectators plenty of time to ogle his corpse.

Not everyone, of course, was able to attend the carnivalesque execution. For those thousands of New Yorkers deprived of the chance to get a firsthand view of the infamous killer, P. T. Barnum offered the next best thing. In the age before the advent of the modern mass media, the "Great Showman" provided antebellum Americans with the sort of vicarious thrills that later audiences would derive from radio crime melodramas, gangster movies, and TV cop shows "ripped from the headlines." Within days of the hanging, newspaper advertisements for Barnum's American Museum began trumpeting the latest additions to this emporium of wonder. In addition to such living curiosities as Samson the Learned Seal, Crowley the Man-Horse, and the Amazing Murray Midgets, viewers could marvel at a "Life-Size Wax Figure of A. W. Hicks, attired in the very clothes worn by him when he butchered his victims with an ax! Acknowledged by all to be a wonderful likeness of the infamous pirate!" The gruesome display instantly became—and for many years remained—one of the museum's biggest attractions.

[*Sources: The Life, Trial, Confession and Execution of Albert W. Hicks, the Pirate and Murderer* (New York: Robert De Witt, 1860); Jay Robert Nash, *The Great Pictorial History of World Crime*, vol. II (Wilmette, IL: History, Inc., 2004).]

"Hicks the Pirate"

Composed by the legendary New York minstrel known as the Saugerties Bard (see p. 102) and printed by one of the city's leading publishers of song sheets, this murder ballad—meant to be sung to the tune of a popular air, "The Rose Tree"—went on sale just days after Hicks' execution.

A mournful tale heart rending
    To you kind friends I will relate;
The solemn truth intending
    Of three that met a tragic fate;
An oyster sloop was sailing
    Upon the ocean's sparkling tide,
In the beautiful breeze regaling,
    She moved upon the waters wide.

But upon this Oyster vessel,
    A pirate bold had found his way,
With wicked heart this vassal
    The captain and two boys did slay;
He seized the gold and silver,
    Which the poor captain had in store;
His watch and clothes did pilfer,
    While he lay struggling in his gore.

He overboard soon threw them,
    The murdered boys and captain too;
The briney deep enclosed them,
    And they were quickly gone from view;
But the eye that never slumbers,
    Did follow on the murderer's track;
And the Vigilance of numbers
    To justice brought the monster back.

In a boat he left the vessel,
    When he the wicked deed had done;
And soon the murderous rascal
    Had far into the country gone;
He soon was overtaken
    And to New York was brought again
A lonely wretch forsaken,
    Who had the boys and captain slain.

By a true and faithful jury,
    He was found guilty of the crime;
Some raved and cursed like fury,
    But he met his fate in time;
'Twixt heaven and earth suspended,
    On Bedloe's Island Hicks was hung,
Some thousands there attended,
    To see the horrid murderer swung.

The Resurrection of Albert Hicks

Not long after Albert Hicks was hanged on Bedloe's Island, a remarkable story began to make the rounds: that the notorious pirate had been brought back to life. According to the rumor—first reported in several New York City newspapers and reprinted in the November 3, 1860, issue of the British medical journal the *Lancet*—Hicks was still alive when, with the connivance of a paid accomplice posing as a deputy marshal, his body was cut down, wrapped in warm blankets, and spirited to the home of Dr. Henry D. O'Reilly of Brooklyn. There, Dr. O'Reilly and a colleague named Crane employed an "electro-chemical bath" devised by a certain Professor Verguès to effect Hicks' resuscitation:

> *The body was at once placed in the electro-chemical bath and while subjected to the battery and the action of the acids, Dr. Crane commenced a series of experiments for the inflation of the lungs. In the course of about two hours, these were partially successful, the pirate beginning to give faint indications of respiration. Very slowly but steadily, Albert W. Hicks regained consciousness, though for several days unable to speak, his throat being too severely injured. It was then found that his left eye—the side on which the noose had been—had lost all power of sight, and that his left arm and left leg were utterly paralyzed. In this condition, he was conveyed to Poughkeepsie, where his sister, Mrs. Gavan, lives, and under her roof he is now sheltered.*

Needless to say, there was not a shred of truth to this humbug (as P. T. Barnum would have called such a flagrant hoax).

Slightly more than a hundred years later, on the evening of April 4, 1963, Albert Hicks really did return to life—in a manner of speaking. It happened on the first network broadcast of "The New Exhibit," an episode of Rod Serling's classic TV series, *The Twilight Zone*.

The program concerned one Martin Senescu, a mild-mannered employee of a run-down wax museum. Informed that his beloved workplace is closing for good—"People aren't interested in wax figures anymore," sighs his boss—Senescu carts home a collection of his favorite criminal effigies: Jack the Ripper, Burke and Hare, Henri Landru ("The French Bluebeard"), and an axe-wielding Albert Hicks. In typical *Twilight Zone* fashion, the figures proceed to come to life and do away with a number of Senescu's nemeses, including his nagging wife and nosy brother-in-law.

For a student of American crime, what's most interesting about this show (one of nearly two dozen *Twilight Zone* episodes penned by writer Charles Beaumont) is the prominence it accords Albert Hicks. Clearly, as recently as the 1960s, Hicks was still regarded as one of history's most infamous killers, a homicidal maniac on the order of Jack the Ripper. Yet in the decades since, the Ripper's fame has only increased; he has entered the realm of undying myth. By contrast, Hicks, for whatever mysterious reasons, has (like Martin Senescu's outdated wax museum) become a dusty relic of the bygone past.

III

POST—CIVIL WAR
MONSTERS

1866-1880

MARTHA GRINDER, LYDIA SHERMAN, AND SARAH JANE ROBINSON: THE "AMERICAN BORGIAS"

PRURIENT RUMORS ABOUT POWERFUL INDIVIDUALS—OFTEN INVENTED BY THEIR political enemies—offer so much in the way of titillating entertainment that, as a general rule, people much prefer them to the humdrum truth. As a result, all sorts of scandalous stories have attached themselves to certain historical figures.

A case in point is the Renaissance noblewoman Lucrezia Borgia. Though revisionist historians portray her as a loving, pious, and charitable woman who was manipulated by her Machiavellian family, she has come down in legend as a ruthless, sexually ravenous *femme fatale* who engaged in incestuous relations with her father and brothers and dispatched her enemies with poison powders dispensed from a special hollow ring.

It was her ostensible fondness for this latter method of homicide that made her name a byword in the nineteenth century, when our country was rocked by a string of serial murder cases involving female poisoners. Each of these killers in turn was known as "The American Borgia."

One of the earliest female psychopaths to be branded with this nickname was Mrs. Martha Grinder, also known as "The Pittsburgh Poisoner." A full-fledged "homicidal monomaniac"—as serial killers were labeled in the Civil War era—Grinder derived "fiendish delight" from serving arsenic-laced food to the people around her, then lavishing loving attention on them while they suffered excruciating deaths. Though convicted and executed for a single homicide—the 1865 murder of her next-door neighbor Mary Caruthers, who was tenderly nursed by Mrs. Grinder while dying horribly from the latter's poisoned soup—"the wretched torturer" (as the *Pittsburgh Post* called her) was believed responsible for at least seven other murders. Her alleged victims included various members of her husband's family, including his two younger brothers, both Union soldiers who died in agony shortly after returning from the war and partaking of meals prepared by Martha.

Her own demise was appropriately gruesome. Owing to a careless adjustment of the noose, her neck didn't snap when the trap was sprung. "She strangled slowly," wrote one spectator. "Struggling fearfully, she caught with her right hand the edge of the fallen trap and grasped and held it firmly for some time. At length, the struggles became feeble, died away to a shrug—and then ceased." It took her a full twelve minutes to die.

MRS. GRINDER'S PRESUMED body count of eight victims was surpassed a few years later by that of another female serial killer, Lydia Sherman, aka "The Poison Fiend," "The Queen Poisoner," and "The Borgia of Connecticut."

Her original name was Lydia Danbury. Born in Burlington, New Jersey, in 1825, she was just seventeen when she married her first husband, Edward Struck, a forty-year-old widower with six children. Within a year of their wedding, she had given birth to a healthy boy. Five more children followed in rapid succession.

With a wife and twelve children to support, Struck—by then living with his family in Manhattan—took a job as a police officer. In 1863, however, he was fired in disgrace after failing to respond quickly enough when a knife-wielding drunkard attacked a hotel bartender.

By then, Struck's children from his first marriage had grown up and left home, and one of Lydia's babies had died of an intestinal ailment. That left five children in the household. With not a penny coming in to feed them, Struck plunged into a state of extreme despondency. Eventually he refused to leave his bed. Deciding that he had become more trouble than he was worth, Lydia killed him with arsenic-laced porridge. The attending physician diagnosed the cause of death as "consumption."

Lydia was a forty-two-year-old widow with no income. Just a month after disposing of her husband, she began to feel disheartened by the difficulty of supporting five children on her own. In the first week of July, she poisoned the two youngest with arsenic.

Freed of these burdens, Lydia's situation improved, particularly since her fourteen-year-old son, George, had gotten a job as a painter's assistant. Unfortunately, George developed a condition known as "painter's colic" and was forced to quit work. His mother gave him a week to recuperate. When he showed no signs of improvement, she killed him with arsenic-spiked tea.

Lydia Sherman murder pamphlet (*Courtesy of New York State Historical Association Library, Cooperstown.*)

Two of Lydia's children still remained above ground: her eighteen-year-old daughter, also named Lydia, and little Ann Eliza, aged twelve. Ann Eliza was a frail child, frequently sick with fever and chills. Lydia began to feel oppressed by the burden of caring for her. In March 1866, she killed the little girl by mixing a few grains of arsenic into a spoonful of patent medicine. The cause of death was given as "typhoid fever."

For the next six or seven weeks, the two Lydias, mother and daughter, lived together in a small apartment on upper Broadway. In early May, after paying an overnight visit to her half sister in lower Manhattan, young Lydia returned home with a fever and took to bed. Her mother did not feel like caring for her. On May 19, 1866, after dutifully taking the foul-tasting medicine her mother had fed her, the eighteen-year-old girl died in convulsive agony and was laid to rest beside the bodies of her father and five siblings.

Shortly afterward, Lydia moved to Stratford, Connecticut, where she met and married an old man named Dennis Hurlburt, a local farmer of considerable means.

Slightly more than one year later, Hurlburt fell violently ill and died after eating a bowl of his wife's special clam chowder. His death was attributed to "cholera."

The forty-six-year-old widow came into a considerable inheritance. If her motives had been entirely mercenary, she could have tossed away her arsenic and never killed again. While Lydia was happy to profit from her crimes, it was not greed that drove her but an addiction to cruelty and death: what her contemporaries described as a "mania for life-taking."

Within months of Hulbert's death, she married Horatio N. Sherman, a hard-drinking widower with four children. In mid-November 1870—just two months after the wedding—Lydia murdered Sherman's youngest child, a four-month-old baby named Frankie. The following month, she poisoned his fourteen-year-old daughter, Ada.

The sudden death of his two children devastated Sherman. He began to hit the bottle harder than ever. After returning from one weekend bender, he took to bed for several days before returning to work on Monday, May 8, 1871. When he came home from the factory that evening, Lydia was waiting with a nice cup of poisoned hot chocolate. Two days later, he was dead.

Mr. Sherman drinks his DEATH POTION prepared by his wife.

The sudden, shocking death of the seemingly healthy Sherman aroused the suspicion of his physician, Dr. Edward Beardsley. Securing permission to conduct a postmortem, Beardsley removed the stomach and liver and shipped them to a toxicology professor at Yale for analysis. Three weeks later, he received the results. Sherman's liver was saturated with arsenic. A warrant was promptly issued for the arrest of Lydia Sherman.

On June 7, 1871, she was picked up in New York City and transported back to New Haven. Her trial was a nationwide sensation. In the end—rejecting her lawyer's suggestion that her despondent husband had taken his own life—the jury found her guilty of second-degree murder and sentenced her to life imprisonment in the state prison at Wethersfield. She died there of cancer eight years later, though not before being immortalized in a popular ditty:

> Lydia Sherman is plagued with rats.
> Lydia has no faith in cats.
> So Lydia buys some arsenic,
> And then her husband gets sick;
> And then her husband, he does die.
> And Lydia's neighbors wonder why.

> Lydia moves but still has rats;
> And still she puts no faith in cats;
> So again she buys some arsenic,
> This time her children, they get sick,
> This time, her children, they do die,
> And Lydia's neighbors wonder why.

> Lydia lies in Wethersfield jail,
> And loudly does she moan and wail.
> She blames her fate on a plague of rats;
> She blames the laziness of cats.
> But her neighbors' questions she can't deny—
> So Lydia now in prison must lie.

*   *   *

So MONSTROUS WERE the crimes of Lydia Sherman that her contemporaries felt certain they would never see her like again. But they were mistaken. Just eight years after the death of America's "Queen Poisoner," another homegrown Borgia succeeded to her vacated throne.

In early February, 1885, a poor, forty-two-year-old South Boston seamstress named Annie Freeman contracted pneumonia shortly after giving birth to her second child. Thanks to the largesse of her mother-in-law, a private nurse was brought in to tend to the bedridden woman. To the immense relief of her husband—an unskilled factory worker improbably named Prince Arthur—Annie slowly began to show signs of improvement. By the second week of February, the family physician, Dr. Archibald Davidson, confidently predicted that, "with proper nourishment," the patient would almost certainly make a complete recovery.

And then Annie's sister showed up.

Her name was Sarah Jane Robinson. Like Annie, she was a skilled seamstress, though she had also done her share of nursing. To be sure, her patients had an unfortunate habit of dying. Just a few years earlier, for example, she had cared for her landlord, Oliver Sleeper, during what turned out to be his final illness. His death had taken his friends by surprise. Until he was stricken with a sudden intestinal ailment, the seventy-year-old Sleeper had appeared in perfectly sound health. Still, he was an old man. Certainly Mrs. Robinson had given him assiduous attention, remaining at his bedside day and night and making sure that he swallowed every last dose of his medication. For her services, she had charged his estate $50 following the old man's intensely unpleasant death—a bill that Sleeper's survivors ultimately settled by remitting Mrs. Robinson's overdue rent.

A few years later, her own husband, Moses Robinson, died of an illness whose symptoms bore a remarkable similarity to those manifested by old Mr. Sleeper during his final, agonized days—violent nausea and vomiting, bloody diarrhea, burning pains in the stomach. She had also lost three of her eight children to the same devastating disease, including both of her twin sons, who died within a week of one another when they were barely eight months old.

Now she had come to take care of her sister, Annie.

Taking care of Annie was nothing new for Sarah. She'd been doing it ever since they were children in Ireland. When their parents, a poor farming couple named Tennent, died within a few months of each other in 1853, it was fourteen-year-old Sarah, all by herself, who took her nine-year-old sister across the ocean to America. Later—after Annie's first husband sliced his hand on a saw blade and succumbed to blood poisoning—it was Sarah who opened her home to the grieving young widow.

To those who knew her, therefore, it came as no surprise that Sarah had hurried to her sister's sickbed the moment she got word of Annie's illness. Of course, in a very real sense, no one knew Sarah Jane Robinson. Even her nearest acquaintances had been deceived by her apparent normality. Several years would pass before she stood revealed to the world as the kind of virulent personality we now describe as a criminal psychopath. Though capable of counterfeiting ordinary human emotions, such beings lack every trace of fellow feeling. Like Sarah Jane Robinson, they may be adept at putting on convincing shows of sympathy and concern. At bottom, however, they care about nothing but their own monstrous needs. And they will happily sacrifice anyone—a husband, a child, or an ailing younger sister—to make sure those needs are gratified.

When Sarah arrived at the Freemans' tenement, she found a family friend, a woman named Susan Marshall, seated at Annie's bedside. Annie herself was much improved. Her coloring was better than it had been in many days, and her coughing had let up significantly. Propped up on her pillow, she greeted her sister with a fond smile.

Sarah, however, seemed strangely dismayed at the sight of her sister. After spending a few minutes quizzing Annie about her health, she asked to speak to Mrs. Marshall in private.

Retreating to the kitchen, Sarah told Mrs. Marshall about a terrible dream she'd had the night before. In it, Annie had gotten sicker and sicker, until she had wasted into a skeleton.

"I just know she'll never get any better," Sarah exclaimed as she finished describing the nightmare.

"But she *is* getting better," Mrs. Marshall replied, seeking to reassure the obviously distraught older woman.

But Sarah would not be consoled. "Whenever I have a dream like that," she said, "there is always one of the family who dies."

Later that day—after Prince Arthur returned home from work—Sarah persuaded him to dismiss Annie's private nurse. Why waste good money when she herself could tend to Annie? To demonstrate the point, she proceeded to fix her sister a nice bowl of oatmeal gruel and a cup of freshly brewed tea. Both appeared to have a strangely bitter quality to Annie, though her sense of taste had been so impaired by her illness that she could not really be sure.

That night, Annie took a sudden and devastating turn for the worse. She was overcome with nausea and seized with savage stomach pains. She lay awake all night, alternately retching into the chamber pot and writhing on her mattress in agony. When Dr. Davidson arrived for his morning visit, he was completely bewildered by her altered condition. Only one day earlier, his patient had been well on the way to recovery. Now she had not merely suffered a setback; she had begun to display an entirely new set of symptoms. Davidson prescribed a common nineteenth-century remedy for acute gastric distress: bismuth phosphate, each dose to be dissolved in three parts water and taken at regular intervals.

In spite of the medicine—faithfully administered by Sarah, who made sure that her sister swallowed every sip of the doctored water—Annie continued to grow worse. In addition to her other symptoms, she was stricken with a ferocious burning in the pit of her stomach. She begged for anything to soothe the pain. Sarah bought her some ice cream, and fed it to her a few spoonfuls at a time. But the ice cream only made Annie's nausea worse and intensified the vomiting until she was bringing up nothing but a thin, blood-streaked fluid.

When Susan Marshall came by several days later, she was shocked at her friend's transformation. The last time she'd visited, Annie had clearly been on the mend, her strength returning, her appearance improved. Now—as Mrs. Marshall would later testify—her "features were very much bloated," and her complexion was of a ghastly "discolored" hue. It was clear to Mrs. Marshall that her friend wasn't suffering from "any ordinary sickness." Her throat was so constricted that she could barely speak, though she did manage to voice a desperate plea for something cold to drink, to ease the dreadful burning in her stomach. She was afflicted with a blinding headache, overwhelming nausea, and another, deeply puzzling, symptom—terrible cramps in the calves of her legs. Even with the opium that Dr. Davidson had prescribed to alleviate the poor woman's suffering, she remained in an almost constant state of agony, groaning miserably and rolling back and forth on her mattress.

Utterly aghast, Mrs. Marshall questioned Sarah about this sudden, inexplicable reversal in Annie's condition. "We have been doing all we can for her," Sarah replied.

"But I do not expect that she will ever leave her bed." Then, after a brief pause, she gave a heavy sigh and added: "It is happening just as in my dream."

On February 27, 1885—slightly more than a week after Sarah came to care for her sister—Annie Freeman died in the presence of her weeping husband, several grief-stricken friends, and her dry-eyed older sister.

Sarah Jane Robinson's dream had come true.

No sooner had Annie emitted her last, tortured breath than Sarah asked to speak to Mrs. Marshall and another family friend, Mrs. Mary L. Moore. Much to the consternation of the two sorrowing women, Sarah—who seemed bizarrely unaffected by her sister's death—wanted to discuss a matter of obviously paramount importance to her. She wanted them to use whatever influence they possessed to persuade Prince Arthur to come live with her, along with his two children. It was, she declared, her sister's last wish. To be sure, no one had ever heard Annie express such a desire in her final days. But then, no one had spent as much time in the dying woman's company as Sarah, who had remained at her sister's side night and day, refusing to allow anyone else to feed her or to administer her medication.

Mrs. Marshall and Mrs. Moore promised to do everything in their power to see that Annie's last wish was honored.

The last shovelful of dirt had barely been tossed onto Annie Freeman's grave when Sarah herself spoke to Prince Arthur, telling him the same flagrant lie that she had told Mrs. Moore and Mrs. Marshall: that Annie had expressly wanted him and the two children to come live in Sarah's home. The stricken man—who had just seen his beloved wife vanish forever into the ground—seemed too stunned to think clearly about the subject, though he did permit Sarah to take his two small children home with her to Boylston Street that night. He himself followed a few weeks later, taking up residence at the home of Sarah Jane Robinson in early April 1885.

Three weeks later, Prince Arthur suffered a second devastating blow when his one-year-old daughter, Elizabeth, developed a sudden case of "intestinal catarrh." Sarah gave little Elizabeth the same watchful care that she had lavished on the baby's mother, and with the same results. In the last week of April, Elizabeth died in great distress and was laid in the ground beside her mother.

Immediately after the child's funeral, Sarah sat her brother-in-law down at the kitchen table and explained what must be done. Like other laboring men of the time, Prince Arthur belonged to a "mutual assessment and cooperative society"—the United Order of Pilgrim Fathers of Boston—whose main function was to provide low-cost life insurance to its working-class members. He owned a policy worth $2,000. Annie, of course, had been the beneficiary. Now that she was gone and Prince Arthur and his remaining child—a six-year-old boy named Thomas—were residing with Sarah, it was only reasonable that *she* be made the beneficiary. That way, little Thomas was sure to be well taken care of. Just in case anything unfortunate should happen to Prince Arthur.

One month later, on May 31, 1885, Prince Arthur's $2,000 life insurance policy was made over to his sister-in-law, Mrs. Sarah Jane Robinson.

Almost immediately, people around Sarah began to notice a dramatic shift in her attitude toward Prince Arthur. Ever since the deaths of his wife and infant daughter, she had treated him with the utmost kindness and consideration. Suddenly, he became a constant source of annoyance to her. It was as though she no longer had the slightest use for him. And she didn't hesitate to let others know exactly how she felt.

During the first week of June, for example, a friend named Belle Clough dropped by Sarah's apartment for a cup of camomile tea and some neighborly gossip. As they sat at the kitchen table, Sarah suddenly burst into a bitter denunciation of her brother-in-law. He was "worthless," "good-for-nothing," "too lazy to earn a living." His wages amounted to only $6 a week, half of which he spent on trolley fare. She ended her harangue with a comment whose sheer vehemence caused Mrs. Clough to raise her eyebrows in surprise. "I wish," said Sarah, "that *he* had died instead of my poor sister."

Just a few days later, Sarah was seated at the same table, this time with her twenty-five-year-old daughter, Lizzie. They were eating a modest supper of boiled beets and codfish. All of a sudden, Sarah gave a violent shudder and went deathly pale.

"Mama, what's wrong?" Lizzie cried.

Sarah passed a hand across her eyes. "I felt a ghost tap me on the shoulder."

Though Lizzie herself had never experienced such supernatural visitations, she knew that her mother was particularly prone to them. Sarah was often possessed by dark forebodings regarding family members, and her premonitions had an uncanny way of coming true.

"Did he say anything?" asked Lizzie.

"He said he would be coming for someone in the family," her mother replied. "I shouldn't wonder if something happened to your uncle very soon."

The ghost proved remarkably prescient. Just a few days later, on June 17, 1885, Prince Arthur and Sarah were seated in the parlor, when—apropos of nothing—she announced that it would be a good idea if he paid an immediate visit to his mother. Given the precarious nature of human existence, it might be his last chance to see her. Prince Arthur was inclined to take his sister-in-law's words to heart. He, too, believed that she possessed a strange, prophetic gift. After all, hadn't she foreseen the death of his wife when everyone else, even Dr. Davidson, had been so optimistic? Now she appeared to have been visited by some dark apprehension regarding his mother. And it was certainly true that the old lady had been in a bad way since taking a fall the previous winter and fracturing her left hip. Early the following day, he set out for Charlestown.

When he arrived at his mother's home, he was relieved to find her in generally sound health and good spirits. When he explained the reason for the unexpected visit, she pooh-poohed Sarah's grim premonition. She felt "fit as a fiddle," she assured him. She planned to be around "for a good many years to come." Prince Arthur stayed long enough to share a meal with his mother before kissing her goodbye and heading back to Cambridge.

It turned out to be their final farewell—just as Sarah Jane Robinson had intended.

On the morning of June 22, 1885, after finishing the bowl of oatmeal and molasses Sarah had prepared for his breakfast, Prince Arthur set off for his job at the Norwegian Steel and Iron Company in South Boston. He hadn't gotten very far when he was suddenly overcome with nausea. Staggering into an alleyway, he threw up his breakfast. Feeling slightly better, he continued on his way. It wasn't long, however, before the sickness returned.

Just then, an acquaintance named F. J. Hayes happened by. At his first glimpse of Prince Arthur, Hayes could see that something was wrong.

"Are you all right, Mr. Freeman?" he asked. "You do not look at all well."

When Prince Arthur confessed that he was feeling "awfully queer in the stomach," Hayes advised him to "turn right around and go home."

Prince Arthur, however, wouldn't hear of it. He had "already missed a considerable number of days on account of sickness," he explained, and could not afford to lose more pay. Fighting back his nausea, he proceeded to the foundry. By the time he arrived, however, he was feeling so wretched that his boss insisted he go home.

A short time later, he arrived back at his sister-in-law's flat on Boylston Street.

Strangely, she seemed unsurprised to see him—almost as if she'd been expecting him to return. She put him to bed and fixed him a cup of tea, which he was unable to keep down. Throughout the day, she fed him small amounts of strange-tasting water, telling him that it was mixed with bismuth phosphate and was certain to make him feel better. But his nausea and stomach pains only grew worse.

That evening, Sarah told her daughter, Lizzie, that the message she had received from her dead husband's ghost appeared to be coming true. "I fear your uncle will never get out of bed again," she said.

The following afternoon, Prince Arthur received a visit from Dr. John T. G. Nichols, a physician who resided on the same block as Sarah. Nichols—as he would later testify—found the patient suffering from "headache, vomiting, pain in the stomach, thirst, quick pulse, and low elevation in temperature." He prescribed the usual remedies—mustard and milk, lime water, soda water, opium. In spite of these measures, however, the symptoms grew worse over the next several days. By Wednesday, June 24, the baffled physician summoned a colleague, Dr. Driver of Cambridge, who—like Nichols—could find no sign of organic disease.

It was Driver who first raised the possibility that the patient might have been exposed to some sort of "irritant poison." Questioning Mrs. Robinson, they discovered that Prince Arthur spent his days at the foundry immersing iron bars in an acid bath, a process known as "pickling." The doctors, however, were inclined to doubt that even prolonged exposure to the fumes of sulfuric acid could produce such a devastating sickness.

Was it possible, they inquired, that her brother-in-law had inadvertently ingested arsenic? Such accidents were not uncommon. People who used it as rat poison were often surprisingly careless in handling the stuff, using household utensils to sprinkle it around the floorboards, then neglecting to wash the implements with sufficient care.

Mrs. Robinson dismissed the notion out of hand. She never kept arsenic around the house. If the doctors wished, they were welcome to examine her cupboards and utensils. Nichols and Driver declined her offer. After all, Mrs. Robinson was clearly such a nice person—so frank and natural in her responses—that there was no reason to doubt her. As Nichols would later put it, "there was nothing in her behavior to warrant the slightest suspicion."

Two days later, Prince Arthur's last hope for survival arrived in the form of his older sister, Mrs. Catherine Melvin, who had just gotten word of his desperate condition. At her first glimpse of her brother, she let out an involuntary gasp. She had heard that he was very sick, but she was unprepared for the sheer ghastliness of his suffering. Face contorted, frame shockingly wasted, he thrashed back and forth on the mattress, while begging for something, *anything*, to ease the terrible pain in his stomach.

Over her sister-in-law's protests, Mrs. Melvin immediately assumed the role of nurse. She sat at Prince Arthur's bedside throughout the night, soothing his forehead with a moist compress and feeding him small sips of brandy, along with the medication prescribed by Dr. Nichols: tincture of nux vomica, two drops every hour.

When Nichols arrived early the next day for his morning visit, he was relieved to find that Prince Arthur's condition had grown no worse. He was even more gratified when he returned that afternoon. For the first time since the onset of his mysterious sickness, the patient actually seemed slightly improved.

That night, Sarah urged her sister-in-law to get some sleep. *She* would resume the care of Prince Arthur. Mrs. Melvin, however, insisted on staying up with her brother again. The next morning, he felt so much better that, for the first time in days, he expressed a desire for food.

Believing that her brother had turned a corner, Mrs. Melvin—who had her own family to take care of—departed that morning, physically exhausted but feeling hopeful about his recovery. She had no way of knowing that she had returned him to the malevolent care of a madwoman, who was more determined than ever to have him hurry up and die.

That same night—after drinking a cup of the odd-tasting tea prepared by his sister-in-law—Prince Arthur took a violent turn for the worse. Shortly before midnight on Saturday, June 27, he went into convulsions and died. Dr. Nichols, who still could not guess what had killed Prince Arthur Freeman, certified the cause of death as "disease of the stomach."

As dreadful as his suffering had been, Prince Arthur at least had the comfort of knowing that his six-year-old son, Tommy, was well provided for. Two months after the funeral, the Order of Pilgrim Fathers made good on his life insurance policy, paying $2,000 to his beneficiary, Sarah Jane Robinson. She immediately paid off her creditors, moved into a larger flat, purchased new furniture and clothing, and took a trip to Wisconsin to visit her brother. When she returned, she used the remainder of the money to take out an insurance policy on the life of her twenty-five-year-old daughter, Lizzie.

Six months later, in February, 1886, Lizzie was stricken with a catastrophic illness and died after several weeks of acute suffering.

In the meantime, little Tommy Freeman had received no benefits at all from the money left by his father. His aunt Sarah—who had been so nice to him while his father was alive—now acted as though she could barely stand the sight of him, treating him like a particularly onerous burden she'd unfairly been saddled with. Visitors to the Robinson household were taken aback by how pale, skinny, and utterly forlorn the little boy looked. When they questioned Sarah about the child, she explained with a sigh that the poor boy missed his parents dreadfully.

"Sometimes," she remarked to one of her neighbors, "I think he would be better off following in their footsteps."

On July 19, 1886, a year and three weeks after the death of his father, Tommy fell ill with uncontrolled vomiting and diarrhea. Sarah had one of her premonitions, telling several acquaintances that the boy would never recover. He died four days later, on July 23.

The terrible fragility of life—the possibility that anyone, no matter how young and healthy, could be struck down at any moment—was a lesson that the inhabitants of the Robinson household could hardly fail to learn. Perhaps for that reason, Sarah's oldest son, twenty-three-year-old William, insured his life with the Order of Pilgrim Fathers shortly after the death of his beloved sister, Lizzie.

One month later, in August 1886, William—who was employed at a commercial warehouse—suffered a minor accident when a wooden crate toppled from a shelf and struck him between the shoulder blades. He shrugged off the mishap: the box was empty, and though the breath had been knocked out of him, he hadn't been seriously injured. Not long afterward, however, he felt suddenly nauseous and threw up the breakfast his mother had prepared for him that morning.

That evening at dinner, his mother fixed him a cup of her special tea. William took a sip and wrinkled his nose. It tasted very strange to him. Still, at his mother's urging, he drank it all down. No sooner had he finished his meal than the nausea returned, worse than ever. He took to his bed and was up all night with racking cramps and constant vomiting.

The next morning, his mother sent for Dr. Emory White, a local physician affili-

ated with the Order of Pilgrim Fathers. White knew about the strange series of tragedies that had befallen the Robinson household—most of them involving family
members insured by the Order—and resolved to keep a close eye on William. When
the young man continued to deteriorate, White shipped a sample of his vomit to a
Harvard toxicologist named Edward Wood. He also informed Police Chief Parkhurst
of his suspicions regarding Sarah Jane Robinson. Parkhurst dispatched a couple of his
men to keep watch over Mrs. Robinson. Two days later, word arrived from Dr. Wood:
William Robinson's stomach was saturated with arsenic. By then, however, the young
man was beyond saving. He died that same afternoon. "The old lady dosed me" were
the last words anyone heard him say.

Sarah Jane Robinson was immediately arrested for the murder of her son.

In the weeks that followed, authorities exhumed the bodies of six more of her
victims: her daughter, Lizzie; her sister, Annie; her brother-in-law, Prince Arthur
Freeman; her nephew, Tommy; her husband, Moses; and her former landlord, Oliver
Sleeper. Arsenic was found in all of the corpses.

For the third time in living memory, America had produced a female "poison
fiend"—a "Modern Borgia" in the monstrous mold of Martha Grinder and Lydia
Sherman. Public excitement over the case was intense, and the newspapers showed
little restraint in their sensationalistic coverage. The *New York Times* placed the
number of her victims at an even dozen, while one widely circulated story claimed
that she'd once poisoned more than a hundred people at a picnic.

Largely as a result of prosecutorial incompetence, her first trial ended with a
hung jury. She was immediately indicted again, this time for the murder of Prince
Arthur Freeman. During her second trial in February 1886, the government argued
that Prince Arthur's killing had been part of an elaborate plot to obtain his $2,000 life
insurance policy, a scheme that also necessitated the murder of both Annie Freeman
and seven-year-old Tommy.

Interestingly, it was the defense attorney, John B. Goodrich, who did a better job
of identifying Sarah Jane Robinson as the homicidal maniac she so clearly was. In his
closing argument, Goodrich argued that money couldn't possibly explain the horrors
of which his client stood accused. "The idea is repellent; it is unnatural; it is unreason-
able to suppose that that would be a sufficient motive," he insisted. The crimes alleg-
edly perpetrated by his client could have only one cause: "uncontrolled depravity." If
"such be the case," he told the jury, "you must pity her. You cannot condemn her."

After all, it took a "monster" to commit such atrocities, said Goodrich, and "I do not know that the law hangs monsters."

In the end, the jury required less than one day to side with the prosecution. Sarah Jane Robinson was found guilty of first-degree murder and condemned to hang, though her sentence was later commuted to life in prison. She lived out the remainder of her days in a narrow cell decorated with engraved portraits of her victims, clipped from local newspapers.

[*Sources:* Marlin Shipman, *"The Penalty Is Death": U.S. Newspaper Coverage of Women's Executions* (Columbia: University of Missouri Press, 2002); Ann Jones, *Women Who Kill* (New York: Fawcett Books, 1988); *The Poison Fiend! Life, Crimes, and Conviction of Lydia Sherman (The Modern Lucretia Borgia), Recently Tried in New Haven, Conn., for Poisoning Three Husbands and Eight of Her Children* (Philadelphia: Barclay Co., 1872); *The Official Report of the Trial of Sarah Jane Robinson: For the Murder of Prince Arthur Freeman in the Supreme Judicial Court of Massachusetts* (Boston: Wright & Potter, 1888); Edmund Pearson, *More Studies in Murder* (New York: Harrison Smith & Robert Hass, 1936).]

"Poison and Pedophilia"

Though the Victorian era was a particularly fertile time for female serial poisoners, the twentieth century also produced a healthy crop of homegrown Borgias. One notable example was Mary Frances Creighton, dubbed the "Black-Eyed Borgia" in the tabloids. A pretty New Jersey housewife with strikingly "dark, luminous eyes," Mary began her lethal career in the early 1920s by bumping off her despised mother-in-law with arsenic-laced hot cocoa. She followed up this homicide by serving poisoned chocolate pudding to her younger brother after persuading him to make her the beneficiary of his $1,000 life insurance policy. She was brought to trial twice but acquitted both times for lack of evidence.

After her second trial, she and her family—her husband, John, and children, Ruth and Jack—relocated to a small cottage on Long Island. By 1935, the once "comely brunette" had coarsened into a "squat and triple-chinned" matron.

With the Great Depression in full swing, the Creightons took in a pair of boarders, an acquaintance of John's named Everett Applegate and his sharp-tongued, morbidly obese wife, Ada. Before long, Everett—or "Uncle Ev," as she called him—had seduced and embarked on a quasi-incestuous affair with fifteen-year-old Ruth Creighton. Obsessed with the underage girl and determined to marry her, he set out to rid himself of his wife by spiking her eggnog with rat poison. He was assisted by Mary, who not only harbored a deep detestation of the foul-tempered Ada but was eager to see her daughter married and out of the house.

Since Ada had tipped the scales at more than 250 pounds, no one doubted her physician's conclusion that she had died of a heart attack—until authorities found out about Mary's involvement with the two earlier poison murders. Their suspicions aroused, they ordered a belated autopsy. When the toxicologist reported that the corpse's vital organs contained eleven grains of arsenic—enough to kill at least three people—Mary and Everett were promptly arrested for murder.

With its irresistibly lurid ingredients (summed up in one memorable headline as "Poison and Pedophilia"), their trial in January

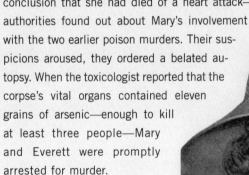

Mary Frances Creighton

1936 was a nationwide sensation. On the stand, Mary confessed that after Everett had prepared the lethal eggnog, she herself had served it up to Ada with the full knowledge that it was poisoned. Everett, hoping to be convicted on the lesser charge of statutory rape, offered graphic details of his affair with the willing teenager, including a detailed account of the time they had engaged in sex while his wife lay beside them on the mattress. Both defendants were convicted and sentenced to die in the chair.

In the days leading up to her execution, Mary worked herself into a state of such hysterical terror that she became semicomatose and had to be trundled to the death chamber in a wheelchair. Moments later—"with the odor of seared flesh still clinging to the chamber"—it was Everett's turn. Standing "tall and ramrod straight," he strode into the chamber and made a final emphatic declaration of his innocence before stoically meeting his doom.

[*Sources:* Deborah Blum, *The Poisoner's Handbook: Murder and the Birth of Forensic Medicine in Jazz Age New York* (New York: Penguin Press, 2010); Dorothy Kilgallen, *Murder One* (New York: Random House, 1967).]

ANTON PROBST,
"THE MONSTER IN THE SHAPE OF A MAN"

DURING THE SECOND HALF OF THE NINETEENTH CENTURY, MAJOR AMERICAN cities such as New York, Boston, Baltimore, and Philadelphia were home to dozens of dime museums—garish showplaces where visitors could gape at a motley assortment of curios, relics, and oddities, from Egyptian mummies to African menageries, dinosaur fossils to human freaks, mechanical marvels to wax-work displays of medieval torture devices. Among the more tawdry of these "palaces of wonder" were the ones that specialized in titillating biological displays: preserved fetuses, wax models of diseased genitalia, and grotesquely deformed taxidermy specimens, along with the skulls, skeletons, and other ostensibly authentic anatomical relics of historical figures.

Perhaps the best-known of these "medical museums" was the New York Museum of Anatomy at 618 Broadway. Advertising flyers for this establishment claimed that it contained twenty thousand "novel and astounding" objects, including the preserved head of a Hungarian with "a perfect deer head growing out of his forehead," a "child with one body, two arms, two heads, and four legs," George Washington's deathbed, a genuine hermaphrodite, and—trumpeted in bold letters on the handbill—"THE HEAD AND RIGHT ARM OF ANTON PROBST, Murderer of the Deering Family, Amputated After Execution!"

For all the tongue-clucking of today's moral crusaders, who are forever decrying the supposedly debased state of American culture, it's clear from this advertisement that things were much worse in the past, when displaying the severed body parts of an executed criminal was a socially acceptable form of commercial entertainment. The flyer also highlights another fact: that Anton Probst, totally forgotten today, was one of the most notorious murderers of his time, perpetrator of a deed so heinous that to the public it seemed the work of an incarnate fiend—"The Monster in the Shape of a Man."

THE LIFE, CONFESSION, AND
ATROCIOUS CRIMES OF

ANTOINE PROBST,

THE CRUEL MURDERER OF THE DEERING FAMILY.

PUBLISHED BY BARCLAY & CO., 602 ARCH ST., PHILADELPHIA.

Anton Probst murder pamphlet

BORN IN BADEN, Germany, in 1842, Probst—a "sullen, brutish" youth who, as he put it, "was never brought up to any trade"—sailed for the United States in May 1863. No sooner had he disembarked in New York City than a Union Army recruiter, spotting the burly young immigrant guzzling beer in a saloon, persuaded him to enlist by promising an immediate cash bounty. Six weeks later, Probst deserted. Then, looking to collect another bounty, he promptly enlisted in a different regiment. He repeated this scam—"bounty jumping," as it was known—a few more times until he was discharged in the spring of 1865 after accidentally shooting off his right thumb while on picket duty in Richmond.

Heading for Philadelphia, he quickly blew all his money in barrooms and brothels, then knocked around the region for a few months, working odd manual jobs until he fell ill and ended up in the almshouse. He was back on his feet by the fall. It was while roaming around the countryside of South Philadelphia, searching for work, that he happened upon the farmstead of Christopher Deering.

An immigrant himself, the thirty-eight-year-old Deering had come to America in 1849 to escape the potato famine ravaging his native Ireland. In 1855, he married Julia Duffy, an Irishwoman seven years his senior who bore him five children in rapid succession. Settled in a rural, sparsely populated area of South Philadelphia known locally as "The Neck," he raised and sold cattle in partnership with a fellow named Theodore Mitchell, who supplied the capital for the enterprise and split the profits with Deering.

Needing a hand, Deering took on Probst for a salary of $15 a month, plus board. Though built for farm labor, the brawny, bull-necked Probst was never one to over-exert himself. He quit after three weeks because, as he later explained, his employer asked him to work in the fields "on a rainy, very rough day." Deering's wife, Julia, wasn't sorry to see him go. According to subsequent accounts, there was something in Probst's "conduct and manner" that made her uneasy.

Following his usual pattern, Probst quickly blew through his earnings on liquor and prostitutes. Broke again, he spent a few days doing menial chores at his favorite saloon, then passed another stretch in the almshouse before showing up at Christopher Deering's place again on February 2, 1866.

"I have no work and no money," Probst explained in his heavily accented English. It was a measure of Deering's kindly nature that he agreed to rehire the young German. He could not know, of course, that Probst—who, during his previous stay, had seen his employer counting cash on several occasions—had returned (as he put it) "to get hold of his money."

EARLY SATURDAY MORNING, April 7, Christopher Deering boarded his buggy and drove into the city, leaving behind his wife, four of his children, and his two employees—Probst and a seventeen-year-old farmhand named Cornelius Carey. Deering was going to pick up his cousin, Elizabeth Dolan, a forty-nine-year-old spinster from Burlington, New Jersey. A frequent visitor to the Deering farm, Miss Dolan had taken the seven o'clock steamboat for Philadelphia. She was wearing "furs and a black coat," sporting a gold chain, and carrying a black carpetbag that, in addition to her personal effects, contained a pocketbook with $100 in cash.

On his way to fetch his guest, Deering stopped to perform several errands. At around 8:30 a.m., he made his weekly visit to the stand of a street peddler named Jane Greenwell to purchase six pounds of meat for his family. He then headed to the home of his partner, Thomas Mitchell, to transact some business. Short of cash, he borrowed $10 from Mitchell. Then—after consulting his pocket watch and seeing that he was running late—he hurried off to the steamboat landing.

By the time he arrived, the boat had already docked and discharged its passengers. Driving back down Second Street, he spotted his cousin and pulled up to the curb beside her. A passerby, one Mrs. Wilson, saw Miss Dolan climb into the buggy beside Deering, who then drove off toward Front Street in the direction of his farm. Mrs. Wilson thus became a key figure in the story: the last eyewitness to see Christopher Deering and his cousin alive.

LIKE OTHER INHABITANTS of The Neck, the Deerings lived in relative isolation. One of their nearest neighbors was Abraham Everett, whose farm lay nearly a quarter mile away. Everett, who liked to keep up with the news, subscribed to several Philadelphia gazettes. Every Saturday afternoon, the Deerings' eight-year-old son, John, hiked the distance to Everett's home and borrowed the previous week's papers.

On Saturday, April 7, however, the boy never showed up. Nor did he appear on succeeding days. By Wednesday, Everett was concerned enough to stop off at the Deering place while on his way into town. No one was in sight when he rode up to the house. Dismounting from his horse, he knocked at the front door, but no one responded.

Proceeding to the barn, he was shocked to find Deering's horses "in a state of starvation and nearly dead from thirst." Immediately he grabbed a bucket, hurried out to a water-filled ditch, and began attending to the horses. "I gave one five buckets of water, another four buckets," he later testified. "I then put water in the trough and another drank the whole lot of it. Another I turned out into the yard and he drank, I suppose, for a full fifteen minutes out of the ditch." Everett then released the adult horses into the meadow to feed and brought a bunch of hay to the starving colt tied up in the stable.

Once he had taken care of the animals, he returned to the house, climbed onto the front porch, and peered through a window. He was startled to see that, as he put it, "things looked as if they had been knocked around considerably inside. The house looked as if someone had ransacked it." Shoving open the window, he climbed inside and headed upstairs, where he found the rooms in the same state of wild disorder, "the beds all torn upside down," clothes scattered about, bureau drawers rifled.

Dashing downstairs again, he made for the house of the nearest neighbor, Robert Wyles. Spotting Wyles' farmhand John Gould at work in a meadow, Everett called to the young man and hurried him back to the Deering place. Inside the barn, Gould spotted something that Everett, in his focus on the suffering horses, had missed. Jutting out from a pile of hay was an object that Gould at first took for a stocking. When he stooped to pick it up, however, he discovered "to his amazement and horror" that there was a foot inside it.

Gould immediately alerted his employer, Robert Wyles, who made for the nearest police station. Within a short time several officers arrived on the scene, led by the city's chief of detectives, a longtime veteran of the department who bore the revered name Benjamin Franklin. Pulling the hay off the protruding limb, Franklin and his colleagues made a horrifying discovery.

"There lay a man who was recognized as Mr. Deering," the newspapers reported. "He was extended on the floor cross-wise with the length of the barn. He was dressed in a suit of dark gray clothes, the same in which he had been seen and known on the last day of his life. His head was crushed into pieces, almost to powdered bone, and his throat was cut, nay chopped, from ear to ear. Beside him was a young woman, unknown to these neighbors, whose appearance showed she had met her fate in the same way. Her head and throat revealed the same wounds as were seen on the man by whose side she was lying."

Another, even more ghastly discovery awaited. Not far from the spot where the two savaged corpses lay was a small corn crib, about five feet wide and eight feet long, half filled with hay. Removing the hay, Franklin and his men uncovered a sight so appalling that they were rendered dumbstruck. There lay the decomposed body of Julia Deering, her skull beaten in, her throat gashed open to the neck bone. Heaped "around her and upon her were her four little ones, slaughtered in the identical manner. The little babe in death, lay upon its mother's breast as it had done in life so often—a sight to make strong men weep."

Apart from the Deerings' oldest child, ten-year-old Willie—spared only because he was visiting his grandparents in Schuylkill—the entire family had been slaughtered. No one could recall a crime of similar magnitude. It was, in the view of one observer, an atrocity without "parallel in the catalogue of mere private murders in the annals of the world."

News of the massacre, trumpeted in the next day's headlines, set off the predictable frenzied response. Within twenty-four hours, the Deering farm was overrun with thousands of morbid curiosity seekers. One local journalist, reporting on the scene, was amazed "to see the vast numbers of persons on foot or running as if it were a race of life and death. There were old men who would not have to travel far to find the graves, and young men who were making a holiday excursion of the fearful pilgrimage. A minister of the gospel on horseback passed us, trotting rapidly along. A cripple on crutches swung his distorted legs over the dusty road, making no slow progress. But the women outnumbered the men of all ages, and in all attires from the fashionably dressed lady in her barouche to the poor seamstress on foot." Though a contingent of police officers prevented the mob from entering the house, a crowd of ghoulish souvenir hunters managed to shove their way into the barn and make off with clumps of bloody straw.

It was one of these individuals who spotted something strange on the property: a man's shirt and a pair of drawers lying beside a large haystack about three hundred yards from the barn. He informed a police officer named Dawson Mitchell, who went to investigate. Making a circuit of the haystack, Dawson noticed a spot that had been hollowed out of the straw. He thrust in his hand and immediately felt a human body. Grabbing it by the arm, he pulled it free. It was the decomposed corpse of the Deerings' seventeen-year-old farmhand, Cornelius Carey. He had been killed like the others, his head "broken into fragments" and his throat hacked open from ear to ear.

By then, the police had found the implements that had obviously been used as the murder weapons: a bloody hammer tossed in the hay just inside the entrance to the barn; a small hatchet, likewise encrusted with blood, lying in a ditch not far from the house; and a full-sized axe with blood upon the blade, found in a woodshed.

They had also identified the Deerings' other employee as their prime suspect. None of the neighbors knew much about him, but they could offer a fairly thorough description: "about thirty, bull-necked, missing his right thumb. His English was poor and his first name was believed to be 'Anthony.'"

*   *   *

IT MIGHT BE supposed that a man who had methodically slaughtered eight people, including three prepubescent children and a fourteen-month-old infant, would lose no time in putting as much distance between himself and the crime scene as possible. For all his low cunning, however, Anton Probst was incapable of prudent calculation. Indeed, from all available evidence, he thought of nothing beyond the gratification of his immediate physical needs.

On the evening of Saturday, April 7, just hours after he had perpetrated his mass butchery, he showed up at a brothel on Front Street, carrying a black carpet-bag containing, among other items, two watches, a gold chain, a snuffbox, a pistol, and a powder flask. After a night of "dissipation and debauchery" with a prostitute named Lavinia Whitman, he left early Sunday morning, paying her $3 in green-backs.

He next took a room at a tavern on Newmarket Street, a favorite hangout of his, run by a man named William Leckfeldt. For the next five days, he was in and out of the tavern, drinking beer and shooting dice when he wasn't making brief excursions around the city to pawn his stolen goods for pocket money.

At around 7:00 p.m. on Thursday, April 12, five days after the massacre, he was seated in the barroom of Leckfeldt's when two police officers appeared to ask the proprietor if he had seen "a suspicious-looking man." Drawing his slouch hat over his eyes and sinking into his seat, Probst made himself as inconspicuous as possible until the policemen departed. The moment they were gone, he leapt from his seat and, without bothering to fetch his possessions, hurried out into the night.

Not long afterward, an officer named James Dorsey spotted a burly fellow with his hat pulled low on his head making for the Market Street Bridge. There was something furtive about the man's bearing that aroused Dorsey's suspicions. Looking closer, he saw that the man was missing his right thumb.

Overtaking Probst before he reached the bridge, Dorsey plucked off his hat for a better look at his face. "Good evening," he said.

"How de do," replied Probst.

Hearing the accent, Dorsey asked: "You're a Dutchman?"

Probst's reply would become the stuff of local legend. "No," he said. "Me a Frenchman."

"You are, are you?" said Dorsey, grabbing Probst by the arm. "Take a walk with me."

Down at the Sixth District station house, a search of Probst's pockets turned up Christopher Deering's pistol and snuffbox. In fact, as the police quickly determined, Probst was wearing Deering's clothes, having exchanged them for his own blood-soaked shirt and pants before fleeing the crime scene. The black carpetbag, retrieved from Leckfeldt's tavern, was identified as the one Elizabeth Dolan had been carrying on her ill-fated visit. Every item it contained, including two straight razors, several spools of thread, and a few "five-penny children's trinkets," had been taken from the Deering home.

Interrogated by Mayor Morton McMichael, Probst, after making the predictable protestations of innocence, admitted that he had slain Cornelius Carey but insisted that the other seven victims had been slain by an accomplice, a Swiss cutthroat named Gauntner who had served with him in the Union Army. With an enraged mob laying siege to the jailhouse, howling for his blood, he was transferred to the safety of Moyamensing Prison to await trial.

PROBST ON TRIAL.

THE PROCEEDINGS BEGAN on Wednesday, April 25, just two weeks after the murders were uncovered. Faced with an impossible task, Probst's court-appointed attorneys, John P. O'Neill and John A. Wolbert, admitted that their client was guilty of larceny but argued that the evidence of murder, being strictly circumstantial, was not strong enough to establish his guilt. Even they clearly knew that their efforts were hopeless. The jury took just over twenty minutes to convict.

In delivering his sentence, Judge Joseph Allison vented the indignation shared by the entire community. "You have been found guilty of the commission of one of the most appalling crimes of which the records of civilized jurisprudence make any mention," he told Probst. "Almost without motive eight innocent victims you slew; not suddenly, not in a tempest of resistless passion, but in the coolness of a premeditated design—one by one, at intervals, with solemn pause, with calm deliberation, and with a quenchless thirst for blood, you ceased not until all that you set out to do was fully accomplished, and when you found yourself alone with the dead, you felt your triumph was complete. And with what horrid mockery of life you grouped these dead together—mother and children close gathered to each other: cheek pressed to cheek as if in calm repose; and like one who lays him down as sentinel to keep his silent watch, husband and father, in company with his friend and relative, you placed, as if to guard his wife and little ones from harm. How all these ghastly countenances and rigid forms and glaring, sightless eyes condemned you, as on them you looked and claimed the work as all your own! Justice now claims you as its own. And that which it requires to be done shall not be long delayed."

With that, Judge Allison ordered Probst to "be taken to the place of execution" and "there hung by the neck until dead," the sentence to be carried out in five weeks, on June 8, 1866.

WHILE AWAITING DEATH, Probst continued to insist that he was innocent of all but one of the eight murders, that of Cornelius Carey. However, after much importuning by his spiritual advisor, the Reverend Gunther of St. Alphonsus' Church, he agreed to make a clean breast of things. On the morning of May 7, he dictated two separate confessions, one to Chief of Detectives Benjamin Franklin, the other to his attorneys, Messrs. Wolbert and O'Neill. Though differing slightly in language, the documents agree in every detail and are equally chilling in the matter-of-fact way Probst recounts his utter annihilation of the Deering household.

According to Probst, his original intention was only to rob Christopher Deering by sneaking into his house and taking all the money he could find. He never had a chance, however, because there were always people around. Finally, "on the Saturday morning of the murder, about 9 o'clock," he "formed the design of killing the entire family." "I could not," he explained, "get the money in any other way."

That morning, he and Cornelius Carey were out in the field by the haystack, loading wood on a cart to take to the barn. There was a big axe in the cart, used for cutting tree roots. "We were standing under the big tree when I killed him," said Probst. "It was raining a little. He sat down under the tree and talked about work, while I stood right behind him with the axe in my hand. I hit him on the left side of the head. He did not holler. He fell down. I gave him one or two more blows and then cut his throat. I put him on the cart. Then I pulled it up to the haystack and lifted him up and laid him in the haystack and covered him up with hay."

Now THAT HE had decided to confess, Probst held nothing back. Casually fingering a rosary as he reclined on his cot, he was, in the words of one person present, "quiet, undemonstrative, cool and unembarrassed," sharing his "bloody reminiscences without the least trace of shame or remorse."

"Then I came down to the stable," he continued. "I took the big axe, the little axe, and the hammer and put them all at the corner of the door, so they would be handy for me. Then I went over to the house. The children were all in the house and the woman was out at the ditch for water.

"I took the oldest boy, John, and told him to go over to the stable and help me with something. I went inside the door, got the little axe in my hand, and then he comes in. I knocked him down and he fell inside. I gave him one or two more of the same and cut and chopped his throat. I carried him to the crib and hauled him inside and put a little hay on him. Then I put the axe at the same place by the door.

"Then I went out and told the woman to come over, there was something the matter with the little horse, the colt. She comes in two or three minutes alone. I stood inside and struck her on the head. She did not holler. I gave her two or three more blows and chopped her throat. I took her on my shoulder and hauled her into the crib. Then I put the axe in the same place as before by the door.

"Then I go over to the house for the other boy, Thomas is his name, the next oldest. I told him his mother wanted him. He said nothing at all and walks right into the stable. I walked behind him. I hit him on the head and he laid down. He didn't holler. I hit him once more. I don't know whether I mashed his whole skull in. I didn't examine him. I brought him in the crib with the others and covered him with hay.

Probst despatching Mrs. Deering.

"Then I went over to the house and took Annie. I told her her mother wanted to see her in the stable. She did not say a word. Then I took the baby on my arm. The little girl walked alongside of me. I left the baby by the corner as you go into the stable playing in the hay. Then I picked up the little axe and went over to Annie as she looked around for her mother. I knocked her down with one blow and cut her throat same as the others. Then I went back and got the little baby and gave it one on the forehead. Then I took the sharp side of the axe and chopped its throat. Then I hauled them into the crib and covered them up with hay. I guess it took me a half an hour to kill the family.

"Then I went in the house and stayed there, watching for Mr. Deering to come home.

"I guess about half-past one o'clock, I looked through the window and saw him coming with Miss Dolan in the carriage. I went out of the house and stayed outside. When he come, I stepped up to the carriage and told him the steer is sick over in the stable, he had better see him. He walked right over with me to the stable while Miss Dolan went into the house.

"He went into the stable. I walked behind him and picked up the small axe and struck him one on the head. He fell right down on his face. He never said a word. I

Barbarous murder of the infant.

turned him over and gave him one or two more on his head and chopped his throat. Then I put a little hay over him and left him laying there. Going out, I put my axe in the same place.

"Then Miss Dolan called me over to the house. She asked me where the woman and children are. I told her they are all in the stable. I said Mr. Deering wanted to see her over there. She walks right in the stable. I took the hammer with my left hand and hit her on the head and she fell right down on her face. I turned her round, hit her once more in the head, then took the little axe and chopped her throat.

"Then I went to Mr. Deering and took the watch and pocket-book from him and put them in my pocket. After that, I took Mr. Deering's boots off and laid him in the place where he was found and put Miss Dolan there and covered them up with hay."

His butchery completed, Probst returned to the house, ransacked the place, then washed up, shaved, and changed his bloody garments for a set of Deering's clothes. Famished from his exertions, he fixed himself some bread and butter and relaxed until sunset, when he snuck out and made for town.

"I feel much better now that I have told the truth about this thing," Probst said with a smile at the end of his appalling recitation. "I feel relieved."

Asked by Chief Franklin why on earth he had perpetrated such an atrocity, Probst gave a little shrug. "I only wanted the money," he said. "I killed the boy Cornelius first so that he could not tell on me. I killed the two oldest children so they would not afterwards identify me. I killed the two youngest as I did not wish to leave them in the house alone without someone to care for them. I had no ill feeling to anyone in the family. They always treated me well."

INCARCERATION AGREED WITH Probst. He slept soundly each night and ate so heartily that, in the five-week span between his sentencing and execution, he gained twelve pounds. Visitors to his cell noted that he had "changed greatly in spirit since giving his full confession. He seemed to realize the enormity of the crime he had committed and often expressed himself as not only willing but anxious to undergo any punishment which the law required."

That opportunity arrived on Friday, June 8, 1866. After a solid night's sleep, he awoke at 5:00 a.m. and breakfasted on two soft-boiled eggs, three slices of bread, and a large cup of coffee. Father Gunther then administered Holy Communion and led him in "prayer and exhortation."

Shortly before ten-thirty, Sheriff Howell and Warden Perkins appeared at his cell. Dressed in simple prison wear—coarse gray pants and muslin shirt, brogans and blue socks—and clutching a crucifix to his breast, Probst was escorted to the gallows, which had been erected at the extreme western end of the prison yard, out of sight of the convicts' cell windows. After ascending the scaffold, he knelt in prayer with Father Gunther, who administered the rite of absolution. Then, "pliant as a child" and displaying "not the least fear," he rose to his feet and bent his head so that the "noose could be properly adjusted to his neck." The white cowl was then slipped over his head. Father Gunther recited a few final words of prayer, then signaled to the sheriff, who immediately released the drop.

Probst plunged, then convulsed for two or three minutes. His body was then allowed to dangle for twenty-five minutes before being cut down and carried to the paint room of the prison.

So universally detested was Probst that the newspapers abandoned any pretense of journalistic objectivity in reporting on his death. "Anton Probst—the greatest criminal of the nineteenth century—shuffled off his mortal and disreputable coil this morning at 10:46 o'clock," wrote the correspondent for the *New York Times*. "For such a thing it was difficult to feel sympathy or pity. His death was easy, and his ugly carcass swung in the breeze."

IN ACCORDANCE WITH the custom of the time—when, as a form of postmortem punishment, the bodies of executed murderers were handed over to anatomists for dissection—Probst's corpse was immediately delivered to Drs. Pancoast, Rand, and McCrea of Jefferson Medical College. Seated upright in a chair in the prison paint room, the naked body was first subjected to a series of bizarre electrical experiments, designed to test "the force of galvanism to induce post-mortem muscular action." One pole of a powerful battery was inserted into the dead man's mouth and the other into an incision made in his face, causing it to "assume various expressions." The battery was then applied to various muscles of his arms and legs, making them "move wildly about."

Afterward, the corpse was transported to the medical college where, at 4:00 p.m. on Saturday, it "was dissected before a crowded audience, composed of men of all professions and vocations." Probst's brain turned out to be of "remarkably small size"—a mere two pounds four ounces, far below the average weight of three pounds two ounces—confirming the view of the reporter for the *New York Times*, who had earlier opined that the brutish killer of the Deering family "was as destitute of brain as he was of heart."

[*Sources:* William B. Mann, *Official Report of the Trial of Anton Probst, for the Murder of Christopher Deering, at Philadelphia, April 25, 1866, as Well as His Two Confessions, One Made on May 6th, to His Spiritual Adviser, the Other on May 7th to His Counsel, Wherein He Acknowledges to Have Killed the Entire Family of Eight Persons, and the Manner in Which He Done It. To Which Is Added a History of His Previous Life, as Well as an Account of His Last Hours and Execution* (Philadelphia: T. B. Peterson & Brothers, 1866); Ron Avery, *City of Brotherly Mayhem: Philadelphia Crimes and Criminals* (Philadelphia: Otis Books, 2003); Andrea Stulman Dennett, *Weird and Wonderful: The Dime Museum in America* (New York: New York University Press, 1997).]

The Eyes of Anton Probst

In addition to the electrical experiments conducted on his still-warm corpse, Anton Probst was treated to a thorough eye examination immediately following his execution. The purpose of this procedure was to test a belief that had gained widespread currency by the middle of the nineteenth century. This was the notion that the last image seen by a person at the moment of death remains imprinted on his retina "as on a daguerreotype plate"—a phenomenon variously known as an "eye-photograph," "death picture," or "optogram."

Based on the common analogy between the eye and a camera, the theory held that "since the retina functioned like the photographic plate of a camera," the "final image viewed before death should remained fixed forever, like a photo, on the dead person's eyes." A "logical extension of this hypothesis" (in the words of scholar Arthur B. Evans) was "that if death were to occur at a moment when the pupils of the eyes were hugely dilated—e.g., because of fear, surprise, anger, or some other strong emotion—the retinal optograms of the deceased would be even clearer and more detailed."

Since there are few, if any, stronger emotions than the terror experienced by someone about to be killed, the theory raised an exciting possibility for police. As one nineteenth-century medical journal put it, "if the last object seen by a murdered person was his murderer, the portrait drawn upon the eye would remain a fearful witness in death to detect the guilty and lead to conviction." This possibility seemed confirmed in 1857 when a physician named Sandford of Auburn, New York—after dilating the pupil of a murder victim named J. H. Beardsley and examining the retina closely with a "powerful lens"—claimed to see "the figure of a man in a light coat, beside whom there was a round stone suspended in the air."

People, of course, see what they expect to see (as the famous French criminologist Alphonse Bertillon put it, "One can only see what one observes, and one observes only things which are already in the mind"). Whatever Sandford perceived was certainly not the image of Mr. Beardsley's killer. Nevertheless, over the course of the next half century—indeed, well into the first decades of the twentieth—police continued to examine and in some cases photograph the eyes of murder victims in the hope that a picture of the perpetrator was preserved on the retina. Perhaps the most famous such instance occurred during the Jack the Ripper investigation, when police pried open and photographed the eyes of his victim Annie Chapman in a desperate effort to identify her killer.

The postmortem examination of Probst's eyeballs revealed no recognizable images from his final moments, no portrait of the hangman's face or any other "optogram." "The popular idea, lately promulgated, that the impression of the object last seen remained on the retina was entirely disproved," wrote E. R. Hutchins, one of the physicians present at the autopsy. Still, the doctors did discover an ocular phenomenon of such "remarkable interest" that, within weeks of Probst's execution, a paper on the subject was presented at a meeting of the American Ophthalmological Society.

In the paper—titled "Fracture of the Lens of One Eye and of the Anterior Capsules of Both Eyes from Death by Violent Hanging"—Dr. Ezra Dyer of Jefferson Medical College recounts how, upon shining a "powerful electric light" into the right eye of the freshly killed Probst, he was startled to see "a line transversely across the lens" that "had an iridescent or opalescent appearance." An examination of the left eye revealed "the same transverse line," resembling "a crack in a cake of clear ice." Dyer, as he reports, was "so much interested in the subject" that, to study it further, he immediately "procured three very large dogs and hanged them." Dog no. 1, which "died without a struggle," showed the same fracture of the lens. So did dog no. 2, which "died with convulsions lasting a short time." Only in the case of dog no. 3, which "died with prolonged convulsions," could "no lesion be observed."

In the end, Dyer concedes that he does not know what conclusion to draw from his fascinating discovery, though he permits himself to wonder if Probst, as a result of the fracture, saw "the beautiful changes of scene and color which people experience when hanged, as so often described." How someone who has been hanged could possibly describe what he saw while plunging to his death, the good doctor never explains.

EDWARD H. RULLOFF,
"THE MAN OF TWO LIVES"

FED BY HOLLYWOOD FANTASY, THE popular imagination tends to conceive of serial killers as evil geniuses: Hannibal Lecter delivering lectures on Renaissance art when he isn't dining on human liver and fava beans, or the diabolical John Doe of David Fincher's *Seven* who arranges his victims in elaborate tableaux based on medieval conceptions of the seven deadly sins. The truth, however, is far less colorful. Far from being criminal masterminds, real-life serial killers tend to possess perfectly average IQs. Many don't rise to even that middling level.

Every so often, however, a serial killer comes along who, if not quite a Lecter-like mastermind, is notably smarter than the common run of humanity. Such exceptional psychos—

Rulloff assaults his wife with an iron pestle.

men with superior brains but profoundly disturbed personalities—tend to exert a deep fascination on the public. One such figure was Edward H. Rulloff, a man whose "marvelous character" (in the view of an early biographer) would have led him to "become a great benefactor and honor to his race" had his mind not "been warped in the other direction."

Born Edward Howard Rulofson in 1819, he came from distinguished stock. His grandfather, an émigré to New Brunswick, Canada, was a wealthy landowner, the first school superintendent of the province, and a justice of the peace. His father was likewise "a most reputable and highly respected citizen"—a prosperous "farmer, horse breeder, and importer of blooded horses from Europe." Edward's two younger brothers would grow up to be highly accomplished men in their respective fields, one an internationally celebrated photographer, the other a lumber magnate.

Edward, of course, would distinguish himself in his own way, earning nation-wide notoriety as the most remarkable criminal of his day, "famous and infamous throughout the world," in the words of one contemporary, "at once the wonder and execration of mankind."

As to his earliest intellectual achievements, the opinions of his nineteenth-century chroniclers differ. According to a journalist named E. H. Freeman—whose 1871 biography was endorsed by the subject himself—Rulloff was a genuine child prodigy, with an "insatiate thirst for learning." Shunning "the usual pleasures and pastimes of the boys of his age," he spent his leisure hours immersed in books, acquiring a "general knowledge of science and literature" and a precocious mastery of ancient and modern languages.

Other biographers, however, dismiss this claim, insisting that Rulloff's childhood studies were both haphazard and superficial. Though possessed of a youthful "passion for desultory reading," writes one commentator, "it does not appear that at this time of life he acquired any special branches of knowledge, or that any were taught him." Even the skeptics, however, concede that Rulloff was a remarkably quick study who, while hardly the great scholar he claimed to be, had an unusually nimble and "sponge-like" mind.

After a few years at the academy in the nearby city of St. John—where, according to Freeman, he "exhibited the same assiduity, the same devotion to study that had distinguished his earlier days"—Rulloff began clerking for James Keator and E. L. Thorne, partners in a local dry-goods firm. Not long after he took the job, however, Keator and Thorne's establishment burned to the ground. A few months later, they reopened their business in a different part of the city, but another "fire shortly followed and the store was again swept from the earth." The two conflagrations, following so close together—and so soon after Rulloff came to work for the merchants—were taken as acts of God. Given what we now know about the psychological development of serial killers—who commonly display a bent for juvenile pyromania—it seems entirely possible that the fires were no accident.

With his nascent mercantile career up in smoke, Rulloff turned his attention to the law, becoming a clerk in the office of an eminent St. John barrister, Duncan Robertson. Within a remarkably short time, he had acquired enough legal expertise to pass as a credible lawyer—an ability he would have ample opportunity to exercise in the coming years.

Nowadays, we take it as a matter of course that a man might lead a profoundly bifurcated existence: that a successful law student, say, might have a hidden life as a homicidal maniac (like Ted Bundy). In the early nineteenth century, however—long before the term "psychopath" was coined—such a phenomenon seemed incomprehensible. It was this duality—this paradoxical combination of scholarly diligence and compulsive criminality—that would make Edward Rulloff such an object of fascination to his contemporaries: "The Man of Two Lives," as he came to be known. And it was during his years as a young law clerk that his bizarre double nature first came to the attention of the world.

Sometime after he went to work for Duncan Robertson—exactly when is impossible to determine—Rulloff's previous employer, E. L. Thorne, opened a new dry-goods store in the same building as the law office. Not long afterward, someone broke into the place and stole a bolt of expensive fabric. Inquiries instituted by Thorne led him to believe that the culprit was none other than his former clerk—a suspicion confirmed when Rulloff, with the brazenness he would display throughout his life, appeared in a new suit made from the stolen cloth.

Thorne, "who had a lingering regard for the lad," offered not to press charges if Rulloff "made an open confession of the matter." When Rulloff haughtily re-

fused, he was arrested, tried, and sentenced to two years in the St. John Penitentiary. He entered the prison in the fall of 1839. He was twenty years old.

Upon his release in late 1841, Rulloff made his way to New York City, where he
briefly studied bookkeeping and penmanship. Failing to find employment in the me-
tropolis, he headed north by steamboat, ending up in the village of Dryden, a few
miles east of Ithaca. Taking a job as a drug clerk, he quickly impressed the locals with
his apparently great erudition, particularly after he began delivering regular lectures
on the supposed science of phrenology, one of the many subjects he had read up on
during his stint in the penitentiary. To the untutored residents of the rural hamlet, he
"seemed a marvel"—"a druggist, an excellent penman, a classical scholar, a lawyer,
and an earnest, fluent speaker." Before long, they had made him headmaster of their
high school.

Among his pupils was a vivacious seventeen-year-old named Harriet Schutt,
daughter of a respectable local family and, by all accounts, a young woman "of most
exemplary character and conduct." Despite (or perhaps because of) the great disparity in their "mental acquirements," Rulloff began paying court to the "tender, pleasant
girl," who reciprocated his attentions. When Rulloff proposed marriage in late 1843,
she eagerly accepted. Though somewhat leery of their prospective son-in-law, about
whom they knew almost nothing, Harriet's parents raised no strong objections. The
wedding took place on the last day of December 1843.

"The marriage feast was scarcely cold," writes one early chronicler, when trouble
began. By then, Rulloff had quit his teaching job and established himself as a practitioner of "botanical medicine," a then-popular system founded by a self-taught herb-
alist named Samuel Thomson who believed in restoring the body's "natural heat" by
the administration of such stuff as cayenne pepper and *Lobelia inflata*, an emetic plant
commonly known as "puke weed." One of Rulloff's local rivals was Dr. Henry W. Bull,
"a respectable physician of the old school" and a cousin of Rulloff's young wife, Harriet.

A few months after the marriage, Bull paid a visit to Harriet and—as was his
custom—greeted her with a peck on the cheek. Spotting this innocent salutation,
Rulloff flew into a rage. Soon he was "charging her with having criminal intercourse"
with her cousin. Harriet laughed off the accusation, a reaction that only drove Rulloff

to new heights of jealous fury. One night soon afterward, while Harriet was crushing peppercorns with a heavy iron pestle, Rulloff snatched the implement from her hands and knocked her out with a blow to the forehead. When she regained consciousness, he was sufficiently contrite "to say that he did not intend to strike her so hard." But his treatment of her "was no kinder after this outrage than before."

In the summer of 1844, partly to put some distance between his wife and her ostensible lover, Rulloff insisted that they relocate to Ithaca. The move did nothing to allay his suspicions. Just weeks after they settled into their new home, several neighbors heard Harriet shrieking for help from her bedroom. Rushing to investigate, they found Rulloff grappling with his wife while brandishing a small amber bottle.

"Quick!" Harriet screamed. "Edward is going to make me take poison and take it himself!"

"By the living God," cried Rulloff, as the neighbors tried to pull them apart, "this poison will kill us both in five minutes and that will put an end to these troubles!"

As the neighbors wrested Harriet from his clutches, Rulloff hurled the bottle through the window, then began to berate his wife about her infidelity.

"Oh, Edward," she said, dropping to her knees and reaching out to him, "I am innocent as an unborn child."

He struck her in the face, knocking her over. "Get away from me, goddamn you," he cried. As she lay there sobbing, he told her "she could go and live with Bull and seek all the pleasure she wished to, for he didn't want to live with her anymore."

Though Harriet's neighbors advised her to leave him, the couple reconciled. A few months later, they moved again, this time to the nearby village of Lansing, where, on the night of April 25, 1845, Harriet gave birth to a daughter, Priscilla. The infant's arrival seemed to have a calming effect on Rulloff, who was, to all appearances, "unusually kind and attentive to his wife. He had by this time acquired quite a library of books which, in that place at that time, seemed the embodiment of all human wisdom. He had gained the confidence of a large portion of the community as a skilled botanical physician, and man of temperate and industrious habits."

He had also—though no one suspected it at the time—embarked on his career as a serial murderer.

His first victims were two relatives by marriage, the wife and infant child of his brother-in-law, William Schutt. During the first week of June 1845, the baby was stricken with "a simple ailment of infancy." Summoned by Schutt, Rulloff administered one of his homemade concoctions. "The next day," reports one chronicler, "the babe died of convulsions." Two days later, the grieving mother, Amelia, who had been given a supposed botanical sedative by Rulloff, "suddenly sickened and died the same way." Thirteen years after the sudden deaths of Amelia Schutt and her newborn, their corpses would be exhumed and distinct traces of copper poison discovered in their organs, confirming what the world had long since learned about Edward Rulloff's monstrous nature. At the time, however, William Schutt and his neighbors—"simple and unsuspecting country-folk who had never been brought into contact with flagrant crime"—attributed the double tragedy to "the inscrutable ways of Divine Providence."

THREE WEEKS LATER, on the evening of June 23, 1845, a young neighbor of the Rulloffs, fifteen-year-old Olive Robertson, dropped by their home. She found Harriet "sitting in a low rocking chair and fondly holding her cooing babe." Rulloff himself was stirring one of his herbal "compounds" in a teacup, which he then carried over and tried to feed to his child. When Harriet objected, "saying the babe was in perfect health," Rulloff replied that he had "detected the seeds of disease in his offspring, and insisted that the dose be given." The normally compliant Harriet stood firm. "Perhaps you need the medicine more than the baby," Rulloff replied with a tight smile, holding out the cup to her. Harriet pushed it away. After a tense moment, "Rulloff desisted, saying he had only been joking." Olive Robertson left shortly afterward. No one except their killer would ever set eyes on Harriet Rulloff and her infant daughter again.

THE FOLLOWING MORNING, at around ten o'clock, Olive Robertson's father, Thomas, heard a knock on the front door. The caller was Edward Rulloff, who had a favor to ask. The previous night—so Rulloff explained—a cousin of Harriet's named Emory Boyce had come to fetch her and the baby for a visit to his home in Mottville, about ten miles away. The uncle's wagon was so small, however, that, to accommodate his passenger and her infant, he had been obliged to leave behind a large chest. Rulloff now wished to borrow Robertson's horse and wagon so that he could return the chest to Boyce.

Though somewhat reluctant because (as he later testified) "it was an extreme hot day," Robertson agreed. After inviting Rulloff to take dinner with his family, he and his son helped their neighbor load the heavy chest onto the buckboard. It was about 3:00 p.m. when Rulloff set off down the dusty turnpike to Mottville, "whistling softly as the horse moved along." At one point, encountering a group of children on the road, he invited them to ride on the wagon and entertained them with "funny songs and quaint whistling." Later, rumors abounded that Rulloff had found it deliciously amusing to see several of the children perched atop the chest that contained the bodies of his murdered wife and infant daughter.

Precisely how he killed them would never be established. According to his own later confession, he and Harriett had gotten into yet another altercation about Henry Bull. As the argument escalated, Rulloff, in a "passion," reached for the thirty-pound iron pestle of the mortar in which he "pounded medicines, and struck her over the left temple. The pestle broke the skull and sunk into her brain." He then took the child, placed it on the bed, and "gave it a narcotic to stop its crying." Another account, given by one of Rulloff's lawyers on his deathbed, claimed that "he suffocated the babe with a pillow and that he gave chloroform to his wife, opened an artery, and then bled her to death, taking up a board in the floor and allowing the blood to drip into the cellar."

How he disposed of the corpses is also a matter of dispute. One wild rumor had it that he sold them to Geneva Medical College for dissection, though his more reliable chroniclers dismiss this "hypothesis" as "too horrible for belief." Far likelier is the explanation Rulloff himself offered his lawyers. After driving the chest to a secluded spot on the shore of Cayuga Lake, he waited until "the dead and middle waste of night." He then removed the bodies from the chest, wrapped them tightly in untempered wire "that could never become unfastened and, attaching the heavy iron mortar to the body of his wife and a flat iron to that of the child," rowed them out "over the silent waters" and threw them overboard, "down into unfathomable depths to remain forever concealed from the eyes of men."

BACK HOME THE next morning, Rulloff unloaded the now empty chest, returned the wagon and horse to Thomas Robertson, and, after throwing a few possessions into a bundle, headed down the road, telling his neighbors that he was off to join his wife. As the weeks passed with no word from Harriet, her family and friends grew increasingly concerned. Entering the abandoned house, her brothers William and Ephraim found it in a state of wild disorder. The bed wasn't made, the kitchen table was piled with dirty dishes, shoes and stockings were strewn around the bedroom floor along with articles of Harriet's clothing, and her traveling basket, which she "always carried with her when she went away," sat on her bureau.

By the time Rulloff reappeared six weeks later, rumors had spread that his wife and infant daughter had met with foul play. Feigning shock and indignation, Rulloff insisted that mother and child were safe and sound, though he offered contradictory accounts of their whereabouts, telling some people that they were staying in a cottage "between Cayuga and Seneca Lakes," others that they were visiting family in Erie, Pennsylvania, and still others that they were settled in Madison, Ohio.

Confronted with the threat of arrest, Rulloff offered to write a letter to his wife, "asking her to dispel the painful rumors in circulation" by dropping him a line to affirm that she was alive and well. After penning the note, he handed it to Ephraim Schutt, who immediately left for the post office.

No sooner had he gone than Rulloff took off by foot, hurrying north toward the railroad depot at Auburn.

WHAT FOLLOWED WAS a real-life version of the kind of interstate chase sequence, featuring a devilishly slippery fugitive and a grimly determined pursuer, that has long been a cliché of Hollywood suspense thrillers.

The moment he heard that his brother-in-law had fled in the direction of Auburn, Ephraim Schutt mounted his buckboard and made for the railway station. Finding no trace of his quarry, he proceeded to Rochester, where he caught sight of Rulloff on the platform, about to board a departing train. Spotting Schutt, Rulloff vanished in the milling crowd. Schutt leapt aboard the train and, after making a thorough search, found him hiding in the rearmost car.

Insisting that he was on his way to rejoin Harriet and the baby in Ohio, Rulloff proposed that his brother-in-law come along "and see for himself how false had been all the suspicions of his conduct." The pair proceeded to Buffalo, where they spent the night at a hotel before heading down to the docks the next morning to catch an early steamboat for Cleveland. It wasn't until Schutt had pushed his way onto the packed upper deck that he realized that Rulloff was no longer with him. Schutt was still searching the vessel when it pulled away from the wharf.

After a brief stopover at Erie, Pennsylvania, where he called on some relatives to see if anyone had heard from Harriet, Schutt made his way to Madison, Ohio, but could turn up no trace of his missing sister. Still convinced that Rulloff was heading that way, Schutt hurried back to Cleveland, arriving at the steamboat landing just as a pair of vessels were discharging their passengers. Sure enough, he spotted Rulloff among the crowd. Realizing he needed help, he enlisted the aid of a local constable named Hayes. Searching the dives near the wharf, "they soon found Rulloff in a low eating saloon," attempting to make himself as inconspicuous as possible by seating himself "behind a large dry goods box."

Though Rulloff did his best to talk his way out of the situation—nearly convincing Hayes of his innocence—Schutt managed to get him aboard a steamer headed back east, keeping him locked up in a "strong room" until the boat docked in Buffalo. Rulloff was then handcuffed and transferred to a train to Ithaca, where he was led through a howling mob to the city jail.

Despite a determined effort to drag Cayuga Lake with "the most approved apparatus"—an undertaking that cost the county an estimated $10,000—the bodies of Harriet Rulloff and her infant would never be found. With not enough evidence to establish the *corpus delicti*, the District Attorney decided to forgo a murder indictment and charge Rulloff with the abduction of his wife, "of which the proof was incontrovertible." At the climax of his trial in January 1846, he was convicted and sentenced to ten years in the state prison at Auburn.

LOCKED UP IN "that great living tomb of culprits," Rulloff quickly impressed his keepers as "a prisoner of remarkable ability and great versatility." Assigned to various workshops, he exhibited "such wonderful skill and knowledge that he soon came to be regarded as a prodigy, a very paragon." Nowhere were his talents more strikingly on display than in the rug-making department, where his original designs resulted in "some of the most beautiful ingrain carpets ever produced in the United States."

During his leisure hours, he immersed himself in books, pursuing "with a tireless zeal all the volumes of science and art that the kindness of his jailers would allow him and his own limited means could procure." He discovered a particular passion for the subject of philology and eventually mastered a number of languages, including ancient Greek.

At some point during this period he hit upon a grand project that, he believed, would earn him a place in the scholarly pantheon: a monumental work that would explain the common origin of all the world's languages. From that moment on, Rulloff confided in his journal, "no man ever lived with a nobler or higher ambition than I."

RULLOFF MAY HAVE been a model prisoner, but the practice of early parole for good behavior had not yet been established, so he was compelled to serve every day of his sentence. Even his full ten-year term, however, seemed excessively lenient to the still-outraged citizens of Tompkins County. No sooner was Rulloff discharged from Auburn prison in January 1856 than he was rearrested for Harriet's murder and transported in manacles to the jailhouse in Ithaca.

Rulloff, familiar with "the fundamental principles and rules of legal practice" from his days as a law clerk, was unfazed. Representing himself in court, he successfully argued that his trial and conviction for abduction precluded his prosecution for murder. Determined to exact full justice, the district attorney immediately indicted him on a completely different charge: the murder of his infant daughter, Priscilla.

Because the manner of the child's death was and would forever be unknown, the indictment needed to cover every possible scenario. It therefore alleged that Rulloff "did stab her in and upon the left side between the short ribs" with "a certain knife of the value of six cents"; "strike, beat, and kick" her "in and upon the head, stomach, back, and sides" with "both the hands and feet of him"; "choke, suffocate, and strangle" her with "a certain silk handkerchief of the value of one dollar"; "put, mix, and mingle" a "large quantity of a certain deadly poison called arsenic" into "half a pint of milk," which the infant did "take, drink, and swallow"; and "strike and thrust" upon "the left side of her head" with "a certain weapon of the value of six cents." In short, this "most curious legal document" (as one contemporary described the indictment) charged Rulloff with having stabbed, strangled, suffocated, poisoned, bludgeoned, beaten, and kicked to death his baby daughter.

He was brought to trial in October 1856. Despite the fact that the child's body had never been found, he was convicted and sentenced to be hanged, a judgment upheld when the court of appeals ruled that "direct evidence is not, in all cases, indispensable for the purpose of proving the *corpus delicti* on a trial for murder."

Confined to the Ithaca jail while awaiting the outcome of his appeal, Rulloff ingratiated himself with the keeper, Jacob Jarvis, who was so taken with the prisoner's

sweeping erudition that he permitted his eighteen-year-old son, Albert, to spend entire "days in the cell of the prisoner, taking lessons from him in Latin, French, stenography, and other branches of learning." It wasn't long before the impressionable
youth had fallen under the spell of the charismatic psychopath. Sometime after dark
on Monday, May 5, 1857, while his parents were asleep, young Albert undid the bolts
of Rulloff's cell, and the two disappeared into the night.

WITH REWARDS TOTALING more than $1,000 posted for his capture and the entire coun-
tryside on the lookout for him, Rulloff made his way to Meadville, Pennsylvania.
Presenting himself as a scholar named James Nelson, he applied for a professorship
at Alleghany College. Though none was available, he "so won the admiration and
confidence" of the college president, the Rev. Dr. Barker, that, through the good offices of that estimable gentleman, he was "received among the most refined and distinguished society of Meadville."

For the next few months, he resided in Meadville, constructing a patent model for
a part-time inventor named A. B. Richmond and impressing his new acquaintances as
"a gentleman of the most brilliant intellect and profound education," who could speak
learnedly about a dizzying range of subjects, from medicine to mineralogy, law to
linguistics, conchology to classical Greek poetry.

With his funds running low, Rulloff left Meadville in January 1858 and headed
back east toward New York. Along the way, he burglarized a string of stores, including a jewelry shop in Warren, Pennsylvania, which he "robbed of every article of
value it contained, including all kinds of watches, gold pens, rings, and breast-pins."

It was while fleeing from this burglary that his feet, clad only in moccasins, became frostbitten in the snow. Arriving in Jamestown, New York, he entered the drugstore of Dr. G. W. Hazeltine, who—impressed with Rulloff's obvious medical
expertise—permitted him to compound his own frostbite remedy. Unfortunately, it
failed to work, and soon afterward, Rulloff was compelled to have the big toe of his
left foot removed, an amputation that would eventually have dire consequences for
him.

With pursuers hot on his trail, Rulloff turned westward again, ending up in a
small Ohio town not far from Columbus where he took a job as a writing teacher in a
country school. Tracked down by a posse of locals, Rulloff tried to hold them off with

a "three-barreled pistol of his own invention and manufacture" but was overpowered, taken into custody, and extradited back to New York.

Wisely deciding not to represent himself, Rulloff retained an extremely capable young attorney named Francis Miles Finch, later a distinguished judge of the New York State Court of Appeals and an accomplished amateur poet. Much to the outrage of the citizens of Ithaca—who openly threatened to take justice into their own hands—Finch eventually succeeded in getting his client released on a series of legal technicalities.

Like all compulsive criminals, however, Rulloff was incapable of staying out of trouble for long. In November 1861—just eighteen months after Finch managed to set him free—he was back behind bars, having been sentenced to two and a half years in Sing Sing for third-degree burglary. During this stint, he forged an intimate bond with a poor, illiterate petty thief named William Dexter, twenty years his junior. Immediately upon their release, the two teamed up with Rulloff's former protégé, Al Jarvis, himself now a small-time burglar. From that point on, the older man and his two young disciples would constitute an inseparable partnership, an intensely close-knit "triumvirate of crime" that would "remain thenceforward unbroken" until its dramatic end in the incident that came to be known as "The Halbert Horror."

FOR THE NEXT six years—when one or another of them wasn't doing a brief stretch in jail—they lived together in and around New York City, subsisting on the proceeds from countless thefts and break-ins. Though Rulloff participated in some of these crimes, he increasingly left the dirty work to his young confederates while he remained at home, working obsessively on his magnum opus, *Method in the Formation of Languages.*

By 1869, he was ready to make his "grand theory" public. Under the name of Professor Euri Leurio—a coded translation of "Edward Rulloff" based on his ingenious (if totally crackpot) linguistic system—he announced his "tremendous discovery" at the annual convention of the American Philological Association in Poughkeepsie, New York, offering to sell his still-uncompleted manuscript for the price of $500,000. There were no takers.

"Disheartened, but with no intention of abandoning his purpose," Rulloff returned home and resumed his labors on the project he believed would earn him immortality. In the meantime, his two devoted disciples—in awe of his brilliance and convinced that his scholarly masterwork would one day make them all rich—continued to provide for their household needs with the income from various rural burglaries, some committed as far away as New England and Western New York.

During one of these "lawless expeditions," Al Jarvis learned that the Halbert brothers, a pair of Binghamton dry-goods merchants, had recently received a big shipment of expensive silks. Their store, he reported to Rulloff, was "very near the river bank, and it was easy to enter it and get away." Though Rulloff expressed some qualms, Jarvis assured him that "there was no danger." He and Dexter "had every-thing fixed" and "expected to make a good haul." Rulloff "reluctantly consented" to the scheme and agreed to "go along with them, not to take an active part but as a lookout, and to help bring back the goods." With that understanding, the trio boarded a train to Binghamton, arriving at around 5:00 p.m. on Monday, August 13, 1870.

Two nights later, at around one in the morning, the three broke into the rear of the store. Down in the basement, they put on masks and slipped out of their shoes. They then stole noiselessly upstairs, where two young clerks, Frederick Merrick and Gilbert Burrows, who slept on the premises, were occupying adjoining cots. Prepared for such a contingency, Dexter took a bottle of chloroform from his coat pocket, doused a rag with the liquid, and applied it to the faces of the slumbering men. Hav-ing "thus secured the continuing unconsciousness" of the clerks, the thieves got busy gathering up the most expensive bolts of silk.

They were just finishing up their operation when Jarvis stumbled over something and crashed to the floor. At the noise, the two clerks—who clearly had not been chlo-roformed enough—sat up with a start. Seeing the masked men, they sprang from their beds and began to grapple with the intruders. The brawny young clerks quickly overpowered their opponents, Burroughs knocking Dexter down with an iron chisel while Merrick throttled Jarvis. Merrick was tightening his chokehold when Rulloff came up behind him, placed the muzzle of a pistol against the back of his skull, and put a bullet through his brain. Rulloff then gathered up his two companions, and the three of them fled the store through the basement, while Burroughs ran out into the street shouting, "Murder!"

Two days later, with police squads patrolling the city and posses scouring the countryside, Rulloff was found hiding in an outhouse. Authorities had no trouble linking him to the crime scene, since he had fled Halbert's without his shoes. There was no doubt that they belonged to Rulloff: stuffed inside the left one were bits of cloth to fill the void made by his missing big toe. Further evidence was provided on the following day when the corpses of Jarvis and Dexter were fished out of the Chenango River and their pockets found to contain a bunch of items connecting them to Rulloff.

Exactly how the two young burglars had died would remain a matter of dispute. Rulloff claimed that they had drowned while attempting to wade across the river during the getaway, though there would always be those who believed that he himself had disposed of them "as impediments to his escape" by beating them to death before dumping them into the water.

His trial in January 1871 was a legal landmark. Because the corpses of Jarvis and Dexter were badly decomposed when they were fished from the river, they had been immediately photographed "before all hopes of recognition were gone." During the trial, the photographs were introduced as evidence over the objections of Rulloff's lawyer, George Becker, who eventually appealed the ruling. Ultimately, a higher court dismissed the appeal, setting a legal precedent for the admissibility of photographic evidence in criminal trials.

In the meantime, reporters digging into Rulloff's past discovered that in February 1865, a silk factory he was known to have patronized had been broken into by three masked burglars, and that its night watchman, Philip Kraemer, had been fatally bludgeoned during the crime. If, as many believed, the perpetrator was Rulloff, then the "learned monster" was responsible for as many as eight homicides: the murder of his wife, Harriet, and their infant daughter; Amelia Schutt and her newborn; Al Jarvis; William Dexter; Fred Merrick; and Philip Kraemer.

CONVICTED AT THE end of the six-day proceedings, Rulloff was sentenced to die in March, though his attorney managed to delay the inevitable for a few months. While awaiting his execution, Rulloff continued to work frantically on his philological treatise, desperate to complete the "great work which," as he proclaimed to all listeners, "will make this epoch illustrious to future generations." Impressed with his seemingly vast mental powers and obsessive devotion to his studies, various luminaries argued publicly for a commutation. In the *New York Tribune*, Horace Greeley described Rulloff "as one of the most industrious and devoted scholars our busy generation has give birth to," an intellectual phenomenon "too curious to be wasted on the gallows." In the same paper, Mark

Twain regretted that Rulloff's "vast capabilities for usefulness should be lost to the world":

> For it is plain that in the person of Rulloff one of the most marvelous intellects that any age has produced is about to be sacrificed, and that, too, while half the mystery of its strange powers is yet a secret. Here is a man who has never entered the doors of a college or a university, and yet, by the sheer might of his innate gifts has made himself such a colossus of abstruse learning that the ablest of our scholars are but pigmies in his presence.... Every learned man who enters Rulloff's presence leaves it amazed and confounded by his prodigious capabilities and attainments. One scholar said he did not believe that in matters of subtle analysis, vast knowledge in his peculiar field of research, comprehensive grasp of subject and serene kingship over its limitless and bewildering details, any land or any era of modern times had given birth to Rulloff's intellectual equal.

All efforts on his behalf, however, failed. His public hanging on May 18, 1871, generated the usual holiday atmosphere as thousands of spectators swarmed into Binghamton, "hungry for the feast of horror that was promised." They did not go away disappointed. The hanging provided a particularly macabre moment. "With characteristic bravado," one eyewitness reported, "Rulloff put his right hand in his pocket before the trap was sprung. The fall jerked the hand free, but Rulloff, still apparently conscious, put it back in his pocket."

Following the execution, Rulloff's corpse was transported to Geneva Medical College, where his head was sawed off, his skull opened, and his brain weighed and measured. He would undoubtedly have been gratified with the findings. His brain was found to be massive, "ten ounces heavier than the average for a man of Rulloff's age" and nearly as weighty as that of Daniel Webster, one of the intellectual titans of his age.

[*Sources: Life, Trial and Execution of Edward H. Rulloff, the Perpetrator of Eight Murders, Numerous Burglaries and Other Crimes* (Philadelphia: Barclay & Co., 1871); E. H. Freeman, *The Veil of Secrecy Removed. The Only True and Authentic History of Edward H. Rulloff, His Biography and Execution. The Mysteries of His Life Revealed. His Confessions of the Murder of His Wife, and the Killing of Merrick* (Binghamton, NY: Carl & Freeman, 1871); Edward Crapsey, *The Man of Two Lives! Being an Authentic History of Edward Howard Rulloff, Philologist and Murderer* (New York: American News Company, 1871); Richard W. Bailey, *Rogue Scholar: The Sinister Life and Celebrated Death of Edward H. Rulloff* (Ann Arbor, MI: University of Michigan Press, 2003).]

"His Side of the Story"

Besides his outstanding courtroom skills, Francis Miles Finch—the young attorney who secured Rulloff's freedom in 1860—was an accomplished amateur poet, best remembered for his Civil War elegy, "The Blue and the Gray." First published in the September 1867 issue of *Atlantic Monthly* and later reprinted in *McGuffey's Reader*, the nation's best-selling schoolbook, this moving memorial to the Union and Confederate dead became one of the most beloved lyrics of its day.

Two years after Finch's death in 1907, his poems were collected and published in a posthumous volume, *The Blue and the Gray and Other Verses* (New York: Henry Holt, 1909). One piece, however, is missing from this volume: a never-published work called "His Side of the Story."

It's no surprise that this poem was not included in the book. For one thing, while none of Finch's published poems is longer than a page or two, "His Side of the Story" is epic-length: sixty-four handwritten pages. Unlike Finch's other verses, moreover—whose conventional subjects range from patriotic celebrations of heroes such as Nathan Hale to sentimental tributes to his six-year-old daughter—"His Side of the Story" is a poem about a serial killer. More specifically, it is a dramatic monologue in the style of Robert Browning's "My Last Duchess," spoken by Edward Rulloff.

The setting is Rulloff's prison cell on the night before his execution. He is visited by someone—possibly a lawyer or journalist, though the listener is never identified—who is eager to learn exactly what became of Rulloff's long-vanished wife and infant daughter. Rulloff proceeds to relate the story of his life in rhymed iambic tetrameter, tantalizing the listener with the promise to reveal the whole truth, though remaining evasive throughout.

This fascinating and exceptionally skillful poem, which exists only in manuscript form, is clearly too long to be quoted in its entirety. The following excerpt is meant to provide a sense of its content and style. In it, Rulloff—speaking of his jealous hatred of his wife's cousin, Dr. Henry Bull—explains why he did not simply kill Bull, while hinting that his frustrated rage was vented on his wife and daughter.

> *One problem, now,*
> *Your eyes have looked, your clouded brow*
> *Suggested oft, I solve.—Why wreak*
> *My sole revenge on young and weak,*
> *And frame a coward's craft and plan?*
> *Why hate the woman; spare the man?*

Why not pursue him round the globe?

A natural question!—Runs a probe,

Deep in this wound. Perhaps you know

How oft I waited chance of blow;

How many hours I dogged his track.

With knife and arm drawn, anxious back;

What patient nights I lurked in shade,

In hope of shot or stab; how laid

The trap of letter, bait of gold

To lure him out of home stronghold!—

Perhaps you know how fate perverse,

And accident I clothed in curse,

Each time distorted aim and plan!—

Suppose I could not kill the man,

Till vengeance, starved and hungry, rose

And fed its hate in safer blows!—

What think you?—If one late returned,

While flame of steady failure burned,

And rage, unslackened, smoked in brain,

To wreck of home, how much of strain

Would bear of storm, and rude debate

Before some reckless burst of hate

Would flash and burn, like powder?—No.—

I do not say the truth was so,

But only natural—if it were!—

Dost see what might have happened, sir?

LOUIS WAGNER,
THE SMUTTY NOSE BUTCHER

JUST SEVEN YEARS AFTER ANTON PROBST HACKED THE DEERING FAMILY TO DEATH, America was rocked by another appalling axe murder, committed, like the earlier one, by an immigrant from the German Empire. His name was Louis Wagner and—until Lizzie Borden dispatched her father and stepmother on a sweltering afternoon in August 1892—he ranked as the most notorious axe murderer in the annals of New England crime.

ABOUT TEN MILES out at sea off the coast of New Hampshire lie the Isles of Shoals, a rugged archipelago of nine tiny islands, a few little more than barren ledges that vanish periodically when the water is high. Most of the isles are utterly inhospitable—desolate chunks of rock visited only by the gulls. Even those most fit for human habitation have never been home to more than a handful of exceptionally hardy souls. In the mid-1800s, between forty and sixty people constituted the entire population of the isles.

The second largest of the isles is Smutty Nose, whose unlovely name, as novelist Anita Shreve explains, originally "derived from a clump of seaweed on the nose of a rock extending into the ocean." It was there that the "monstrous tragedy" occurred on March 5, 1873.

*   *   *

In her 1997 bestseller, *The Weight of Water*, Shreve invents a photojournalist named Jean Janes who, while researching a magazine piece on the Smutty Nose case, discovers a lost manuscript composed by its lone survivor, Maren Hontvet. Shreve's imaginative reconstruction of the crime is undeniably gripping—a steamy brew of incest, adultery, and a soupçon of lesbian sex. Dramatic as it is, however, her version is not nearly as compelling—or as sheerly appalling—as the truth.

At the time of the murders, Maren Hontvet was twenty-six years old, a petite woman with a "gentle and courteous" demeanor who had emigrated from a small fishing village in Norway five years earlier with her husband, John. They shared their small cottage with four other family members: Maren's older sister Karen, described as a "rather sad-looking woman" in perpetual mourning for a lost lover in Norway; the two women's adored brother, Ivan, "tall, light-haired, and rather grave"; Ivan's new bride, Anethe, a radiant twenty-four-year-old much doted on by her husband; and John's brother, Matthew. The six members of this close-knit clan were the only residents of the wild and lonely island, though they occasionally took in a boarder who assisted the three men with their fishing business. His name was Louis Wagner.

A native of Prussia, Wagner was a ruggedly built twenty-eight-year-old who had struggled to support himself as a fisherman since his arrival in America seven years earlier. Possessed of a dark, brooding manner and the bottomless self-pity typical of psychopaths, he owed money to various acquaintances and had grown increasingly embittered over his hard-luck existence. A few weeks before the Smutty Nose horror, he had displayed his worn-out shoes to a shipmate and declared, "This won't do any longer. I am bound to have money in three months if I have to murder for it."

Wagner was intimately familiar with the Hontvets, their financial circumstances, and the layout of their little home, having boarded with them for several months. By his own later admission, they had always treated him "like a brother." During one of his recurrent bouts of illness, he had been nursed back to health by the women, who, in his words, "were most kind to him." He would repay that kindness with the sort of atrocious cruelty that defies easy psychological explanation and tempts even rationalists to speak of pure evil.

*   *   *

ON MARCH 5, 1873, the men of the Hontvet household—Maren's husband, John; her brother, Ivan; and her brother-in-law, Matthew—set sail at daybreak, leaving the women alone on the island. The three fishermen intended to draw their trawls, take their catch into Portsmouth, and be back home in time for dinner. Owing to a combination of circumstances, however, they were delayed in Portsmouth.

While there, they ran into Louis Wagner, who asked if they planned to return to Smutty Nose that night. By then, the three fishermen had decided to remain in Portsmouth until morning. Shortly after Wagner learned this fact, he repaired to a bar and fortified himself with a drink. He then headed down to a wharf where a dory belonging to one of his acquaintances, a fisherman named James Burke, was tied up. When Burke came to fetch his boat an hour later, it was gone.

It had been taken by Wagner, who by that time was rowing steadily through the calm moonlit waters toward Smutty Nose Island, where the three women of the Hontvet household waited alone in their unprotected cottage, wondering what had become of their men. At around ten o'clock, the women retired for the night, Karen sleeping on a makeshift cot in the kitchen, Maren and Anethe sharing a bed in the adjacent room. Though it was the first time in all the years they had lived there that—as one writer puts it—"the house was without a man to protect it," the women felt secure enough to leave the curtains undrawn and the doors unlatched.

Sometime around midnight, Louis Wagner arrived at Smutty Nose. Tying up his boat, he moved stealthily over the rocks, silently reconnoitering to make sure that he was alone with his helpless prey. He then made his way to the cottage, quietly opened the door, and stepped inside.

Tiptoeing across the darkened kitchen, he fastened the door leading to the adjacent bedroom by pushing a length of wood through the latch. At that moment, the Hontvets' little dog, Ringe, began to bark sharply. Startled awake, Karen—assuming that the three men had returned—exclaimed, "John? Is that you?" Her cry roused Maren in the next room, who called out, "What's the matter?"

Karen—still groggy and unable to make out the looming figure in the night-shrouded room—answered: "John scared me!"

She had barely gotten the words out of her mouth when Wagner picked up a wooden chair and delivered a savage blow to her head. "John kills me! John kills me!" she shrieked as Wagner continued to bludgeon her.

Hearing the sounds, the bewildered Maren sprang to her bedchamber door, only to find it inexplicably latched. She shook it frantically, trying in vain to come to her sister's aid. Just then, on the other side, the badly injured Karen staggered from her bed and fell heavily against the door, dislodging the wooden bar. Throwing the door open, Maren burst out, seized her semiconscious sister, and dragged her toward the bedroom while Wagner rushed at the two women and rained maddened blows on them with his makeshift weapon.

"With the strength of frenzy" (in one historian's words), Maren—wounded now herself—managed to get her sister into the bedroom and shut the door against Wagner, who rattled it furiously while Maren held it closed with all her strength.

Anethe, in the meantime, lay cowering in bed. Now, as Maren shouted at her to escape, she rose unsteadily to her feet and crawled out the low window.

"Scream!" Maren cried, hoping that Anethe's shouts for help might carry to nearby Star Island. But—standing there barefoot in the frozen night, clad only in a flimsy nightdress and paralyzed with fear—Anethe was unable to obey. "I cannot make a sound," was all she managed to say.

At that moment, Wagner stepped around the corner of the house.

As he strode toward Anethe, the moonlight illuminating his face, a shriek finally burst from the throat of the terror-stricken young woman: "Louis! Louis!"

That moment of recognition would prove fateful for Louis Wagner, though the retribution that ultimately befell him, however deeply deserved, seemed insufficient reprisal for the atrocities he was about to commit.

Leaning against the house was an axe that Maren had used earlier that day to chop away ice from the well. Wagner grabbed it. "Oh, Louis, Louis, Louis," Anethe sobbed as he advanced upon her. As Maren, standing at the window only a few feet way, watched in thunderstruck horror, he brought the axe down on Anethe's head, cracking it open. She sank without a sound, blood pouring into the snow. The blow was undoubtedly fatal, but Wagner was taking no chances. He stood over her, striking her shattered skull again and again.

In a frenzy of terror, knowing that Wagner would be coming for them in a matter of seconds, Maren begged her sister to get up and run. "I cannot," Karen moaned. "I haven't the strength." At that instant, footsteps sounded from the kitchen; the killer had reentered the house. Now it was either flee or die for Maren. Grabbing the nearest garment, a skirt, she threw it over her shoulders, climbed out the window, hurried past the slaughtered corpse of Anethe, and—with the little dog, Ringe, following close on her heels—searched desperately for a hiding place.

As she stumbled barefoot over ice and rocks toward the farthest end of the island, she could hear her sister's anguished shrieks as Wagner continued his butchery, delivering such powerful blows that the axe handle broke, then garroting the dying woman with a scarf. Half frozen, almost beside herself with fear, Maren climbed down toward the ocean and, on hands and knees, wedged herself between two rocks at the water's edge, clutching Ringe to her body for warmth. Wagner, meanwhile, had begun a frantic search for the last surviving witness to his atrocities. It was a situation so nightmarish that it has become a staple of horror movies: an implacable monster hunting for a young woman who huddles nearby in absolute terror, barely daring to breathe for fear that her hiding place will be discovered.

Unable to find his prey, Wagner returned to the cottage, where he dragged Anethe by her feet into the kitchen. He then began to ransack the house, breaking into boxes and trunks, emptying bureau drawers. From his familiarity with the Hontvets' fishing business, he had expected to find as much as $600, but his rummaging turned up less than $20. Then came an act that, even more than the murders themselves, struck later observers as indicative of Wagner's utter depravity. With the corpses of his two victims lying a few feet away, he prepared a pot of tea and sat down at the kitchen table to refresh himself with a meal before setting off on his long row back to Portsmouth.

In the morning, Maren waited until the sun was fully risen before crawling from her shelter and making her way on torn and frozen feet to the northernmost tip of Smutty Nose, where her frantic shouts brought help from the neighboring island of Appledore. Bloody, bruised, and in a state of near-delirium, she was ferried across the water to the home of a family named the Ingebertsens, where she was sheltered and cared for, while a group of armed men from Appledore scoured the island for Wagner. By then, however, the killer was long gone.

AFTER MAKING HIS way to Portsmouth, Wagner had eaten a meal, changed his clothing, then boarded a train for Boston. There, he purchased a new suit of clothes, a hat, and a pair of boots, got his long beard shaved and his hair trimmed, and holed up in a room at a sailors' boardinghouse. Within twenty-four hours, however, word of the Smutty Nose atrocities had spread via telegraph throughout the country, and Wagner's name was in newspapers throughout New England. Arrested that same afternoon, Thursday, March 6, 1873, he was transported back to Portsmouth, where a mob of ten thousand people, bent on a lynching, had to be kept back at bayonet point by a company of marines.

Owing to a jurisdictional dispute, Wagner was tried in Maine. Put on the stand, he tearfully protested his innocence, asserting his faith that God would save him while suggesting that the real culprit was John Hontvet, who had murdered the women because "he was tired of having to feed so many relatives." At the end of the nine-day proceedings, the jury took less than an hour to convict him of murder in the first degree. At the announcement of the verdict, the courtroom erupted in cheers. Wagner was placed in a carriage and driven back to the county jail, while jeering throngs lined the route, pelting the vehicle with stones. Arrived at the newly built jailhouse, he reportedly announced to his guards that he would "be out of here a free man within one week."

He made good on his boast on Wednesday, June 26, 1873, when he managed to jimmy open the lock of his cell with some wooden implements and slip away into the night, leaving a "well-constructed dummy made of a variety of objects" lying beneath the blanket of his cot. The ruse wasn't discovered until guards came to distribute breakfast the following morning. A massive manhunt was immediately launched. After contriving a cunning escape, however, Wagner "did not know what to do with his liberty." Wandering aimlessly around the countryside, he subsisted on wild berries and slept in the open until, "ragged and weary," he was captured four days later and returned to jail.

After two years of legal delays, he was finally put to death on June 25, 1875, alongside another multiple murderer named John True Gordon who, on the morning of the scheduled execution, attempted suicide by severing his femoral artery with a smuggled-in shoemaker's knife. Though Gordon was bleeding to death, officials decided that the legalities must be observed. He was carried, semiconscious, to the gallows and held upright by a couple of deputies until the noose was placed around his neck and the trap sprung. Wagner, standing on his own two feet, offered one final proclamation of innocence before plunging to his death. The spectacle was so ghastly that it led to the abolition of capital punishment in Maine.

[*Sources: Report of the Trial and Conviction of Louis Wagner for the Murder of Anethe Christenson* (Saco, ME: William S. Noyes, 1874); Edmund Pearson, *Murder at Smutty Nose and Other Murders* (Garden City, NY: Doubleday, Page & Co., 1926); Celia Thaxter, "A Memorable Murder," *Atlantic Monthly*, May 1875; Richard Dempewolff, *Famous Old New England Murders* (Brattleboro, VT: Stephen Day Press, 1942).]

"A Memorable Murder"

As chance would have it, one of the minuscule number of people residing on the Isles of Shoals at the time of the Smutty Nose murders was a significant literary figure, America's most widely read woman poet of her time. Her name was Celia Laighton Thaxter.

Thaxter grew up on the isles. Between the ages of four and ten, she and her family were the sole inhabitants of White Island, where her father, Thomas Laighton, served as lighthouse keeper. In 1841, the Laightons moved to the largest of the islands, Appledore, where Thomas undertook the construction of a guesthouse, said to be the first summer resort on the Atlantic coast. Appealing to the sort of sightseer who, as one writer puts it, responds to "that strange beauty which dwells in desolate places," Laighton's hotel, Appledore House, began attracting a small but steady stream of vacationers, among them some of New England's most eminent artists and writers, including Nathaniel Hawthorne, Henry David Thoreau, Childe Hassam, James Russell Lowell, and Richard Henry Dana.

Laighton's partner in this enterprise was a twenty-seven-year-old Harvard graduate, Levi Lincoln Thaxter, who also served as an occasional tutor to Celia and her two brothers. In 1851, not long after Celia's sixteenth birthday, he took her as his wife.

Four years later, after trying and failing at a variety of pursuits, Thaxter moved his family—which now included two young sons—to Newtonville, Massachusetts. Celia, who had rarely set foot on the mainland since the age of four, suddenly found herself trapped in what she described as a "household jail." Pining for the stark beauties of her childhood home, she vented her homesickness in verse, composing an autobiographical poem called "Land-locked" that appeared to great acclaim in the March 1861 issue of the *Atlantic Monthly*.

Soon Thaxter was publishing poetry in all the leading periodicals of the day and hobnobbing with the likes of Charles Dickens. Even as her literary career flourished, however, her marriage grew increasingly strained. While Levi—who had developed a taste for warmer climes—made extended visits to the South, Celia took to spending long stretches back on Appledore. As a result, she was there in March 1873 when her beloved isles became the site of Louis Wagner's atrocities, a crime so appalling that her own estimate of it—"one of the most monstrous tragedies ever enacted on this planet," she would claim—seems only slightly hyperbolic.

On the morning after the atrocity, Thaxter was working at her desk on the second floor of her family house on Appledore when she became aware of a commotion outside her window: men hurrying back and forth, some armed with guns. Alarmed shouts of "Trouble at Smutty Nose!" Then the sound of women wailing: "Karen is dead! Anethe is dead! Louis Wagner has murdered them both!"

Rushing downstairs, Thaxter, upon hearing that Maren Hontvet had been taken to the Ingebertsen cottage, hurried to her side and found her lying in bed, "half crazy," her eyes "wild, glittering, dilated." Clutching Thaxter's hand, Maren, in her broken English, cried: "Oh, I am so glad to see you! I so glad I save my life!" Then she related the horrible tale to Thaxter, the first to hear it from the survivor's own lips.

Two years later, Thaxter's lengthy account of the crime, based on her direct, firsthand knowledge of the Smutty Nose horror, appeared in the May 1875 issue of *The Atlantic Monthly*. Titled "A Memorable Murder," it stands as the first genuinely modern work of American true crime literature, predating Truman Capote's *In Cold Blood* by nearly a century. Though Capote is widely regarded as the first American writer to apply a sophisticated aesthetic sensibility to true crime writing, legitimizing a genre that had always been viewed with critical contempt, that honor really belongs to Celia Thaxter, the once renowned, now forgotten poet who transformed a case of real-life horror into a bona fide work of literary art.

FRANKLIN EVANS,
THE NORTHWOOD MURDERER

IT'S A COMMON MISCONCEPTION THAT SERIAL MURDER IS A RELATIVELY RECENT phenomenon that began roughly in the Victorian era with the depredations of Jack the Ripper. Anthropological evidence makes it depressingly clear that human beings have been butchering each other since the days when our pre-historic ancestors dined on each other's brains and collected human body parts as hunting trophies. That our species has always indulged in extraordinarily barbaric behavior is made clear in everything from ancient Greek myths such as the story of Atreus (who butchered his brother's sons and baked them in a cannibal pie) to fairy tales such as "Little Red Riding Hood" (which, in the view of many scholars, re-flects the atrocities of real-life lycanthropes such as Peter Stubbe, a medieval lust killer who preyed on more than a dozen children, ripping them to pieces with the savagery of a wolf).

Decades before Jack the Ripper embarked on his ghastly spree, a sexual mutila-tion murderer every bit as monstrous as the Whitechapel fiend was at large in our own country. Precisely why he has been so thoroughly forgotten while the Ripper has achieved mythic status is a mystery. The killings he confessed to matched the Ripper's tally, their savagery was no less extreme, and the nature of his crimes was arguably even more shocking, since (like Peter Stubbe) he preyed primarily on children. His name was Franklin Evans, and in the eyes of his contemporaries, he was "the most monstrous and inhuman criminal of modern times—or indeed of any time."

ON MONDAY, JUNE 12, 1865, fifteen-year-old Isabella Joyce and her twelve-year-old brother, John—children of a recently widowed seamstress residing in Lynn, Massachusetts—paid a visit to their grandmother in Roxbury. At around eleven in the morning, they expressed a desire to explore a nearby forested area known as May's Woods. After some initial reluctance, the grandmother finally relented. She packed them a lunch, gave them ten cents each for trolley fare, and told them to return no later than 2:00 p.m. She never saw them alive again.

When the children failed to return, their grandmother became frantic. For the next five days, search parties scoured the woods around Roxbury. It wasn't until Sunday, June 18, however, that two men, John Sawtelle and J. F. Jameson—while hiking across the estate of the Bussey family in West Roxbury—stumbled upon the remains of the missing children.

From the evidence, it seemed clear that Isabella and her little brother had been playing happily in the woods, creating little hillocks of moss and fashioning wreaths out of oak leaves and twigs, when they were unexpectedly set upon. Their assailant—a "fiend in human shape," as the newspapers called him—attacked the girl first, savaging her body with a dagger, then tearing off her undergarments and raping her. There were twenty-seven stab wounds on her torso and another sixteen on her neck. The ground all around her corpse was clotted with blood. She had apparently put up a desperate fight, grabbing the long blade of the dagger and attempting to wrest it from her killer. The index finger of her right hand was completely severed and the rest of her fingers nearly cut off. Her clothes were soaked in blood, and clumps of grass had been shoved into her mouth to stifle her cries.

Apparently her brother had stood paralyzed for a few moments with terror. When he finally turned to run, it was too late. He was found lying facedown, having evidently tripped over a tree root while attempting to escape. His killer had pounced on the prostrate boy and stabbed him through the back a half dozen times. The wounds were so deep that, in several instances, the blade had gone all the way through the little victim's body, coming out the skin in front.

There were two houses within a few hundred yards of the scene. But the inhabitants were so accustomed to shouts, laughter, and yells from picnic and excursion groups that, as the newspapers noted, "they would not have paid any attention even if they had heard screams on this occasion."

The appalling savagery of the Joyce murders provoked a statewide furor. From their pulpits, ministers decried the murders as a sign of the growing degeneracy of the age—of the country's deplorable descent into vice, immorality and crime. Rewards totaling $4,500 (more than $60,000 in today's money) were offered by the citizens of Roxbury, while an enormous manhunt was mounted for the "inhuman wretch" responsible for the outrage. Newspapers issued confident pronouncements that the perpetrator of the diabolical deed would be "speedily arrested" and "subjected to summary vengeance." But, though various suspects were interrogated in the immediate aftermath of the crime, no arrests were made.

The case appeared to be broken in March 1866 when an inmate of the Charlestown State Prison, a small-time crook who went by the colorful name of "Scratch Gravel," told a cellmate that he had "done that job in Roxbury." In the end, however, Gravel was judged to be nothing more than a "blustering braggart" who had not even been in Massachusetts at the time of the killings. As the months and years passed with no arrests in the case, it seemed that the murder of the Joyce children—"one of the most horrible and revolting crimes which has ever occurred in New England," as the *New York Times* described it—would forever go unsolved.

EARLY IN THE summer of 1872, seven years after the murder of the Joyce children, Franklin Evans came to board with his elderly sister, Mrs. Deborah Day, at her farmhouse in Northwood, New Hampshire.

A gaunt and grizzled sixty-four-year-old, Evans had led a shiftless existence for much of his adult life. "He belonged," wrote one contemporary chronicler, "to that numerous class of dead beats that are always broke." Wandering the New England countryside, he subsisted by sponging off his adult children, borrowing (though rarely repaying) small sums from acquaintances, and begging handouts from strangers.

What little honest money he made came from supplying a Manchester physician, Dr. F. W. Hanson, with healing roots and herbs. His vagabond life had given the old

EVANS, THE NORTHWOOD MURDERER.

man an intimate knowledge of the landscape, and "his reputation for obtaining the medicinal products of the woods and fields was unsurpassed." Even in this enterprise, however, Evans could not keep from betraying his mendacious nature. Claiming that he himself was a "botanical physician," he peddled worthless "miracle cures" to rural families desperate for medical aid.

He also passed himself off as an itinerant preacher. Exploiting the religious fervor of the age, he joined the Second Advent Society, declared himself a minister of the Gospel, and managed to raise money from his brethren to support himself in his mission. He was "denounced as a mean, sneaking hypocrite," however, when he was arrested for consorting with prostitutes. The incident wasn't his only brush with the law. At various times, he was charged with petty theft, attempting to pass crudely forged ten-dollar bills, and—most serious—scheming to defraud the Travelers Insurance Company of Boston of $1,500.

If these crimes were the sum of his transgressions, Evans would have been nothing more than a small-time scoundrel, a snake oil salesman and confidence trickster on the order of Mark Twain's Duke and Dauphin. But as the world would eventually learn to its horror, he was something far worse: a creature so depraved that, to his contemporaries, his crimes seemed the work of supernatural evil—"too horrible," as one newspaper put it, "for anything in human form to have perpetrated."

Four people resided at his sister's farmhouse when Evans showed up that summer: Mrs. Day and her husband, Sylvester; their widowed daughter, Susan Lovering; and Susan's daughter, Georgianna. A blooming thirteen-year-old, tall and "well developed for her age," Georgianna—Evans' grandniece—immediately became the object of the depraved old man's lust. Within days of his arrival, he had set about trying to seduce the girl. When she repulsed his odious advances, he concocted a diabolical scheme—a "deeply laid plan," as one account put it, "designed for no other purpose than to lure his victim into his lecherous grasp."

Not far from the Day farmhouse lay a deep forest, the largest tract of woodland in the county, covering an area of nearly two thousand acres. Late on Monday, October 21, 1872, after being absent for much of the day, Evans returned to his sister's home, explaining that he had been off in the forest setting snares for partridges. The following morning, he invited his niece to accompany him into the woods to see if he had caught anything. The traps turned out to be empty. He showed Georgianna how they worked—little hoops concealed inside the hedges, designed to snag the birds by the throat as they scrambled through the foliage. Georgianna was intrigued by the cunning little traps, never suspecting, of course, that they had been placed there to snare *her*.

Early Friday morning, October 25, Evans asked his grandniece for a favor. He had agreed to perform some chores for a neighbor, a farmer named Daniel Hill, and would be gone all day. Would she go into the forest and check the bird snares for him? Surely he must have caught something by now.

Though the girl was reluctant at first, she allowed herself to be persuaded. Evans left soon afterward, presumably for Hill's farm several miles away. A short time later, Georgianna stuck a comb in her thick brown hair to hold it in place, threw on a shawl, tied on her bonnet and—like Little Red Riding Hood off to visit Grandma—disappeared into the forest.

When Georgianna failed to return by lunchtime, her grandfather went out to look for her. Unable to find her, he came back home and told her mother, who immediately became alarmed. The two hurried back to the woods. As they made their way through the forest, shouting the girl's name, they spotted her apron caught on a tree branch. A short distance away, they came upon her comb, broken in half, with some strands of her hair stuck in the teeth. The soft earth all around was trampled with two sets of prints, one made by a man's boots, the other by a girl's shoes—evidence, as Grandpa

Day would later testify, of a "squabble." Frantic with anxiety, Day and his daughter pushed ever deeper into the woods but could turn up no other trace of the missing girl.

Racing back home, they alerted the neighbors. All day Saturday and into Sunday morning, hundreds of people scoured the woods, but to no avail. By then, suspicion had fallen on Franklin Evans. Checking with Daniel Hill, authorities discovered that, contrary to Evans' claim, he hadn't gone to Hill's farm that day—in fact, Hill hadn't seen him for a week. Another witness, a young man named James Pender, testified that he had seen Evans cross into the forest at around eight-thirty on Friday morning, just a half hour before Georgianna herself disappeared into the woods.

When Evans, under intense questioning by County Sheriff Henry Drew, could offer no convincing account of his whereabouts on the day his grandniece went missing, he was taken into custody. Inside his pockets, Drew (as he later testified) found "a wallet, money, obscene books, a bottle of liquor, and a common bone-handled knife with two blades, blood-stained and keen as a razor."

At first Evans denied all knowledge of Georgianna's whereabouts. When Drew assured the old man that "no harm would come to him if he would confess," Evans changed his story. Georgianna, he insisted, was alive and well. He had arranged to have her "carried away by a man from Kingston," a farmer named Webster, who wanted her as his bride.

Though Drew was skeptical, he immediately started for Kingston, where he confirmed that the story was a "base falsehood." Back at the jailhouse, he continued to press Evans, plying him with liquor and promising to help him escape to Canada if he told the truth. Finally, on Halloween night, the old man gave in. Asked by Drew "whether the girl was cold in death or not," Evans replied, "She is, and I've done wrong."

"With this admission, on Thursday, about midnight, six days after her disappearance," writes one contemporary chronicler, "Evans told the Sheriff he would go with him and show where the girl was. Through the dark forest at midnight they silently pursued their way, over rocks and decayed logs, through swamps and glades, and there, in the recess of this deep wood, beneath the roots of an upturned tree, this worse-than-criminal pointed to a pile of dried leaves and coolly said, 'There she is.' The Sheriff gently moved away the leaves and by the dim light of his lantern were revealed the mangled remains of Georgianna Lovering."

By then, two other townsmen, Eben J. Parsley and Alonzo Tuttle, had arrived on the scene, followed closely by the local physician, Dr. Caleb Hanson. Gaping in shock at the naked, savaged girl, Parsley asked Evans: "How did you come to do such a bloody deed?"

The old man shrugged and replied, "I suppose the evil one got the upper hand of me."

A glance at the girl's face, with its bulging eyes, swollen and protruding tongue, and dark bruises around the windpipe, told Hanson that she had been strangled. Her body had been hideously mutilated. Evans, as he later confessed, had raped the corpse, then torn open the belly with his jackknife to get at her uterus. He had also excised her vulva, which he carried off some distance and hid under a rock. When a stunned Sheriff Drew asked Evans why he had committed such butchery, the old man calmly explained that he "did it to gain some knowledge of the human system that might be of use to me as a doctor."

As he led Evans back to the jail, Drew had one more question for him. "What did you set those snares for, Frank?"

If the sheriff had any doubts that he was in the presence of some unaccountable evil, they vanished with the old man's response.

"I set them to catch the girl," said her uncle with a self-satisfied smirk, "and I catched her."

FRANKLIN EVANS' TRIAL, which opened on February 3, 1873, was a perfunctory affair, its outcome a forgone conclusion. Only one moment of drama occurred during its three-day duration. Early on the morning of Tuesday, February 5, while his keeper was off fetching him a glass of water, the old man took one of his suspenders, tied it around his neck, attached the other end to a clothes hook nailed to the wall, and tried to hang himself. Just then, as newspapers reported, the keeper returned, "seized Evans, and disengaged him from the hook."

The halfhearted nature of this suicide attempt convinced most observers that Evans—hoping to get off on an insanity defense—was merely trying to convince the jurors of his mental instability. If so, the effort failed. He was convicted of murder in the first degree and sentenced to be hanged for real on the third Tuesday of February 1874. For "his unnamable and incredible crimes, he will be swung like a dog," exulted one local newspaper, which went on to recommend that those wishing to attend the hanging should make "early application in order to secure 'reserved seats,' which will be scarce."

Accompanied by the high sheriff of Rockingham County, J. W. Odlin, Evans was transported by train to the state prison at Concord. A crowd of more than eight hundred gawkers, "excited to a remarkable pitch of feeling," gathered at the station to catch of glimpse of him. Their frenzied fascination was not entirely based on Evans' notoriety as the slayer of Georgianna Lovering. By then, he had confessed to other crimes as well—atrocities that marked him as one of the most appalling killers of the age, a monster whose like would not be seen again in this country for another fifty years, when the pedophiliac madman Albert Fish prowled the land.

Evans' "inconceivable career of crime" had begun fifteen years earlier, during a visit to Derry, New Hampshire. Passing by the dwelling of a family named Mills, he peered through a window and spotted a little girl, approximately five years old, playing on the floor. No adults were to be seen. Possessed by the urge "to procure a body to examine for surgical purposes" (in his words), he snuck into the house, snatched the child, then "took her to the woods at some distance and strangled her." When he stripped off her clothes, however, he discovered that "one hip and part of her spine were deformed." Seized with revulsion, he abandoned his plan to "examine her"—his euphemism for postmortem rape and sexual mutilation—and buried the corpse beneath a rotten chestnut stump.

Three years later, while staying in Augusta, Maine, he waylaid a fourteen-year-old named Anna Sibley on her way to school. Carrying her deep into the woods, he raped her, cut her throat, then hid her corpse beneath a pile of leaves. In May 1872, just weeks before arriving at his sister's home in Northwood, Evans also raped and murdered a woman whose body was found in the woods near Fitchburg, Massachusetts.

His most sensational admission, however, was that he had slain little John and Isabella Joyce in Lynn, Massachusetts. Though some law officers involved in the case were skeptical of his claim—and though Franklin himself retracted it shortly before his death—the similarities between the Lovering outrage and the murders in Bussey's woods convinced most observers that the crimes had indeed been perpetrated by the same "inhuman wretch." Headlines around the country trumpeted the news that the eight-year-old Joyce mystery had finally been solved.

* * *

FRANKLIN EVANS PASSED the last night of his life quietly, falling asleep around midnight with his spiritual advisor, the Rev. Mr. Church of Providence, Rhode Island, at his side. Awakening around 5:30 a.m., he ate a hearty breakfast and drank a mug of hot tea. "I have confessed everything," he replied when Church asked if he had any last-minute statements to make. "If the people don't believe it, I can't help it."

Outside the prison walls, a large, excited crowd had gathered. At 10:50 a.m., they were admitted into the building, where the gallows had been set up in the corridor between the guardroom and the cells. Within minutes, every available inch of space was packed with spectators, some positioning themselves on the stairways leading up to the cells, others crowding around the scaffold.

At eleven o'clock, Evans, dressed in a black suit, was led through the crowd by Warden Pittsburg. Mounting the scaffold, he muttered something inaudible under his breath while his arms and legs were pinioned. He appeared "quite calm and possessed," though the people standing closest to the scaffold observed that his knees were trembling slightly. The noose was carefully adjusted around his neck and the black hood pulled down over his head. After reading the death warrant, Sheriff Odlin placed his foot on the spring of the drop and—at precisely 11:06 a.m., Tuesday, February 17, 1874—the sixty-seven-year-old serial murderer "was launched into eternity."

He dangled for nearly twenty minutes before his heart stopped beating and the attending physician declared him dead. In view of his outrageous claim that he had mutilated his victims to gain anatomical knowledge that would "aid him as a doctor," the final disposition of his own corpse couldn't have been more fitting. It was transported to Dartmouth Medical College for dissection by students.

[*Sources:* Randolph Roth, *American Homicide* (Cambridge, MA: Harvard University Press/Belknap, 2009); *The Northwood Murder: A Complete Report of the Trial of Franklin B. Evans for the Murder of Georgianna Lovering at Northwood, October 25, 1872, Together with a Portrait and Sketch of the Career of the Murderer* (Manchester, NH, 1873).]

"Georgianna Lovering, or the Northwood Tragedy"

Franklin Evans was still awaiting trial when a local poetaster named Byron DeWolfe composed and printed a broadside ballad about the sex slaying of Georgianna Lovering. Unlike the typical "murdered-girl ballad," which tends to play fast and loose with the facts, DeWolfe's piece, despite its thick coating of sentimentality, offers an almost journalistic account of the crime. Consisting of more than two dozen eight-line stanzas, it is too long to reprint here in its entirety, though the following excerpt offers a good sense of the whole. Interested readers can find an image of the original broadside by going to "An American Time Capsule: Three Centuries of Broadsides and Other Printed Ephemera" on the Library of Congress' "American Memory" website: http://memory .loc.gov/ammem/rbpehtml/.

Dark were the eyes of a beautiful maiden,
Like music her voice, and her cheeks were in bloom;
Her mind seemed to be with the purest thoughts laden;
Her breath was as sweet as the rose's perfume;
Her mother worked hard for her child's education,
And brought for her many a well-written tome;
Her father had died for the flag of his Nation;
And she was the sunlight and comfort of home!

She with her grandparents and mother resided;
Two miles from the Centre of Northwood the cot;
The villagers loved her and in her confided;
And girls near her age her companionship sought;
She was her mother's one, chief earthly treasure;
Oft her sweet voice had the weeping one cheered;
Sorrow itself seemed to turn into pleasure,
And grief unto gladness where Georgie appeared!

She had an uncle too deep steeped in error
To learn in her presence the way to improve;
His sinister look would fill children with terror;
Few hearts could towards him affectionate move;

He looked sanctimonious for certain occasions,
  And words big with honor came to him at ease,
Yet he was her uncle, and she must have patience,
  And do all she could to relieve him and please.

True, his mean soul she was quick to discover,
  Yet knew not how fiendish her uncle could be,
The angels of love seemed about her to hover;
  A word was unkind for no mortal had she;
So when he told her he'd work on the morrow,
  And asked her if she'd to his bird-snares attend?
"O, yes!" she replied, though she told him in sorrow,
  As if she was dreading some terrible end.

The next morn arrived, a bright day in October,
  The maiden was up to look after the snares,
And grandmother saw that young Georgie looked sober,
  As if she was weary of earth and its cares!
"O, what is the matter my darling, this morning?
  What makes you look sad, when so often you're gay?
Have you had a terrible dream or a warning?
  O, what has come over you, pretty one, say?"

"Granny, to uncle last night I was telling
  I'd go to the wild woods his bird-snares to see,
But somehow I dread to leave your homely dwelling,
  For horrible thoughts really linger with me;
Oft to me did those old woods look delightful;
  I oft liked to go at the bird-snares to look;
But now, despite sunshine, the forest looks frightful,
  And lately with joy I've no trip in it took!"

Old granny, no doubt, thought the girl superstitious,
  And having no reason for trouble or fear,
And Georgie gave her a sweet kiss and delicious,

Then these were the words the old lady did hear,
"I promised my uncle his snares I'd attend to;
    This morning I'll go and I'll look them all o'er,
But when I've done that, O such work there's an end to,
    I'll go in the woods for my uncle no more!"

The uncle went not to his labor that morning!
    His thoughts were all evil, his ways all defiled,
Religion—truth—honor—humanity scorning,
    He stands on the hill-top—he watches the child!
He comes down the hill! In the forest does enter!
    The watcher knows not on what mission he's bound,
But soon the news spreads from the cot to the Centre,
    How young Georgie Lovering can nowhere be found!

In the wild wood had her grandfather sought her,
    Though "Georgie" he called, he received no reply;
The mother, too, searched for her beautiful daughter,
    Until she was ready with anguish to die;
How wildly—how deeply her mother lamented,
    And said, "Tell me, Georgie, where you roam!"
No wonder the woman was almost demented,
    When she found the apron, and with it her comb!

Yes, there was the comb, it had Georgie's hair in it,
    The sight seemed to prove that her earth-life had fled;
The searchers with horror did stand for a minute,
    And each of them feared Georgie Lovering was dead;
Continue the search—get more men from the Centre—
    We must know her fate, and the end we must see.
And farther and farther the forest we'll enter,
    No sleep will we crave, and unwearied we'll be.

And when Sheriff Drew at last forced the confession
    From Evans, the uncle a fiend among men,

That he had done wrong, and great was his transgression,
　　That search was abandoned; but not until then!
Abandoned! but 'twas for the sake of another,
　　To be in the night—in the darkness intense;
For one that would bring a dead child to its mother,
　　But for a lost idol make small recompense.

With lantern in hand went the Sheriff with Evans;
　　The wind in the forest did dismally moan;
No bright moon or star could be seen in the heavens;
　　Around all was darkness—and darkness alone,
Save the small light by the lantern was given;
　　And on went the Sheriff, his eye on the wretch,
Who, if caught by a crowd could no prayer-time be having;
　　His form from the nearest stout tree-branch would stretch!

"Lead!" said the Sheriff. "I lead!" said the trembler;
　　He led; for he knew not what else he could do,
He'd been a deceiver—a murderer—dissembler—
　　And somehow he was in the power of Drew!
He led to a swamp where the bog-holes looked fearful!
　　He left it—returned—reached a desolate spot
Which even the sunshine could never make cheerful,
　　And midnight upon it great loneliness wrought.

There the fiend stooped, ay, he almost was kneeling,
　　He scraped away leaves and THERE WAS SOMETHING WHITE!
The Sheriff the form of the dead girl was feeling!
　　Feeling it there on that terrible night!
Feeling it there with her murderer near him,
　　And standing as calm as a man at his gate,
Feeling it there! Was he wild? Was he dreaming?
　　He thought even this was a terrible fate.

Assistance was near, for that had been provided;
    Men came to the spot just as quick as they could;
The prisoner, surely, by that time decided
    That nothing about was foreboding him good;
There lay the form of the girl he had strangled,
    And probably dragged to that horrible spot;
There lay the body, all lifeless and mangled,
    Ah, never a tiger such bad work had wrought.

"Was It a Ghost?"

The 1865 slaying of the Joyce children, ultimately confessed to by Franklin Evans, inspired what has to be one of the weirdest true crime books ever published, Henry Johnson Brent's *Was It a Ghost? The Murders in Bussey Wood. An Extraordinary Narrative* (Boston: Loring, 1868).

A well-known landscape painter and founding editor of the *Knickerbocker Magazine,* the preeminent literary journal of its day, Brent was vacationing ("rusticating," he puts it) at the country home of a friend only a short distance from the crime scene at the time the murders took place.

Three weeks after the discovery of the two butchered children, he was out for an evening stroll in the forest when—so he claims—a strange "misty figure" appeared before him. "He looked dark gray from head to foot," Brent writes. "Body he had, and legs, and arms, and a head; but the face I could not distinctly see." This weird apparition stood frozen for a moment, then—"as quick as the flash of gunpowder"—vanished into thin air, leaving Brent convinced that he had seen a ghost, possibly of the unknown murderer himself.

The book then alternates between a detailed re-creation of the double murder and an argument for the existence of ghosts. The result is a bizarre hybrid—part true crime book, part meditation on spiritualistic phenomena—that drew widespread scorn from contemporary critics. "We are disposed to consider this a very unsubstantial pretext for making a book," sniffed one reviewer. "What good it accomplishes, what end it serves, it is impossible to discover. It does not help the identification of the murderer. It throws no light on any of the supernatural speculations so prevalent in these days. The curious public will probably hang with fresh interest on the horrible details of the crime. But no one, so far as we can see, will be benefited by its perusal."

JOSEPH LAPAGE,
"THE FRENCH MONSTER"

L ESS THAN TWO YEARS AFTER FRANKLIN EVANS WAS HANGED FOR THE SEX murder of thirteen-year-old Georgianna Lovering, another shockingly similar crime occurred in New Hampshire. Its perpetrator was a French Canadian woodcutter named Joseph Lapage. Like Evans, Lapage was a classic lust killer—the type of extreme sexual psychopath who attacks with the ferocity of a wild beast, subjecting his victim's body to unspeakable mutilations. His contemporaries described him in less clinical terms. To them, he was a creature of infernal evil: a "fiend incarnate," a "demon from the bottomless pit."

HIS BIRTH NAME was Joseph Paget. Born in 1837, he grew up on a farm about fifty miles northwest of Montreal. At the age of twenty he married a local woman three years his senior from a family named Rousse. They had five children in rapid succession.

Sometime around 1862, he and his family moved to Saint Beatrice, "a little French provincial town in the bleak rolling hills of Quebec." By then, as the *New York Times* would later report, "he had gained a very bad reputation. He abused his wife shamefully and associated with the vilest company." It was during his years in Saint Beatrice that he also committed his first known sex crime: the rape of his wife's thirteen-year-old sister, Julienne, a girl he had known since her early childhood.

It happened in June 1871. At around 7:00 a.m. on the day in question, Julienne—who was working as the hired girl for a family named Lajeunesse—went off to milk the cows, her regular early morning chore. She was walking through a pasture well out of sight of the nearest dwelling when she was stopped cold by a sinister sight.

About fifty feet way stood a stocky man dressed in a red flannel shirt and baggy linen trousers held up by a leather belt. Beneath his black slouch hat, his face was concealed by a mask fashioned of buffalo skin, and in one hand he carried a pine-root cudgel about two and a half feet long and as thick as her own arm. Suddenly the man

Joseph Lapage murder pamphlet
(*Courtesy of New York State Historical Association Library, Cooperstown.*)

came hurrying toward her, so fast that his hat flew off his head.

Letting out a scream, Julienne turned on her heels and ran, but the man overtook her, grabbed her by one arm, and spun her around. As he did, the adolescent girl reached up with her free hand and tore off his mask. "I knew him very well," she later testified. It was Joseph Lapage, her brother-in-law, his face contorted into a grimace of lust.

Gripping her around the throat, Lapage began to choke her, then threw her to the ground and straddled her. As she struggled, he snatched up a handful of sandy soil, shoved some into her mouth to silence her, and ground the rest into her eyes. Then he pulled up her skirt and raped her. She lost consciousness before he was through.

When she came to, she staggered back home and told her employer, Joseph Lajeunesse, what had happened. An arrest warrant was issued for Lapage, but he managed to elude the law. Julienne, unable at first to hold down food or drink, took "a long month" to recover from her physical injuries. By then, her assailant had fled Canada with his wife and children.

THREE YEARS LATER, at around three-thirty on the afternoon of Friday, July 27, 1874, a young teacher, Miss Marietta Ball of St. Albans, Vermont, closed up her one-room schoolhouse and set out along a lonely stretch of road to visit a friend on the south side of town. She never arrived.

The following day, search parties scouring the woods discovered her naked corpse—"hideously violated and mangled in the most fiendish manner"—lying in a little gully beneath a pile of leaves. At the inquest, the coroner, Dr. H. H. Farnsworth, determined that her skull had been crushed with a rock, though whether she was raped pre- or postmortem was impossible to say.

Determined to find the perpetrator of the outrage, her neighbors pooled their resources and brought in a detective from Boston. Interviewing everyone who knew her, including her pupils, the investigator soon learned about one suspicious character who had been "asking the schoolchildren about Miss Ball's route home" in the weeks prior to her disappearance and who had been seen with "deep scratches and bruises" on his face immediately following her murder. Known for his generally crude character, especially toward women, the suspect had been residing in St. Albans' "French settlement" since his arrival from Quebec three years earlier. His name was Joseph Lapage.

Lapage was promptly arrested but managed to bring forth witnesses who testified (falsely, as it would eventually appear) that he was working in a hayfield at the time of the murder and supported his claim that he had scratched his face on thorns while berry picking. With no hard evidence against him, he was released. The following March, he and his family suddenly packed up and left town. Not long afterward, they showed up in Pembroke, New Hampshire.

*   *   *

DURING THE WANING days of September 1875—just six months after Lapage moved to Pembroke—a number of townspeople spotted a strange figure lurking alongside the road that led to the local high school. Seventeen-year-old Clarence Cochran, for example, was headed for class on the last Friday of the month when, as he later testified, he "saw a man jump into the bushes on the left side of the road" about fifty feet ahead of him. Believing it was a friend named John Colby—a practical joker who liked to hide in the bushes and spring out at his unwary schoolmates—Cochran shouted: "Get out of there, you long-legged son of a gun, you can't scare me." When Clarence reached the spot where the figure had leapt into the undergrowth, however, no one was there.

The following day, Mrs. Albersia Watson and her youngest daughter, Annie, a student at Pembroke Academy, were walking along the same deserted stretch of road. Suddenly sensing that someone was behind them, they turned and saw "a man standing by the side of the road about a hundred feet away, holding a stick in his right hand." Though Mrs. Watson could not make out his features, she saw that he was of stocky build with "black hair and whiskers, tan-colored overalls, and a black slouch hat." As the mother and daughter continued on their way, the man began to follow at a rapid pace. Throwing a protective arm around her daughter—who was now whimpering in fear—Mrs. Watson hurried the girl onward. By now, the man was "partly running." He was almost upon them when, round-

Josie Langmaid

ing a bend, Mrs. Watson spotted a neighbor, George Mack, picking berries in a nearby field. As Mrs. Watson steered her daughter toward Mack, she threw a quick glance over her shoulder and saw her pursuer vanish into the woods.

That same weekend, Hiram Towle and his wife, Harriet, were driving their buggy along Academy Road when they saw "a man coming, carrying a stick behind him in a peculiar way." As they drew up beside him, he glanced at Mrs. Towle with a look that made her quail. "I thought he might be crazy," she would later testify. "I felt afraid of the man." Though she had never laid eyes on Franklin Evans, she had read descriptions of the infamous "Northwood Monster" in the papers. Now, as they drove past the grubby, club-wielding figure making his way toward the high school, Mrs. Towle turned to her husband and said: "I should think that was old Evans himself if he was still alive."

By the time the Towles passed him on the road, Lapage had already set his sights on another victim—not a teacher this time but one of the female students attending Pembroke Academy. Exactly which student is unclear. It appears that his original target was either Litia Fowler, the sixteen-year-old daughter of a farmer named Trueworthy L. Fowler, or her schoolmate Sarah Prentiss.

On September 22, while threshing rye for Mr. Fowler, Lapage noticed Litia as she crossed the front yard and entered the house. He immediately began asking her twenty-year-old brother, Andrew, about the girl: who was she, where did she go to school, what road did she take to get there? Oblivious to the sinister import of the questions, "Andrew obligingly answered, even pointing out the school" when he and Lapage drove past it in a wagon a few days later.

Sarah Prentiss also caught Lapage's prurient eye while he was working for Fowler. Spying her as she walked past the farm, he pulled aside a thirteen-year-old boy named Edwin Mahuir and grilled him about the girl, asking her name, where she lived, "who was going with her." When he made a crude remark about "certain parts of the girl's anatomy, young Edwin was so startled that he turned and fled."

Evidence suggests that Lapage intended to waylay either Litia Fowler or Sarah Prentiss on the morning of Monday, October 4, 1875, as they made their way to school. Somehow his plan miscarried. By the time he arrived at the spot he had picked for the ambush, both girls were already safely seated at their desks. Their classmate Josie Langmaid wasn't as lucky.

Just two months shy of her eighteenth birthday, Josie was a "pretty and popular girl" who usually made the two-and-a-half-mile hike to the school with her younger brother Waldo. On that fateful morning, however, Josie had promised to wait for a friend. Waldo, growing increasingly impatient, hung around with his sister until eight-fifteen when he headed off by himself. Fifteen minutes later, when the first reminder bell tolled from the academy, Josie's friend had still not arrived. Snatching up her books and kissing her stepmother goodbye, Josie started up the road alone. At around nine o'clock—five minutes after the last reminder bell sounded—a farmer named Bernard Gile passed her as she was hurrying in the direction of the schoolhouse. He was the last villager to see her alive.

When Waldo returned from school that afternoon and informed his parents that his sister had never shown up, an anxious Mr. Langmaid hurried around to the neighboring homes to see if Josie might be with one of her friends. Except for Bernard Gile, however, no one had seen her all day. Within an hour, word of her disappearance had spread throughout the community. Dozens of men began scouring the countryside. When darkness fell, the search continued by torchlight.

It was a farmer named Daniel Merrill who stumbled upon Josie's savaged corpse while moving through a marshy patch of woods about eighty feet from the main road. The time was around 8:00 p.m. The body was "lying on its back with the right arm doubled under and the left crossed over the breast," he later testified. "The right foot was drawn up. The clothing appeared to have been removed and thrown back, all saturated with blood. The breast was bare." Her vulva had been cut away and carried off by her butcher, never to be found. Her head, cleanly severed, was nowhere to be seen.

It wasn't until the following morning that another searcher, Horace Ayer, discovered Josie's head, rolled in her blue cape and dumped in the woods about a quarter mile from where her body was found. A postmortem examination revealed that before hacking off her head with an axe, her killer had crushed her skull with a club, then stomped on her face for good measure, leaving a clear imprint of his boot heel on one cheek. So savage was the bludgeoning he inflicted that every bone in Josie's left hand had been shattered when she tried to shield her head from the blows.

* * *

AT FIRST SUSPICION fell on a twenty-four-year-old stonemason named William Drew, who—though married with children—was reputed to have made "improper advances" toward a number of schoolgirls, including Josie Langmaid. Ultimately, however, various witnesses supported Drew's claim that he had been mending a wall on a neighbor's farm at the time of the murder.

A few days later, Pembroke officials received a letter from Coroner Farnsworth of St. Albans, Vermont, who had read about the Langmaid case in the papers and noted its striking similarity to the rape and murder of Marietta Ball a year and a half earlier. Police immediately paid a visit to the home of Ball's accused killer, where a search of Lapage's bedroom turned up a bloody overcoat, a bloodstained hat, and a pair of trousers "bespattered with blood from the belt line all the way down to the cuffs." A comparison of his boots to a tracing of the heel print left on Josie's face revealed a precise match.

Despite Lapage's insistence that he had been "lost in the woods" at the time of the murder, a high school girl named Hattie Gault swore that she had seen him striding down Academy Road with an axe in his hand at eight-thirty that morning. Another witness, Thomas Gardiner, told police that on the afternoon of October 4—after Josie was reported missing but before her body had been found—he and his wife received a visit from Lapage. When Mrs. Gardiner remarked on Josie's disappearance, Lapage blurted, "It's too bad that the girl has been killed." Then—seemingly aware of his blunder—he turned and "hurried away as quick as he could."

Taken into custody, Lapage was indicted for the murder, rape, and mutilation of Josie Langmaid. During his incarceration, a newspaper reporter sought out Lapage's long-suffering wife and questioned her about the earlier murder of Marietta Ball. She claimed that she had "no evidence that would link him" to the crime, "but since she had foiled an attempt by him to ravish their own fifteen-year-old daughter, she had to admit that he was capable of committing it."

In the meantime, Lapage was busily trying to dig his way to freedom with a makeshift tool fashioned from a piece of his metal bed frame. He managed to pry loose seventeen bricks from the wall of his cell before his jailers became aware of his efforts.

An "immense throng" showed up at the Concord City Hall for the start of his trial on the morning of Tuesday, January 4, 1876. Before the actual proceedings began, the jurors, along with the defendant, were taken by carriage to the scene of the murder. As Lapage looked on indifferently, the dozen men were led into the woods and shown "the precise locality where the headless body" had been found. A large stake,

Condemned to death!
Berurtheilt zum Tod!

Lapage condemned. (*Courtesy of New York State Historical Association Library, Cooperstown.*)

marking the spot, had been driven into the earth, and the surrounding trees and shrubs were festooned with pieces of black crape—tokens of mourning from Josie's friends and neighbors. From that somber place the jurors were led to the spot where her head had been discovered. On a nearby tree, someone had whittled away a section of bark and, on the exposed wood, inscribed the following with a lead pencil: "J. Langmaid's Head found here, October 5, 1875. Poor Josie, may her soul rest in peace."

The proceedings themselves lasted six days and produced one particularly dramatic moment: the appearance of Lapage's French-speaking sister-in-law Julienne Rousse, who—testifying through a translator—vividly described the terrifying morning five years earlier when Lapage had (as she put it) "outraged her person." In the end, the jury took just ninety minutes to convict him. Unfortunately for the prosecution, the appeals court ruled that Judge Foster had erred in admitting Rousse's testimony since it had no direct bearing on the Langmaid murder. The reversal, however, proved only a temporary setback for the state. A second trial in March 1877 culminated in another swift conviction.

A year would pass before his execution on March 15, 1878. Confined in the state prison in Concord, New Hampshire, Lapage—according to the *New York Times*—was a "perfectly docile" prisoner, "giving no trouble to the Warden or any of his keepers. He made no complaints about his treatment, nor asked for anything." On the Monday before his scheduled hanging, he had a final meeting with his family, but—apart from a few tears shed by one of his daughters—"little emotion was manifested by any of them. At parting, he kissed his wife and daughters but only shook hands with his two boys."

On the evening before his execution, Lapage received a visit from his spiritual advisors, the Revs. Mr. J. E. Barry and Mr. J. B. Millette. They prayed together in his cell until nearly midnight. No sooner had they taken their leave than Lapage—who had never wavered from his protestations of innocence—summoned the warden to his cell. Throwing himself to his knees and speaking in broken English, he tearfully confessed to the murder of the "two gals." "After making his confession," reported the *New York Times*, "he felt greatly relieved."

When the two priests returned early the next morning, they found Lapage enjoying a hearty breakfast. After receiving the sacrament, he was led to the gallows, which had been erected in the corridor of the prison's north wing. A large crowd was assembled at the foot of the scaffold. Among the witnesses was Josie Langmaid's father, James, still devastated not only by his daughter's murder but also by a second terrible blow: the death of his thirteen-year-old son, Waldo, who had succumbed to consumption only two months after Josie was killed.

At a few minutes past 11:00 a.m., Lapage was led to the scaffold by Sheriff Dodge, who—after reading aloud the death warrant—adjusted the noose around the prisoner's neck, drew the black hood over his head, pinioned his arms, and sprang the trap. "A slight twitching of the legs was the only motion observable after he fell," the *Times* reported. The officiating physicians, Drs. A. H. Crosby, C. P. Gage, and J. W. Barney, closely monitored his fading heartbeats. Nearly twenty minutes passed before he was pronounced dead. His corpse was then delivered to a local undertaker named Crow and interred in Blossom Hill Cemetery.

Two weeks later, a "party of young scamps" stole into the graveyard at midnight, unearthed the corpse, and left it hanging from a water pipe in the statehouse yard, where it greeted the citizens of Concord, New Hampshire, the next morning, April Fool's Day.

[*Sources: The Trial of Joseph Lapage the French Monster, for the Murder of the Beautiful School Girl, Miss Josie Lang-maid. Also, the Account of the Murder of Miss Marietta Ball, the School Teacher, in the Woods, in Vermont* (Philadelphia: Old Franklin Publishing, 1876); Richard Dempelwolff, *Famous Old New England Monsters and Some That Are Infamous* (Brattleboro, VT: Steven Day Press, 1942); Milli S. Knudsen, *Hard Time in Concord, New Hampshire: The Crimes, the Victims, and the Lives of the State Prison Inmates* (Westminster, MD: Heritage Books, 2008).]

The Langmaid Memorial

The Langmaid Memorial

Though the world at large has forgotten the horror perpetrated by Joseph Lapage, it seems unlikely that the people of Pembroke, New Hampshire, ever will, since they live with a constant reminder of it. In 1875, local townsfolk erected a memorial to the slain schoolgirl: a fifteen-foot stone obelisk located near the spot where her headless corpse was found. Regarded by aficionados of such things as one of New England's most bizarre attractions, the monument is inscribed with the following tribute:

> ERECTED
>
> BY THE CITIZENS OF PEMBROKE
>
> AND VICINITY, TO COMMEMORATE
>
> THE PLACE OF THE TRAGIC DEATH
>
> AND MEMORY OF
>
> JOSIE A. LANGMAID
>
> A STUDENT OF PEMBROKE ACADEMY
>
> WHO WAS MURDERED ON HER WAY
>
> TO SCHOOL, ON THE 4TH DAY OF
>
> OCTOBER, 1875, AGED 17 YEARS
>
> 10 MONTHS, AND 27 DAYS

Also included are helpful directions to the precise spot in the woods where her decapitated head was found.

For those interested in paying a personal visit to the Langmaid Memorial, Eric Jones, author of *New Hampshire Curiosities: Quirky Characters, Roadside Oddities, and Other Offbeat Stuff* (Guilford, CT: Globe Pequot, 2006), offers the following directions: "Follow Route 3 North out of the village of Pembroke for about a mile, then take a right onto Academy Road. The monument is 0.75 miles on the north side of Academy Road, just across from the Three Rivers School."

The Mystery of Serial Murder

Fifty years before a German physician coined the term "psychopath," some of America's greatest authors were portraying these cold-blooded, conscienceless criminals in their fiction. Edgar Allan Poe's classic horror story "The Tell-Tale Heart," for example, presents a frighteningly persuasive portrait of such a creature, a killer who derives keen sadistic pleasure from toying with his elderly victim before murdering and dismembering the harmless old man. Nathaniel Hawthorne wrote repeatedly about the criminal type he called the "unpardonable sinner," the man full of intelligence but devoid of conscience or compassion, who—with the malignant narcissism typical of sociopaths—sees other human beings as mere objects to be exploited for his own pleasure. And in his final masterpiece, *Billy Budd,* Herman Melville creates a diabolical character named Claggart who employs his "cool, sagacious" judgment to accomplish acts "that in wantonness of atrocity would appear to partake of the insane": a description that applies perfectly to psychos such as Ted Bundy, Jeffrey Dahmer, and John Wayne Gacy.

Melville viewed such evil as ultimately inexplicable—"a mystery of iniquity," in scriptural terms. Searching for a more scientific theory, nineteenth-century psychologists came up with the concept of "moral insanity" (or "moral imbecility") to describe the behavior of rational, intelligent individuals who use their cleverness and cunning to commit unspeakable crimes. The phrase was applied, for example, to the post–Civil War "boy fiend," Jesse Pomeroy, America's youngest serial killer, whose "sharp wits," "knowledge of right and wrong," and "above-normal intellectual capacity" coexisted with a complete "absence of moral sense and human sentiments and feelings." It was also the label given to Jane Toppan, confessed poisoner of thirty-one victims and, until John Wayne Gacy, America's most prolific serial murderer.

By the early twentieth century, however, psychologists had come to realize that while the expression "moral imbecile" might accurately describe the kind of criminal we now call a sociopath, it didn't explain the cause of such aberrant behavior. In 1921, for example, two California psychiatrists, Ernest Bryant Hoag and Edward Huntington Williams, published a remarkable paper about a then-notorious, now long-forgotten "Bluebeard" killer named J. P. Watson, who confessed to murdering more than nine of his twenty-one wives (see p. 333). "To call such a man a 'moral imbecile' means nothing and leads to no solution to such problems," the authors concluded. "We freely admit the entire inadequacy of such a diagnosis."

In exploring Watson's past, Hoag and Williams did discover one very interesting fact about Watson, a classic sadistic sex killer incapable of empathy or remorse. On at least three occasions, he had suffered significant head injuries. At ten years old, "he had a blacksmith's anvil tip over on him, pinning him to the ground with a considerable portion of the weight of the anvil resting on his head." Some years later, "he was thrown from a motorcycle, striking the back of his head." And in 1913, "he fell out of the upper berth of a steamship, again striking directly on the top of his head."

At virtually the same time Watson was perpetrating his crimes, another West Coast serial killer was on the loose: Earle Leonard Nelson, the "Gorilla Murderer," who strangled nearly two dozen women before he was finally captured. Interestingly, Nelson too suffered a severe head injury in his youth when he was thrown from his bicycle after being hit by a trolley car and ended up in a coma for nearly a week.

These and similar cases (like that of John Wayne Gacy, who developed a blood clot on the brain after being struck in the head with a playground swing as a boy) accord with the latest findings of neuroscientists exploring the sources of criminal behavior. Deploying state-of-the-art MRIs and other high-tech devices to scan the brains of imprisoned psychopathic killers, researchers such as Kent Kiehl of the University of New Mexico and Jim Fallon of the University of California have become convinced that damage to those areas of the brain responsible for compassion, inhibition, and moral choice can significantly reduce a person's reluctance to harm others.

Even proponents of this theory, however, concede that other factors have to be present to turn someone into a serial killer. Extreme parental maltreatment is prominent among them. John Wayne Gacy, for example, might have suffered a brain injury, but he was also raised by a viciously demeaning father who subjected him to unrelenting ridicule and humiliation, creating in the boy a bottomless well of fury, hatred, and malice toward the world. Some genetic component might also be at work. In short, it appears to require a witch's brew of three toxic ingredients to produce a serial murderer: damage to particular brain areas, extreme childhood abuse, and an inheritance of specific genes thought to be associated with aggression and violence.

CHARLES FREEMAN
AND THE "POCASSET HORROR"

IN THE EARLY DECADES OF THE NINETEENTH CENTURY, WHEN A WAVE OF REVIVALISM swept the land, the teachings of William Miller—an upstate New York farmer and amateur biblical scholar who believed that the Second Coming of Christ could be determined with mathematical precision—gained thousands of adherents throughout the Northeast. Based on his interpretation of Scripture, Miller calculated that Christ would return on Wednesday, October 22, 1844. As the great day approached, as many as a hundred thousand Millerites (as they were then called) eagerly awaited the end of the world and the inauguration of the Millennial Kingdom. Many had sold their homes and quit their jobs in expectation of Christ's return.

The failure of Jesus to appear at the predicted time—"the Great Disappointment," as it quickly came to be known—did not, as might be supposed, spell the end of Miller's sect. Miller himself conceded that he had been wrong to fix an exact time for the Second Coming but continued to insist that it would take place on some imminent, if indeterminate, date. The "Great Disappointment," he told his followers, was a divine test of their faith, analogous to the experience of Abraham. His adherents remained devoted to his prophetic vision long after his death in 1849. They became known as the Second Adventists.

By the end of the Civil War, a small group of Second Adventists had set up a

church in Cataumet, Massachusetts, a picturesque little village at the extreme western end of the Cape Cod peninsula, on the shores of Buzzards Bay. Among its members was a man named Charles Freeman, a local farmer who lived in the neighboring
town of Pocasset with his wife, Harriet, and two young daughters—six-year-old Bessie Mildred and four-year-old Edith, her father's favorite.

A man of "upright life and conduct" (as the newspapers would later report), Freeman was much admired—even revered—by his fellow believers for the fervency of his
convictions. He had frequently spoken of the need to prove his faith through sacrifice,
and declared that "he had
given his whole family to
God." None of his associ-
ates doubted his sincerity—
though they could hardly
have guessed at the dreadful
fixation that was growing
stronger in him by the day.

DURING THE LATTER half of
April 1879, Freeman became
obsessed by the notion that
God required an ultimate
test of his faith. He was perfectly willing to offer himself in sacrifice. After two
weeks of prayer, however,
he decided that God was demanding something even
more extreme: the life of
one of his children.

He shared this revela-
tion with his wife, who did
all she could to dissuade
him—but to no avail. On the
evening of April 30, 1879,

Charles Freeman murder pamphlet
(*Courtesy of New York State Historical Association Library,
Cooperstown.*)

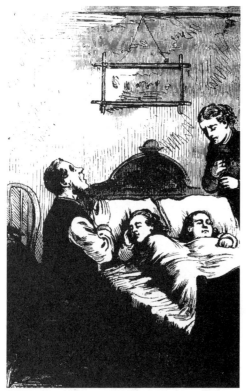

Charles Freeman prays at the bedside of his doomed daughter, Edith.

after attending a gathering at the home of a fellow Adventist, Freeman returned to his own "large and comfortable" cottage, where he tucked his daughters into the bed they shared and kissed them good night. "They never seemed so dear to me as then," he would later testify. He then retired to his own bed and quickly fell asleep.

At about half past two in the morning, he awoke with a start, shook his wife's arm, and told her that the time had come. "The Lord has appeared to me," he said. "I know who the victim must be—my pet, my idol, my baby Edith."

Weeping, her teeth chattering in horror, Harriet made one final plea. Her husband, however, would not be deterred. "The Lord has said it is necessary," he declared.

In the end, it was she who relented. "If it is the Lord's will, I am ready for it," she said at last. Her words seemed to lift a terrible burden from his heart.

Singing praises to the Lord, he rose from bed, rapidly dressed, then repaired to the shed, where he got a large sheath knife. With a buoyant heart, he returned to the house, lighted an oil lamp, and stepped inside his daughters' bedroom. Bessie, the older child, awoke at his entrance. Freeman instructed her to go into the other room and get into bed with her mother.

He then placed the lamp on a chair, pulled down the bedclothes covering Edith, and lowered himself to his knees. Silently, he prayed that Edith not awake, and that God might stay his hand at the last moment, as Abraham's had been stayed. Getting to his feet, he stood over the body of his four-year-old child and raised the knife high above his head.

At that instant, Edith opened her eyes and gazed up at her father. The look on her face did not stay Freeman's hand. Nor did divine intervention. He drove the blade deep into her side.

"Oh, Papa," she gasped. A moment later, she was dead.

Climbing into bed beside his child's corpse, Freeman took her into his arms as though lulling her to sleep and remained there until daybreak. For the first two hours—as he would later state—he suffered "a good deal of agony of mind." Eventually, however, a great feeling of peace, even exultation, came over him. "I never felt so happy in my life," he said afterward. He had been tested and found worthy. He had done God's will.

The following day, several dozen of Freeman's neighbors were summoned to his home, where—according to his message—they would be vouchsafed a great revelation. In the end, about twenty-five people, nearly all of them Adventists, showed up at his home at the appointed time.

The group crowded into the parlor, where Freeman proceeded to deliver a rambling, hour-long harangue, interrupted by stretches of silence and bouts of weeping. He spoke of the imminent coming of Christ, as foretold in the twenty-fourth chapter of Matthew, and of the overwhelming conviction that had taken possession of his soul during the preceding fortnight. Then—with his sobbing wife beside him—he led them into the adjoining bedroom, where a little form lay draped beneath a stained sheet. Reaching down, he drew back the covering and revealed to his neighbors the glorious sacrifice that he had made at God's behest.

As his fellow church members looked on in confusion, Freeman assured them that they need have no concern for the child. In three days, Edith would rise again. Her resurrection would be a sign that the Son of Man had come.

Shaken by the sight of the butchered child—but inspired by the rapturous intensity of Freeman's belief—the crowd soon dispersed to their homes and, without mentioning the awful scene they had just witnessed to anyone outside their little sect, returned to their daily affairs.

"It is almost impossible to conceive of an assembly of people in such a state of mind as to attempt to conceal such an atrocious deed," the *Boston Journal* would later report, "but they told no one and went about their usual vocations."

Despite the silence of Freeman's co-religionists, it didn't take long for word of the atrocity to reach the ears of the constable. By the following day, Freeman and his wife were under arrest and lodged in the Barnstable jail.

The horrific nature of the deed—combined with the complicity of Freeman's fellow Adventists, several of whom were highly vocal in their support of the filicide—set off a firestorm of outrage throughout New England. The pulpits rang with sermons on the dangers of religious fanaticism, a phenomenon seen as a growing social threat. The New England Adventist Association, put on the defensive, quickly distanced itself from any association with the Pocasset sect, denouncing Freeman's act "as redhanded wickedness, diabolical bigotry, and inexcusable religious frenzy." Throughout the Northeast, newspapers trumpeted "The Pocasset Horror" in lurid headlines, "The Fanatical Father!" "Freeman's Ghastly Crime!" "Sheath-Knife into the Bosom of His Sleeping Child!" "Oh, Papa! Dying Words of the Martyred Girl!"

From his cell, Freeman calmly, even cheerfully, assured visitors that he would soon be vindicated. "I can't conceive of such a thing as God failing to justify me," he proclaimed. "His power is about to be revealed in an astonishing manner to the world, and all disbelievers will be humbled in the dust at His feet." Edith, he insisted, would shortly be "restored to earth-life."

Contrary to his expectations, however, his slaughtered child did not reawaken. Three days after her murder—on the morning of her promised resurrection—the dead girl disappeared forever into the sod of Pocasset cemetery. A plaque on her coffin read: *Little Edie—lived only 57 months. She shall surely rise again—John vi. 39.*

ONE DAY AFTER the burial of their daughter, Freeman and his wife—displaying "not the slightest regret at the commission of their sacrificial act"—were brought before Justice Hopkins at Barnstable and charged with murder. They were then returned to their cells to await the action of the next grand jury, which, at its October session, indicted Freeman but set Harriet free.

At a special session of the Supreme Court in January 1880, after listening to the testimony of assorted alienists and other medical specialists, the justices ruled that Freeman was insane and incapable of standing trial. Freeman himself scoffed at the ruling, insisting that, far from being insane, he embodied "the spirit of Truth."

"I represent Christ in all his parts, prophet, priest, and king," he declared to reporters. "All good is represented in one person, and that person is me. I feel sure that my name will be honored above any other name except Jesus."

Asked how he felt about the death of his daughter, he calmly replied, "I feel perfectly justified. I feel that I have done my duty. I would not have her back." He was promptly committed to the State Lunatic Asylum at Danvers "to remain until the further order of the court."

A few years in the madhouse gave Freeman a new perspective on things. Interviewed by some of Boston's leading alienists in the spring of 1883, he acknowledged that he had in fact been "an insane man" when he slew his daughter and now regretted it "as the most dreadful act that was ever perpetrated." Having seemingly recovered from his violently delusional state, he was ordered to stand trial. The proceedings, held in Barnstable on Monday, December 3, 1883, lasted all of one day. After hearing from several expert witnesses—all of whom testified to the defendant's derangement at the time of the murder—the jury took only ten minutes to find him not guilty by reason of insanity. He was sent back to the lunatic asylum, presumably for life. Four years later, however, by order of the governor, he was pronounced "cured of his delusion and harmless" and set free. Exactly what became of him is unknown, though rumors persisted that, like the countless others who heeded Horace Greeley's call, "he went West to begin life anew."

[*Sources: A History of the Pocasset Tragedy, with Three Sermons Preached in New Bedford by Rev. William J. Potter, Rev. C. S. Nutter, and Rev. W. C. Stiles* (New Bedford, MA: Chas. W. Knight, 1879); Evan J. Albright, *Cape Cod Confidential: True Tales of Murder, Crime, and Scandal from the Pilgrims to the Present* (Dennis, MA: On Cape Publications, 2004).]

The Woman Who Killed Her Child for God

Charles Freeman's dreadful act of religious mania wasn't the only such case in the annals of American crime. Indeed, a shockingly similar murder occurred as recently as 2004. At the time, it generated nationwide media coverage, though it has already faded from public memory. Exactly why is hard to say. Certainly it was every bit as horrific as other atrocities that have achieved more enduring notoriety.

That Dena Schlosser was in the throes of a severe postpartum breakdown should have been glaringly evident to everyone around her. Twenty-four hours after giving birth at home to a daughter named Margaret, the thirty-five-year-old housewife cut her own wrist and was treated at the hospital emergency room. Five days later, she was seen running down the street of her West Plano, Texas, neighborhood, shrieking that there were spirits in her apartment. Responding to a call from a neighbor, police officers found the newborn alone in the Schlossers' bedroom.

Social workers from the Texas child protective services were called in to monitor the situation, but by August the agency closed its books on the case, having deemed Mrs. Schlosser recovered. As for her husband, John—follower of a local evangelist who preached that all mental illness "is a manifestation of demonic activity"—he had shrugged off her growing religious delusions—her conviction that a neighbor was constructing an ark, her belief that "a TV news report about a boy being mauled by a lion" was "a sign of the apocalypse." And he had apparently seen no need for psychiatric intervention when, on the night of November 21, 2004, she declared that she had decided "to give her child to God."

It wasn't until the next morning—when she called him at his office to say that she had just cut off the arms of their infant daughter—that he took action. He immediately phoned the day care center where his wife had worked prior to Maggie's birth, explained the situation to the woman who answered, and asked her to check on Dena while he drove home. The woman immediately called Dena and spoke to her briefly. She then dialed 911 and reported an emergency to operator Steve Edwards.

Edwards promptly called the Schlosser home. Dena answered. In the background he could hear music coming from the radio—the church hymn "He Touched Me" (Something happened and now I know, / He touched me and made me whole"). Edwards asked if there was an emergency.

"Yes," said Dena, sounding perfectly calm.

"Exactly what happened?"

"I cut her arms off," said Dena.

"You cut her arms off?" Edwards repeated, as if unable to grasp what he had heard.

"Uh-huh," Dena replied.

Police officers were immediately alerted and arrived on the scene within minutes. They found Dena seated in a chair in her kitchen, clutching a large knife and covered with blood from a deep wound she had inflicted on her own shoulder. Eleven-month-old Maggie lay in her crib in the bedroom, soaked in blood. Her severed arms lay beside her, her right hand open, her left clenched in a fist. She was rushed to the hospital, where she died.

Dena—who later explained to psychiatrists that she had been commanded "to cut Maggie's arms off and her own arms off, and her legs and her head, and give them to God"—recovered nicely from her wound. Tried in 2006, she was found not guilty by reason of insanity and sent to North Texas State Hospital, where she became roommates with Andrea Yates, the Houston housewife who drowned all five of her children in a bathtub to protect them from Satan. In November 2008, Schlosser was released into outpatient care but was ordered back to Terrill State Hospital two years later for violating the terms of her release.

EMELINE MEAKER,
"THE VIRAGO OF VERMONT"

ONE OF THE MOST APPALLING AMERICAN CRIMES OF THE TWENTIETH CENTURY WAS the 1965 murder of sixteen-year-old Sylvia Likens, tortured to death by a bunch of neighborhood kids under the depraved supervision of her paid caretaker, Gertrude Baniszewski. A hatchet-faced, thirty-six-year-old divorcée and mother of seven whose grim, brutalized existence had transformed her into a premature crone, Baniszewski inhabited a run-down clapboard house in a poor section of Indianapolis. With her meager income from assorted odd jobs—ironing, babysitting, hawking soda pop at the local speedway—she and her kids subsisted on a diet of canned soup, warmed on a hot plate (the house had no stove). Evidently the family took turns eating, since—according to reliable reports—there were only three spoons in the household.

In the summer of 1965, a neighbor named Lester Likens, who barely knew Baniszewski and never bothered to inspect her home, offered her twenty dollars a week to board his teenage daughter Sylvia and her younger, polio-crippled sister, Jenny, while he and his wife hit the road with a traveling carnival. Within weeks, Baniszewski began subjecting Sylvia to ever-intensifying abuse, progressing from slaps to punches to savage thrashings with a heavy leather belt, a broom handle, and a wooden paddle. In her spiraling sadism, she recruited her own children along with a group of their young friends to participate in the awful violation of the pretty teenager until, as *Time* magazine reported, "torturing Sylvia became a neighborhood sport." Over the next few months, Sylvia was beaten, starved, burned, and compelled to eat her own feces and to sexually debase herself before an audience of her juvenile tormentors. The climax occurred when Baniszewski heated up a needle and, with the assistance of several neighborhood boys, branded Sylvia's shrunken belly with the words, "I'm a prostitute and proud of it." Death, when it finally came to the victim, was undoubtedly a mercy.

THOUGH BANISZEWSKI (WHO was paroled in 1985 after serving twenty years of a life sentence and died of lung cancer later that year) was a uniquely monstrous figure, her crime was not entirely without precedent. A century earlier, America was shocked by a strikingly similar case: a paid female caretaker who, with the aid of her own son, savagely abused and murdered a young girl in her charge.

The victim in this case was eight-year-old Alice Meaker of Charlotte, Vermont, whose brief, tragic life was blighted from the very start. She had barely turned three when her father died in 1873, leaving his family—his third wife, Mary, and their two children, Alice and Henry—in abject poverty. Unable to maintain the little ones, Mary placed them in the town poor farm, where, according to later reports, the young girl was subjected to sexual abuse.

Relief from this dire situation seemed to arrive in 1879 when Alice's uncle, Horace Meaker of Duxbury, was offered $400 by town officials to take Alice and Henry into his household and off the public dole. The sum was a powerful inducement to the fifty-year-old Horace, a perpetually down-at-the-heels farmer who had spent his adulthood dragging his family around the state in a vain struggle to make a go of it. Contemporary accounts describe him as "a man of good character." In light of later events, this seems like a generous assessment. At the very least, he was guilty of turning a totally blind eye to the dreadful doings of his wife, Emeline.

Married to Horace since she was eighteen, forty-five-year-old Emeline was (according to newspapers of the time) a "coarse, brutal, domineering woman," a "perfect virago," a "sullen, morose, repulsive-looking creature." To be sure, these characterizations were deeply colored by the horror provoked by her crime. Still, there is little doubt that, as with Gertrude Baniszewski, Emeline's grim, hardscrabble life had left her deeply embittered and seething with suppressed rage—"malignant passions" (in the words of one contemporary) that would vent themselves against her helpless niece.

The abuse started shortly after Alice came to live with the Meakers. The "timid, shrinking" girl was treated like a household slave, forced "to do far more drudgery than her slender strength was equal to," as one newspaper reported. At the slightest provocation—a whimper of complaint or a task not performed to her guardian's satisfaction—Emeline would subject the child to a savage whipping with a broom or heavy stick. Before long, the hateful woman required no excuse at all. Calling the eight-year-old "a little bitch," she would strip the child naked and "beat her without cause until she bled."

Though Emeline herself suffered severe hearing problems and was literally deaf to her little niece's anguished cries, the same could not be said of the neighbors, some of whom later testified that they "could hear the child's screams half a mile away." Their reluctance to intervene in any way would itself become a public scandal, anticipating the outrage provoked by the Kitty Genovese murder a century later. "The Duxbury people who allowed the Meaker woman to torture, unchecked, the little waif placed in her care," editorialized one Vermont daily, "were guilty of culpable neglect, and must take a share of the blame as well as of the disgrace which this horrible crime has brought upon their community."

WITHIN THAT SAME community, stories would eventually circulate that Alice was murdered to prevent her from revealing a scandalous secret: that Emeline Meaker and her twenty-five-year-old son, Almon, were "guilty of the revolting crime of living in an incestuous relationship. . . . Having observed that the two occupied the bedroom while Horace slept upstairs, Alice declared that she would tell, and this made the little girl the victim of terrible abuse, till she was finally killed." However deliciously titillating, this rumor probably says less about the Meakers than about prurient fantasies of their neighbors, who—in the wake of what was generally regarded as the most heinous murder in Vermont history—were ready to imagine the worst about the perpetrators.

Almon himself, described in one newspaper as "a harmless appearing young man not over bright," offered a very different motive. Alice, he explained, "wasn't a very good girl; no one liked her, and she was hard to get along with." Persuaded by his mother that Alice "would be better off if she were dead," he consented to assist in her murder.

At first, Emeline proposed that her son "take Alice out and abandon her to starve on a remote mountain." When he rejected that idea as overly risky, she came up with a more straightforward plan.

On Friday evening, April 23, 1880—less than a year after Alice and her brother came to live with the Meakers—Almon, acting on his mother's orders, purchased fifteen grains of strychnine at a local drugstore, telling the proprietor that he "wanted to kill some rats in the buttery." He then proceeded to a nearby livery stable, where he hired a horse and a buggy. Back home, he and his mother stole into the sleeping girl's bedroom, slipped a sack over her head, bundled her into the carriage, and drove northward to a remote hilltop, where—after mixing the poison with some sugar-sweetened water—they forced the girl to drink the lethal potion from her own favor-ite crockery mug, a gift from her long-dead mother inscribed with the words "Remember Me."

It took about twenty minutes for the strychnine to work. As the little girl con-vulsed and cried out for her mother, Emeline clamped a hand over her mouth to muffle the noise. When Alice stopped breathing, Almon drove the buggy to a spot outside Stowe, where he buried her in a swampy thicket about forty-five feet off the road, stomping the body down into the muck and covering it with some brush. He then drove the rig back to the livery stable, dropping off his mother along the way.

It didn't take long for neighbors to notice that Alice was gone. When asked about the girl's disappearance, Emeline claimed that the "damned critter" had run away in the middle of the night. Her tone made it clear that, as far as she was concerned, it was a case of good riddance to bad rubbish. For whatever reason, however (sheer stupidity seems the likeliest explanation), Emeline hadn't bothered to share her cover story with Almon, who not only offered a completely contradictory account—that he had dropped Alice off at a friend's house in a nearby town and hadn't seen her since—but kept changing the details. (In another version, he "had driven Alice to Richmond, Vermont, and given her $6.50 for train fare to Montreal.")

Their suspicions aroused, a few of the neighbors finally conveyed their concerns to town officials. On Monday, April 26, a deputy sheriff named Frank Atherton showed up at the Meaker farm and subjected the suspects to an intense grilling. Before long, the weak-willed Almon had cracked and spilled out the awful truth. Atherton immediately ordered Almon to show him the body. Climbing into the deputy's buggy, the pair drove out to the swampy woods, where (as Vermont historian John Stark Bellamy reconstructs the scene):

> Atherton alighted from the buggy and waded into the mire, splashing a path about forty-five feet to a two-foot-deep pit of water. After kicking aside some covering branches, he knelt down and plunged his arm into the water. Seconds later, he withdrew it. Clenched in his fist was the arm of nine-year-old Alice. Her dead body had lain hidden in that "muck pit" for almost exactly three days. Atherton dragged the muddy corpse back to the buggy and heaved it onto the seat next to Almon. There was scant room there, and Atherton told Almon he would have to hold the corpse upright to keep it from falling off the buggy. It took almost three hours to take the body back, and Almon whimpered with terror as he tightly embraced the corpse, its head on his shoulder.

At first, the murderous pair—guilty of what the newspapers immediately branded "one of the most diabolical and revolting murders known in history or fiction"—displayed a touching loyalty to each other. Emeline initially insisted that "Almon is innocent, I am the guilty one." For his part, Almon altered his original story and now claimed that "he and he alone had planned and committed the murder."

By the time the case came to trial in November 1880, Emeline's protectively maternal impulse had been replaced by craven self-interest. Proclaiming her innocence, she placed the entire blame on Almon. The evidence against her, however—including the testimony of fifty-three witnesses who described in chilling detail her monstrous mistreatment of Alice—was overwhelming. At the end of the seven-day proceedings, the jury needed less than two hours to arrive at a decision. Unable to hear the foreman, Emeline broke into hysterical shrieks when her lawyer wrote out the verdict on a slip of paper—"guilty of murder in the first degree"—and showed it to her.

In the meantime, Almon—who had pleaded guilty at the commencement of the trial and was sentenced to hang along with his mother—underwent an eventual change of heart. Four months before the scheduled execution, he recanted his confession and—while admitting his part in the murder—"insisted it was all his mother's idea." His desperate, last-minute bid to save his own skin succeeded, and his sentence was commuted to life in prison. As for his mother, she would go to her death bitterly complaining that "his lies had sent her to the gallows."

THOUGH VERMONT HAD never executed a female before, no outcry was raised over Emeline's death sentence. Even opponents of capital punishment failed to rally on her behalf, such was the abhorrence provoked by her crime. "It is indeed an awful thing to hang a woman," editorialized the Burlington *Free Press*, "but still more awful is the spectacle of a woman devoid of the natural instincts and affections of her sex." The world "would breathe freer with the execution," said the paper, adding the devout wish that future generations would never again see the like of "such a monster."

Locked up in the state prison at Windsor while her appeals made their long and ultimately futile way through the courts, Emeline passed her time feigning madness,

State Prison, Windsor, Vt.   Stone, Tracy Co's Series

Vermont State Prison at Windsor, Emeline Meaker's last home and site of her execution attacking attendants, and in general (as one paper reported), acting "like a wild beast." As her execution date approached, however, she quieted down, spending "much of the time calmly knitting in her cell," as the *New York Times* reported.

On the eve of her execution, she grudgingly agreed to a visit from Almon. At the end of the hour, she even allowed him a goodbye kiss, though she made it clear that she still held him responsible for her predicament. The following morning—after a breakfast of beefsteak, potatoes, bread and butter, mince pie, and coffee—she asked to see the gallows. "Inspecting it," writes author Kelly Segrave, "she walked up the stairs, studied the mechanism, and had the working of the drop explained to her by the sheriff." "Why, it's not half as bad as I thought," she remarked as she was led back to her cell.

Her death on March 30, 1883, was witnessed by 125 spectators—a fraction of the number that had clamored for passes to the singular spectacle. Handsomely attired in a black cambric dress made especially for the occasion, she ascended the scaffold with firm steps and a stolid demeanor. "May God forgive you all for hanging me, an innocent woman," were her final words. Her neck broke instantly when she plunged through the trap, though it took twelve minutes for her heart to stop beating. Such was the public's ghoulish fascination with the case that, in its account of the execution, the *Free Press* published the minute-by-minute record of her subsiding pulse rate. In the following days, one early collector of what we now call "murderabelia" wrote to the prison, requesting one inch of the hangman's rope, "properly certified," for his collection of crime relics.

Emeline's last request was that her body be returned home for burial. Fearing the fury of his neighbors, however, her husband refused, and her corpse was interred in the prison cemetery. Ten years later, on November 18, 1893, her son Almon died of tuberculosis after a prolonged illness.

[*Sources:* John Stark Bellamy II, *Vintage Vermont Villainies: True Tales of Murder and Mystery from the 19th & 20th Centuries* (Woodstock, VT: Countryman Press, 2007); Martin Shipman, *"The Penalty Is Death": U.S. Newspaper Coverage of Women's Executions* (Columbia: University of Missouri Press, 2002); Kerry Segrave, *Women and Capital Punishment in America, 1840–1899: Death Sentences and Executions in the United States and Canada* (Jefferson, NC: MacFarland & Co., 2007).]

Hangings Public and Private

One hundred and twenty-five witnesses—the number that packed the prison yard when Emeline Meaker was put to death on March 30, 1883—might seem like a sizable crowd. Extrapolating from historical precedent, however, one may safely assume that a far greater number would have shown up if her execution had been held in public.

Four decades earlier, in a sensational case, a Bennington farmer named Archibald Bates was sentenced to death for "the barbarous murder of his sister-in-law by shooting her through the head with a rifle ball as she was sitting in her room, nursing her babe in the dusk of the evening" (to quote one early Vermont historian). When Bates was hanged atop Bennington Hill on February 8, 1839, fifteen thousand spectators showed up and turned the occasion into a "gala affair."

Revulsion against such "disgusting open-air spectacles" had been building for a number of years. In April 1834, "Pennsylvania became the first state to legislate against public hangings," writes Professor Negley K. Teeters in his fascinating book *Hang by the Neck: The Legal Use of Scaffold and Noose, Gibbet, Stake, and Firing Squad from Colonial Times to the Present* (Springfield, IL: Charles C. Thomas, 1967). "New Jersey was not far behind, on March 3, 1835, followed by New York on May 9 of the same year and Massachusetts on November 4. New Hampshire followed on January 13, 1837."

The festive atmosphere surrounding the Bates hanging prompted Vermont lawmakers to join this growing list. Shortly after his execution, the state legislature abolished public hangings and decreed that all subsequent executions take place within the walls of the Vermont State Prison at Windsor. A pair of wife murderers, Sandy Kavanaugh and William Barnett, became the first two criminals executed under the new law when they were hanged together in the prison yard on January 20, 1864. Nineteen years later, Emeline Meaker became the tenth.

Mad Dorothy Talby

For reasons perhaps best explained by Freudian analysts, untold millions of loving, law-abiding wives and mothers find few things more titillating than true-life tales of so-called monster moms: seemingly ordinary married women who cold-bloodedly murder their own children. Infamous recent examples of such modern-day Medeas include Susan Smith, the South Carolina divorcee who killed her two young sons by strapping them into their car seats and sending the vehicle into a lake, and Andrea Yates, the Houston housewife who methodically drowned her five small children in a bathtub.

As with every other kind of unspeakable crime, however, there is nothing new about this one. In our own country, the earliest recorded instance of such maternal mania goes all the way back to the days of the New England Puritans. In the early 1600s, a resident of Salem, Massachusetts, named Dorothy Talby—held by her neighbors in "good esteem for godliness"—began showing signs of extreme mental instability after giving birth to her fifth child, a daughter christened with the bizarre name "Difficulty." From our own perspective, it seems clear that Mrs. Talby was suffering from a textbook case of postpartum psychosis. Her contemporaries, however, had a different diagnosis: Satanic possession.

In June 1637, authorities ordered her chained to a post for physically abusing her husband, John—"laying hands on him to the danger of his life," in the language of the time. Unsurprisingly, this treatment failed to achieve a cure. When she continued to commit "misdemeanors against her husband," she was first excommunicated, then ordered to be whipped. The tragic culmination of her brief tormented life occurred in September, when, ostensibly acting under orders from God, she murdered little Difficulty by breaking the infant's neck. Brought before the Salem court, she refused to utter a word until threatened with slow torture, at which point she offered a full confession. Sentenced to be hanged, she asked to be beheaded instead but was sent to the gallows in December 1638.

To later New England writers, her case would stand as a prime example of the cruelly benighted attitudes that reigned in Puritan Salem. In his story "Main-Street," for example, Nathaniel Hawthorne pictures "Dorothy Talby . . . chained to a post at the corner of Prison Lane, with the hot sun blazing on her matronly face, and all for no other offense than lifting her hand against her husband." And in his survey "The Medical Profession in Massachusetts," Oliver Wendell Holmes laments: "See poor Dorothy Talby, mad as Ophelia, first admonished, then whipped; at last, taking her own little daughter's life; put on trial, and standing mute, threatened to be pressed to death, confessing, sentenced, praying to be beheaded; and none the less pitilessly swung from the fatal ladder . . . the poor lunatic, who would be tenderly cared for today in a quiet asylum, is judged to be acting under the instigation of Satan himself."

IV

TURN-OF-THE-CENTURY PSYCHOS

1892–1896

CARLYLE HARRIS,
THE LIBERTINE

WHAT SERIAL MURDER IS TO OUR OWN AGE, POISON MURDER WAS TO VICTO-rian America—the signature crime of the era, reflecting its darkest anxieties. In a time before food and drug regulation—when doctors prescribed formaldehyde for the common cold, over-the-counter "cure-alls" contained opium and strychnine, babies were fed rancid "swill milk," and U.S. soldiers were supplied with tins of tainted "embalmed beef"—the figure of the secret poisoner personified the culture's worst nightmare, the fear of ingesting something toxic with every bite of food or spoonful of medicine.

Of course, not every jealous lover, embittered spouse, or disgruntled servant who relied on arsenic or cyanide to satisfy a long-simmering resentment achieved nation-wide infamy in nineteenth-century America. To become a true newspaper sensation, a poison case had to include some additionally juicy element, preferably a generous dollop of sexual titillation. It was just such a combination of irresistibly lurid ingredients that made the Carlyle Harris case one of the most notorious crimes of 1890s America.

IN THE FORMAL photographic portrait that appears on the title page of his published trial transcript, twenty-three-year-old Carlyle Harris is the very picture of Victorian respectability. With his slicked-down center-parted hair, pince-nez eyeglasses, and prim little moustache, he looks as dignified and upright as the high, stiff collar of his dress shirt. Indeed, it was the extreme disparity between his impeccable façade and his profoundly amoral character that made him such an object of appalled fascination to his contemporaries. If ever there were a real-life Jekyll and Hyde, it was Carlyle Harris.

He had the kind of background that would have made interesting fodder for psychoanalysts, had any existed back then. At a time when there was a serious social stigma attached to divorce, his parents split up during his boyhood, and Carl—as he was known to intimates—was taken to live with his mother, a formidable individual. Known to the public by her pen name, Hope Ledyard, she was a best-selling author of children's books, as well as a popular lecturer on a range of topics, including religion, homemaking, and childrearing, a subject about which she had unorthodox ideas. Believing Carl to be a singularly sensitive lad, she "denied him the companionship of the boys of his age in the neighborhood" (as the newspapers later reported), with the result that "his playmates were mostly girls."

From Carl's earliest years until the day of his death, Mrs. Ledyard was a constant, not to say overpowering, presence in

Carlyle Harris murder pamphlet (*Courtesy of New York State Historical Association Library, Cooperstown.*)

his life. That such extreme, if not suffocating, maternal devotion could breed in its recipient hostile feelings toward the female sex in general was a notion that would have seemed far-fetched in that pre-Freudian, mother-worshipping age.

With his dynamic mother as a model, Carl quit school at thirteen and worked at a variety of odd jobs. A few years later, he tried his hand at acting—a congenial vocation for a young man so gifted at dissembling. Though he showed some promise in his first role—a French revolutionary in the historical melodrama *Paul Kauvar* at the Standard Theatre in Manhattan—he was forced to abandon the stage at the insistence of his mother, who (as she later wrote in a memoir) was "very much averse" to the theatrical profession. For a while, he drifted from job to job—as an assistant purser at a steamship company, a clerk for a sugar importer, a book salesman.

It was through the offices of his maternal grandfather, Dr. Benjamin W. McCready, that Carl finally found his calling. An emeritus professor at Bellevue and one of the country's leading physicians, McCready encouraged his grandson to pursue a medical career, offering to pay his expenses and helping to secure his admission to New York's prestigious College of Physicians and Surgeons. Carl entered the program in the autumn of 1888 and—working under the tutelage of the eminent surgeon Dr. Robert Abbe—quickly distinguished himself as a bright and conscientious student. By the end of his second year, he was assisting in the operating room. His particular field of interest was obstetrics and gynecology.

WHILE HARRIS LIVED in Manhattan with his grandfather during the school year, he summered with his mother at the seaside resort of Ocean Grove, New Jersey, a Methodist stronghold where Mrs. Ledyard offered lectures on the subject of temperance. To the neighbors, the handsome, well-spoken medical student seemed like a paragon of manly virtue. It would come as a shock, some time later, when the local papers reported that even while his mother was sermonizing on the evils of alcohol, young Harris was secretly operating a "rum and poker" joint called the Neptune Club in nearby Asbury Park, a place (as the press described it) "where men and women of questionable character congregated" and "orgies were a nightly occurrence." He was arrested for keeping a "disorderly house" and spent a night in jail before being bailed out by his mother.

Still, with the cool aplomb characteristic of psychopathic personalities, Harris was able to convince the world that he was an innocent victim, guilty only of youthful

naiveté. Eager to earn money to pay his own way through medical school, he had borrowed $600 from his grandfather and set up a café in Asbury Park to cater to the
summer crowd. At some point, he was approached by the proprietors of the Neptune
Club, who offered to lease the second floor from him, "pay him a good rent, and guarantee him a hundred dollars' worth of custom in his café." Harris had leapt at the
chance, never suspecting the truth about the den of iniquity operating directly over-
head.

So forthright and sincere was Carlyle's manner that his neighbors could not help
but believe him. His mistake was chalked up to his overly trusting nature, and he
continued to be welcomed into the best homes in Ocean Grove.

ONE EVENING DURING Carl's first summer in Ocean Grove, he attended a dance at the
Coleman House, a sprawling beachfront hotel in Asbury Park. It was there that he
first set eyes on Helen Neilson Potts. A vivacious eighteen-year-old who had just
graduated from high school with honors, Helen was the beloved only daughter of
doting parents: a well-to-do-father, George Potts, who had made his fortune in railroad construction, and a mother, Cynthia, whose primary concern was keeping a
watchful eye on her high-spirited daughter.

Carl, already a practiced seducer, instantly set his sights on the radiant young
woman. "She was the most beautiful girl I ever saw," he would later recall. "She was
tall, with remarkably large, dark eyes, an olive complexion, and possessed that crown-
ing glory of all, a mass of chestnut hair." Before the evening was out, the handsome
young medical student had won her over with his smooth-spoken charm.

Within weeks of that fateful first meeting, Carl had become a regular visitor to
Helen's stately Ocean Grove home. That summer, they were seen everywhere
together—boating excursions, tennis parties, picnics on the beach. They also spent
hours in private, during which Helen—though deeply infatuated with Carl—doggedly
rebuffed his increasingly importunate sexual demands.

In the fall of 1889, the Potts family rented an apartment on West Sixty-third
Street in Manhattan so that Helen, a gifted pianist, could begin classes at the New
York College of Music. In the meantime, Carl returned to his medical studies at the
College of Physicians and Surgeons on West Fifty-ninth Street. Working just a few
blocks from the Pottses' new residence, he was constantly coming by to spend time

with Helen. "We were always pleased to see him," Mrs. Potts would later testify. "We were homesick, and it seemed like seeing someone from home."

Even so, as her daughter and Harris saw more and more of each other, Mrs. Potts began to have misgivings. Sometime that November, after Carl had passed yet another long Sunday afternoon in Helen's company, Mrs. Potts took him aside. "I said I thought he was coming rather often, more so than I approved of," she later recounted. Though she regarded him as "a very pleasant friend," she felt "it was wrong to call as often as he was calling." She worried that "something might grow of the friendship that would be a disadvantage" to her susceptible daughter.

Carl seemed taken aback at the implication that he might have dishonorable designs on Helen. Looking at Mrs. Potts in a "frank, open, innocent way," he "assured her so candidly that nothing could be further from his thoughts" that Mrs. Potts "was ashamed at having spoken of it."

Though Carl "promised to call less frequently," his pursuit of Helen continued unabated. In January 1890, Mrs. Potts felt compelled to speak to him again. She was shocked when Carl brought up the subject of marriage. "You cannot be engaged to my daughter," she exclaimed. "She is fond of you, but you are still a medical student, and Helen is much too young to think of such a thing. I am glad that the two of you are friends, but you must not call on her with any such idea."

Seemingly chastened, Carl assured Mrs. Potts that he would put all such thoughts out of his mind. But as was so often the case with the duplicitous young medical student, he was telling a lie.

AT AROUND TEN o'clock on the morning of February 8, 1890, Carl called at the Pottses' home and asked permission to take Helen downtown to see some of the sights in lower Manhattan. Mrs. Potts had no objections. When the couple returned at around three, they sat down in the front parlor with Mrs. Potts and told her all about their outing. After visiting the New York Stock Exchange and Richard Morris Hunt's magnificent Tribune Building, they had lunched at an elegant restaurant, and had an altogether delightful time.

In earnest tones, Carl then asked permission to remain there with Helen for the rest of the afternoon. The request was made so courteously—and Helen seemed so eager for his company—that Mrs. Potts could not bring herself to refuse. For the next few hours, while the older woman busied herself with her household tasks, the handsome young couple sat beside each other on the sofa, chatting merrily, though occasionally their voices would drop and they would whisper together in excited, conspiratorial tones.

THAT WOULD BE the last time Mrs. Potts saw the two of them so happy together. Over the next few weeks, as she later recalled, she "noticed a difference in Carl's manner towards my daughter. He did not call as frequently as he used to, nor was he as pleasant as he had been."

Though Mrs. Potts was by no means displeased over the apparent cooling of the relationship, she was concerned about her daughter, who seemed deeply distressed about Carl's sudden indifference. In an effort to reassure the girl, Mrs. Potts suggested that the young man was merely preoccupied with his studies. The end of the school year, however, brought no change in Carl's strange new behavior. Though he continued to call on Helen at the Pottses' summer home in Ocean Grove, "he did not make himself nearly as courteous and agreeable as he had been. When there were musicals or concerts or anything of the kind, he did not care to go. He made appointments with my daughter to take her out to church twice and did not keep those appointments. His manner was as if he was bored and tired of their friendship."

One afternoon in early June, Carl arrived at the Pottses' home and invited Helen for a walk. Though Mrs. Potts expected them back in an hour or so, Helen did not reappear until that evening. As soon as she walked in the door, her mother was struck by how "pale and ill" she looked. Assuming that her daughter had been stricken with one of her recurrent "sick headaches"—as migraines were called back then—Mrs. Potts asked why she had "taken so long a walk." Without answering, Helen headed upstairs, got into bed, and stayed there until the next morning.

She was still feeling unwell the following week when she arranged to go visit her uncle, Dr. Charles Treverton, in Scranton, Pennsylvania.

MARRIED TO CYNTHIA Potts' sister, Charles W. Treverton was relatively new to his profession, having gotten his degree from Bellevue College less than six years earlier. It didn't require long years of medical experience, however, to see that there was something seriously wrong with Helen. Pallid and weak, she had virtually no appetite and suffered severe bouts of nausea, especially in the mornings. Despite her illness, she was unwilling to let her uncle examine her. Given her reluctance and the nature of her symptoms, Treverton believed he knew what was wrong. When she finally agreed, his suspicions were confirmed. His niece (as he put it) "was in the family way."

But that was hardly the most startling revelation. Tearfully, Helen spilled out the truth. The previous February, on an afternoon when her mother believed that she was off on an innocent outing in downtown Manhattan, she and her companion, Carlyle Harris, had actually gone to City Hall and gotten secretly married under assumed names. In June, after learning she was pregnant, Harris had persuaded her to undergo an abortion at his hands—a procedure that, judging from her current condition, the young medical student had clearly bungled.

Treverton immediately dashed off an indignant note to Harris, summoning him to Scranton at once. When Harris arrived by train a few days later, he displayed none of the emotions—worry, guilt, contrition—Treverton expected. He spoke as if the secret marriage and subsequent abortion were the most natural things in the world and breezily explained that he had performed the same procedure on five previous girlfriends, all of whom had recovered "very nicely." He was surprised to learn that Helen was unwell. Though "there was a good deal of hemorrhage at the time" of the operation, he "thought that he had removed everything that was there" and assumed that "this matter of her sickness was all over."

Treverton was taken aback by the young man's blasé tone, especially after Harris declared that he had brought along his valise of surgical implements in anticipation of doing a follow-up procedure on Helen. Treverton let it be known that he had no intention of allowing the young cad to participate in any further operations on his niece.

It was a conversation that took place the following day, however, that revealed the true depths of Carlyle Harris' depravity. Eager to do a little sightseeing while he was visiting Scranton, Harris persuaded a young man named Charles Oliver to take him on a tour of some nearby coal mines and steel mills. On their way back that evening, Harris, for whatever unaccountable reasons, began boasting of his amorous exploits, telling Oliver that he "had had sexual intercourse with a great many women." He then proceeded to explain "that it was a very easy matter to administer a strong drink of intoxicating liquor with a glass of ginger ale. When it had its effect, he had no trouble in getting his desire with the women."

True, there had been two instances where this method hadn't succeeded. In both those cases, he had "overcome the women's scruples by a secret marriage ceremony." The first time he had resorted to this expedient, things had worked out well for him. After impregnating the young woman (whose identity would never be disclosed), he had performed an abortion on her, after which she disgustedly declared that "she wanted nothing more to do with him."

Helen Potts, of course, was the second of his secret wives. As with the first, he had married her solely to get her into bed. Once she had given herself to him, he immediately lost interest in her.

HARRIS REMAINED IN Scranton for less than a week. As soon as he left, Treverton focused his full attention on Helen, who had taken a turn for the worse. Assisted by an older, more experienced colleague, Dr. D. B. Hand, Treverton administered a combination of drugs intended to induce labor. Two days later, a decayed fetus, four or five months old, emerged from Helen's womb. As far as Treverton and Hand could judge, it had been dead for several weeks. There was a wound on its partially decomposed head, evidently made by the implement wielded by Carlyle Harris during the botched abortion.

Helen remained at her uncle's home for the rest of the summer, slowly regaining her strength. Later, it would emerge that during her convalescence Carl took up with another woman, a beautiful twenty-year-old named Queenie Drew, who traveled upstate with him to Canandaigua, New York, where they spent several nights together in the fanciest hotel in town, sharing a bed.

IN MID-AUGUST, MRS. Potts, in response to an urgent telegram from her brother-in-law, traveled to Scranton, where she finally learned the shocking truth about her daughter's secret marriage and the clumsy abortion that had almost cost Helen her life. Under the tender ministrations of her mother and the watchful care of her uncle, Helen made a complete recovery. By the first of September, she was well enough to travel back home to Ocean Grove.

By then, Carlyle Harris had returned to his grandfather's home in the city. Since his visit to Scranton, he had made no effort see his wife. As the fall approached, Mrs. Potts—who had kept the news of the marriage from her husband "because she could not bear to tell him of their daughter's shame"—grew increasingly agitated over the situation. Finally, in early October, she arranged to meet Harris in New York City.

Over lunch at a downtown restaurant, she demanded to know why Carl had married her daughter in such an underhanded fashion. His explanation was so outrageous that, for a moment, Mrs. Potts merely gaped at him in dumbfounded silence.

"I did it that way for this reason," he said with his usual nonchalance. "I thought we might someday get tired of each other, and if we were married under false names, we could just drop the matter and no one would be the wiser."

"With my daughter!" Mrs. Potts finally sputtered. "You were going to drop the matter once you got bored with her? I call that legalized prostitution! I insist that you be made a legitimate marriage under your right names."

Harris assured his mother-in-law that he would obey her wishes, though he asked for a brief delay since he was just beginning his new semester at the medical college and had to concentrate on his studies. In the meantime, he urged Mrs. Potts to bring Helen to New York City and enroll her at the select Comstock School for Girls on West Fortieth Street (the school's alumni included the future Mrs. Theodore Roosevelt). He "expected to make a good position in New York," Carl explained, and Comstock would "train Helen for the society he hoped they would live in."

Two months later, on December 8, 1890, Helen became a pupil at the school.

DESPITE HIS PROMISE to Mrs. Potts, Harris continued to find reasons for putting off the ceremony she had demanded. By mid-January 1891 her patience had run out. "Now listen to what I say," she wrote to him on the eighteenth of the month. "The 8th of February will be the anniversary of your secret marriage. I set that day as the day on which you shall go to a minister of the Gospel and be married in a Christian manner."

On January 20th, Harris penned a reply, assuring her that "all your wishes shall be complied with."

That same afternoon, he appeared at a pharmacy on the corner of Eighteenth Street and Broadway and wrote out a prescription for six capsules, each to contain four and a half grains of quinine and one-sixth grain of morphine. Two days later, he gave four of the capsules to Helen, who had been troubled with her sick headaches, instructing her to take one each night before going to bed. He retained the other two capsules himself. The following morning, Harris left town for a week's vacation, taking a steamer to the Old Point Comfort resort on Virginia's Chesapeake Bay.

On Saturday morning, January 31, Mrs. Potts took Helen on a shopping expedition to Macy's. The two then returned to the Comstock school, where they had lunch. Afterward, Mrs. Potts accompanied Helen to her room, where her daughter showed her the box of pills Carl had given her. She had taken three of the capsules so far, she explained, "but they made her feel so ill" that she was "tempted to throw the last one out the window."

"I told her that quinine was apt to make one feel wretched," Mrs. Potts later testified, "but I thought it would do her good, so I advised her to take it. I left her at around three o'clock in the afternoon." That was the last time she saw her daughter alive.

HELEN'S THREE ROOMMATES, Frances Rockwell, Rachel Carson, and Henrietta Cookson, spent that Saturday evening at a symphony. Returning to the Comstock School at around ten-thirty, they found Helen already asleep. As they lit the gas jets and chatted about the concert, Helen awoke and said groggily: "Girls, I have had such beautiful dreams. I wish they could go on forever."

Completing their toilets, the three young women extinguished the lights and retired. No sooner were they in bed, however, than they heard Helen groan. Rising, Frances and Rachel hurried to her side.

"I feel so queer, girls," Helen said hoarsely. She was having trouble swallowing and was numb all over. "I can't feel your hand at all," she moaned when Frances tried calming her by stroking her head. "I believe I am dying."

By then, Rachel had relit the gas lamps. Returning to Helen's bedside, she was shocked at what she saw. "She looked like death," the young woman later recalled. "She was very pale and the veins all stuck out on her forehead and were blue."

Terrified, Rachel roused the headmistress, Lydia Day, who immediately summoned the school physician, Dr. Edward Fowler. By then, Helen, drenched in cold sweat and barely breathing, had lapsed into a deep coma. Recognizing the symptoms of profound opium poisoning, Fowler, assisted by two colleagues, labored throughout the night, applying artificial respiration, administering black coffee enemas, injecting atropine, whiskey, and digitalis, and employing electric shocks and oxygen gas—to little avail. Scouring the room for clues, Fowler turned up the empty box of pills prescribed by Carlyle Harris, who—having just returned from his pleasure jaunt to Old Point Comfort—was immediately sent for.

Harris' response to the crisis—typical of the "malignant narcissism" that criminal psychologists now recognize as a hallmark of sociopathic behavior—would turn out to be one of the most damning bits of evidence against him. Arriving at 6:00 a.m., he seemed shockingly indifferent to Helen's dire condition. Insisting that the pills he had prescribed were harmless, he expressed concern only for himself. "Do you think I will be held responsible?" he repeatedly asked Dr. Fowler, who—appalled by the young man's self-centeredness—snapped: "I am not interested in who is responsible. I am trying to save this girl's life."

Fowler and his colleagues labored heroically but futilely for another four hours. When, at around 10:00 a.m., Helen was finally pronounced dead, Harris responded in his predictably shameless way. "My God," he cried. "What will become of me?"

In heartbreaking contrast to her husband's reaction, Helen's parents were devastated, particularly her father, who refused to believe that his daughter was gone. Insisting that he saw a flush on her cheek as she lay in her open coffin at her funeral service, he would not permit her to be buried, in the desperate conviction that she was not really dead and would arise at any moment. It was not until three days after the service that he accepted the truth and allowed her to be lowered into the ground.

Several theories were put forth about Helen's death. Some speculated that, in filling the prescription, the pharmacist had committed a terrible mistake and reversed the relative proportions of quinine and morphine. Others suggested that, after taking the first pill and finding it had no effect, Helen had swallowed the remaining three at once and died from an accidental overdose. There was even talk of deliberate suicide.

As reporters for the yellow press dug deeper into the case, however, they began uncovering scandalous facts about Carl Harris, including his arrest for running a liquor and gambling joint and his proclivity for performing abortions on his pregnant girlfriends. He was promptly expelled from medical school and denounced from city pulpits as "the vilest wretch ever vomited out of hell." On March 5, the body of his "girl-wife" (as the papers consistently referred to Helen) was exhumed and the viscera turned over to the country's leading toxicologist, Prof. Rudolph Witthaus, who confirmed that the otherwise healthy young woman had been poisoned. Five days later, Carlyle W. Harris was indicted for murder.

*   *   *

AT THE TRIAL, which began in mid-January 1892 after a protracted delay, Assistant District Attorney Francis Wellman built a devastating case against Harris, depicting him as one of "the greatest libertines of the age"—a "human wolf" who, after satisfying his "unbridled and unholy lust," had concocted a diabolical plan to rid himself of his all-too-trusting victim. Harris had evidently hit on his scheme while attending a lecture on poisons by one of his professors, Dr. George Peabody, who "laid particular stress upon the difficulty of detection in cases where morphine had been used feloniously." During the talk, "samples of the drug were handed around in wide-mouthed bottles, and the students were permitted to take out and could examine the contents." Evidently, when Harris' turn came, he managed to steal some of the opiate and smuggle it out of the classroom.

A few days later, he went to the pharmacy and procured a half-dozen capsules of quinine and morphine compound, ostensibly for Helen's headaches. Bringing them home, he "removed the mixture contained in one, substituting in its place pure morphine to the amount of at least five grains—a frightful quantity when half that much is considered a lethal dose.

"He then delivered the box containing the four capsules to his loving young wife," continued Wellman. "On the very next day, he started for Old Comfort, Virginia, where he remained a week. It was safe to assume that the deadly pill would not be taken last, so that there would be one or more left for analysis when the questions as to Helen's death were raised. As only a harmless mixture would be found, it would be assumed that natural causes were responsible. Then again, the direction to take the capsules before retiring would insure her passing away in her sleep, with no opportunity to observe the symptoms. Harris being away at the time, no one would think of connecting him with the catastrophe."

As an added precaution, however, Harris made sure to retain two of the original six capsules, so that "if any suspicion *were* to attach to him afterwards," he could prove that the medicine he had prescribed for Helen could not possibly have killed her. "Truly," Wellman declared, "a cold-blooded plan worthy of its callous inventor." That it had not succeeded was proof of an eternal truism. "The plans of the shedder of human blood always fail," thundered Wellman. "Murder will out because God wills it so!"

* * *

THROUGHOUT HIS THREE-WEEK trial, Harris observed the proceedings with a look of unflappable calm that was in marked contrast to the demeanor of his mother, who sat devotedly by his side, making no effort to conceal her feelings. When, after deliberating for less than ninety minutes, the jury returned a guilty verdict on February 2, Mrs. Ledyard (according to contemporary accounts) "uttered a piercing cry and dropped to the floor in a dead faint," while Harris himself "did not betray any reaction by so much as a flutter of the eyelash."

He went to the electric chair the following year with the same unnatural composure, coolly declaring his innocence even as the guards adjusted the straps. He was buried in a handsome casket to which his mother had affixed a metal plate inscribed with the words:

CARLYLE HARRIS
MURDERED MAY 8TH 1893

[*Sources: The Trial of Carlyle W. Harris for Poisoning his Wife, Helen Potts, at New York* (New York: 1892); Charles Bosworth and Lewis Thompson, *The Carlyle Harris Case* (New York: Collier Books, 1961); Hope Ledyard, *Articles, Speeches and Poems of Carlyle W. Harris* (New York: J. S. Ogilvie, 1893); Francis L. Wellman, *Luck and Opportunity: Recollections* (New York: Macmillan, 1938).]

Dr. Robert Buchanan, Copycat

Carlyle Harris was still awaiting execution in Sing Sing when New York City was riveted by another murder trial involving a member of the medical community, a physician named Robert Buchanan. That the two cases occurred so close together was no coincidence. Buchanan was a classic copycat, a poisoner who paid close attention to his predecessor's MO and set out to prove that he could do better.

Born in Nova Scotia, Buchanan studied in Edinburgh, Scotland, before moving with his wife to Manhattan, where he established a thriving practice. Like Carlyle Harris, he led a Jekyll-and-Hyde existence, maintaining a respectable façade by day while passing his evenings at a posh New Jersey bordello run by a middle-aged madam named Anna Sutherland. Though Sutherland was no beauty—one historian reports that "she was obese, sported a wart on her large nose, had dyed orange hair, and was twice his age"—she possessed a substantial fortune that, in Buchanan's avaricious eyes, more than made up for these flaws. The two soon became lovers. In short order, Buchanan had divorced his wife, persuaded Sutherland to draft a new will leaving everything to him, and took the former brothel keeper as his bride.

Tensions immediately developed between the newlyweds. Though fond of her fortune, Buchanan was so put off by his wife's coarse manners and unsightly looks that he tried to conceal the marriage from the world, claiming that the "old hag" now occupying his Manhattan residence was his housekeeper. He continued to spend his nights carousing in various dens of iniquity. For her part, Anna seethed with resentment over her husband's incorrigible ways and his obvious distaste for everything about her except her money.

It was the trial of Carlyle Harris in January 1892 that showed Buchanan a way out of his predicament. From Buchanan's point of view, the young medical student had had the right idea when he tried ridding himself of his unwanted wife by slipping her poison. But Harris had carried out his scheme like "a bungling fool," "a stupid amateur." As Buchanan observed to various acquaintances, morphine poisoning was too easily detected from its effect on the pupils, which were contracted to pinpoints by the drug. Such a telltale sign could easily be disguised by putting a few drops of belladonna in the victim's eyes, causing the pupils to dilate.

Three months later, in April 1892, Anna Buchanan fell ill after finishing breakfast, quickly slipped into a coma, and died. The attending physician attributed her death to a cerebral hemorrhage. A few days after her funeral, Dr. Buchanan—now richer by $50,000 (more than $1 million in today's money)—traveled to Nova Scotia, where he promptly remarried his first wife and brought her back to New York.

In his absence, however, friends of the late Anna Sutherland, suspicious of her sudden death, had contacted a reporter for Joseph Pulitzer's *World,* who began his own investigation, turning up a wealth of incriminating information. Under pressure from the paper, the coroner ordered Anna's body exhumed. When an analysis of her viscera confirmed the presence of morphine, Buchanan was arrested.

After the high drama of the Harris case, New Yorkers must have experienced a keen sense of déjà vu when Buchanan's trial opened in March 1893, since a number of the same figures were involved, including the eminent toxicologist Dr. Rudolph Witthaus, who asserted that "treatment of the eyes with atropine"—a derivative of belladonna—"might very well eliminate the narrowing of the pupils which otherwise follows morphine poisoning." His testimony led to a dramatic and unusually gruesome demonstration. A live cat was brought into the courtroom and injected with a fatal dose of morphine. Then, as jurors closely observed the effects on the dying animal's pupils, drops of belladonna were placed into its eyes. District Attorney Francis Wellman, who had successfully prosecuted Carlyle Harris, helped seal Buchanan's fate when he called the nurse who had attended Anna in her final hours and who confirmed that the defendant "had put some drops into his wife's eyes for no apparent reason."

Believing that Carlyle Harris' attorneys had made a strategic error by not putting their client on the stand, Buchanan insisted on testifying on his own behalf, only to be torn apart by Wellman's ferocious cross-examination. Convicted and sentenced to the electric chair, he languished on Sing Sing's death row for two years before his final appeal was denied. He was electrocuted on July 2, 1895.

[*Sources:* Francis Wellman, *Luck and Opportunity: Recollections* (New York: Macmillan, 1938); Jay Robert Nash, *Murder, America* (New York: Simon & Schuster, 1982); "Morphine," in *Crimes and Punishment,* vol. 18 (Westport, CT: H. S. Stuttman, Inc., 1994).]

HARRY HAYWARD,
"THE MINNEAPOLIS SVENGALI"

AS A GENERAL RULE, CELEBRATED PSYCHO KILLERS ACHIEVE THEIR NOTORIETY BY committing some form of multiple homicide: family annihilation, mass murder, serial slaughter. Occasionally, however, a killer comes along who earns widespread infamy by doing away with a single victim. Harry Hayward was one of these rarities. More unusual still is that Hayward himself did not do the actual killing. To his contemporaries, however, that fact only added to his dark mystique. In their eyes, he was a figure of unprecedented evil: "the most depraved, the most cold-blooded murderer that ever walked God's footstool, the most bloodthirsty soul that ever usurped the human frame."

AT THE CORNER of Thirteenth Street and Hennepin Avenue in the Loring Park neighborhood of downtown Minneapolis stands a handsome building known today as the Bellevue. A popular restaurant called Eli's Bar and Grill occupies the ground floor, along with another trendy eatery, the Espresso Royale. The four stories above consist of airy condos whose prices extend into the quarter-million-dollar range. Real estate ads tout the elegant features of these apartments: the high ceilings, the hardwood floors, the splendid fireplaces and spectacular skyline views. Potential buyers are also informed that the Bellevue itself is a "historic building," though the precise details of its history are rarely given—an understandable omission since its significance derives largely from its connection to one of the city's most sensational murder cases.

Built in 1891 as a residential hotel, the Bellevue—or the Ozark Flats, as it was originally called—was owned and managed by a local real estate magnate, William W. Hayward, who resided in the building with his family. Among the other early occupants was a woman named Catherine Ging—Kitty to her friends—soon to achieve a kind of grim immortality as the subject of a popular murder ballad, "The Fatal Ride."

Even in the age of the statuesque "Gibson girl," when the ideal female physique was considerably fleshier than it is today, Kitty Ging—standing five feet seven inches tall and weighing 150 pounds—was regarded as a bit on the hefty side: "grand in figure," as one chronicler gallantly puts it. Nor was she particularly beautiful: "passably good looking, though of a masculine type" is the way one contemporary describes her. Still, with her luxuriant black hair, striking gray eyes, bright smile, and vivacious manner, she had no trouble attracting male attention.

Born and raised in upstate New York, she had moved to Minneapolis in her early twenties—reportedly "to escape a persistent suitor"—and opened a dressmaking shop on Nicollett Avenue. A skilled seamstress and ambitious young businesswoman, she quickly attracted a wealthy clientele.

Harry Hayward
(*Minnesota Historical Society. Used by permission.*)

In 1893, she received a marriage proposal—along with a diamond ring—from a department store clerk named Frederick Reed. The engagement didn't last, but the experience wasn't a total loss for Kitty, since she got to keep the ring, which she wore upon her person at all times, tucked inside the bodice of her dress in "a little chamois bag." There was nothing sentimental about this gesture. Rather, it reflected a fundamental fact about Kitty Ging's character: money was exceptionally dear to her heart, and she was not overly particular about the way she obtained it.

In keeping with the precept of speaking no ill of the dead, most of Kitty Ging's contemporaries insisted that she was a person of spotless virtue. Still, even her staunchest defenders had to admit that she led a somewhat free and easy life for a young unmarried woman in late Victorian America. Moralists of the day read her tragic fate as a cautionary tale: "a terrible warning to the class of young womanhood which delights in nightly carriage rides with male companions and private party suppers in places where wine and cigarettes can be made part of the bill of fare." Indeed, according to the earliest chronicler of the Ging murder, a journalist named Oscar F. G. Day, on the very afternoon of Kitty's death she remarked to a male companion that she had recently come into a substantial sum of money and intended to use it "to paint the town red." In view of subsequent events, the statement was seen as grimly prophetic.

"Alas poor girl," writes Day, "how little did she know that on that very night she would 'paint the town red,' not in the common acceptance of the term, but with her very life blood!"

AT AROUND HALF past eight on the clear, moonlit evening of Monday, December 3, 1894, a young railway employee named William Erhardt, on his way home from work, alighted at a streetcar stop on the outskirts of the city and proceeded by foot along a lonely stretch of road. Almost immediately, he heard the sound of fast-approaching hooves. He stepped to one side just as a buggy sped past, drawn by a galloping horse. With the leather top of the buggy raised, Erhardt couldn't see the driver. Glancing after the rig as it vanished from sight, Erhardt wondered "why a man should be driving at such a reckless pace." Then, dismissing the matter from his mind, he continued on his way.

He hadn't gone far when, as he later testified, he nearly stepped on a large object lying in the middle of the road. Peering closer, he saw that it was the body of a woman. She was sprawled on her side, her limbs entangled in a carriage robe, her head in a pool of still-steaming blood.

Instantly thinking of the galloping horse, he assumed that she was the victim of a runaway accident, thrown from the buggy when the driver lost control. Dashing to the nearest telephone, he notified a physician named William Russell, who, arriving a half hour later, pronounced the woman dead.

The corpse was transported to the Hennepin County morgue and laid out, fully clothed, on a marble slab. She was clearly a young woman "of the better class," as revealed by her stylish outfit: blue woolen skirt, striped shirtwaist, fine sealskin jacket, and jaunty sailor's hat. Stripping off her garments, morgue keeper John W. Walsh found a laundry mark on an item of her underclothing. It consisted of a single word: "Ging."

It was nearly 11:00 p.m. when coroner Willis P. Spring arrived at the morgue to examine the corpse. It didn't take him long to discover that her death was no accident. There was a "round, ragged wound" behind her right ear and her left eye protruded from the socket. When Spring pushed the eyeball back into place, he felt a small hard object. Even before he pulled it out with his fingers, he could tell it was a bullet.

AT ROUGHLY THE same time that the body of the murdered woman was on its way to the morgue, Henry Gilbert, foreman of the Palace livery stable in downtown Minneapolis, heard a horse enter the barn. Crossing the floor to meet it, he saw that it was a bay mare named Lucy, hitched to a buggy that had been rented out earlier that evening. No one was inside the buggy.

After unhitching the horse and sending it to its stall, Gilbert peered into the buggy and noticed something peculiar on the center of the cloth seat cushion. In the dim light of the stable, he thought it was a scarf. Leaning in for a closer look, he was startled to see that it was "a pool of clotted blood, a half-inch thick and as large as a sheet of legal paper." Pulling the buggy closer to a lantern that hung from the wall, he saw that there were splashes of blood everywhere—"on the back cushion, on the buggy bottom, on one of the bows that supported the top."

The police were summoned, the stable owners notified. A check of the register quickly disclosed the name of the person who had rented the rig for the evening: Catherine Ging of the Ozark Flats.

REPAIRING TO THE Ozark Flats, police broke the bad news to Kitty's next of kin, her seventeen-year-old niece, Mary Louise Ireland, who shared her rooms and helped with her dressmaking business. "Frantic with grief," Mary was in no condition to talk. The police had given up hope of gleaning any useful information from her when another resident of the building—an intimate acquaintance of the murder victim— arrived: Harry Hayward.

The youngest child of the building's owner, twenty-nine-year-old Harry conformed to a familiar type: the dissipated, ne'er-do-well son of a powerful, prominent father. Broad-shouldered, deep-chested, and imposingly tall, he was a fine figure of young manhood—"a man to be looked at twice when met," in the words of one contemporary. A dandy in dress, he sported a neatly trimmed blond moustache and—despite prematurely thinning hair, horsey teeth, and an ocular tic that caused his right eye "to roll upwards at intervals"—was considered dashingly handsome. He had smooth, polished manners and was welcomed in that "level of society acquainted with evening dress."

He was also, as he himself would later confess, a Jekyll-and-Hyde personality. Though he enjoyed mingling with Minneapolis' social elite, most of his time was spent in the company of petty crooks, cardsharps, and the habitués of billiard halls. He had taken up gambling at an early age and—despite his father's efforts to involve him in the real estate business—had never done an honest day's work in his life. Every cent that came his way was squandered at the faro table. Like other addicts, he was constantly on the lookout for the funds to support his habit. As the world was soon to learn, one major source was Kitty Ging.

When informed of Kitty's death, Harry had an odd response. "Goddamn it," he cried. "My money is gone to hell! What a fool I've been!" Asked to elaborate on this "strange exclamation," he explained that he had loaned Miss Ging nearly $10,000 to expand her millinery business and was now afraid that he would never see the money. When pressed for more details about their financial dealings, Harry admitted that, as security for the loan, Kitty had taken out two life insurance policies of $5,000 each—one from the New York Life Insurance Company, one from Traveler's Accident Insurance Company—and assigned them to him.

From the moment it broke on the follow morning, the story of Kitty Ging's murder—"the most wonderful tragedy of modern times," as one journalist called it—became a newspaper sensation, dominating the headlines for months. Several suspects were quickly identified: an unemployed man named Constant J. Warnecke, who "was known to have boarded at the same house with the murdered woman and to have known her intimately"; Kitty's former fiancé, the dry-goods clerk Frederick Reed, whose diamond ring she still carried in her corset; a "pretty, petite brunette" named Lillian Allen, said to have been a rival for Reed's affection; Ed Conway, a rakish young man who lived in the Ozark Flats; and a traveling salesman named Harvey Axelrod, whose affair with Kitty had come to an acrimonious end when she learned that he was married. Tracked down by police, all had no trouble proving their innocence.

As the beneficiary of Kitty's two life insurance policies—both of which had been written only ten days before her death—Harry himself was an obvious suspect. But he too had a seemingly airtight alibi. At the time of the murder, he was at the Grand Opera House, enjoying Charles Hale Hoyt's popular musical comedy *A Trip to Chinatown* in the company of Miss Mabel Bartelson, daughter of a prominent attorney.

By then, the mayor of Minneapolis, William Henry Eustis, had become actively involved in the investigation. Summoning Harry to his office, Eustis, in the company of several police detectives, questioned Harry closely about his relationship with the murder victim.

The suave young man replied without the slightest hesitation. He had met and befriended Kitty Ging when she became his neighbor in the Ozark Flats the previous January. Soon he was regaling her with tales of his gambling prowess. Infatuated with the debonair young man—and tempted by the prospect of easy money—she had bankrolled his ventures at the gaming tables to the tune of several thousand dollars. After Harry lost a sizable sum of her money playing faro in Chicago, however, she had ceased to stake him.

Increasingly suspicious of Harry—and frustrated by his imperturbable manner—authorities resolved on a scheme to rattle his composure. Conveying him to the morgue, they confronted him with the disfigured corpse of Kitty Ging, stretched out upon the marble slab. If they hoped that he would betray his guilt by quailing at the ghastly sight, they were disappointed. Like other psychopaths, whose bizarre emotional makeup renders them immune to anxiety, Harry had the ability to remain utterly calm and unruffled under the most nerve-racking circumstances.

Gazing down at the corpse, he shook his head sadly and said: "Poor girl—poor dead girl. If you could only speak now, you could tell us who he was."

"Not a particle of color left his face," Day reports. "Every eye was upon him, every nerve was strained to catch the slightest quiver of his muscular frame, the slightest pallor of his face. Yet he stood the test. Not one of the party could say that the sight of the poor murdered girl caused him a moment of guilt and remorse." Assuming that their suspicions were misplaced, they let him go.

The following morning, December 5—two days after Kitty Ging's death—a funeral service was held at the Church of the Immaculate Conception. Harry brought a large floral tribute to place on the casket and announced his intention to accompany the remains back to Kitty's hometown of Auburn, New York, where she would be laid to rest in the State Street Cemetery.

He never made the trip.

That very afternoon, even as Harry was returning from the church, assistant county attorney Albert H. Hall got a remarkable letter from an elderly attorney named Levi M. Stewart, one of the city's most prominent men and a close family friend of the Haywards. In it, Stewart revealed that, three days prior to the Ging homicide, he had received a visit from Harry's older brother Adry, "a pathetically dependent man of thirty-two" (in the words of one historian) who worked in his father's real estate office for a pitifully small salary and was always in need of money.

Adry was in a highly agitated state. "He told me," Stewart's letter explained, "that Harry and a confederate were going to murder Miss Ging in order to get money from her life insurance . . . and he wanted to know what could be done to prevent it."

Stewart was incredulous. "I hadn't the least belief that there was any foundation for his fears and told him it was only some of Harry's big talk. . . . I repeated to him again and again that while Harry was wicked he was not a fool, and that he certainly would not have given himself away in advance in that way if there had been any intention to perpetrate such a crime."

Adry, however, was adamant, insisting that "the murder was certainly planned and would be accomplished in a very few days." Events, Stewart now sadly conceded, had "proved conclusively that Adry was right."

"If I had supposed there was the most remote possibility of his story, or rather belief being founded on a genuine intention to commit a crime, I should have advised him at once to go to the superintendent of police and lay the matter before him, but I had no belief whatever in its being anything but bluster and bluff on the part of

Harry. . . . I knew long ago that Harry was one of the most mendacious liars and dishonest rogues I had ever seen, but I had no idea of his being such a criminal."

Hall lost no time in showing the letter to his superior, state's attorney Frank M. Nye. A few hours later, both Harry and Adry were arrested and locked up in the Central Police Station.

At first, Adry was tight-lipped. Under advice from Levi Stewart, however, he finally opened up about his brother's diabolical scheme.

ONE AFTERNOON IN early September, Adry was at work in his father's office when Harry dropped in and, after a bit of aimless chitchat, asked if Adry "wanted to make good money" by performing a simple task.

"I am always willing to make good money, but it depends upon what it is," said Adry.

As if it were the most natural thing in the world, Harry then explained that he was prepared to give Adry $2,000 if he "would kill a woman." It would be "a very simple thing." Harry would "get her out somewhere, take her out driving or something like that," and all Adry had to do was shoot her. Since Adry had no connection at all to the woman—whose name Harry did not reveal at the time, referring to her only as "the dressmaker"—"nobody would ever suspect me of the crime."

When Adry refused, Harry derided him for not having "any nerve."

"I have nerve enough," said Adry.

"Prove it," Harry sneered. "Go out and kill somebody and I'll give you a hundred dollars. If you are too afraid to kill a woman, kill a child. Or kill a cripple; they are better off dead than alive anyway."

When Adry stood firm in his refusal, Harry stormed out of the office, declaring that he was "through with me, that I was no good." Over the ensuing weeks, however, he kept Adry abreast of his plans. In early November, Harry revealed that he had persuaded his intended victim to take out life insurance policies amounting to $10,000 and make him the beneficiary. A few weeks later, on the day after Thanksgiving, he appeared in Adry's office and announced that the time had come "to sacrifice the dressmaker." By then, he had found someone to do the job that Adry was too "chicken-hearted" to perform. His name was Claus A. Blixt.

* * *

DESCRIBED BY ONE historian as a "dim-witted immigrant," the Swedish-born Blixt had come to America as a seven-year-old and settled with his parents in southeast Minnesota. He had spent the next twenty years on the family farm, where—after acquiring a threshing machine—he became adept at stationary engineering. Moving to Minneapolis in 1886, he worked at various odd jobs—bartender, streetcar conductor, steam engine operator at a rock quarry—before being hired as the handyman for the Ozark Flats. Forty-one years old at the time of the Ging murder, he and his third wife lived in the basement, where, among his other duties, he tended the furnace and kept the hydraulic elevator in working order.

Knowing an easy mark when he saw one, Harry immediately recognized that the simpleminded Blixt had the makings of a pliable tool. Throughout the fall of 1894, he made nightly visits to the basement and—using a combination of bribery, blackmail, and bullying—did everything in his power to bend the handyman to his will. By mid-November, Blixt had so fallen under Harry's malign spell that, when challenged to prove his courage by setting fire to a barn across the road, Blixt readily agreed. According to some accounts, he also poisoned a neighbor's dog at Harry's behest as a further demonstration of his mettle.

Satisfied that Blixt was fully in his power, Harry broached the subject that was foremost on his mind: getting rid of Kitty Ging. He intended, he told Blixt, "to take her down." Everything about her revolted him. "Whenever I go up to her room and she puts her arms around me," he said, "I feel like putting a knife into the goddamned bitch."

Blixt, who adored his third wife, was appalled. "If a girl loves you like that, how could you do such a thing? It is awful. I don't understand it."

"I would rather kill her than shoot a dog," said Harry. "If there was a dog and her, I'd shoot her and let the dog go."

His personal aversion to Kitty, however, wasn't the most important consideration. Mostly it was a matter of money. He was "going to make ten thousand dollars on her," said Harry, explaining his life insurance scheme.

"But Harry," Blixt protested, "can't you try to make money some other way than by killing the poor girl?"

But Harry would not be dissuaded. "Don't you want to make some money easy?" he asked Blixt, proposing the same deal he had offered Adry: $2,000 to "kill the woman for me." When Blixt refused, Harry accused him of cowardice and promised to have him arrested for arson. "You know that barn you fired for me? I can have you sent to prison for ten years for that. You must help me if you want me to keep quiet." It wasn't until Harry issued the ultimate threat, however—"If you don't help me, I will kill your wife"—that a tearful Blixt relented.

Harry's first, outrageously gruesome plan was to orchestrate an elevator "accident." He would get in the elevator with Kitty, he explained, and knock her senseless from behind with a hammer. He would then arrange her body so that her head was "over the edge of the elevator." At a signal from Harry, Blixt—who did nighttime duty as the elevator operator—would "start it up and it will tear her head off."

When Blixt recoiled in horror and insisted that he "would not do any such thing," Harry contrived a less ghoulish scheme. Certain aspects of it, known only to Harry, would forever remain a mystery. On the evening of December 3, the day he had set for her death, Harry met with Kitty and laid out the details of a supposedly surefire moneymaking deal he had set up for that night. Kitty—in thrall to the seductive sociopath and never averse to fattening her bank account, even by questionable means—agreed to help out. At 7:00 p.m., she hired a buggy and drove it to the corner of Lyndale Avenue and Kenwood Boulevard, where Harry had arranged to meet her. She was surprised to find him accompanied by another man, introduced by Harry as "one of the gang." It was, of course, Claus Blixt, who—unbeknownst to Kitty—had been fortified with a half pint of whiskey and equipped with a Colt revolver.

Ordering Blixt into the buggy, Harry gave them directions, telling the two of them to drive out to "the west side of Lake Calhoun," where he would meet them with another team. They would then "exchange horses" before proceeding with their mission—a necessary precaution, he explained, to "confuse anyone trying to follow us."

As Kitty and Blixt drove off into the night, Harry hurried by foot to Mabel Bartelson's home, picked up his date, and escorted her to the opera house. He and Mabel were enjoying the show when Blixt, following Harry's instructions, drove Kitty to a deserted spot, shot her in the back of the head, dumped her body into the road, abandoned the buggy and took a streetcar back home.

BLIXT DID NOT reveal all of this information at once. Taken into custody on Friday, December 7, he initially claimed total ignorance of the murder. On the following day, after intense grilling, he altered his story, claiming that he had been a mere accessory to the crime, helping to dispose of the corpse after Harry had done the killing. It wasn't until the following day that he broke down and made a full confession. On December 13, both he and Harry were indicted for murder. Adry was not charged.

THOUGH ALL BUT forgotten now, the trial of Harry Hayward was a nationwide sensation—"one of the greatest legal battles the world ever saw," in the estimation of one contemporary chronicler. Having been whipped into a "fever of excitement" by the frenzied attention accorded the case, the public turned out in droves for the opening day of the proceedings, January 21, 1895. The scene, wrote one reporter, "would have cast in the shade a Republican convention in a presidential year." More than five thousand people jammed the streets around the courthouse, waiting to see the prisoner escorted from the jailhouse a half block away. At their first glimpse of Harry, they broke into catcalls and chants of "Hang him! Hang him!"—a sentiment seconded by Minnesota congressman Ignatius Donnelly, who expressed his belief that "Harry should be hung at once, and if he is acquitted, the public had better turn out and hang his attorneys."

Though the seven-week trial got off to a slow start, with the first nine days devoted entirely to jury selection, it produced its share of memorable moments. Particularly dramatic were the testimony of Claus Blixt, which held the audience spellbound for nearly three days, and the riveting revelations of Adry. "Never before on the witness stand," exclaimed one reporter of Adry's recital, "was there ever such a story told for mortal ears!" Harry's defense team—hired at great expense by his doting father, who had sold off much of his property to pay the legal expenses—attempted to discredit Adry's devastating testimony by showing that he was insane. In the end, however, the jury needed less than three hours to reach a guilty verdict. Three days later, on March 11, 1895, he was sentenced to death.

CONFINED TO HIS cell in the Hennepin County jail while his appeal made its way through the courts, Harry maintained the air of cool bravado that had served him so well at the gaming tables. He joked with his jailers, charmed visiting journalists with his "cordial and gentlemanly" manners, and—notwithstanding two attempted escapes—professed perfect contentment with his surroundings. His sleep was deep and untroubled, his disposition serene, and his appetite so hearty that he began to grow seriously stout. The prospect of hanging seemed to hold no terror for him. He made wisecracks about his impending "necktie party" and speculated humorously about "what his sensations at the last moment would be."

On only one occasion did Harry's affable façade crack open, exposing the madness beneath. Ever since Adry's testimony against him at the trial, Harry had made no secret of his "unbounded hate" for his brother. Finally, at the urging of his heartbroken parents, he agreed to send for Adry and reconcile with him. Penning a brief note, he dispatched it to Adry's home via a messenger:

Dear Brother Adry:

My days are numbered, and I hope and trust that you will grant this my last request. I would like to have you come and see me as soon as you receive this. I wish to forgive you for any injury I have fancied you have done me, and I hope you will extend a like forgiveness.

Your loving brother,
Harry

The note turned out to be a trap. No sooner had Adry arrived than Harry began to berate him in a tone that grew increasingly maniacal as he went on.

"I will be with you, Adry, as long as you live," he cried. "I will haunt you to your last day. You will see me every night for the rest of your life. You will see me as a corpse with the rope around my neck. I will make life a living hell for you. How do you like it?

"Ah, this is glorious!" he shrieked, striding back and forth across the cell and waving his arms wildly. "If I could have your brains, Adry, I would stick them on an iron and roast them in the fire. I would clench them in my hands and tear them to pieces. This is my forgiveness!"

As his horrified brother leapt to his feet and hurried from the cell, Harry shouted after him: "Goodbye, Adry. I will meet you at the gates of hell!" For nearly an hour, he continued to pace up and down his cell, exclaiming "in exultant tones how he had fooled Adry into coming to hear his curse."

To those who witnessed it, the outburst gave weight to an opinion shared by a number of medical experts: that Harry Hayward, for all his charm and intelligence, was "actually insane."

* * *

AT NO POINT during his year in jail did Harry display the slightest remorse. Nor would he admit to any role in Kitty Ging's murder. It wasn't until the evening of December 9, 1895—after his appeal had been denied, the governor had refused to grant clemency, and a bill to abolish the death penalty in Minnesota had been voted down by the state legislature—that Harry, with nothing to lose and death only twenty-six hours away, agreed to open up.

His confession—made to his cousin Edward Goodsell and transcribed by a court stenographer—took place over three lengthy sessions lasting a total of twelve hours. In it, Harry portrayed himself as a criminal mastermind, "coursing the byways of this world and twisting its supine inhabitants to the requirements of his will." Most shocking was his claim that, in the course of his wide-ranging travels as an itinerant gambler, he had murdered three people besides Kitty Ging.

The first was a pretty twenty-year-old "sporting girl" he had met in Pasadena. Luring her to a remote spot in the Sierra Madre, he had shot her in the back of the head, buried her in the woods, and made off with the $700 she carried in her purse. Sometime later, on the opposite coast, he had shot a "consumptive" in Long Branch, New Jersey, and taken $2,000 from the man before disposing of the corpse.

His most brutal crime, however, was the slaying of a "Chinaman" in a New York City gambling joint on Mulberry Street. Getting into an altercation over a card game, Harry "knocked the Chinaman down and kicked him in the stomach." He then picked up a chair and jabbed the pointed end of one wooden leg into the man's eye. Then, while the man "was down and howling," Harry sat down on the chair. "His skull was kind of thin," Harry related with a chuckle, "and I heard the chair leg smash down through his skull."

He admitted that, before committing his first murder, it had "always been in my head to kill a person," and that the impulse to "do away" with different victims had "passed through my mind dozens and dozens of times." Describing a "good, nice girl" he had briefly wooed some years earlier, Harry claimed an affinity with the infamous San Francisco sex killer Theodore Durrant. "I can tell exactly how he felt," he told Goodsell. "He did it with pleasure." Taking the trusting girl out for a buggy ride one evening, Harry "could hardly keep from choking her to death. I would have just liked to. She don't know how close she came to kicking the bucket."

To the horrified Goodsell, it seemed clear that his cousin Harry—a man capable of committing the most awful atrocities without the slightest twinge of conscience or remorse—was no "ordinary assassin" but a being "possessed of a frightful homicidal mania," a "Dr. Jekyll and Mr. Hyde" character "totally devoid of all moral sensibility": in short, what a later age would call a serial killer.

Throughout the confession, Harry does in fact display many of the traits that we now know are typical of serial murderers: overweening narcissism, juvenile sadism ("in early life," we are told, "he was recognized by his school mates for his brutal instincts, delighting in the torture of domestic animals"), pyromania, a total lack of empathy for his fellow human beings. Like other serial killers, he experienced his "murderous impulse" as a kind of autonomous second self that would suddenly "come over him." Interestingly, he also seems to have suffered from convulsions as an adolescent, possibly as the result of a head injury—a factor found in the background of many serial killers.

To be sure, it is hard to know how much credence to give to Harry's claims of multiple murder. Like all psychopaths, he was an inveterate liar, constitutionally incapable of telling the truth. Typical of his breed, he also took a perverse pride in his criminal celebrity. It is possible that, in his eagerness to ensure a place in the pantheon of infamy, he grossly exaggerated his crimes. Goodsell himself refers to Harry's desire "to go down in history as the 'Napoleon of crime.'"

And then there was the matter of money. As Harry understood, the more lurid the confession, the more copies it would sell. Since the profits would go to Goodsell, his "favored cousin," Harry was only too happy to give the public what it wanted. Certainly his own older brother, Dr. Thaddeus Hayward, regarded the confession as a hoax. "Harry regarded his whole life as a big joke, and he decided to top the climax with a joke," Thaddeus told reporters. "I place but little faith in the confession. He intimated to me regarding his confession that it was his intention to give the public their fill of blood and thunder."

In the end, it is impossible to know whether Harry Hayward killed one victim or (as he claimed) four. All that can be said with certainty is that, as a case of criminal psychopathology—"moral insanity," in the terms of his contemporaries—Harry Hayward was, as Goodsell and others saw it, one of the most remarkable specimens of his age.

AFTER COMPLETING HIS confession late on Tuesday evening, December 10, Harry summoned his brother, Adry, again, apologized for his previous outburst, shook his hand, and bid him farewell. He then sat down for a hearty supper. A few hours later, nattily dressed in a cutaway coat, pinstripe trousers, turndown collar, and white necktie, he was escorted to the gallows, which—at his request—had been painted a holiday red.

As he ambled to the scaffold, he bid the spectators a cheerful "good evening" and asked "for three cheers for himself." Ascending the stairs with a firm step, he stood upon the drop and proceeded to crack so many jokes about his imminent death that the spectators, according to one eyewitness, "looked upon him almost as if he were a stage performer who would soon take his bow, receive his modicum of applause, and retire." It wasn't until the sheriff reprimanded him for his undignified behavior and urged him "to die like a man" that Harry brought his flippant monologue to a close.

Very swiftly, his arms and legs were pinioned, and the noose was thrown around his neck. "Keep up your courage boys," Harry said with a sneer. "Pull her tight. I stand pat."

With that, the trap was sprung. The noose, however, had not been adjusted correctly. The fall did not break Harry's neck. Thrashing in midair, he slowly strangled, taking fifteen long minutes to die.

AMONG THE WITNESSES gathered at the foot of the scaffold were two enterprising Minneapolis businessmen, H. Benedict and T. C. Hough, who—with the help of some judicious bribes—had smuggled an early phonograph machine into the jail and managed to record Harry's last words on a wax cylinder. Within days of the execution, copies of this macabre souvenir were being marketed to the public.

As for Claus Blixt, he pleaded guilty at a separate trial and was sentenced to life in prison. He died behind bars in August 1925 at the age of seventy-two, having reportedly descended into total insanity.

[Sources: The Ging Murder and the Great Hayward Trial. The Official Stenographic Report Containing Every Word of the Wonderful Trial from Its Opening to Sentence of Death; the Rulings of the Court; Speeches of Frank M. Nye [and Others] the Court's Charge, etc. Supplemented by a Dramatic Story of the Great Crime by Oscar F. G. Day (Minneapolis: Minnesota Tribune Company, 1895); Walter N. Trennery, Murder in Minnesota: A Collection of True Cases (St. Paul: Minnesota Historical Society Press, 1985); Stewart H. Holbrook, Murder Out Yonder: An Informal Study of Certain Classic Crimes in Back-Country America (New York: Macmillan, 1941); Olive Wooley Burt, American Murder Ballads and Their Stories (New York: Oxford University Press, 1958); Tim Brooks, "The Last Words of Harry Hayward (A True Record Mystery)," Antique Phonograph Monthly 1, no. 6 (June-July 1973): 1–8.]

"The Fatal Ride"

Like so many other sensational homicides of the past, the murder of Kitty Ging—"Minnesota's best-known, carefully planned crime," as historian Walter N. Trennery calls it—was commemorated in a widely distributed ballad. Anonymously written and variously known as "The Harry Hayward Song" and "The Fatal Ride," the lyrics go like this:

Minneapolis was excited, and for many miles around,
For a terrible crime committed just a mile or so from town.
It was on a cold and winter's eve, the moon had passed away,
The road was dark and lonely when found dead where she lay.

The stars were shining brightly and the moon had passed away,
The roads were dark and lonely where her form had turned to clay.
Then tell the tale of a criminal, Kit was his promised bride,
Just another sin to answer for, just another fatal ride.

When for pleasure she went riding, little did she know her fate,
That was to take place on that lonely night on the road near Calhoun Lake;
She was shot while in the buggy, and beaten ('Tis true to speak!)
Until all of life had vanished—then was cast into the street.

He was at heart a criminal and a coward of a man!
And so he sought another to execute his plan.
The bargain it was struck, the villain did reply,
"Tonight she takes that fatal ride—Yes, she will have to die!"

Oh, how could he have done that deed, so terrible to do?
Or how could he have killed a girl with a heart so pure and true?
It was a cold and bloody plot—likewise a terrible sin,
To take a life so kind and true as she had been to him.

A Hypnotic Villain

Published in 1894, George Du Maurier's novel *Trilby* tells the tragic story of a lovely young artist's model, Trilby O'Ferral, who falls under the sway of a brilliant musician with sinister hypnotic powers. Though completely tone-deaf, Trilby is transformed through the evil genius of her mentor into a world-famous soprano, only to find her life fatally entwined with his. The book not only became an international sensation but, as historian Judith Pintar notes, "set off a marketing frenzy, during which the heroine's name was bestowed upon a hat, several shoe designs, candy, toothpaste, soap, a brand of sausage, and even a town in Florida. Trilby's face appeared on dolls, fans, writing paper, puzzles, and there were ice cream bars made in the shape of her feet." Though the Trilby fad eventually faded, the book left a lasting mark on the English language. The villain's name immediately became a synonym "for one who exercises a controlling or mesmeric influence on another, frequently for some sinister purpose": Svengali.

At the time of Harry Hayward's trial—just a year after *Trilby* was published—certain sensationalistic newspapers began referring to him as the "Minneapolis Svengali." The reason was the supposed mesmeric influence he had exerted over his victims. According to widely circulated reports, it was Harry's irresistible hypnotic power that had caused Kitty Ging to conspire in the plot that led to her murder and compelled Claus Blixt to carry out the "desperate deed." Even Adry was quoted as saying that he had refrained from alerting police to his brother's nefarious plan "partly from fear of Harry and partly as a result of the hypnotic influence he held over me." Needless to say, there was not a shred of truth to these wild stories, though Harry himself, always eager to enhance his Mephistophelian image, did nothing to discourage them.

SCOTT JACKSON,
WHO SLAUGHTERED POOR PEARL BRYAN

APPLE TREES HAVE BEEN ASSOCIATED WITH EVIL SINCE THE PRIMAL SERPENT persuaded Eve to sample the forbidden fruit. In more recent times, orchards have been the locale of various heinous happenings. In 1873, for example, the killer clan known as the "Bloody Benders"—a family of frontier serial murderers who set up a crude roadside inn in Kansas where unwary travelers were slaughtered, then stripped of their possessions—used their newly sown apple orchard as a makeshift cemetery. A hundred years later, the California serial sex killer Juan Corona also planted his many victims in local orchards (albeit peach, not apple). And one of the most sensational murder mysteries of the twentieth century had its start in an orchard: the double slaying of the married Reverend Edward Wheeler Hall and his choir-girl mistress, Mrs. Eleanor Mills, whose savaged corpses were found side by side in a New Jersey crabapple grove on a September morning in 1922, igniting a case that transfixed Jazz Age America.

Though it has long since faded into obscurity, one of the grisliest and most highly publicized American murders of the late nineteenth century also came to light in an apple orchard. Early on the morning of Saturday, February 1, 1896, sixteen-year-old James Hewling—a hired hand for a farmer named James Lock, owner of a sizable spread near Fort Thomas, Kentucky—was cutting across his employer's property when he spotted a woman's body sprawled in the grass beneath some apple trees. The young man was not especially alarmed. After a night on the town, carousing soldiers sometimes brought their doxies into the fields for a tumble, and on more than one occasion Hewling had come upon a drunken female sleeping off her debauch. Even so, he made sure to notify his boss upon arriving at the farmhouse. Lock immediately conveyed the information to Sheriff Jule Plummer, who dispatched one of his deputies to the scene. County coroner Robert Tingely, who was in the sheriff's office at the time, thought it best to tag along.

As he approached the body, which lay on its stomach, Tingely noticed signs of a violent struggle, including a torn and bloody man's shirtsleeve lying nearby in the grass. Though young James Hewling had assumed, as he later testified, that the woman was "asleep or just drunk," Tingely could tell, even before he reached her, that she was dead. It wasn't until he knelt by the corpse, however, that he saw, to his horror, that she had been beheaded. Turning the body over, he found that her outer clothing had been ripped open and her corset torn off, exposing her breasts. The palm and fingers of her left hand had been sliced nearly to the bone. A large pool of blood soaked the ground beneath the stump of her mangled neck.

While Tingely continued inspecting the corpse, the deputy raced back for Sheriff Plummer, who arrived a short time later. Examining the crime scene, Plummer and his deputy discovered several sets of footprints. From these markings and other physical evidence—the scattered clothes, trampled ground, widely splattered blood—they deduced that the woman and a male companion "had walked side by side for a short distance when, for some reason, the woman had attempted to flee." Overtaking her, the murderer had "choked her into silence and dragged her toward the bushy bank. She struggled desperately and he tore handfuls of clothing from her dress. He threw her to the ground and slid over the bank with her." Drawing a knife, "he slashed at her throat." Defensively, she clutched the blade with her left hand and it "laid her palm and fingers open to the bone. Her struggles were useless, and in a moment her life blood was pouring from a gaping wound in her throat." Afterward, the killer had sawn through her neck below the fifth vertebra and carried off her head.

While the body was loaded onto a wagon and driven to a nearby undertaker's establishment to be autopsied, a pair of Cincinnati detectives, Cal Crim and John McDermott, were assigned to the case. By the time they arrived at Lock's orchard, however, the site had been overrun by curiosity seekers who—driven by the perennial human craving for the kind of grisly souvenirs known nowadays as "murderabilia"—had effectively destroyed the crime scene. As one contemporary account described it:

> Relic hunters were out in great numbers, and they almost demolished the bush under which the body was discovered, breaking off branches upon which blood could be seen. They peered closely into the ground for blood-spotted leaves, stones, and even saturated clay. Anything that had a blood stain upon it was seized upon eagerly, and hairs of the unfortunate woman were at a premium, men and boys, and even young women, examining every branch and twig of the bush in the midst of which the struggle took place in the hope of finding one. The inherent morbid love of the horrible the mass of humanity possesses was well illustrated in the scenes witnessed. The heavy rain which fell nearly all afternoon was not a deterrent to these relic hunters' zeal.

The scene outside W. H. White's undertaking parlor in Newport was equally frenzied. "All day long and up to a late hour at night, the place was besieged with people anxious to get a look at the remains of the unfortunate woman." With Coroner Tingely and several other physicians in attendance, Dr. Robert Carothers of Newport conducted the postmortem examination, which revealed that the victim was carrying a fetus "of between four and five months' gestation" that had clearly been alive when the victim was butchered. The fetus was removed and taken to a nearby pharmacy, where it was placed in alcohol for preservation. The stomach was also excised and turned over to Dr. W. H. Crane of Ohio Medical College, who was able to ascertain that the victim had ingested seventeen grains of cocaine shortly before her death. All the victim's blood had gushed out through her open neck; not a single drop was found in her veins, arteries, or heart.

Following the autopsy, Carothers issued a statement that proved to be remarkably accurate. "I judge that it was a premeditated and cold-blooded murder," he told reporters. "The girl, in my opinion, was from the country and comparatively innocent. She was brought to Cincinnati to submit to a criminal operation. Once here she was taken to Fort Thomas and murdered. Her head was taken away, horrible as it may seem, merely to prevent the identification of her body."

News of the atrocity set off shock waves that reverberated throughout the nation—and beyond. "The awful deed struck horror to the hearts of the people, and they were worked up to a pitch that had never been witnessed," wrote one observer. "The entire country was startled from center to circumference and aroused as it never had been before. Telephones and telegraph were called into service, and the finding of the headless body of a young and doubtless beautiful woman in a sequestered spot near Fort Thomas was flashed around the world."

With criminal science still in a primitive stage (even the forensic use of fingerprints was still more than a decade away in the United States), detectives resorted to the only means at their disposal. Three "famous bloodhounds" named Jack, Wheeler, and Stonewall—responsible for the apprehension of more than twenty criminals then serving time in midwestern penitentiaries—were given a scent of the dead woman's clothing, then brought to the murder scene by their owner, Arthur Carter of Seymour, Indiana. After following the trail to Covington reservoir, however, they lost the scent. Thinking that the missing head might have been tossed into the water, authorities had the reservoir drained at considerable expense. "But the head," as one paper reported, "was not discovered."

In the end, it was the victim's shoes that broke the case open. In contrast to her handmade and nondescript clothing, the new black button-topped shoes were factory produced and carried the manufacturer's marking: "Louis & Hays, Greencastle, Ind., 22–11, 62,458." With assistance from a local dry-goods merchant named L. D. Poock, detectives were able to trace the footwear to their source and determine that the shoes had been purchased by a local girl named Pearl Bryan.

Born into one of "the oldest and best connected families in the state of Indiana," twenty-two-year-old Pearl was the youngest of twelve children of Alexander S. Bryan, owner of a large and prosperous farm in the town of Greencastle. As the baby of the family, she had grown up "petted and feted"—the darling late-life child of doting parents who showered her with love and worldly goods. Despite her coddled upbringing, she had grown up to be entirely unspoiled, a vivacious young woman "of a lovable, affectionate disposition, liked by all." Besieged by wealthy young men who "would have eagerly jumped at the opportunity to claim her as their wife," she rebuffed all suitors—until, in the spring of 1895, she was introduced to a debonair young dental student named Scott Jackson.

Son of a navy commodore, the widely traveled Jackson was an affable, smooth-talking charmer with a "most winsome countenance"—"dimples on his chin and cheeks, a childish smile on his lips, frank, beautiful, pale violet-blue eyes." Women found him irresistible, and Pearl Bryan was no exception. From their initial meeting, wrote an early chronicler of the case, "it was love at first sight. She who had refused to listen to the wooing whispers of men in high rank and station in life by the scores, fell at once a victim to the darts from cupid's shaft sent from Jackson's lips."

Pearl undoubtedly would have been less taken with the prepossessing dental student had she known of his unsavory secret history. Just a few years earlier, he and an accomplice had embezzled $32,000 from the Pennsylvania Railroad Company—an amount equal to more than $800,000 in today's money. Jackson had avoided a long stretch in the penitentiary only by turning state's evidence against his cohort. He also possessed a highly developed taste for debauchery, which he had freely indulged during his wide-flung travels. To those who knew the truth about Jackson, he was "a natural monster, a whited sepulcher, one of those unaccountable freaks of nature," beneath whose "fine form and features" there lurked a diabolically cunning creature "absolutely incapable of any expression of remorse." In the language of his time, he was a "very demon in human form." In the clinical terms of ours, he was a classic criminal psychopath.

Smitten with his charms—his "honeyed words and protestations of love"—the virginal Pearl gave herself to the cold-blooded seducer. It wasn't long before she discovered, to her horror, that she was pregnant. By then, Jackson, his "lustful desire" slaked, had abandoned her and moved to Cincinnati.

In a panic, she wrote to him, describing her desperate condition. He in turn suggested various medicinal concoctions that would produce a miscarriage—"recipes calculated to prevent the evil results of their indiscretion," in the euphemistic language of the time. When those failed "to have the desired effect of reversing the laws of nature," he directed her to come to Cincinnati, where he would arrange for an abortion. She left home on January 27, telling her parents that she was off to visit friends in Indianapolis. Her family had not heard from her since.

Nine days had elapsed without a word from Pearl when Detectives Crim and McDermott showed up at the Bryan farmhouse, carrying the bloodied clothes of the murder victim. Shown the hand-sewn garments, her parents immediately identified them as Pearl's. Desperately clutching at the hope that their daughter might yet be alive, they "argued that she might have given her clothes to some else." When the detectives described some distinguishing features found on the body, including webbed toes and a small wart on one hand, her parents could no longer fend off the terrible truth. "Pearl, my poor Pearl!" sobbed her mother, burying her face in her hands.

In short order, Scott Jackson was arrested, along with his roommate and accomplice, Alonzo Walling. At first both men vehemently denied any knowledge of the crime. For days they were subjected to constant interrogation. In an effort to make them crack, they were taken to a local undertaking establishment and confronted with Pearl Bryan's headless corpse, clothed in the white silk dress she had worn for her high school graduation and laid out in a satin-lined casket. Though neither culprit would ever make a wholehearted confession, the central facts of the murder eventually came to light.

CARRYING A PAIR of satchels, one made of tan leather, the other of alligator skin, Pearl arrived in Cincinnati on Monday afternoon, January 27. She was met at the station by Jackson, who took her to a nearby women's hostel, the Indiana House, and got her settled in a room. She spent the next few days in the company of Jackson and his roommate, Alonzo Walling, waiting anxiously for the promised procedure. By Thursday, she had grown so impatient with the protracted delay that she threatened to return home if Jackson did not immediately make good on his obligation. Assuring her that arrangements had been made for the following evening, Jackson told Pearl to meet him at a nearby saloon.

Both he and Walling were there when she showed up shortly before seven o'clock on Friday night. Seated at a secluded table in the rear of the saloon, Jackson, who had brought along a vial of cocaine he had purchased at a local pharmacy, managed to slip the drug into Pearl's sarsaparilla soda during dinner. By the time they left the place, she was so groggy that she had to be half lifted into a cab by the two men.

Directing the driver to take them over the river and into Kentucky, Jackson had him stop at a remote spot just outside the wooden fence bounding James Lock's farm. He and Walling then got Pearl out of the carriage, helped her over the fence, and led her deep into the apple orchard. Even in her drugged state, Pearl suddenly understood what was happening. Breaking away from the men, she tried to flee but was quickly overtaken by Jackson, who dragged her into some bushes and began slashing away with a razor-edged dissecting knife he had brought along. In her frenzied effort to save herself, Pearl clutched at the blade, which sliced her fingers to the bone. Yanking her head back by the hair, Jackson opened her throat. She collapsed in the grass and bled out within seconds.

Jackson then knelt beside her and sawed off her head, which he wrapped in his overcoat, carried back to his boardinghouse room, and placed inside one of Pearl's satchels. A few nights later, he carried the satchel to the Covington Suspension Bridge and tossed the head into the swirling current of the Ohio River.

SCOTT JACKSON'S THREE-WEEK trial began in late April 1896 and featured a number of sensational moments, including the display of a grotesque headless dummy dressed in Pearl Bryan's blood-soaked clothing. Walling was tried separately a month later. Both men were found guilty and sentenced to death. On May 20, 1897, they were hanged together for what the newspapers touted as "The Crime of the Century."

Like similar nineteenth-century homicides involving pregnant young women slain by their lovers, the savage killing of Pearl Bryan was promptly commemorated in a highly sentimentalized ballad. Scholar Anne B. Cohen has identified six different versions of the song. The most popular goes like this:

> Deep, deep in yonder valley
> Where the flowers fade and bloom,
> There lies poor Pearl Bryan
> In a cold and silent tomb.
>
> She died not broken hearted,
> Nor lingering ill befell,
> But in an instant parted
> From one she loved so well.
>
> One night the moon shone brightly,
> The stars were shining too,
> When to her cottage window
> Her jealous lover drew.

"Come Pearl, let's take a ramble
O'er the meadows wide a gay,
Where no one will disturb us
We'll name our wedding day."

Deep, deep into the valley
He led his love so dear,
Says she, "It's for you only
That I am rambling here.

"The way seems dark and dreary
And I'm afraid to stay,
Of rambling I've grown weary
And would retrace my way."

"Retrace your way? No, never!
These woods no more you'll roam,
So bid farewell forever
To parents, friends, and home.

"You have not the wings of an eagle,
Nor from me can you fly,
No human hand can aid you,
Pearl Bryan you must die!"

"What have I done, Scott Jackson
That you should take my life?
You know I've always loved you,
And would have been your wife."

Down on her knees before him,
She pleaded for her life,
But into her snow white bosom
He plunged a fatal knife.

"Farewell my loving parents,
My happy peaceful home,
Farewell my dear old schoolmates,
With you no more I'll roam.

"Farewell my dear, dear sister,
My face you'll see no more,
Long, long you'll wait my coming,
At the little cottage door.

"But Jackson, I forgive you
With my last and dying breath."
Her pulse had ceased its beating,
Her eyes were closed in death.

The birds sang in the morning,
But doleful were their songs,
A stranger found Pearl Bryan
Cold headless on the ground.

[*Source: The Mysterious Murder of Pearl Bryan, or: The Headless Horror* (Cincinnati: Barclay & Co., 1897).]

Murdered-Girl Ballads

The tear-jerking ditty of Pearl Bryan belongs to a genre that folklorists call the "murdered-girl ballad," a type of traditional song about a trusting young woman done in by a cold-hearted seducer. Scholar Eleanor R. Long-Wingus has identified four central elements that make up the murdered-girl ballad formula:

1. An innocent young woman is seduced by an unscrupulous lover.

2. When she becomes pregnant, he arranges a tryst on the pretext of discussing plans for their marriage.

3. Over her protests, he succeeds in luring her to a remote area.

4. Though she begs for mercy, he kills her in a particularly vicious manner, then disposes of her body.

The best-known of all American murdered-girl ballads is "Poor Naomi Wise" (aka "Omie Wise"). During the folk music craze of the late 1950s—when the pop charts were ruled by clean-cut vocal groups warbling "This Land Is Your Land" and every self-respecting baby boomer could strum the chords to "Kumbaya"—the song was a coffeehouse standard. Scores of artists, ranging from Bob Dylan to Elvis Costello, have recorded it. Inspired by a real-life murder that happened in Randolph County, North Carolina, in 1807, the ballad exists in many versions, though the earliest known printed lyrics are these:

> Come all good people, I'd have you draw near,
> A sorrowful story you quickly shall hear;
> A story I'll tell you about N'omi Wise,
> How she was deluded by Lewis's lies.

> He promised to marry and use me quite well;
> But conduct contrary I sadly must tell,
> He promised to meet me at Adams' springs;
> He promised me marriage and many fine things.

> Still nothing he gave, but yet flattered the case.
> He says we'll be married and have no disgrace,

Come get up behind me, we'll go up to town,
And there we'll be married, in union be bound.

I got up behind him and straightway did go
To the banks of Deep River where the water did flow;
He says now Naomi, I'll tell you my mind,
Intend here to drown you and leave you behind.

O pity your infant and spare me my life;
Let me go rejected and not be your wife;
No pity, no pity, this monster did cry;
In Deep River's bottom your body shall lie.

The Wretch then did choke her, as we understand,
And threw her in the river below the milldam;
Be it murder or treason, O! what a great crime,
To drown poor Naomi and leave her behind.

Naomi was missing they all did well know,
And hunting for her to the river did go;
And there found her floating in water so deep,
Which caused all the people to sigh and to weep.

The neighbors were sent for to see the great sight,
While she lay floating all the long night;
So early next morning the inquest was held;
The jury correctly the murder did tell.

Like other specimens of the genre, "Poor Naomi," while based on an actual homicide, takes considerable liberties with the truth. Though the historical record is scanty, scholars have determined that—far from being a virginal maiden brought to ruin by a heartless cad—the real Naomi Wise was a household menial of dubious "carnal conduct" who had already borne two illegitimate children before she became involved with her eventual killer, a younger man named Jonathan Lewis. After getting pregnant by Lewis—a well-to-do clerk from a respectable local family—the shameless Naomi, evidently proud that she was with child by a man of "so high rank as Jonathan," let the world know that he was the father-to-be. Infuriated at being exposed to disgrace—and worried that he would have to support the child under Kentucky's "bastardy" laws, which required fathers of illegitimate babies to put up money for the future maintenance of their offspring—Lewis "charged Naomi upon peril of her life to remain silent." When she blithely ignored his warnings, he lured her to a river and drowned her. Arrested and jailed, Lewis managed to escape and remained at large until his recapture four years later. He was ultimately tried and acquitted for lack of evidence, though it is said that he confessed to the murder on his deathbed.

The most complete account of the case is Robert Roote, "The Historical Events Behind the Celebrated Ballad, 'Naomi Wise,' " *North Carolina Folklore Journal* 32, no. 2 (Fall-Winter 1984): 70–81. For more on the subject of murdered-girl ballads, see Eleanor R. Long-Wingus, *Naomi Wise: Creation, Re-Creation, and Continuity in the American Ballad Tradition* (Chapel Hill, NC: Chapel Hill Press, 2003) and Anne B. Cohen, *Poor Pearl, Poor Girl! The Murdered-Girl Stereotype in Ballad and Newspaper* (Austin: University of Texas Press, 1973).

Cal Crim,
"Sleuth-Hound of the Law"

At the time of its occurrence, the slaying of Pearl Bryan was trumpeted in the press as "the most diabolical, cold-blooded, premeditated outrage ever committed in a civilized community"—"a murder so horrible and revolting as to appear to place it beyond the civilization of today," "one of the most terrible tragedies of the nineteenth century." Nowadays, hardly anyone remembers it. In this respect, the Bryan case is typical of many murders that dominate the front pages for a while, only to fade from public memory. But it's not just the crimes themselves that are quickly forgotten. Often the celebrated lawmen who solve them are too.

Such is the case with the once legendary Cincinnati detective, Cal Crim. Christened David Calvin Crim at his birth in 1864, he was raised in a Maryland orphanage and moved to Cincinnati at the age of fifteen. At the time, according to historian Catherine Cooper, "crime in the city was rampant. The year before his arrival, police arrested more than 1,300 prostitutes and 2,000 drunks, and it was discovered that for years thieves had been stealing bodies from the Colored Cemetery and selling them to medical schools. Brutal murders shocked the community. By January 1, 1885, the jail held twenty-three accused murderers." One of these cases—the savage bludgeoning murder of a livery owner by his two young employees—triggered the worst rioting in the city's history when a mob of ten thousand citizens, outraged over the lenient sentence given to one of the killers, ransacked the courthouse and set it on fire in March 1884. The riots—which lasted three days, until they were quelled by the combined forces of the sheriff's department, city police, and state and local militias—left fifty-four people dead and more than two hundred injured.

Two years after the courthouse riots, Crim—who had worked his way up from shoeshine boy to bellhop to desk clerk at a luxury hotel—joined the Cincinnati police force as a patrolman. He made a rapid ascent through the ranks and was supervising the vice squad (or "Purity Squad," as it was known at the time) when he was called in to investigate the Pearl Bryan case. His brilliant work on the case, which led to the arrest, conviction, and execution of the killers, first brought him to national attention and won him renown as an ace "sleuth-hound of the law."

Five years later, he was shot twice while attempting to apprehend a notorious sneak thief, John Foley, whose favorite street-fighting tactic—a vicious head butt—had earned him the nickname "Foley the Goat." By then, Crim was such a revered figure that a year later, following his lengthy recovery, the grateful citizens of the community chipped in to buy him a home.

Though he would carry two bullets inside him for the rest of his life, Crim never slowed down. In 1913, after twenty-eight years on the force, he retired from public service and founded the Cal Crim Detective Bureau, the first private detective agency in Cincinnati. Still in existence today (under the name Cal Crim Security), the company "solved many murders, kidnappings, and lesser crimes" and played a major investigatory role in the notorious Black Sox baseball scandal of 1919, "for which Cal received a gold-plated lifetime pass to any major league ballpark," as Catherine Cooper writes.

In 1953, Cal Crim died at the age of eighty-nine, forgotten by the world at large but still esteemed among crime cognoscenti as "Cincinnati's super-sleuth."

[*Source:* Catherine Cooper, "Cincinnati's Super-Sleuth," *Cincinnati Magazine* 16, no. 11 (August 1983): 96.]

V

A YEAR OF
HORROR

1927

ANDREW P. KEHOE, "THE WORLD'S WORST DEMON"

THE ANNALS OF CRIME PROVIDE GRIM CONFIRMATION OF THE SCRIPTURAL SAYING "There is no new thing under the sun." In April 1995, anti-government fanatic Timothy McVeigh committed the most heinous act of domestic terrorism in U.S. history when he bombed the Alfred P. Murrah Federal Building in Oklahoma City, killing 168 people. Four years later, almost to the day, a pair of teenage sociopaths, Dylan Klebold and Eric Harris, turned their Colorado high school into a killing field, making its name synonymous with adolescent mass murder: Columbine.

To a stunned American public, both these enormities seemed symptomatic of specifically contemporary social ills: the proliferation of right-wing extremists dedicated to the overthrow of the federal government, the epidemic of random school shootings by disaffected, gun-obsessed teens. Seventy years earlier, however, a crime occurred that combined the most appalling aspects of both the Oklahoma City catastrophe and the Columbine massacre (with an added element of another modern-day terror, the suicide bombing). It was known as the Bath School Disaster.

THE PERPETRATOR OF this outrage was a man named Andrew P. Kehoe, who would forever after be known by a variety of epithets: "fiend," "monster," "maniac," and—in the phrase of his earliest chronicler—"the world's worst demon." Born outside Tecumseh, Michigan, in 1872, one of thirteen children of a prosperous farmer, Kehoe was from his earliest years an inveterate tinkerer who enjoyed experimenting with electricity "the way other children indulged in sports."

Following the death of his beloved mother in 1890, Kehoe enrolled in Michigan State College in East Lansing, where he studied electrical engineering. Though biographical details are vague, he appears to have transferred to a school in St. Louis, where he reportedly suffered an unspecified head injury that left him in a coma for almost two weeks—a trauma that may or may not have contributed to his subsequent descent into homicidal mania. At all events, after some years of drifting around the Midwest, working as an electrician, he returned to the family farm in 1905.

By then, his sixty-year-old father had taken a much younger wife, Frances, toward whom Kehoe developed an intense and reciprocated loathing. In September 1911, an incident occurred that was viewed as a tragic mishap at the time, though it would take on a far more sinister aspect in light of subsequent events.

Returning from an afternoon outing, Frances set about making dinner preparations. When she put a match to the oil stove, it exploded, engulfing her in flames. Kehoe, hearing the explosion and his stepmother's shrieks, ran into the kitchen, grabbed a pail of water, and doused her with it, which only caused the burning oil to spread over her body, "liquefying what little skin she had left." Her "muscles roasted to the bone," she died in agony a few hours later, "little more than a blackened lump." The tragedy was attributed to a defect in the stove. Only later, when the world learned exactly what Andrew Kehoe was capable of, would people come to believe that he had deliberately rigged it to explode.

KEHOE REMAINED A bachelor until the age of forty, when he married thirty-seven-year-old Nellie Price, a local woman he had known since their undergraduate days at Michigan State. Seven years later, they bought an eighty-acre farm, putting down half the $12,000 purchase price and taking out a mortgage for the balance. Shortly thereafter, they moved into their new home in the township of Bath, a tight-knit little farming community situated about twelve miles from Lansing.

To the villagers of Bath, Kehoe seemed like an unusually smart, capable, and friendly fellow, always willing to lend a hand, particularly when it came to mechanical matters. "Any favors we asked of him, he was perfectly willing to do," one neighbor would later testify. "If anything was wrong, he'd come to our place and fix it." When Monty Ellsworth, who operated a wholesale butcher business, needed a steam boiler installed in his slaughterhouse, he "asked Mr. Kehoe to come up and help me, which he did very readily. He ran the pipes to the scalding tanks and showed me all about the boiler. Being no mechanic, I had some trouble from time to time with the boiler and I would always call Kehoe and he would come right up and fix it and would never take any money for his work."

To be sure, the man had his eccentricities. Unlike other farmers, who toiled in dirt-crusted coveralls and work boots, Kehoe kept himself as neatly groomed as a banker, riding his tractor in a business suit, vest, and polished shoes. He would hurry home to wash up if his hands got too greasy, and he was known to change his shirt in the middle of the day if he noticed a sweat stain or smudge of dirt. When finished with his tools, he made sure to put them back in perfect order. His barn, as Monty Ellsworth observed, was "cleaner than many houses." His neighbors marveled at his meticulous ways. Nowadays, a psychologist would take a more pathological view of such compulsive behavior.

His insistence on perfection extended to other areas of his life. Though sociable enough to participate in weekly card games, he was bitterly intolerant of any perceived infractions, snapping at other players who didn't stick strictly to the rules or who committed inadvertent errors. Though capable of generosity, he also displayed flashes of cruelty that bordered on outright sadism. On one occasion, he killed a neighbor's dog whose incessant barking had gotten on his nerves. Another time, in a fit of frustration at a recalcitrant horse, he beat the overworked animal to death.

And then there was his obsession with taxes.

From the time of Bath's founding in 1843, its children had attended one-room country schoolhouses where students of different ages shared the same teacher and their education ended with tenth grade. By the early 1920s, such an outmoded system no longer served the needs of the community. In the summer of 1921, the townspeople voted to build a modern new school with separate classes for every grade level from kindergarten through high school. To fund the project, household taxes were raised to $12.26 per $1,000 of property valuation. Construction began at once on a handsome two-story building and, in the fall of 1922, the Bath Consolidated School opened with 236 students bused in from throughout the township.

Though the majority of residents took enormous pride in the school—viewing it, in the words of one historian, as "a shining landmark overlooking the town, symbolically representing a higher ideal and bright future"—it was a source of resentment to others, who bridled at the increased tax burden, which grew heavier by the year. Andrew Kehoe, who had taken an increasingly active role in civic affairs, was from the first an outspoken critic of the school and the expense it imposed on the community, particularly on those, like himself, who were childless. In 1924, representing those disgruntled farmers who wanted tighter control exerted over educational expenditures, he got himself elected to the school board and was appointed treasurer.

Over the course of his three-year term, Kehoe found himself in constant conflict with other trustees and on the losing side of most battles. He clashed repeatedly with the school superintendent, Emory Huyck, a dedicated and much-admired administrator who seemed to inspire a peculiar loathing in Kehoe.

In 1926, following the sudden death of town clerk Maude Detluff, Kehoe was asked to fill the vacancy for the remainder of Detluff's term. His confrontational style proved so alienating that—though he was eager to hold on to the post—his fellow party members refused to nominate him in the next general election. The following year, he made a final, futile bid for public office, running unsuccessfully for county justice of the peace. His defeat only added to his growing bitterness. By then—though he gave few outward signs of it—Andrew Kehoe was harboring a deep and growing hatred of his community, the world, and life itself.

Though it used to be a catchall phrase for any homicidal maniac who claimed multiple victims, the term "mass murderer" is now reserved for the type of profoundly embittered individual who—blaming the world for all that has gone wrong with his life—resolves to go out with a bang and take as many people with him as possible. In a single, sudden burst of apocalyptic violence, he explodes without warning, wiping out everyone within range and turning a safe, familiar environment into the site of a corpse-strewn massacre. Whereas the serial killer can be defined as a predator, a "hunter of humans" who slakes his bloodlust by stalking one victim at a time, the mass murderer is stereotypically described as a "human time bomb"—a metaphor that, in Andrew Kehoe's case, would prove to be especially, horrendously apt.

By 1926, a toxic brew of emotions—resentment, humiliation, powerlessness, paranoia—was simmering in Kehoe's breast. His hopes for political office had been met by mortifying rejection. His wife had contracted tuberculosis and required constant and increasingly burdensome medical care. His personal finances were in such a shambles that he could no longer keep up his mortgage payments. In the fall of 1926, a deputy arrived at his farm to deliver a foreclosure notice.

"If it hadn't been for that three hundred dollar school tax," Kehoe remarked after examining the document, "I might have paid off the mortgage." The comment was striking enough to stick in the deputy's mind, though its full ominous import would only become clear later.

GIVEN HIS AVERSION to slovenliness and disorder—stemming from his obsessive need to exert absolute control over his environment—it was not surprising that Kehoe devoted much of his energy to making his property as tidy and well-tended as his tool shed. Among other things, this entailed clearing the land of tree stumps, boulders, and other such obstructions. To accomplish this goal, he relied on dynamite and pyrotol, an explosive made from surplus World War I gunpowder. Neighbors grew accustomed to the frequent detonations emanating from Kehoe's farm. What none of them knew or suspected, however, was that in late 1925 Kehoe began accumulating and storing away large quantities of both explosives, for reasons that had nothing to do with farming.

BECAUSE OF HIS electrical know-how, Kehoe was asked, while still serving on the school board, if he would perform some repairs on the school's wiring system. When he agreed, he was given a key and free access to the building, day or night.

It was during some of those nights, beginning in late 1926, that he smuggled into the basement more than six hundred pounds of pyrotol in thirty-pound sacks, ten bushel baskets full of dynamite, a dozen blasting caps, and the simple components— wiring, battery, alarm clock—needed to fashion a crude homemade timer.

AS APPALLING AS the events of Wednesday, May 18, 1927, were, they might have been—and indeed were meant to be—much worse. With only one day to go before commencement, many seniors stayed home from school. Others weren't scheduled to arrive until late in the morning for a final exam. Even so, there were more than 250 children in the building when the bomb went off at eight forty-five, ten minutes after classes began.

The whole building rocked on its foundation, and the entire north wing, which housed grades three through six, was reduced to rubble. "Dynamite and pyrotol combined in a powerful ball of energy," writes historian Arnie Bernstein, describing the detonation. "This forced the walls of the north wing upward about four feet. They fell back to earth, collapsing outward with a crash of wood, glass, plaster, and iron. The roof of the building slammed down onto the crumbling walls. A cloud of dust hovered above the ruins. For a moment there was silence. And then a cacophony of screams."

The terrible blast "sounded throughout the farmlands of Bath Township, and continued to echo for miles beyond." Such was the force of the explosion that windows of nearby houses were shattered, people were knocked to the floor, and "horses, terrified by the roar, broke loose from their plows and scattered."

Within minutes, hundreds of people had arrived on the scene. While Emory Huyck supervised the rescue of the children still trapped inside the east wing, other villagers tore through the smoldering wreckage. As they brought out the small bodies—some terribly injured, others lifeless, a few miraculously unscathed—"the piercing lamentations of mothers" mingled with "the heartrending cries of the sufferers and the terror-stricken screams of children." Altogether, two teachers and thirty-six children (some from the same family) died in the explosion.

But the horrors wrought by Andrew Kehoe—"the fiend in human form," as one newspaper described him—were not yet at an end.

KEHOE HAD BEEN a busy man.

In the weeks before the disaster, a few visitors to his home noticed that he had been stringing copper wires between his farm buildings. Knowing that he was an inveterate tinkerer, they thought nothing of it. No one had the slightest inkling of the truth: that Kehoe, in his all-consuming rage, had resolved not just to wreak a terrible vengeance on his community but to obliterate his entire world.

Sometime between May 16, when he drove his wife home from a brief stay at the local hospital, and the morning of May 18, Kehoe murdered Nellie by crushing her skull with a blunt object. He then loaded her body onto a cart and wheeled her behind the chicken coop. Inside his barn, he hobbled his horses by wrapping wire around

Postcard showing "Small Portion of the Destruction Caused by the Crazed Maniac" at the Kehoe farm.

their ankles. With a saw, he cut down the beautiful old shade trees surrounding his house and severed his grapevines.

Finally, he packed the rear seat of his Ford pickup with old tools, nails, nuts, bolts, and assorted scraps of metal and placed a few sticks of dynamite atop the junk pile. With the vehicle thus converted into a massive shrapnel-filled bomb, Kehoe's preparations for his personal Armageddon were complete.

At roughly the same moment that the explosives detonated in the basement of the Bath Consolidated School, Kehoe activated the ignition devices he had set up throughout his property, turning his house, barn, and assorted outbuildings into an inferno. He then jumped into his truck and headed for town.

KEHOE'S NEMESIS, SUPERINTENDENT Emory Huyck, was leading the rescue effort when the pickup pulled up in front of the demolished school. Stepping out of the vehicle, Kehoe called Huyck over. As Huyck approached, Kehoe grabbed either a pistol or a rifle from the cab of his truck (eyewitness accounts differed) and fired into the backseat.

The car bomb went off in a devastating blast that ripped apart the bodies of both men and sent hot metal fragments tearing through the flesh of a half dozen men, women, and children standing nearby. Seventy-five-year-old Nelson McFarren was killed outright. His son-in-law Glen Smith, the village postmaster, had one leg sheared off at the thigh and bled to death on the scene while reassuring the rescuers who were frantically trying to save him that they shouldn't "feel bad if I go." Another victim, eight-year-old Cleo Clayton, was struck in the stomach with a large bolt and died a few hours later.

As APPALLING AS the bloodbath was, Kehoe's plot, had it fully succeeded, would have wrought even greater destruction. Searching the basement of the ruined school, police found more than five hundred pounds of explosives that had failed to go off, owing to a faulty timer. Had the device worked as intended, the entire building would have blown up, killing or maiming everyone inside.

He had done a more complete job on his farm, where his house had been reduced

Postcard of "Unexploded Dynamite Found in Ruins of Bath School"

to cinders, his tractor and other equipment utterly destroyed, his horses incinerated, and his wife's corpse charred to a blackened lump.

Wired to a fence at the edge of the farm, investigators found a small wooden sign with these stenciled words: *Criminals are made, not born.* It was a final, self-justifying message from the psychopathic Kehoe, who seemed to be suggesting that he had become a killer through no fault of his own—that the townspeople had only themselves to blame for the horror that had befallen them.

LIKE THE SITES of other sensational killings, Bath became an instant tourist attraction, drawing hordes of the morbidly curious. According to one contemporary estimate, no fewer than eighty-five thousand cars passed through town on the Sunday after the catastrophe. After a titillating afternoon of viewing the wreckage of the school building and the scorched remains of the farm, many of the visiting voyeurs returned home with souvenir postcards showing the bushels of unexploded dynamite, the twisted remnants of Kehoe's truck bomb, and the precise spot where his wife's blackened corpse had been found.

Because nothing like the Bath disaster had ever happened before, there seemed to be no adequate language to describe it. One prescient pundit, recognizing that Kehoe's mad act represented the advent of a uniquely modern form of violence, proposed adding a new word to the language. According to an item in the May 27 edition of the *Lansing State Journal*, an unnamed member of the editorial staff had "coined the verb 'kehoe' " to cover any such future cases. "Applications of the idea would cause any person who destroys another or others by means of explosives to be termed a 'kehoe,' the act committed would be a 'kehoe,' while the victim would be considered as having been 'kehoed.' "

Far from entering the language, Kehoe's name quickly faded into obscurity. In the immediate aftermath of the tragedy, the story was front-page news across the nation. Within days, however, it was supplanted by an event of far greater magnitude: Charles Lindbergh's epochal flight across the Atlantic. When Lucky Lindy's plane touched down at Le Bourget field outside Paris on the evening of May 21, the world erupted into celebration, leaving the stricken citizens of Bath to mourn and remember on their own.

[*Sources:* M. J. Ellsworth, *The Bath School Disaster* (Bath, MI, 1927); Arnie Bernstein, *Bath Massacre: America's First School Bombing* (Ann Arbor: University of Michigan Press, 2009); "Maniac Blows Up School, Kills 42, Mostly Children," *New York Times*, May 19, 1927, 1.]

The Wall Street Bombing

Until the Bath School Disaster, the worst act of U.S. domestic terrorism occurred on September 16, 1920. Shortly before noon on that cool, late summer Thursday—the beginning of lunch hour, when the streets were crammed with clerks, secretaries, messengers, and other office workers—a horse-drawn wagon came to a halt at the corner of Wall and Broad Streets in lower Manhattan, directly across from the headquarters of the J. P. Morgan bank, the fortress-like symbol of American capitalism. Concealed inside the weatherbeaten wagon were one hundred pounds of dynamite and five hundred pounds of scrap iron designed to act as shrapnel.

As the bells of Trinity Church tolled noon, the driver leapt from the wagon and fled through the surging crowds. One minute later, the wagon exploded.

"The bomb," writes historian Kevin Baker, "was an immeasurably cruel device. It blew people apart, tore arms and legs, hands and feet and scalps off living human beings. Others were beheaded or eviscerated, or found themselves suddenly engulfed in flames. Still more injuries were caused by a cascade of broken glass and the terrified stampede that followed." Thirty people died immediately, and nine more would succumb in the coming weeks. More than three hundred were injured.

The timing of the act—less than a week after Ferdinando Nicola Sacco and Bartolomeo Vanzetti were indicted for murder—led investigators to suspect that it was the work of anarchists, a suspicion apparently confirmed the very next day when a message was found inside a mailbox a block away from the site of the explosion: *Remember. We will not tolerate any longer. Free the political prisoners or it will be death to all of you. American Anarchist Fighters!* Despite an intensive investigation by the Bureau of Investigation, however—the forerunner of the FBI—the crime was never solved.

To this day, the building that formerly housed J. P. Morgan & Company at 23 Wall Street bears the scars of the bombing, its lower portion pockmarked with small craters from the shrapnel. The incident itself, however—like the Bath school massacre that would horrify the nation seven years later—quickly faded from public memory and is barely remembered today.

ADA LeBOEUF,
"THE SIREN OF THE SWAMPS"

FROM THE PROSECUTION OF HARRY K. THAW FOR THE SHOOTING OF STANFORD White in 1906 to the O. J. Simpson circus of 1995, nearly every decade in the hundred-year stretch between 1900 and the dawn of the new millennium witnessed a sensational court case touted as the "trial of the century." Appropriately enough for an age of excess, the Roaring Twenties produced no fewer than three such extravaganzas: the 1924 trial of the college-age "thrill killers," Leopold and Loeb; the 1926 trial of Mrs. Frances Hall for the double murder of her minister husband and his choir-girl mistress, Eleanor Mills; and the Ruth Snyder–Judd Gray "Double Indemnity" trial of 1927.

As it happens, another sensational homicide took place in 1927, one that bore striking similarities to the brutal slaying of Albert Snyder by his brassy wife and her milquetoast lover boy. While the Snyder-Gray trial remains one of the defining events of the era, however, the subsequent case—though it generated nationwide coverage at the time—has been largely forgotten, relegated to a mere footnote in the official histories of Jazz Age crime.

IT WAS A scene straight out of a Southern Gothic melodrama, one of those lurid B-movies set in the Louisiana swamps. On the night of July 6, 1927, three local trappers were rowing a small skiff around Lake Poularde, deep in the heart of Cajun country. The men, armed with spears and a flashlight, were gigging frogs to sell to New Orleans restaurants.

Suddenly, as they navigated close to the bank, their boat bumped into something odd, "an obstacle apparently snagged by a submerged tree branch." Whatever it was, its stench left no doubt that it was dead.

One of the men beamed the light on the object, revealing (in the words of historian Charles M. Hargroder) "a mass of what he first took to be the water-whitened carcass of an animal." As the men peered closer, they were startled to see that the carcass was a partially clothed human body, its face eaten away by crabs, its belly slit open, its neck and feet weighted with heavy metal brackets—150-pound railroad angle irons.

Hastening back to town, the men notified Chief Louis Blakeman of the Morgan City police, who immediately roused the assistant parish coroner, Dr. C. C. DeGravelles. Before long, a small flotilla had returned to the scene and wrangled the loathsome remains onto one of the boats. The corpse was transported to the local mortuary. Thanks to the work of the crabs, the man's face was so disfigured that he could be identified only by his distinctive club-shaped thumbs. He was Jim LeBoeuf, general manager of the local utility company, Morgan City Power & Light, and a pillar of the community.

Though LeBoeuf had been missing from his home for five days, no alarms had been sounded. When family members inquired about his sudden absence, his wife, Ada, had breezily told them that he was "probably on an out-of-town trip." From the condition of the corpse, however, it was clear that LeBoeuf had been floating in the brackish lake all that time. He had been killed by two shotgun blasts to his left side, one just below the heart, then slit "from gullet to groin" by someone apparently skilled in field-dressing game.

Exactly how a corpse weighted with three hundred pounds of iron had floated to the surface was at first unclear, though the explanation soon became apparent. "The body had not floated at all," writes one chronicler of the case. "Enormous floods on the Mississippi River in 1927 caused the water level in the lake to rise. The body, thrown into what was at the time deep water, was in shallow water when the river receded." There were those, of course, who saw the matter in very different terms, as an act of divine providence: God's hand abating the floodwaters to bring the dreadful deed to light.

* * *

IT DIDN'T TAKE long for suspicion to fall on Ada, a thirty-eight-year-old homemaker who, though no great beauty, "had that certain something" (in the words of one male observer). To casual acquaintances, she and Jim "were comfortably wed"—a respectable, modestly well-off couple occupying a decent two-story clapboard house in a good part of town. Their more intimate friends, however, knew that the marriage was troubled. Jim was a wildly jealous husband, resentful even of Ada's female intimates, and he'd been known to express his displeasure with his fists.

In recent years, his deepest suspicions had focused on one person in particular: the LeBoeufs' family doctor, Thomas E. Dreher. Married with three children, Dreher was one of Morgan City's "sterling citizens," as the papers described him—a "leading physician" who, in addition to his medical practice, was co-owner of the town's largest drugstore, played a prominent role in civic affairs, and (as the papers proudly noted) had "once held high office in the Ku Klux Klan."

Dreher and LeBoeuf had, in fact, been close friends at one time, going off together on frequent hunting and fishing expeditions. A few years before LeBoeuf's gutted corpse was found floating in Poularde Lake, however, the two had a major rift. Its cause was an anonymous letter sent to Dreher's wife. "Two nights ago," it read, "there was a lady and a man in that empty shack in the bayou. One of them was Ada LeBoeuf and the other was your husband."

In her shock and confusion, Mrs. Dreher—a "petite, dignified" woman utterly devoted to her husband—made an unfortunate decision. Not knowing what to do or where to turn, she paid a visit to Jim LeBoeuf's office and showed him the letter. It was a fateful act, setting off a chain reaction that would climax with the destruction of three lives.

Given LeBoeuf's hotheaded temperament, it's no surprise that he was driven to new heights of jealous fury. Confronting Ada with the note, he reportedly laid into her with his fists and threatened to kill both her and her lover if the story proved to be true. Neighbors would later testify that, in the throes of his obsession, "he forced his wife to drive their automobile through the back streets of town while he crouched in the back seat with a shotgun, waiting for the hapless physician to speak to her." It is certainly true that at one point he approached Chief Blakeman and "insisted that Dreher be prevented from driving past his home." When Blakeman pointed out that "he could not keep Dreher off a public street," LeBoeuf vowed that if the physician ever attempted to contact his wife again, he would kill them both.

Throughout all this, Ada stoutly protested her innocence. As it happened, however, the information provided by the anonymous busybody—an unnamed "lady from across the tracks," as Ada would later describe her—was more than idle gossip. Ada and Dr. Dreher really were carrying on a secret affair. And by the summer of 1927, Jim LeBoeuf—with his constant threats and unceasing vigilance—had become an intolerable obstacle to the two illicit lovers.

While insisting to the end that her friendship with Dr. Dreher was purely platonic, Ada herself later testified that her life with Jim had been unbearable ever since Mrs. Dreher showed him the anonymous letter. "Jim went wild," she said. "Since that day, God only knows the agony I lived in. Jim forbade Dr. Dreher the house and forbade me to speak to him when he passed me on the street. My husband's mind was poisoned. He saw meanings in the simplest doings of everyday life. At last, I came to the end of my endurance. I had to have it over."

There would be various conflicting accounts of exactly what transpired on the evening of Friday, July 1, 1927. All agreed, however, that the sequence of events that culminated in the mutilation murder of Jim LeBoeuf began earlier that day when Dr. Dreher got a note from Ada informing him that she and her husband would be out boating on Lake Poularde at around 8:00 p.m. There was general agreement on another point, too: that immediately after receiving this information, Dreher paid a visit to his friend Jim Beadle.

A plainspoken, rough-hewn "man of the soil" (as the local papers described him), Beadle earned his meager keep as a hunter and trapper. He was deeply loyal to Dr. Dreher, who was known for his generosity to his less prosperous patients, often treating them without charge in particularly tough times. Word had it that his benevolence to his hunting partner Beadle extended even further—that Dreher's charity "kept bread in Beadle's kitchen and his seven children in shoes."

At around dusk on the evening of Friday, July 1—just a few hours after Ada's letter was delivered to Dreher's office—a teenager named Morris Trahan was sitting on his front porch when the doctor's automobile drove by on the way to Lake Poularde with Dreher behind the wheel and Jim Beadle in the passenger seat. Lashed to the side of the car was Beadle's green pirogue—a lightweight flat-bottomed boat resembling a dugout canoe, a standard piece of household equipment in that watery part of the country. What Trahan couldn't see, of course, was Dreher's double-barreled shotgun lying on the rear seat.

Sometime later, at approximately 8:00 p.m., Alec Comeaux—a trapper who lived in a shack on the shore of Lake Poularde not far from what the newspapers invariably identified as the "colored schoolhouse"—heard two gunshots echoing across the water. He would later testify that they occurred "about half a second apart" and that they were unmistakably made by a shotgun.

QUESTIONED BY CHIEF Blakeman on the night her husband turned up dead, Ada began by insisting that the corpse couldn't possibly be Jim's. True, she hadn't seen him for a week. She wasn't in the least bit worried, however, since "he was in the habit of leaving home every now and then without saying a word to anybody. He would go to Lafayette, Lake Charles, and over to Texas and stay there for a few days and then come back." She was "sure he would return alive and well."

Under intense questioning by Blakeman, Ada's defenses began to crumble until she had "proceeded from absolute denial" to a qualified confession that underwent several significant revisions in the course of the lengthy interrogation. Ultimately, she admitted that she had sent the note to Dreher telling him that she and Jim would be out "riding on the lake tonight." She insisted, however, that she was merely arranging a kind of peace parley on neutral territory—trying to get the two men to have a civilized talk and "fix this up friendly," as she put it.

On the night of the murder, she and Jim "paddled out the old shell road. We had gone about fifty feet on our way back when another boat approached." Seated inside were Dreher and Jim Beadle. "The other boat came up about four feet. The doctor said, 'Is that you, Jim?' My husband said, 'Yes, who is that?' The doctor said, 'This is me—Doc. Your wife told me to meet you here and we would be friends again.' 'Friends, hell,' my husband said, 'you've got that damned Beadle with you,' and fired a shot. Two shots came from the other boat and my husband fell dead. Jim Beadle, I judged, fired them. In my excitement, I just turned my boat around and came on back and never said a word about it to anyone." The next morning, when her children inquired as to their father's whereabouts, she told them that he had "rushed out of town after a violent quarrel" but would return home in a few days, after he had cooled off.

AFTER LOCKING ADA up in the local jail, officers proceeded to the home of Dr. Dreher, who met them with a combination of anguish and relief.

"I have been expecting you for a week," he said when presented with the arrest warrant they carried. "I knew you would come and get me. This is hell. I have been in hell. Oh, why didn't I do what I started out to do?—shoot my head off. I waited too long."

Leading the sheriff out of earshot of his stunned wife and children, Dreher spilled out the story he would stick to until the end. Jim LeBoeuf, he claimed, had threatened his life "so often that I have been in fear at all times. I have kept my home in darkness for fear he would take a shot at me through the windows at night."

After receiving Ada's note a week earlier, he had gone and "told Jim Beadle that LeBoeuf meant to kill me, and Jim Beadle said to me, 'You bring that son of a bitch out somewhere and I will put him away where he will never bother you or anyone else so long as you live.'

"I did not kill Jim LeBoeuf," Dreher insisted. "Jim Beadle killed him. But he did it all for me, and I am just as guilty as he is."

JIM BEADLE WAS the last of the trio to be picked up that night. In stark contrast to Dreher, who had broken down at his first sight of the lawmen, Beadle maintained a stoic silence, steadfastly denying any knowledge of the brutal affair. Taken to the jail for further questioning, he was brought face-to-face with the physician, who advised him that the "jig was up" and that he "might as well tell the whole thing."

"I don't know what you're talking about," Beadle blandly replied. In a nation that equates true manhood with reticence, Beadle would win many admirers, who saw him as an epitome of the "strong, silent" workingman, unshakably loyal to his more privileged benefactor. In the end, however, that loyalty would prove to have its definite limits.

* * *

IN AN AGE that couldn't get enough of tabloid-ready sex and murder scandals, the press had a field day with the story. For a full month, the New Orleans *Times-Picayune* plastered its front pages with blaring headlines on the case, proclaiming it "one of the most brutal crimes in Louisiana history" and the South's very "own Snyder-Gray love murder." Reporters scrambled to come up with lurid nicknames for Ada, labeling her "Louisiana's love pirate," "the bucolic Lorelei," "the small-town Cleopatra," "the automobile-riding vampire," and "the siren of the swamps." The public was whipped into a state of such frenzied excitement that within two weeks of the arrests, a seven-verse song about the murder began making the rounds. Catchily titled "Boat Riding Mamma, Don't You Try to Angle-Iron Me," its chorus went like this: "Sweet piroguing mamma, don't you/Angle iron me."

Local residents were "almost giddy" at the prospect of the trial, widely expected to be the most sensational criminal proceedings in the history of the state, an event that, as the *Times-Picayune* put it, would rival "the Snyder-Gray case in the public interest" and draw national attention to the sleepy town of Franklin, site of the county courthouse. By the time the trial began on July 24, 1927, every hotel room was "booked to overflowing and restaurants were geared for the onslaught" of out-of-town visitors. Though the courtroom could accommodate no more than three hundred spectators, town officials predicted that at least five thousand curiosity seekers would descend on the town—a number exceeding the entire population of Franklin.

In the event, the twelve-day trial turned out to be something of a bust, devoid of the high drama that had made both the Hall-Mills and Snyder-Gray cases such media sensations. For all its lurid potential, the case—so one reporter groused—devolved into a "drab, dull, and commonplace affair."

The biggest bombshell was dropped by Jim Beadle, who, in a bid to save his own skin, dictated a confession that was read to the jury. In it, he placed all the blame on Dreher. "The doctor asked me to go hunting, and after we started he said he was going to kill Jim LeBoeuf," Beadle claimed. "I said, 'No, don't do that,' and he said if I didn't row him, he'd kill me too. When we got on the lake and met their boat, he said, 'Jim, is that you?' 'Yes, who's that?' LeBoeuf answered. Then the doctor shot him. Dr. Dreher said, 'Let's go get that iron. I want to sink that son of a bitch in the lake.' " According to Beadle, it was Dreher who also gutted the corpse.

Taking the stand in his own defense, the doctor offered a very different version. At half past three on July 1, he testified, he had received Ada's note saying that "her husband had agreed to meet me on the lake and clear up all this foolishness in a friendly way." A few hours later, at about six o'clock, he drove to Beadle's house and asked if he "could take me out" in his boat. To Dreher's surprise, Beadle insisted on bringing along his shotgun. "I said, 'Jim what do you want with a gun?' He said, 'Times are hard and we might see an alligator and that might mean two or three dollars for its hide.' "

Rowing far out onto the lake, they came upon Jim LeBoeuf and Ada, who were in separate boats. "As we got close, I called out, 'Hello, is that you, Jim?' and he said, 'Yes, who's that?' I said, 'It's me, Doc. I got a message from your wife this afternoon that we were to meet on the lake and talk over this foolishness and be friends.' He said, 'Friends, God damn, no! You know I told you if you ever spoke to me again, I'd kill you. And there's that Beadle, too. I got the pair of you just where I want you now.' " With that, LeBoeuf had pulled out a small automatic pistol and fired a shot.

"At the same instant," Dreher continued, "Beadle grabbed his shotgun and made two shots and LeBoeuf fell in the pirogue. I said, 'Oh my God, what are we going to do?' Jim said, 'He made the first shot and there wasn't anything else to do but shoot him.' "

Dreher proposed that, "since the man was killed in self defense," they should "take him into town and turn him over to the authorities." Beadle, however, had other ideas. " 'I'll fix him so that nobody will ever find him,' he said. He said he knew where there was some angle irons and suggested that we get them and weigh him down."

After getting the angle irons, the pair "went back to the lake. Jim pulled the boat up to where he could reach the body and after he tied the irons on, he said, 'Well, there ain't anything to do but sink his body in the lake. I suppose a man's just like a deer. If a deer sinks, in just a couple of hours gas forms in the stomach and the body rises. I guess I better cut his body open so the body won't rise up.' He slit the stomach open. While he slit it, I turned my head and didn't see how he did it.' "

IN THE END, Beadle's strategy worked. Despite widespread predictions that no southern jury would send a white woman to the gallows, Ada and Dreher were both sentenced to hang, while Beadle, though convicted, was spared the ultimate penalty and given life imprisonment.

If the trial itself was disappointingly short of drama, the aftermath more than made up for that deficiency. When the Louisiana Supreme Court rejected an appeal for a new trial, public sentiment suddenly "turned in favor" of the condemned pair. "Hundreds of women in the Franklin area circulated petitions to the state pardon board and governor for clemency," while "newspapers that had previously played up the gory details of the murder began whipping up opinion to demand mercy." As historian T. Harry Williams points out in his Pulitzer Prize–winning biography of Huey Long:

> Some people who supported the demand had honest doubts about the guilt of the accused; they argued that the circumstantial nature of the evidence did not justify a death sentence. But with the majority, maudlin sympathy was the ruling emotion. The doctor and his alleged paramour suddenly became romantic figures, devoted lovers who were the victims of local jealousy and malice. The most ridiculous contention of the advocates of clemency was that Ada should not be executed because she was a white woman. No white woman had ever been hanged in Louisiana, and if one were, the Southern code of chivalry would be violated, even though the woman was guilty of murder.

Even the men who had voted for their conviction joined in the crusade. Along with other jurors, foreman L. S. Allen petitioned the state pardon board for clemency, attesting that the "death verdict had been unduly influenced by the high feelings existing at the time against" the two defendants. New exculpatory evidence was also introduced. A prison guard named Wright swore that he had overheard Jim Beadle admit to the killing. At around the same time, two crawfishermen happened upon a discarded pistol not far from the murder site. Jim LeBoeuf's eldest son, Joe, testified that it was identical to the model owned by his father. One of its chambers, moreover, had been discharged, supporting the contention of Ada and Dreher that LeBoeuf had fired first.

On December 21, 1928—the date originally set for their execution—the prisoners received the happy news that the pardon board had voted for clemency. Though "the board itself could not commute the sentence to life imprisonment, it could recommend the commutation to the governor, and hardly ever had a governor refused to follow the board's advice."

Unfortunately for Ada and Doc, they had become pawns in a nasty political power struggle. The head of the pardon board was Paul Cyr, the state's lieutenant governor and a bitter foe of Huey Long. After "several sleepless days and nights trying to figure out what to do," Long—partly out of genuine conviction but mostly to thwart his hated rival, Cyr—rejected the board's recommendation. "This was a cold-blooded murder," he announced, "and the law should be allowed to take its course." The new execution date was set for January 5, 1929.

The climax of the tragedy had all the nail-biting suspense of one of those classic prison movies that keeps the audience on the edge of their seats, wondering if the last-minute reprieve will arrive before the executioner throws the switch. No sooner had Long issued his announcement than another of his opponents intervened: Charles O'Niell, chief justice of the state supreme court. The lone dissenter in the tribunal's earlier decision, O'Niell now took it upon himself to issue a writ "directing the sheriff of St. Mary parish not to carry out the order for execution." Long was forced to grant a temporary reprieve while O'Niell's unprecedented maneuver was reviewed by the full court.

In the meantime, word reached Lieutenant Governor Cyr that Jim Beadle had undergone a change of heart and was "hysterically begging to confess." Cyr rushed to the state penitentiary at Angola to interview Beadle, only to be informed that "Governor Long had issued an order that no one could speak with the prisoner."

On January 18, exactly two weeks after O'Niell had issued his stay, the state supreme court ruled that the chief justice had "overstepped his authority in granting the earlier reprieve." Ada and Dreher's lawyers made a last-ditch effort to persuade the U.S. District Court that their clients "were now insane and should not be hanged because new Louisiana law prohibited the hanging of the insane." When this desperate bid failed, Long promptly "set the execution for February 1" and "warned the sheriff of St. Mary that, if he had to, he would call out the militia to enforce the order."

THE HANGING TOOK place, as scheduled, on Friday, February 1, 1929. Ada went first. Wearing a pink housedress, she was led to the gallows at a few minutes past noon. "Oh God, isn't this a terrible thing?" she sobbed as the hangman slipped the black hood over her head and her skirt was tied around her knees "to prevent it from parachuting immodestly when she fell." Dreher died with Christ's words on his lips: "Oh God in heaven, forgive them for they know not what they do."

The following day, a lengthy farewell note composed by Dreher on the eve of his execution and entrusted to a local reporter was released to the Associate Press. "Poor Mrs. LeBoeuf and I go to our doom tomorrow," it read in part.

> It is a bitter cup we have to drink, but we are going to face our God with our hearts washed clean of hatred. We were overruled on everything that might work in our favor when we fought to keep out of the record much that might hurt us. God knows, and I know we are both innocent, and yet we never had the benefit of the faintest shadow of doubt. It is hard not to grow bitter when you stand face to face with a shameful death you have not deserved as I do tonight. I will try not to be bitter. I have forgiven those who have lied about me, and I have prayed to God to forgive them. Mrs. LeBoeuf has done the same. We can face our God with clear consciences.

Jim Beadle spent just ten years behind bars. Released in April 1939, he died a few years later of natural causes.

[*Sources:* Charles M. Hargroder, *Ada and the Doc: An Account of the Ada LeBoeuf–Thomas Dreher Murder Case* (Lafayette: University of Louisiana at Lafayette, 2000); Marlin Shipman, *"The Penalty Is Death": U.S. Newspaper Coverage of Women's Executions* (Columbia; University of Missouri Press, 2002); Milton Mackaye, *Dramatic Crimes of 1927: A Study in Mystery and Detection* (Garden City, NY: Crime Club, 1928).]

"Rules for Murderesses"

Regarded by aficionados as the preeminent American practitioner of the true crime genre, Edmund Pearson (1880–1937) brought a highly sophisticated, often wickedly funny sensibility to his favorite subject. His macabre wit is on full display in his classic 1930 essay "Rules for Murderesses."

According to Pearson, a woman "may murder whom she likes" and get away with it, provided she takes "care to observe a few simple restrictions." This conclusion, he says, is based on his careful review of criminal history. Having surveyed several dozen cases of "more or less charming ladies" tried for murder over the span of 170 years, Pearson found that the vast majority either went "scot-free" or, if convicted, escaped "the hands of the executioner." Only a handful ended up paying "the law's highest price." These unfortunate few, he writes, came to their ill-fated end because they foolishly disregarded "one of the great rules for murderesses." These four "obvious rules" are:

1. If you decide to murder your husband, you must never act in concert with a lover.

2. It is inadvisable for a maidservant to murder her mistress under circumstances of extreme barbarity.

3. Even in the murder of a father or mother, the astute murderess will take care that no lover appears upon the scene.

4. If you commit murder for insurance money or for mere pleasure, make it wholesale. Never stop at one.

Pearson illustrates each of these precepts with various examples, from Belle Gunness, the infamous "Lady Bluebeard" of La Porte, Indiana (whose successful career of serial slaughter proves the validity of Rule #4), to Lizzie Borden (a sterling exemplar of Rule #3).

As for Rule #1, among the foolhardy women who paid the ultimate price for ignoring this fundamental "regulation" was, writes Pearson, "Mrs. LeBoeuf of Louisiana, whose name figured grimly in newspapers in 1927."

WILLIAM EDWARD HICKMAN, "THE FOX"

THOUGH THE ABDUCTION AND MURDER OF THE LINDBERGH BABY IN 1932 REMAINS the single most infamous case of its kind in American history, it was preceded by a number of sensational child snatchings, beginning with that of little Charley Ross, regarded as our country's first kidnapping for ransom.

Sometime on the afternoon of Wednesday, July 1, 1874, four-year-old Charley and his five-year-old brother, Walter, sons of a prosperous Philadelphia merchant, were playing on the sidewalk in front of their house when they were enticed into a buggy by two men who offered them candy and promised to buy them fireworks for the Fourth of July. Walter was later released. Charley was never seen again.

Three days later, Mr. Ross received the first of an eventual twenty-three crudely misspelled letters, demanding $20,000 (roughly $400,000 in today's dollars) and threatening Charley with "instant anihilation" if "yu put the cops hunting for him." Warned by authorities that paying the ransom would only encourage other kidnappings, Ross stalled for time while the Philadelphia police, aided by Pinkerton detectives, embarked on a massive—and ultimately futile—search for the missing child.

Five months after the abduction, a pair of career criminals named William Mosher and Joseph Douglas were shot while attempting to burglarize a house in Brooklyn. The mortally wounded Douglas lived just long enough to confess that he and his partner were the ones who "stole Charley Ross from Germantown." He could not, however, say where the little boy was. Only Mosher knew Charley's whereabouts. And Mosher had been slain on the spot.

Not long afterward, a third man, an embittered ex-policeman named William Westervelt, was arrested, tried, and convicted of conspiring in the kidnapping, described by the presiding judge as "the worst crime of the century." Westervelt, however, maintained his innocence to the end. Christian Ross spent the rest of his life and his entire fortune searching for his lost son. But Charley would never be found.

IN SUCCEEDING DECADES, other child abductions became nationwide sensations. In December 1900, sixteen-year-old Ed Cudahy, son of a Nebraska meatpacking tycoon, was snatched from the streets of his fashionable Omaha neighborhood by a pair of men in a buggy. The following morning, a ransom note was left on the front lawn of the Cudahy mansion. In it, the kidnappers demanded $25,000 for the safe return of Ed, threatened to "put acid in his eyes and blind him" if the money wasn't paid, and advised his father not to repeat the mistake of Christian Ross, who by refusing to "give up the coin" had "died of a broken heart."

Nine years later, another child of wealth—eight-year-old Billy Whitla, nephew of a Pennsylvania steel millionaire—was allowed to leave school with a man who claimed to be picking him up for his father. The following day, a letter arrived at the Whitla home, demanding $10,000 and leaving no doubt as to the consequences of refusal. "Dead boys are not desirable," read the note's chilling final line.

The ordeals of Ed Cudahy and Billy Whitla ended happily for both victims: the ransoms were paid and the boys released unharmed. Infinitely more tragic was the fate of Marion Parker, whose 1927 abduction—overshadowed by both the murder of Bobby Franks at the hands of Leopold and Loeb and the Lindbergh baby kidnapping—nevertheless stands as one of the most appalling cases in the annals of twentieth-century American crime.

IN LATER YEARS, after he had gained nationwide notoriety for the most sickening atrocity of his time, psychiatrists who examined William Edward Hickman—Ed, as he liked to be called—found ample evidence of madness in his family history. His maternal grandmother, Rebecca Buck, was certifiably psychotic. Convinced that her neighbors "had it in for her" and that her husband meant to poison her, she would run screaming through the fields of her Arkansas farm or huddle weeping for hours in a corner of the barn. Paul Buck, Hickman's grandfather, was known to beat his own livestock half to death during one of his frequent "mad fits" of rage.

Most unstable of all was their daughter, Eva—Hickman's mother. The torturous pain accompanying the delivery of her first child left her with a terror of pregnancy and a deep abhorrence of sex. Persuaded by her zealot father that it was her duty to obey St. Paul's admonition—"Wives submit yourselves unto your husbands as you would unto the Lord"—she gave in to her husband's conjugal demands. Each of her subsequent pregnancies only drove her further into "puerperal mania." When she found herself pregnant with Ed, her fourth son, she threatened to carve the baby out of her womb. "I am going to get it out of me," she shrieked to her husband. "I am going to take a knife and rip myself open."

Ed's premature birth in 1908 was particularly nightmarish. Eva, in labor for thirty-six hours, had to be chloroformed, and the infant—delivered in a breech position—emerged from the womb black and apparently stillborn. Only the heroic efforts of the attending physicians brought him to life.

Eva gave birth to one more child, a girl named Mary. Soon afterward, she attempted suicide by swallowing carbolic acid and was committed to the state insane asylum at Little Rock. Upon her release, she seemed much improved. Gradually, however, her madness returned. When her husband left for work in the morning, she would tell him that when he "came home, he would find the children all cut up and piled like cordwood in the middle of the floor." At night, sleeping in a room with all five children, he would awaken to find her standing at his bedside, a butcher knife in hand. He began to barricade the door with a chair. Eventually the situation became more than he could handle. In 1915 he abandoned the family and moved to New Mexico. At the time, his son Ed was seven.

LIVING IN CRUSHING poverty with a frighteningly unstable mother, Ed was taken under the wing of his fanatically religious grandfather. Accompanying the old man to frenzied, fire-and-brimstone tent meetings, the impressionable boy soon was infused with

298   HAROLD SCHECHTER

a burning zeal that, with his grandfather's encouragement, developed into a fierce determination to become a minister of the Gospel.

His sense of high spiritual calling did not prevent him from indulging in extreme forms of juvenile cruelty. Boyhood acquaintances would later testify to Hickman's "mania for capturing and torturing stray dogs and cats." On one occasion, he strangled the pet kitten of a neighbor girl who, even as a grown-up, vividly recalled the "apparent delight" he derived from the act.

Ed was still a preadolescent when Eva, in an effort to stave off starvation, uprooted herself and her brood and moved to Kansas City, Missouri. Her two oldest sons quickly found good-paying jobs, while Ed devoted himself to his studies. By the time he entered high school, he had become convinced that God—pictured in his mind as a rugged old revivalist with a white suit, white tie, white shoes, and "eyes that would burn a hole through you"—meant him "to become America's most influential clergyman."

From his freshman through his junior years, he was an academic star, achieving a straight-A average, while serving as vice president of the student body, editor of the school newspaper, staffer on the yearbook, and member of the debating team. During his senior year, however, he underwent a bizarre transformation. The charming and ambitious young student, admired by his schoolmates and considered a "dormant genius" by his teachers, turned into a surly and paranoid loner, cutting himself off from friends, ignoring his studies, and quitting his extracurricular activities. At the time, his acquaintances blamed this "strange reversal in attitude" on the bitter disappointment he suffered when he lost by one vote in the annual oratorical contest sponsored by the *Kansas City Star*, which he'd set his heart on winning. Forensic psychiatrists, however, would later opine that Ed's "insidious degeneration" was an early symptom of latent insanity.

Following graduation, Ed was still toying with the idea of a life in the ministry and applied to a local seminary, Park College, but he withdrew his registration before the semester began. After working at a few dead-end jobs—including a stint at a poultry house where he spent several months disemboweling and disjointing chickens—he took a part-time position at the Kansas City Public Library. There he made the acquaintance of another employee, a budding young sociopath named Welby Hunt. Despite a gap in their ages (Hunt, fourteen at the time, was four years younger than Ed), the two were soon inseparable companions. On the day after Thanksgiving,

1926—less than two months after they met—they armed themselves with handguns and robbed a downtown candy store, making off with $70.

A few days later, in the first week of December, they set off by car to Los Angeles, where on Christmas Eve, just days after their arrival, they held up a pharmacy at gunpoint. When a neighborhood patrolman happened into the store, a shootout erupted that left the proprietor, Clarence Thoms, mortally wounded. Deciding to lie low for a while, Hickman—who, like other psycho killers before and since, concealed his malevolent self beneath a clean-cut, college-boy persona—found work as a messenger at the First National Trust and Savings Bank in downtown L.A. It wasn't long, however, before his criminal compulsions asserted themselves. He began to forge small checks, using the proceeds to purchase a used motorcycle. Caught and arrested in mid-June 1927, he was tried in juvenile court and—largely because the bogus checks were for such paltry sums—let off with probation. With the stunning brazenness typical of psychopaths, he immediately applied for reinstatement to his former job at the bank. Unsurprisingly, he was rejected.

By August he was back in Kansas City, working nights as an usher at a movie theater and thinking vaguely of returning to school. He did, in fact, enroll in Kansas City Junior College but once again withdrew before attending a single class. Shortly afterward, he was fired from his job "because of unsatisfactory work." According to Hickman's later accounts, he then stole a car and embarked on a month-long odyssey that began in Chicago and took him through Detroit, Philadelphia, New York City, Indianapolis, and St. Louis, financing the trip by knocking over a succession of small shops along the way. Whatever the truth of this claim, it is certain that he was back in Kansas City by November 7, when he stole a Chrysler coupe at gunpoint from a physician named Herbert Mantz and drove it to California, arriving in Los Angeles on November 18. Over the next few weeks, he committed yet another string of drugstore holdups.

Even while engaged in this crime spree, the increasingly delusional Hickman felt infused with a renewed sense of religious vocation and resolved to reenroll in the Park College seminary. Tuition, however, was $1,500 (more than $18,000 in today's money), far more than he was able to realize from his penny-ante robberies. To fulfill his holy mission, he came up with a diabolical plan.

* * *

PERRY M. PARKER was chief cashier at Ed's former workplace, the First National Bank. Some historians of the case claim that Ed nursed a grudge against Parker for opposing his probation and denying him a second chance at his job. Others insist that Parker had no strong feelings about Ed's sentence and had nothing to do with the bank's refusal to rehire him. Indeed, Parker appears to have taken little notice of Hickman during the latter's brief stint as a messenger boy.

Hickman, on the other hand, was keenly aware of certain facts about Parker. He had learned, for example, that the chief cashier had a substantial savings account at the bank. He also knew, from her frequent visits, that Parker was the doting father of a twelve-year-old daughter named Marian, a student at Mount Vernon Junior High School.

Shortly after noon on Thursday, December 15, 1927, a nicely groomed, well-spoken young man appeared at the attendance office of Mount Vernon Junior High and introduced himself to the secretary, Naomi Britten, as a friend and co-worker of Mr. Perry Parker. The banker, he explained, had been "gravely injured in a traffic accident" and wanted his daughter by his hospital bedside.

Unbeknownst to Hickman, there were two Parker girls in attendance: Marian and her sister Marjorie. When Mrs. Britten asked which daughter he meant, Hickman—though completely caught off guard—didn't miss a beat. "The youngest," he said. Since Marian and Marjorie were twins—another fact Hickman didn't know—this was a peculiar answer. It was also odd that a critically injured father would summon only one of his girls to his side.

Still, the young man was so obviously trustworthy and the situation so urgent that the secretary dismissed whatever doubts she might have entertained. Assuming that Mr. Parker wanted Marian—the younger of his twins by a few minutes—she summoned the girl from her homeroom, where a Christmas party was under way. Repeating his story to the little girl, Hickman then led her outside to the dark blue Chrysler coupe he had stolen the previous month from Dr. Herbert Mantz and spirited her away.

WHEN MARJORIE PARKER returned home from school without her sister, her parents were perplexed, though not overly alarmed. It wasn't until the first telegram arrived at around 4:45 p.m. that terror gripped the household. "Do positively nothing till you receive special delivery letter," read the ominous message. About two hours later, at a few minutes before 7:00 p.m., a second telegram was delivered to the door. "Marian secure," it said. "Use good judgment. Interference with my plans dangerous." It was signed "George Fox."

Prostrated by the realization that her daughter had been kidnapped, Mrs. Parker was put under the care of a physician, while her anguished husband consulted with the authorities. The following morning—with police staking out the residence, patrol cars scouring the community, and descriptions of Marian's abductor distributed to telegraph offices throughout the area—a special delivery letter arrived for Perry Parker. Across the top of the sheet the word "death" had been inscribed in pseudo-Greek letters with a triangular delta substituting for "D." The letter itself read:

> Use good judgment. You are the loser. Do this. Secure 75 $20 gold certificates U.S. Currency 1500 dollars at once. Keep them on your person. Go about your daily business as usual. Leave out police and detectives. Make no public notice. Keep this affair private. Make no search. Fulfilling these terms with the transfer of the currency will secure the return of the girl.
>
> Failure to comply with these requests means no one will ever see the girl again except the angels in heaven.
>
> The affair must end one way or the other within 3 days. 72 hours.
>
> You will receive further notice.
>
> But the terms remain the same.

This time, the sender had signed with a different alias: "Fate."

There was another sheet folded in the letter, a note in Marian's handwriting. "Dear Daddy and Mother," it read. "I wish I could come home. I think I'll die if I have to be like this much longer. Won't someone tell me why this had to happen to me. Daddy please do what this man tells you or he'll kill me if you don't." Following Marian's signature was a heart-wrenching P.S.: "Please Daddy, I want to come home tonight."

Defying the advice of the police, Parker hurried to his bank and secured the money. That night, at around eight-thirty, he received a phone call. The menacing male voice on the other end instructed him to drive at once to a particular location and not "bring any police if you want to see your child alive." Parker set off immediately, unaware that he was being tailed by a pair of police cars. He waited at the designated spot for four hours, but his daughter's abductor never appeared.

The following morning, Saturday, December 17, an infuriated letter arrived from the kidnapper, who had spotted the previous night's police trap and laid the blame entirely on Parker's shoulders. "Mr. Parker, I'm ashamed of you! I'm vexed and disgusted with you!" the writer raved. "You're insane to betray your love for your daughter, to ignore my terms, to tamper with death. You remain reckless, with death fast on its way. . . . A man who betrays his own daughter is a second Judas Iscariot—many times more wicked than the worst modern criminal."

Once again, the madman had enclosed a brief, plaintive note from his little captive:

> Daddy, please don't bring anyone with you today. I'm sorry for what happened last night. We drove wright by the house and I cryed all the time last night. If you don't meet us this morning you'll never see me again.
>
> Love to all,
> Marian
>
> P.S. Please Daddy: I want to come home this morning. This is your last chance. Be sure and come by yourself or you won't see me again.

A second special delivery envelope arrived later that day, this one containing two letters from the kidnapper. Though calmer in tone than the earlier message, they were no less threatening. "Please recover your senses," the first began. "I want your money rather than kill your child. But so far you give me no other alternative . . . I'll give you one more chance to come across and you will or Marian dies." It closed by reminding Parker that he was dealing with no "common crook or kidnapper" but "with a master mind"—a boast picked up in the second letter, which began: "Fox is my name. Very sly, you know. Set no traps. I'll watch for them."

During the next few nerve-racking hours, the authorities agreed that it was best to conform to the kidnapper's demands. Parker would be allowed to go by himself to the meeting place, pay the ransom, and get his daughter back alive. Whatever clues he could glean from his contact with the kidnapper would, the law officers hoped, lead them to the criminal.

The climactic call finally came at around 7:45 p.m. The familiar voice instructed Parker to drive to the corner of Fifth Street and Manhattan Place in northwest Los Angeles. It took the banker only twenty minutes to arrive at the destination, a shadowy, residential neighborhood with little traffic and no pedestrians in sight.

He had been sitting in his parked car for only a few minutes when a blue Chrysler coupe, its headlights off, pulled up alongside him. The driver wore a handkerchief over his lower face, bandit-style. One of his hands was on the steering wheel. The other clutched a sawed-off shotgun. Beside him sat a huddled figure, tightly bundled in a blanket.

"You know what I'm here for," said the masked man, aiming the gun at Parker. "No monkey business."

"Can I see my little girl?" Parker asked.

"She's asleep," said the driver, indicating the swaddled figure in the passenger seat.

In the dim light, Parker could barely make out his daughter's face. He thought she had been chloroformed. Passing the package of twenty-dollar bills across to the masked driver, Parker waited, as instructed, while the blue coupe edged forward about two hundred feet before coming to a halt. Suddenly the passenger door flew open and his daughter was shoved into the street. An instant later the coupe roared away into the night.

Leaping from his car, Parker rushed to the inert bundle lying in the gutter and scooped it in his arms. Wrapped in the blanket was Marian's limbless and disemboweled torso, her face hideously rouged and her eyes sewn open to make it appear as if she were alive.

The following day, a stroller in nearby Elysian Park would come upon several newspaper-wrapped bundles containing Marion's severed arms and legs. Later that afternoon, her viscera would be found in another neatly wrapped package in the tall grass of the park.

News of the atrocity, trumpeted from every radio station on the West Coast and blazoned across the front pages, set off a panic among the residents of Los Angeles.

School attendance plummeted and playgrounds were deserted as terror-stricken parents kept their children at home. More than eight thousand local, state, and federal lawmen—assisted by untold numbers of outraged citizens—threw themselves into what quickly became the largest manhunt in California history. Rewards topping $60,000 (about $750,000 in today's money) were posted for the killer's arrest. Scores of suspects were hauled in for questioning. One young man who matched a published description of the kidnapper was arrested seven times in eight hours by different policemen. Another even less fortunate look-alike was nearly torn to pieces by a mob and had to be rescued by police. Tossed into jail, he was set upon by other inmates and found hanging in his cell the next morning.

In the meantime, the autopsy on the victim's butchered remains had turned up a macabre clue. Stuffed inside Marian's hollowed-out abdominal cavity was a bloody towel with a label from the Bellevue Arms apartments, off Sunset Boulevard on the fringe of downtown L.A. Descending on the building, police learned that a young man calling himself Donald Evans had occupied rooms there for the previous three weeks. A search of the apartment turned up, among other incriminating evidence, scraps of human flesh in the bathtub drain and a milk bottle with fingerprints matching those on the letters sent to Perry Parker.

By then, Hickman was long gone. After ditching the Chrysler coupe, he had carjacked an olive-green Hudson sedan and headed north. On the afternoon of Thursday, December 22, a week after the abduction, his vehicle was spotted by sharp-eyed police officers in Pendleton, Oregon, and pulled over after a high-speed chase. There was a sawed-off shotgun on the seat beside the driver and a suitcase stuffed with the ransom money in back. Taken into custody, Hickman reportedly wondered aloud if he "would be as famous as Leopold and Loeb."

EXTRADITED TO CALIFORNIA, Hickman made a full confession on the train carrying him back to L.A. Marian, he explained, "did not hesitate" to accompany him when he showed up at her school with the trumped-up story about her father's accident. It was not until he had driven her out to Glendale that he "stopped the car on a quiet street" and "told her that she had been deceived." Explaining that he "would have to hold her for a day or two and that her father would have to give me $1500," he proceeded to blindfold the girl and bind her hand and foot.

"She did not cry out or even attempt to fight," said Hickman. "She pleaded with me not to blindfold her or tie her and promised not to move or say anything. I believed her and took off the blindfold and the bandages from her arms and ankles."

As Hickman headed back to Los Angeles, Marian "sat right up in the seat beside me and talked in a friendly manner." By evening, they were having such a "jolly time" that—after sending out the initial warning letters and telegrams to Perry Parker—Hickman took his little captive to the movies. "Marian enjoyed the picture and we both laughed very much during the vaudeville which followed the picture."

William Hickman handcuffed to Detective Raymond of the LAPD. (© *Bettmann / Corbis. Used by permission.*)

Hickman drove her back to the Bellevue Arms and smuggled her into his apartment, where she promptly fell asleep on the couch while he retired to his bedroom. He awoke the next morning to find the little girl sobbing. He consoled her by "telling her that she could write a letter to her father and that I would also." After going out to post the letters, he returned with the newspapers. Tickled by her newfound celebrity, she kept "looking at her picture and reading the accounts of her abduction."

When she complained about feeling cooped up, Hickman "promised to go out driving again." Leaving around noon, they drove all the way out to San Juan Capistrano. On the way back, Hickman stopped to place several phone calls to Perry Parker and arrange for the ransom payment. After spotting the police trap, however, Hickman had headed back to the Bellevue Apartments. "Marian sobbed a little because she couldn't go home that night, but she saw everything and was content to wait till the next morning."

The next day, Hickman had Marian "write to her father that he must not try to trap me or something might happen to her." Though she was aware that in his own letters to her father Hickman had threatened to kill her, she didn't take the threats seriously. "She knew I didn't mean it and was not worried or excited about it," said Hickman. "In fact, I promised Marian that even though her father didn't pay me the money, I would let her go back unharmed. She felt perfectly safe."

When Hickman made that promise on Saturday morning, December 17, he was entirely sincere. It took him by surprise, therefore, when, as he was on his way out to mail another letter to Perry Parker, he was "completely gripped" by the "intention to murder." Grabbing a dish towel from the kitchen, he returned to Marian, who was tied to a chair, then "gently placed the towel about her neck and explained that it might rest her head." Before she "had time to doubt or even say anything," Hickman "pulled the towel about her throat and applied all my strength to the move. She made no audible noise except for the struggle and heaving of her body during the period of strangulation, which continued for about two minutes."

His exertions having left him somewhat sweaty and disheveled, Hickman washed his face, combed his hair, and straightened his clothing. He then left the building and proceeded to the nearest drugstore, where he purchased rouge, lipstick, and face powder, explaining to the salesgirl that he was purchasing the cosmetics for his sister. Back in the apartment, he set about dismembering the child's corpse for easy disposal, applying the techniques he had learned back in Kansas City while working in the poultry house.

Stripping the body, he carried it into the bathroom and laid it facedown in the tub, head over the drain. He then slit the girl's throat with a butcher knife, turned on the water, and returned to the kitchen for a snack of sardines and crackers while the blood drained from the carcass.

Returning to the bathroom, he stripped down to his undershorts and went to work on the body with a set of "improvised surgical instruments"—the butcher knife, a pocket knife, a kitchen fork, an icepick, and a package of razors. He began (in the words of Hickman's defense lawyer, Richard Cantillon, who would go on to write a powerful account of the case) by effecting "a disjunction from the body of the arms at the elbows and the legs at the knees. Then he cut an opening in the abdomen, removing the viscera. The odor from the entrails made him sick to his stomach and he vomited into the toilet bowl."

After standing by an open window in the living room until his "stomach settled down," he returned to the bathroom and wrapped the viscera in a "thick newspaper bundle." He then went back to butchering the body. As he sawed through the backbone,

> the upper portion of the body jerked violently, nearly throwing itself out of the tub. Hickman was momentarily shocked but when he recalled seeing chickens jump high in the air on being decapitated, he dismissed his fright with the idea that this strange action of the torso had some relation to severing the spinal cord. When all the blood was washed from the hair, the torso was removed and wiped dry. Then all available towels were tightly packed into the cavity of the torso to effect rigidity. Hickman, gently cradling the head to protect it from becoming disconnected, removed the upper portion of the torso into the living room and sat it upright on the davenport.

After wrapping the severed limbs in newspapers, Hickman thoroughly scrubbed the bathroom floor, washed out the tub, and took a warm bath. Once he was dressed, he "picked up the cosmetics and with the ineptitude of an amateur beautician, applied the rouge, lipstick, and face powder to the dead face. He slipped her school dress over the head and torso, carefully pinning it so it would remain in place and cover the wound on the throat." As a final touch, he sewed open her eyelids with two fine strands of picture wire, "brushed and fixed Marian's hair in a ponytail, held in place with her hair ribbon, tied in a neat bow.

"The entire effect," observes Cantillon, "was quite lifelike."

HICKMAN'S THIRTEEN-DAY TRIAL, which opened on January 25, 1928, drew hordes of curiosity seekers, including a few Hollywood celebrities. Roughly one hundred journalists were also in attendance, among them Edgar Rice Burroughs, creator of Tarzan, who had been hired by the *Los Angeles Examiner* to cover the proceedings and whose controversial commentary was syndicated in Hearst newspapers across the country. A devotee of the dangerously crackpot theory of eugenics—the belief that the human species can be improved by eliminating genetic undesirables—Burroughs saw Hickman as a type of "instinctive criminal," a born "moral imbecile" whose execution would remove "a potential menace to the peace and happiness of countless future generations, for moral imbeciles breed moral imbeciles, criminals breed criminals, murderers breed murderers just as truly as St. Bernards breed St. Bernards." In Burroughs' view, the psychiatrists who testified that Hickman was insane were even crazier than the defendant.

In the end, the jury shared his opinion of Hickman's mental state, finding him guilty of first-degree murder after deliberating for all of forty-three minutes. Days later, in a separate trial, Hickman and Welby Hunt were found guilty of murdering pharmacist Clarence Thoms during the drugstore holdup in December 1926.

Hickman spent eight months on San Quentin's death row while his appeals made their way through the courts. During that time, he converted to Catholicism and—proclaiming himself a "contrite and humble sinner"—wrote apologetic notes to his victims' families.

His hanging, on October 19, 1928, was a grisly affair. As he plunged through the trap, his head struck the side of the gallows. Instead of dying cleanly with a snapped neck, he "hung there, violently twitching and jerking" as he slowly strangled to death. The spectacle was so ghastly that three witnesses fainted, "toppling from their wooden chairs."

[*Sources:* Christian K. Ross, *The Father's Story of Charley Ross, the Kidnapped Child: Containing a Full and Complete Account of the Abduction of Charles Brewster Ross from the Home of His Parents in Germantown, with the Pursuit of the Abductors and Their Tragic Death; the Various Incidents Connected with the Search for the Lost Boy; the Discovery of Other Lost Children, Etc. Etc.* (Philadelphia: Joseph E. Potter and Company, 1875); Paula S. Fass, *Kidnapped: Child Abduction in America* (Cambridge, MA: Harvard University Press, 1997); Milton McKaye, *Dramatic Crimes of 1927: A Study in Mystery and Detection* (Garden City, NY: Crime Club, Inc., 1928); Kurt Singer, *Crime Omnibus* (London: W. H. Allen, 1961); Richard H. Cantillon, *In Defense of the Fox: The Trial of William Edward Hickman* (Atlanta, GA: Droke House/Hallux, 1972); Michael Newton, *Stolen Away: The True Story of California's Most Shocking Kidnap-Murder* (New York: Pocket Star Books, 2000).]

Cashing In

Nowadays, when a notorious criminal is captured or killed, the heroes responsible for taking him down can expect, at most, their proverbial fifteen minutes of media fame. The situation was different in the pre-TV past. Back then, when the public had no other way of seeing such prodigies or hearing the thrilling accounts of their exploits, these instant celebrities could make good money by appearing live onstage.

The most famous example was Jesse James' assassin, Robert Ford, who, for several years after shooting his former gang leader in the back, re-created the moment in a touring show called *The Outlaws of Missouri*. Forty-five years later, a pair of old-fashioned lawmen named Tom Gurdane and C. L. "Buck" Lieuallen briefly found themselves in theatrical demand after nabbing the most infamous criminal of the day, William Edward Hickman.

A rugged westerner who, when not in uniform, favored classic frontier garb—"cowboy boots, fringed leather jacket, and sombrero"—Gurdane had served as police chief of Pendleton, Oregon, since 1917. On Thursday, December 22, 1927, after learning that the fugitive had been spotted in a nearby town, Gurdane enlisted the help of state highway patrolman Lieuallen, a former professional bronco buster, amateur wrestling champion, World War I veteran, and future five-term state legislator.

With Lieuallen behind the wheel of his police car, the two men drove twenty miles to the outskirts of Echo, where they parked on the side of the main road. When Hickman's stolen Hudson roared past a short time later, the men switched on the siren, chased him down, and arrested him at gunpoint.

Such was the public's fascination with the infamous "Fox" that, a week after his capture, newspapers announced that Gurdane and Lieuallen had signed a contract to appear on the vaudeville circuit, beginning with matinee appearances at the Pantages Theater in Los Angeles. Their salary was reported as $5,000 a week (approximately $62,000 today) with a fourteen-day guarantee and "an option of continuing for a longer period."

VI

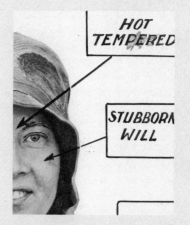

DEMONS OF THE
DEPRESSION

PEARL O'LOUGHLIN, WICKED STEPMOTHER

A S EVERYONE KNOWS, FAIRY TALES ARE FULL OF WICKED STEPMOTHERS, FROM THE black-hearted shrew of "Cinderella," who treats the title character like a galley slave, to the wicked queen of "Snow White," who plots against the young heroine's life, and the greedy wife of "Hansel and Gretel," who persuades her weak-willed husband to abandon the two siblings in the forest. Perhaps scariest of all is the villainess of "The Juniper Tree," who—after decapitating her stepson with the heavy lid of an iron chest—chops up his body, bakes it into a meat pie, and feeds it to his father.

Of course—as psychoanalytic critics assure us—these nightmarish creatures are figures of pure infantile fantasy, rooted in childhood fears of maternal rejection. Such monsters, they argue, couldn't possibly exist outside the pages of the Brothers Grimm. Unfortunately, criminal history proves otherwise. As the 1930 case of Pearl O'Loughlin demonstrates, fairy tales really can come true. And not in a good way.

AT THE HEIGHT of her notoriety, when accounts of her crime dominated the regional newspapers, one eminent psychologist diagnosed Pearl O'Loughlin with the same character flaw that afflicted the evil queen in "Snow White": "overweening vanity." And it is certainly true that the thirty-one-year-old wife and mother took inordinate pride in her

OVERWEENING VANITY

HOT TEMPERED

ABOVE THE AVERAGE of HER CLASS in INTELLIGENCE

STUBBORN WILL

PRONE TO JEALOUSY

AMAZING VITALITY

Character analysis of murderess Pearl O'Loughlin
(© *Stanley B. Burns, M.D. and The Burns Archive.
Used by permission.*)

appearance and the impression it made on others. A tall and slender redhead with big dark eyes and a brilliant smile, she was—as one contemporary reported—"famous in her Denver neighborhood for her good looks."

She and her eight-year-old son, Douglas—the offspring of her failed first marriage—had moved into the neighborhood in January 1929 when she wed for a second time. Her new husband, city detective Leo O'Loughlin— "one of the ace sleuths of the Denver police department"—had his own child from an earlier marriage, a pretty, blue-eyed ten-year-old named Leona. The four lived in a modest house on Tremont Street, which they shared with Leo's bachelor brother, Frank.

The union of Leo and Pearl was troubled from the start. Within months of their wedding, they were already quarreling so bitterly that on at least three occasions, Pearl—screaming threats of divorce—stormed out of the house with Douglas in tow and didn't come back for several days.

She also had problems with her brother-in-law, Frank. After one particularly nasty argument between them, a mysterious fire broke out in Frank's bedroom closet, scorching much of his clothing. Though Pearl professed innocence—the garments, she claimed, had burst into flame as a result of "spontaneous combustion"—Frank would have nothing more to do with her and stopped taking his meals with the family.

On the evening of Tuesday, October 14, 1930, during a relatively tranquil time in the household, Pearl prepared a special supper for Leo and the children. Precisely what she served is a matter of dispute. Some accounts describe the main dish as lamb chops, others as fish. All agree, however, that it was accompanied by roasted potatoes, plus a big bowl of rice that Pearl carefully placed on the table between her husband and stepdaughter.

Leo, a strapping six-footer, helped himself to two heaping mounds of the rice. At Pearl's urging, little Leona also ate a hearty portion. When Douglas, however—after polishing off his meat and potatoes—held out his plate for some rice, his mother declared that he had eaten enough and refused to serve him any. She herself did not touch the rice.

Shortly after dinner, at approximately 6:50 p.m., Leo—who'd been assigned to the night shift—left for central headquarters. He got home around midnight, slept fitfully, and awoke with what felt like a bout of food poisoning. Despite the cramps and nausea, he headed to work around 7:00 a.m. By midmorning, however, he was feeling so ill that he returned home.

No sooner had he walked in the door than Pearl informed him that something worrisome had happened. Leona was nowhere to be found. Normally, the little girl arose, ate a solid breakfast, bid her stepmother goodbye, then went off to school in the company of her friend Betty Scott, who lived across the street. That morning, however, Pearl had not seen Leona at all.

Though not excessively alarmed, Leo was concerned. His daughter was a creature of habit, not the kind to dash off on an empty stomach or without a word of goodbye. Fighting back his sickness, he telephoned the Cathedral School and asked if Leona was there. The nun who answered told him to hold while she checked. She was back in a few moments with unsettling news. The little girl had not appeared in class that morning.

Putting in a call to Betty Scott's parents, Leo learned that, after waiting as long as possible for Leona, Betty had gone off to school by herself that morning. His anxieties intensifying by the moment, he telephoned around the neighborhood. No one had seen his daughter.

By then, Leo was seriously worried. True, children sometimes ran away from home in a snit. But as far as he knew, Leona had been in a perfectly happy mood.

Sick as he felt, Leo rushed back to headquarters, where he informed his superior, Captain Albert Clark, that his daughter was missing. Though Clark believed there was no cause for panic—perhaps, he suggested, the child was just playing hooky—he ordered his dispatchers to spread the word about Leona.

It wasn't long before one of Leo's colleagues, a detective named Clarence Jones, called in with a disturbing report. Going from door to door in the O'Loughlins' neighborhood, he had come upon a fellow named Amos Johnson, who testified that while lying awake the previous night, he had heard a "muffled scream," followed immediately by the "racing hum of an automobile." The noises, said Johnson, had come from the direction of the O'Loughlin home.

For Captain Clark, Johnson's testimony put a much more serious complexion on the case. The previous decade had witnessed a rash of high-profile child abductions (a terrifying trend that would culminate in 1932 with the Lindbergh baby kidnapping). It now seemed as if Leona O'Loughlin might have been snatched from her home—perhaps by someone with a grudge against her policeman father.

Clark immediately contacted the police identification bureau and requested a list of all offenders arrested by O'Loughlin within the past few years. At the same time, he put out a general alarm that swiftly mobilized officers from law enforcement agencies across the state.

One person, however, was unable to assist in the search. By midafternoon, Leo O'Loughlin's intestinal sufferings had become so acute that he'd been forced to return home, where he lay moaning in bed, racked with abdominal pain.

THE DISAPPEARANCE OF Detective O'Loughlin's ten-year-old daughter—followed by his own mysterious collapse—was front-page news by the next day. Like all such highly publicized stories, this one brought a deluge of imaginary sightings, false leads, and wild reports. "Leona was seen in this mountain town and that," wrote crime reporter Ray Humphreys. "She was captive of a gypsy band in Southern Colorado; she had been spirited away by killers of the Leopold-Loeb type; she was 'spotted' in Kansas, New Mexico, Nebraska, Utah." Psychics, fortune-tellers, and the usual assortment of cranks kept the police switchboard lit up with a variety of crackpot solutions.

One presumably reliable witness, a National Guardsman named C. I. Mosier, swore he'd seen the bound and gagged little girl in the back of a gray Ford roadster zooming down a road near Golden, Colorado. The car, Mosier reported, had Arizona plates and was driven by "a male about twenty-three years old, six feet tall, weighing about 135 pounds, with dark hair and a swarthy complexion." Acting on the tip, state troopers managed to track down the suspected vehicle, only to discover that the supposedly trussed-up child in the backseat was actually a small pile of suitcases with a white sweater tossed over it.

In the meantime, Leo's health had been steadily deteriorating. By Friday morning, his condition was so dire that he was rushed by ambulance to St. Joseph's Hospital. He was still being examined by the admitting physicians when his missing daughter was finally found.

It was a grocer named William McLeod who made the discovery. McLeod, who worked near Berkeley Park in the northwest section of Denver, was out for an afternoon stroll by the lake when he spotted a small body, garbed in a schoolgirl uniform, floating facedown in the water. He phoned police headquarters immediately. Within minutes, a small fleet of vehicles—including a squad car, an ambulance, a fire department rescue truck, and an automobile carrying the coroner, George Bostwick—were racing to the scene. No sooner had they arrived than the body was fished from the water and positively identified as Detective O'Loughlin's daughter.

Bostwick's preliminary examination indicated that the girl had not drowned. She had apparently been beaten on the head with a blunt instrument, then suffocated to death before being dumped in the lake.

Leo was in such bad shape that the doctors thought it best to withhold the news from him. Pearl was the first to be informed. Escorted to headquarters, she was ushered into the office of a grim-faced Captain Clark, who told her that her stepdaughter had been located.

"Oh, is she dead?" Pearl responded.

Clark confirmed that the child's corpse had been found in Berkeley Park Lake.

"Poor little dear," said Pearl.

Despite her weirdly blasé reaction, suspicion did not immediately alight upon Pearl. Clark still held to the belief that the child had been killed by one of Leo's gangland enemies. He began to change his mind when the full autopsy results came in. An analysis of the contents of Leona's stomach revealed that the little girl had ingested several spoonfuls of ground glass on the night of her death.

Almost simultaneously, Clark received a startling report from the hospital, where Leo lay alive and suffering. In an effort to determine the cause of Leo's illness, his stomach had been pumped. It, too, contained a quantity of ground glass.

Questioned from his hospital bed, Leon recalled that, at dinner on Tuesday evening, he and his daughter had been the only ones to eat rice. Very quickly the murder

investigation shifted focus from the hypothetical kidnapper to the person who'd prepared the meal—Pearl.

A search of the O'Loughlins' kitchen turned up particles of crushed glass scattered on the floor beneath the sink. In the trunk of the O'Loughlin car, police also
found a tire iron stained with what appeared to be dried blood. A few strands of soft
blond hair, matching Leona's in length and color, were stuck to the clot.

Brought back to police headquarters for protracted questioning, Pearl put on
such a convincing display of wounded innocence that even Captain Clark began to
doubt his suspicions. Then David O'Loughlin, Leo's seventy-four-year-old father,
showed up.

Six weeks earlier—so the old man related—Leo, Pearl, and the kids came to his
Fort Collins home for Sunday dinner. After they left, David, who liked to satisfy his
sweet tooth with a few spoonfuls of granulated sugar, took some from his bowl. As
soon as he put it in his mouth, he knew something was wrong. It was as if, he told
police, "someone had put sand" in it. Curious, he took another spoonful and stirred it
into a cup of warm water.

"Some of it didn't dissolve," he said, "and when I looked at this closely, I saw it was
glass—pounded up, ground glass, maybe—and not sand."

Hoping to get to the bottom of the mystery, David had not disposed of the adul-
terated sugar. Retrieving it from his home, police turned it over to a chemist, who
confirmed that the substance was a mixture of sugar and coarsely ground glass.

And there was more. Pearl's own sister, Marybelle, came forward to testify that
on the evening of October 10, Pearl had dropped by her home with some food scraps
for Marybelle's pets—a cat and a dog. Later that night, the cat went into convulsions
and died. The dog, also stricken, expired two days later. Curious, the family vet performed a postmortem on the dog and discovered ground glass in its viscera.

Despite her continuing protestations of innocence, Pearl was taken into custody
and held without bail. Her reaction to the arrest was revealing. Most people in such
distressing circumstances would respond with anger, fear, or outrage. By contrast,
Pearl—displaying the kind of extreme narcissism characteristic of psychopathic
personalities—was primarily concerned with her appearance.

"I want the pink dress that goes with the pink coat I wore when I came down
here," she told Captain Clark from her cell on the morning after her arrest. "I want
some silk nightgowns because I could never get used to the one furnished by the city.

Above all, I want my vanity case with powder, rouge, mascara and lipstick. You'll find it in the upper drawer of the dresser in my room at home."

In an effort to wrest a confession from her, authorities resorted to various tactics. Shortly after her arrest, for example, she was brought to the city morgue and interrogated in full view of Leona's corpse—a gambit that elicited a few crocodile tears from Pearl but no admission of guilt. Police also planted a female informant in her cell, but to no avail. Apart from a few tantalizing hints—"I could tell you things but I won't," Pearl remarked at one point—she remained tight-lipped about her stepdaughter's death. "I got as chummy with her as I could," the informant reported to Captain Clark, "but I didn't even get the time of day from her."

Beginning at around 10:00 p.m. on Wednesday, October 22, Clark, his patience at an end, subjected Pearl to a brutal six-hour grilling at the climax of which—so he announced—"she cracked. She admitted responsibility." In truth, Pearl's "confession" consisted of little more than a few vague and disjointed remarks: "I have done a great wrong," "I alone am to blame," "When you get ready to hang me, I'll tell a priest everything." By the following afternoon, she had already recanted, telling Clark that she had only "made the statements to get away from you and get some sleep."

Public opinion remained bitterly divided on the question of her guilt. For every person who saw her as a monster there was someone else convinced that the Denver police—unable to catch the real killer—were railroading Pearl. One family friend claimed that Leona hadn't been murdered at all. Describing the girl as an "impulsive," "quick-tempered," and "queerly morbid" child who resented the uniform she was forced to wear to school, this woman insisted that Leona had committed suicide—a theory undermined only by the victim's head wounds, the cause of death, and the fact that ten-year-old girls rarely kill themselves because they are unhappy with their clothing.

"The Ground Glass Murder Case" (as the tabloids dubbed it) came to trial on November 28. An enormous crowd of curiosity seekers turned out for a glimpse of Pearl, who basked in the attention. Escorted into the courthouse, she flashed her dazzling smile at the mob of cameramen assembled at the entrance. "Go ahead boys," she said breezily, "take my picture if you want to." Seating herself at the defense table, she made sure to keep her skirt hiked above her knees, giving the jurymen an eyeful of her shapely, silk-clad legs.

During the week-long trial, the district attorney built a strong circumstantial case, exhibiting, among other damning pieces of evidence, the bloodstained tire iron found in the trunk of the O'Loughlins' car and the crushed glass removed from Leona's stomach. Pearl was ably defended by a prominent Denver attorney, John Keating, who persuaded the judge to bar any testimony relating to her confession on the grounds that it had been wrung from her under duress. Pearl, Keating argued, had absolutely no motive for the crime; it was her traditionally reviled role that had led to her persecution.

"Everyone is prejudiced against a stepmother," he told the jurors. "There has been a mad rush to convict Pearl O'Loughlin. Everyone said, 'That stepmother did it. Get that stepmother,' and the police and everyone else went after the stepmother."

For all his skill and ingenuity, however, Keating couldn't repair one of the most damaging holes in Pearl's story: her inability to account for her whereabouts between 7:00 and 10:30 p.m. on Tuesday, October 14—the hours when, according to expert witnesses, Leona was murdered and dumped in the lake.

It took the jury less than two hours to convict her. Pearl was sentenced to life imprisonment at hard labor. By the time she was removed to the Colorado State Penitentiary, she had been divorced by Leo, who had made a full recovery. The newly single, ruggedly handsome detective was besieged by letters from female admirers, offering themselves as replacements for Pearl. As far as marriage went, however, Leo—as he told an interviewer—was "all through. Since my last experience, I am no longer matrimonially inclined."

[*Sources:* Lee Casey, ed., *Denver Murders* (New York: Duell, Sloan and Pierce, 1946); Betty L. Alt and Sandra K. Wells, *Mountain Murders: Homicide in the Rockies* (Indianapolis, IN: Dog Ear Publishing, 2009); Frances Melrose, "Ramsey Case Reminiscent of 1930 Denver Murder," *Rocky Mountain News* (May 18, 1997, 22D); Stanley Burns, *News Art: Manipulated Photographs from the Burns Archives* (New York Burns Archive Books, 2009).]

Can Ground Glass Kill?

If murder mysteries and crime dramas are to be believed, finely ground glass is invariably lethal when used as a food additive. In "The Perfect Murder," for example—a classic episode of the old *Alfred Hitchcock Presents* TV series—two greedy French brothers plot to dispatch their elderly aunt (and inherit her fortune) by mixing pulverized glass into her dinner. More recently, an episode of the hard-hitting cable-TV prison drama *Oz* featured a character who comes to a gruesome end after being furtively fed crushed glass. In truth, however, adding a few tablespoons of freshly ground glass to a recipe is hardly a surefire way of getting rid of someone.

To be sure, swallowing large shards or splinters of glass can do serious damage to the gastrointestinal tract, "cutting the esophagus, the stomach, and the intestines with most unpleasant consequences, including death," as British anthropologist Ashley Montagu puts it. The problem is that it's very difficult to slip large chunks of glass into someone's food without arousing suspicion. Responding to a query from a crime novelist who was plotting a tale about "an abused wife who decides to kill her husband by feeding him ground glass from a salt shaker," Dr. D. P. Lyle, author of *Murder and Mayhem,* a handy forensic reference guide for mystery writers, explains that "the glass would have to be very finely ground, or the victim would notice it as he ate. As we chew, we sense even tiny pieces of gravel, sand, glass, gristle, and so forth. Salt dissolves but glass doesn't, so the food would seem gritty unless the glass was ground into a powder. But very fine glass is unlikely to cause any lethal damage to the GI tract. It would be more of an irritation, with minor bleeding if any at all."

Dr. Lyle is hardly the first to make this point. As far back as the seventeenth century, the great British scientist-philosopher Sir Thomas Browne dismissed the belief "that glass is poison" as a popular misconception—a "vulgar error," as he called it. In short, while powdered glass is not recommended as a dietary supplement, it makes for a poor murder weapon.

HARRY POWERS,
"THE BLUEBEARD OF QUIET DELL"

H E WAS, IN THE WORDS OF HIS EARLIEST BIOGRAPHER, "THE MOST FIENDISH human being of his day"—perpetrator of "one of the most monstrous mass murders in world history, the most horrible tragedy in American annals." Yet this Depression-era psycho, whose crimes appalled and titillated millions of his contemporaries, is barely remembered today. He stands as a prime example of the curious workings of infamy—the mysterious forces that bestow near-mythical status on some notorious killers while consigning others to near-total oblivion.

IN THE BYGONE days before Internet dating services, singles looking to meet prospective mates sometimes availed themselves of the services of matrimonial bureaus— mail-order matchmaking agencies that provided subscribers with lists of potential partners. One of these operations was the American Friendship Society of Detroit, which lured customers with classified ads in pulp true-romance magazines: "LONELY HEARTS—Join the world's greatest social extension club, meet nice people who, like yourself, are lonely (many wealthy). One may be your ideal. We have made thousands happy. Why not you?"

Among the many desperate love seekers who replied to this come-on was a fifty-year-old Danish-born widow named Asta Buick Eicher, resident of Oak Park, Illinois, and mother of three children—fourteen-year-old Greta, twelve-year-old Harry, and nine-year-old Annabelle. In early 1931, Mrs. Eicher—a cultivated, artistically inclined woman who had reputedly inherited a tidy sum from her late husband, a prosperous silversmith—received a letter from a gentleman who identified himself as Cornelius O. Pierson of Clarksburg, West Virginia.

Pierson, so he claimed, was a successful civil engineer with a net worth of $150,000 (more than $2 million in today's dol-

Harry Powers aka Herman Drenth

lars) and "a beautiful ten-room house, completely furnished." Because his heavy business responsibilities prevented him "from making many social contacts," he had turned to the American Friendship Society to help him "make the acquaintance of the right type of woman." From Mrs. Eicher's listing, he felt she might be a suitable partner. "My wife," he wrote, "would have her own car and plenty of spending money."

Before long, the two had embarked on a long-distance, mail-order courtship. As their epistolary romance heated up, Pierson plied the full-fleshed widow with his particular brand of sweet talk. In response to a Kodak photograph she sent, he exclaimed over how "well preserved" she was, and assured her that he "preferred plump women." He also let her know that he understood the deepest needs of the opposite sex. "The great trouble is that men are so ignorant that they do not know that women must be caressed," he purred.

Sometime in the spring of 1931, at Mrs. Eicher's invitation, Pierson made the first of several trips to her home in suburban Chicago. History does not record how she reacted to her first glimpse of her long-distance suitor. From his letters, she expected a tall, handsome, distinguished-looking gentleman with dark wavy hair and "clear blue eyes." What she saw was a bespectacled, beady-eyed, moon-faced fellow standing barely five feet seven inches tall and weighing just under two hundred pounds—"squat, pig-eyed, and paunchy," as one contemporary described him. Nevertheless, she appears to have been quite taken with him, inviting him back for several more visits in the following months and proudly introducing him to her neighbors as a man of substance, with investments in oil and gas wells, farmland, and "stocks and bonds paying from six to forty percent dividends."

Those same neighbors were the ones who notified the police when Mrs. Eicher and her children mysteriously disappeared in late June. Searching her house, detectives discovered twenty-seven letters from Cornelius Pierson. Two months passed before authorities managed to trace Mrs. Eicher's love interest to his home in Clarksburg, West Virginia. His name turned out not to be Pierson at all. It was Harry F. Powers. And far from being a wealthy bachelor with money from oil wells, dairy farms, and high-yield bonds, he was a married vacuum cleaner salesman whose wife, Leulla, supplemented their meager income by selling sundries from a little shop adjacent to their cottage.

At first Powers denied any knowledge of Mrs. Eicher. Confronted with the incontrovertible evidence of his more than two dozen love notes, he admitted that they had corresponded but insisted that he knew nothing about her disappearance.

It wasn't long, however, before investigators learned that Powers and his wife owned a small plot of land, inherited from her father, in a place called Quiet Dell, a bucolic little village nestled in the hills just a few miles outside Clarksburg. Proceeding to the property, detectives discovered a tumbledown wooden bungalow that clearly had been vacant for years. Directly across the narrow dirt road, however, stood a large, shed-like structure that appeared to be a newly built garage. The door was secured with a pair of heavy padlocks that were quickly pried open with a crowbar. The interior was big enough to accommodate three automobiles. But there were no cars inside—just a pile of cartons and trunks that turned out to be packed with the personal belongings of Mrs. Eicher and her three children.

One of the officers noticed a trapdoor in the concrete floor. Swinging it open, he was assaulted by a heavy stench wafting up from below. Beaming their flashlights into the darkness, several officers descended the wooden steps. As they swept their lights around, they saw at once that the cellar had been used as a prison. The space was divided into four cramped, soundproofed cells, each fitted with a heavy wooden door. Small, iron-grated apertures in the exterior walls allowed some weak rays of sunshine to penetrate the gloom. Otherwise, there was no light or ventilation. Nor were there any furnishings—just a bare, filthy mattress on the concrete floor of each cell.

Apart from a few bloodstained articles of clothing scattered about, there was no sign of the victims.

The corpses weren't discovered until the following day, when officers from the sheriff's department and the state police—supplemented by a road gang from the county jail—began excavating the property. Stuffed in burlap sacks, the bodies were buried in a shallow drainage ditch that ran from the rear of the garage to a nearby creek. That same evening, the diggers came upon the remains of a fifth victim. She was quickly identified as fifty-one-year-old Dorothy Lemke of Northboro, Massachusetts, who had not been seen since the previous month, when she withdrew $1,555 from her bank and went off with her mail-order fiancé, Cornelius Pierson.

Based on the autopsy results, authorities concluded that Mrs. Eicher and her children had been starved and tortured before being put to death. Evidence in the "death dungeon"—as the tabloids promptly dubbed the cellar—suggested that the mother had been hanged from a ceiling beam, perhaps in full view of her children. When the boy, Harry—who had been bound with rope and gagged with "garage waste"—had tried to struggle free to save his mother, his skull had been beaten in with a hammer. He had also been castrated. His sisters, like Dorothy Lemke, had been strangled.

Informed of these grisly finds, Powers continued to maintain his innocence, insisting that the bodies must have been buried on his property by someone else. At that point—around eight-thirty in the evening of Friday, August 28—his interrogators began applying the third degree. For the next eight hours, Powers was punched, kicked, flogged with a rubber hose, beaten with a ball-peen hammer, burned with cigarettes, and jabbed with needles. His left arm was broken and hot boiled eggs were pressed under his armpits. Finally, at around four o'clock Saturday morning, he broke. "I did it," he sobbed. "My God, I want some rest." His face badly swollen, his flabby body a mass of bruises, burns, puncture wounds, and welts, he was taken to the infirmary, where he signed a statement confessing to the murder of Mrs. Eicher and her children "by using a hammer and strangulation."

In the meantime, news of the atrocities had spread across the region. Throughout the night, hundreds of people streamed through the Romine Funeral Home in Clarksburg for a glimpse of the five victims, who had been laid out in open coffins. The following day, Sunday, August 30, an estimated thirty thousand curiosity seekers overran the "murder farm" (as the papers immediately dubbed the property), turning that sweltering summer Sabbath "into a morbid holiday." A dozen county policemen were dispatched to the scene to direct traffic, while a few enterprising locals attempted to erect a six-foot wooden fence around the "death den" and charge an admission fee. Outraged at having the site of the tragedy transformed into what one observer called a "mass murder amusement park," an angry mob tore down the barricade, "and everyone was then free to visit the death spot without charge or restraint."

Over the following weeks, investigators dug deep into the background of the man now known in the tabloids as "the Bluebeard of Quiet Dell." It quickly emerged that "Harry F. Powers" was merely another pseudonym, one of many that the lifelong criminal had employed over the years. His real name was Herman Drenth. Born in Holland in 1892, he had immigrated to New York in 1910. Over the next dozen years, he had led a rootless life, residing for brief periods in Indiana, Ohio, Virginia, Illinois, and Pennsylvania before ending up in West Virginia in 1926. During that period, he had done two stints in jail, once in Iowa for burglary, the second in Indiana for defrauding a widow of $5,400.

In 1929, he had married the former Leulla Strother of Clarksburg. A forty-one-year-old divorcée with an unfortunate marital track record, Strother had previously been wed to a local farmer named Ernest Knisely, who was arrested and tried for murder after fracturing the skull of a neighbor during a violent altercation. It was not long after she and Powers exchanged vows that he hit on his matrimonial-bureau scheme, joining a number of these mail-order services (including one that advertised itself as "Cupid's Headquarters") and securing the names of several hundred potential victims. At the time of his arrest, five letters—sealed, stamped, and addressed to women in New York, Maryland, Detroit, and North Carolina—were found in his possession.

As the investigation dragged on, rumors began to swirl that the outraged citizens of Clarksburg planned to take matters into their own hands. The crisis came to a head on the night of Saturday, September 19—nearly a month after Powers' arrest—when a lynch mob of more than four thousand men and women surrounded the jailhouse, crying out for the monster's blood. They were met by a contingent of heavily armed lawmen—the sheriff and all his deputies, the entire city police force, and a detach-ment of state troopers—who warned the crowd "to stay back or they would be shot down in their tracks." Ignoring the threat, the mob surged forward. After firing a few warning shots over the crowd, the police let loose a barrage of tear gas. In the ensu-ing confusion, eight of the rioters were grabbed and arrested, while the rest, "choking and crying from the fumes," fell back and eventually dispersed. In the midst of this uproar, Powers was hustled out the rear of the building into a waiting automobile and—escorted by a pair of police cars—driven to the state penitentiary at Mounds-ville a hundred miles away, where he would remain locked in solitary until the start of his trial.

Anticipating an insanity plea on the part of the defense, prosecutors called in a well-known forensic psychiatrist, Dr. Edwin H. Meyers, to examine Powers. After examining Powers in his cell for several hours, Meyers pronounced him legally sane, someone who "knows right from wrong," but clearly psychopathic—"possessed of an exaggerated lust to kill which dominates his entire personality." Though motivated partly by financial greed, Powers derived his deepest gratification from contemplat-ing, planning, and then carrying out his atrocities—"tormenting, torturing, and pun-ishing his victims before strangling or beating them to death." He was driven, in short, "by the mere love of killing."

Knowing how many spectators would flock to Powers' trial, county officials de-cided to conduct it in the largest venue available—the city opera house. The show opened on December 7, 1931, with the principal players—the judge and jury, the wit-nesses, the defendant and his lawyers, and the prosecuting attorneys—seated on-stage. For the five days of its duration, it drew a standing-room-only crowd who watched with rapt absorption. Powers, by contrast, sat through the proceedings with a look of utter indifference—"a bland gum-chewing observer of a drama that seemed to bore him," as one reporter wrote.

His expression remained impassive even when the jury returned a guilty verdict on the afternoon of December 11, after less than two hours of deliberation. Nor did he evince the slightest emotion three months later when he was led to the gallows in Moundsville State Penitentiary. The town itself, as the local paper reported, "had taken on a holiday festive appearance in preparation for the execution of the man whose crimes startled the world. Outside the prison a crowd gathered along the curbs. Automobiles were lined up for blocks."

Nattily dressed in a black pinstripe suit, white broadcloth shirt, and gaudy blue necktie, the condemned man ascended the scaffold with absolute composure and gazed steadily at the forty-two assembled witnesses before the black hood was slipped over his head. Asked if he had any last words, he calmly replied, "No." A moment later, at precisely 9:00 a.m. on Friday, March 18, 1932, the trap was sprung. Neck broken, he dangled from the end of the rope for eleven full minutes before the prison physicians declared him dead.

[*Sources:* Evan Allen Bartlett, *Love Murders of Harry F. Powers: Beware Such Bluebeards* (New York: Sheftel Press, 1931).]

Cover page of 1931 sheet music, "The Crime at Quiet Dell"
(*Southern Folklife Collection, Wilson Library, University of North Carolina at Chapel Hill. Used by permission.*)

"The Crime at Quiet Dell" (Version One)

Ballads about high-profile homicides continued to be created well into the twentieth century. In contrast to earlier broadsides—single sheets of crude doggerel verse often printed by the authors themselves—the more modern versions took the form of professionally published sheet music.

There have actually been two songs based on the Harry Powers case, both titled "The Crime at Quiet Dell." The first, credited to A. H. Grow and Leighton D. Davies, appeared in 1931. Appended to the printed lyrics was a note explaining that the song "was not written to appeal to the morbid fancies" of listeners. Rather, it was "intended to serve as a warning that it is folly to listen to the alluring wiles and extravagant promises of total strangers and also to remind some of the old moral, CRIME DOES NOT PAY!" Given the song's loving attention to the most gruesome details of Powers' crimes, the reader may well question this high-minded claim.

A widow and her children three
At Park Ridge, Illinois,
Was happy and contented
With two daughters and her boy;
And all was well until one day
A letter to her came
Which said she would be wealthy,
If she only changed her name.

Then came the stranger to her home
And told her of his love;
And promised her that life would be
Like heaven up above.
This winsome stranger she believed
And with him she did go,
To meet a fate so horrible
No one on earth will know.

Mid hills of West Virginia fair
Near village Quiet Dell,

A foul crime was committed there
That shocked the depths of hell.
Upon this scene a place was built
Away from sight and sound
With gallows in the upper part
And prisons underground.

The prison poor without a door
Devoid of air and light,
With deadly gas jets on the walls
Presents a gruesome sight.
The bloodstains on the prison floor,
The graveyard just outside,
When taken all together tells
Just how the victims died.

Upon this fatal summer night,
The crime-bent coward crept
Toward the prison down below
Where little Harry slept.

Then took him to the floor above,
Up through the crude trap door;
But little did he realize
His life would soon be o'er.

The poor boy's mother next he brought,
And as the trap door banged,
He said, "Now boy I've brought you up
To see your mother hanged."
The cruel rope went around her throat
And as she dangled there,
A scream from little Harry came
That rent the midnight air.

With tearful eyes the poor lad cried,
"My own life I will give.
Please have some mercy, Mister,
Let my own dear Mamma live."
The demon seized a hammer near
And struck with all his brawn,
And as his life ebbed away,
A little soul passed on.

The poor starved sisters next were brought
Upon this horrid scene,
To see their murdered loved ones
And to face their captor mean.
Upon their knees they pleaded but
He heeded not their wails;
And answered, "No, you two must go,
When dead you'll tell no tales."

The other widow, fifth in turn,
Was soon to learn her fate.
To be mourned by her loved ones

Up in Massachusetts state.
And when the sun arose next day
In splendor o'er the land,
It shone upon five shallow graves,
Wrought by a murderous hand.

The stealthy fiend in human form
From justice felt secure,
But when confronted with the truth
His nerve could not endure.
The monster of this heinous crime
Now ponders in his cell,
And shudders at the fate he'll meet
For deeds at Quiet Dell.

This is a solemn warning then
To all the ladies fair
Do not confide in strangers that
You meet from everywhere.
The moral lesson this shall teach
For one can never tell
Lest you be lured unto your doom
Like those at Quiet Dell.

"The Crime at Quiet Dell" (Version Two)

Country singer Chris Stuart first learned about the Harry Powers case from an article in *Goldenseal*, a magazine devoted to the history, folklore, and culture of West Virginia. The result was his own original song on the subject, a piece that—though composed for his 2008 CD *Crooked Man*—has the timeless feel of a traditional murder ballad. In contrast to the 1931 version, which lingers to an almost prurient degree on the sufferings of the victims, Stuart's is more concerned with the "little pig-eyed" perpetrator himself and the community outrage provoked by his atrocities.

Gather round good people, of evil I will tell,
Did you hear about the crime at Quiet Dell?
A little pig-eyed grocer is sittin' in his cell,
Did you hear about the crime at Quiet Dell?
So if you love your neighbor, go home and get your gun,
We'll drive the devil out of West Virginia in 1931.
Up around Clarksburg, there's a little piece of hell,
Did you hear about the crime at Quiet Dell?

The police sent a message from Park Ridge, Illinois,
About a widow, two girls, and a boy,
They said a Mr. Pierson might be to blame,
But down here Harry Powers is his name.
They found that little coward and they dragged him in,
They beat him through the night 'til he told them what he did,
Then he led them to the farmhouse and pointed down the well,
Did you hear about the crime at Quiet Dell?

He lured them with love letters and told them pretty lies,
They saw his fancy roadster and silk ties,
The women and their children, he brought to Quiet Dell,
And he kept them where no one could hear them yell.
So go and tell your neighbor, he's sleepin' at the jail,
We're gonna hang the evil out of Harrison County so good folks will prevail,
Up around Clarksburg, there's a little piece of hell,
Did you hear about the crime at Quiet Dell?

The Night of the Hunter

From the earliest days of our national literature, American authors have been creating fictionalized versions of notorious murders. As far back as 1798, Charles Brockden Brown—the "Father of the American Novel"—used the widely publicized case of a family annihilator named James Yates as the basis for his classic Gothic romance *Wieland*. "The Tell-Tale Heart," by Brown's admirer Edgar Allan Poe, was partly inspired by the shocking 1840 crime perpetrated by Peter Robinson, who buried his victim beneath the floorboards of his New Brunswick, New Jersey, home (see p. 41). Theodore Dreiser scored a bestseller with his 1925 masterpiece *An American Tragedy,* a thinly disguised exploration of the sensational Chester Gillette–Grace Brown drowning case of 1906 (see p. 336). Perhaps best known of all is Robert Bloch's *Psycho,* the basis for Alfred Hitchcock's landmark 1960 horror film, which sprang from the enormities of Wisconsin ghoul Ed Gein (who also served as the model for *The Texas Chainsaw Massacre*'s Leatherface and the serial killer Buffalo Bill in Thomas Harris' horror masterpiece *The Silence of the Lambs*).

Though relatively few people are aware of the fact, Harry F. Powers also inspired a best-selling book: the 1953 thriller *Night of the Hunter* by Davis Grubb, a native of West Virginia who grew up near Powers' home in Clarksburg and set his novel in Moundsville, where "the Bluebeard of Quiet Dell" was incarcerated in the state penitentiary. Set during the Depression, Grubb's novel centers on a psychopathic ex-con named Harry Powell, who passes himself off as an itinerant preacher. In his relentless hunt for $10,000 in stolen cash, he woos, weds, and murders a widowed young mother, then pursues her orphaned children, who take flight with the money.

Two years after Grubb's novel was published to great commercial success and critical acclaim (including a National Book Award nomination), a darkly brilliant movie version—directed by renowned British actor Charles Laughton and adapted by James Agee—hit the screens. Though this highly stylized film noir proved too offbeat for contemporary audiences, it is now recognized as a classic of the genre. As the Harry Powers–inspired serial sex killer Harry Powell, Robert Mitchum—his knuckles tattooed with the words "love" and "hate," his honeyed voice oozing menace—turns in one of the most chilling performances ever recorded on celluloid.

Bluebeard: Fact and Fantasy

A lovely young woman—courted by an older, physically repulsive, but enormously wealthy nobleman who has already married and lost several wives—overcomes her aversion to his off-putting looks and agrees to wed him. Not long after their marriage, he departs on a journey, leaving her the master key to all the locks in his castle and instructing her that she is welcome to enter any room except one: a "little closet at the end of the great gallery on the ground floor. Open them all," he tells her, "go into all and every one, except that little closet, which I forbid you."

No sooner has he gone, of course, than curiosity overcomes her and she sneaks into the forbidden chamber. As her eyes adjust to its gloom, she is assaulted by a fearful sight: "the floor was covered over with clotted blood on which lay the bodies of several dead women ranged against the wall." These, she realizes to her horror, are the dismembered corpses of her husband's former wives. When he returns from his journey and discovers her disobedience, he draws his cutlass and informs her that since she was so eager "to go into the closet," she will remain in there forever, taking her "place amongst the ladies you saw there." Only the timely arrival of her brothers, who ride to her last-minute rescue, saves her from becoming another butchered relic in the madman's hideous trophy room.

This is the plot of the famous story "Bluebeard," as recounted by the seventeenth-century French author Charles Perrault in his classic collection *Contes du temps passé* (*Tales of Past Times*), more commonly known as *Mother Goose's Tales*. Some scholars have traced the origin of this gruesome story to various real-life sources, particularly a sixth-century Breton chieftain known as Cunmar the Cursed, who was in the habit of decapitating his pregnant wives, and the depraved fifteenth-century French nobleman Gilles de Rais, who was ultimately hanged for the torture–murder of hundreds of young boys.

Other scholars see "Bluebeard" not as a historically based legend but as a version of an ancient and widely distributed type of folktale known as "The Bloody Chamber." *Grimm's Fairy Tales,* for example, contains a very similar story called "Fitcher's Bird," in which a young woman unlocks the one door that her wizard husband, before leaving on a brief journey, forbids her to enter in his absence. "But what did she see when she went in? A great bloody basin stood in the middle of the room, and therein lay human beings, dead and hewn to pieces, and hard by was a block of wood and a gleaming axe lay upon it." When her husband discovers her transgression, he throws her down, drags her by her hair into the chamber, cuts off her head, and "hews her in pieces so that the blood ran on the ground. Then he threw her into the basin with the rest." Another nineteenth-century folklore collection, Richard Harris Barham's *Ingoldsby Legends,* features an analogous story in ballad form, "Bloudie

Jack of Shrewsberrie," in which the heroine discovers a locked cabinet containing the amputated "wedding fingers" and severed "great toes" of the villain's earlier, butchered brides.

Whatever its source—historical fact or archetypal fantasy—the name "Bluebeard" quickly became a byword. At times it has been used facetiously to describe the kind of metaphorical lady-killer who marries and dumps a succession of women, acquiring a new, younger bride whenever he tires of the older one. At others, it has served as a synonym for the kind of homicidal sex maniac we now call a serial killer. The protagonist of the 1944 movie *Bluebeard,* for example, is a sexually warped serial strangler who preys on beautiful young women in nineteenth-century Paris, and contemporary advertisements for the film made direct comparisons between the character and Jack the Ripper.

Nowadays, the term "Bluebeard" is used in a more restricted sense to describe a specific variety of psycho killer: the type who marries and murders a succession of wives. Unlike most serial killers, who tend to target random strangers, Bluebeards are, for the most part, only interested in doing away with their mates. They differ from the usual run of serial killers in another way, too. Though they undoubtedly derive sadistic gratification from their crimes, they are also motivated by financial greed. Wedding and bumping off a series of well-heeled (or heavily insured) women is their means of maintaining an affluent lifestyle.

The first American serial killer to be tagged with the "Bluebeard" label appears to have been Dr. J. Milton Bowers, a San Francisco physician accused of poisoning three of his wives between 1873 and 1885. A decade later, the nickname was attached to Herman Mudgett, aka Dr. H. H. Holmes, the notorious Gilded Age "multi-murderer" who perpetrated an indeterminate number of homicides at the time of the great Chicago World's Fair of 1893. To his contemporaries, Holmes was a "modern Bluebeard" (as the papers called him) not only because he killed so many women—various girlfriends, mistresses, and fiancées—but also because his victims met their deaths within his Gothic "horror castle": a massive turreted building equipped with all manner of bizarre features, from soundproof vaults and secret passageways to a medieval torture dungeon and a private crematorium.

The atrocities of another so-called modern Bluebeard came to light in 1920. The perpetrator was a seemingly mild-mannered, middle-aged Californian named J. P. Watson, who over the span of just three years managed to bigamously marry twenty-one women up and down the West Coast and murder at least nine of them. Though Watson made sure that each new wife signed her property over to him as soon as they were wed, he was, by his own admission, driven less by greed than by an irresistible homicidal compulsion—an overwhelming impulse to kill that would suddenly take hold of him and leave him, once he had bludgeoned his latest victim to death, "with a great sense of mental and physical relief and an actual spirit of elation." His confession revealed him to be a classic psychopath. "At no point during the narrative of his promiscuous murders, even when giving the most harrowing and revolting details, did he show the least emotion," wrote the psychiatrists who examined him. "Moreover, he made no pretense of feeling any remorse." The sheer enormity of his crimes, combined with his bizarre personality, made him, in the view of these experts, "the most astounding case of criminality ever known in America."

[*Sources:* Maria Tatar, *Secrets Behind the Door: The Story of Bluebeard and His Wives* (Princeton: Princeton University Press, 2006); Jonathan Goodman, *Medical Murders* (New York: Carol Publishing, 1992); Ernest Bryan Hoag and Edward Huntington Williams, "The Case of J. P. Watson, the Modern 'Bluebeard,' " *Journal of the American Institute of Criminal Law and Criminology* 12, no. 3 (Nov. 1921): 348–59.]

ROBERT EDWARDS,
THE "AMERICAN TRAGEDY" KILLER

WHEN SHE TRAVELED TO THE ADIRONDACKS IN MIDSUMMER, 1906, GRACE Brown—twenty years old, single, and several months pregnant—believed that she would return a respectable married woman. She had spent the past few months at her parents' home, writing desperate letters to her boyfriend, Chester Gillette, her co-worker at an upstate shirt-collar factory. Terrified that her life would be ruined once her condition became obvious, she begged him to make her his lawful wife. "Oh Chester," she wrote, "please come and take me away. I am so frightened, dear."

Despite his professions of love, however, Chester seemed in no rush to settle down. In Grace's absence, he had happily pursued other women, including a well-to-do beauty named Harriet Benedict. When Grace got wind of his dalliances, she threatened to expose him as a heartless seducer. If her life was ruined, she wrote, *his* would be too.

Her warning seemed to work. In early July, Chester invited her to join him on an Adirondacks vacation—a trip that would culminate in their wedding. Or so Grace assumed.

On the brilliantly sunny morning of July 11, 1906, the couple arrived at the Glenmore Inn, a picturesque hotel on the shore of Big Moose Lake in Herkimer County.

After checking in under an assumed name, Chester—carrying his suitcase and tennis racket—escorted Grace down to the water, where they rented a rowboat for the day.

Precisely what happened in the following hours will never be known. At various times during the afternoon, the two were spotted on the lake by other boaters. At one point they were seen picnicking onshore. When they failed to return at sundown, Robert Morrison, who had rented out the rowboat, was not especially alarmed. Tourists often misjudged the sheer size of the lake and, finding themselves too far away to make it back before nightfall, rowed to the nearest shore and spent the night at another inn.

It was not until the following morning that Morrison, by then seriously concerned, organized a search party. Setting off in a steamer, they scoured the lake and eventually came upon the rowboat, floating upside down on the water. Peering into the depths, one of the searchers spotted a strange object caught in the weeds on the bottom. Hauled up with a long, spiked pole, it turned out to be the drowned corpse of Grace Brown, her face and head savagely battered.

Three days would pass before Chester Gillette—still going under an alias—was arrested. At first he maintained that Grace had drowned accidentally when the boat overturned. Later he changed his story, claiming that, in her despair, she had deliberately thrown herself overboard. Neither explanation, however, accounted for the terrible wounds on her face, caused—according to the autopsy report—by a bludgeoning implement, very possibly a tennis racket.

Chester's trial in November 1906 was a media sensation. Despite the uncertainties surrounding Grace's death, the jury took only six hours to vote for a conviction. Sentenced to the electric chair, Chester went to his death in March 1908, still protesting his innocence.

For all its notoriety, it seems likely that the sad tale of Grace Brown and Chester Gillette would have faded into obscurity were it not for the great American author Theodore Dreiser. For years, Dreiser had been poring over the newspapers in search of a crime that embodied his own personal obsessions with sex and social ambition. In the figure of Chester Gillette, he found the perfect raw material for his literary purposes. The result was his 1925 masterpiece *An American Tragedy*. An enormous bestseller, the book brought Dreiser the fame and fortune he had always hungered for. He became even richer when the novel was made into a major Hollywood movie, released in 1931.

* * *

THREE YEARS LATER, on the evening of July 30, 1934, Robert Allen Edwards—a clean-cut, church-going twenty-one-year-old whose striking good looks made him wildly popular with the opposite sex—took his former flame, a homely but vivacious twenty-seven-year-old named Freda McKechnie, for a drive to Harvey's Lake, twelve miles west of Wilkes-Barre, Pennsylvania.

Children of respectable local families, Freda and Bobby (as everyone called him) lived next door to each other and had spent a great deal of time in each other's company—far more time, in fact, than their parents suspected. Besides the usual small-town activities they attended together—church socials, Sunday school picnics, and the like—they had passed many a romantic hour in various secluded trysting places, including the town cemetery. Despite their age difference and the glaring disparity in their relative physical attractiveness, everyone assumed that the two long-time sweethearts would get married.

Bobby, however, had other ideas. Three years earlier he had gone off to a state teaching college, where he'd met a demure, musically inclined young woman named Margaret Crain, from a well-to-do upstate New York family. Though Margaret was, by all accounts, even plainer than Freda (one contemporary described her as possessing "about as much sex appeal as a pound of chopped liver"), Bobby found her entrancing. She, in turn, succumbed to his charms. Before long, they had embarked on a passionate affair.

With the country in the grip of the Depression, Bobby was forced to drop out of college in his junior year. Moving back in with his parents, he took a job at a coal mining company. By then, Margaret had graduated and was working as a high school music teacher in her hometown of East Aurora, New York. Separated by more than two hundred miles, they kept up a steady correspondence, exchanging frequent, fervent letters. Margaret also gave Robert money for a down payment on a car. Over the next year, he made regular weekend trips to her home, where he impressed her parents as an upstanding fellow and a fine prospective son-in-law.

What neither Margaret nor her parents knew, of course, was that during his time away from his true love, Bobby was still sleeping with the infatuated Freda McKechnie. Matters reached a crisis on July 23, 1934, when, during a visit to her family doctor, Freda learned that she was four months pregnant.

When she broke the news to Bobby the following day, he agreed to do the honorable thing and marry her. The date was set for August 1, a week away. Elated, Freda immediately broke the news to her family and began making preparations. Witnesses would later attest that they had never seen her so happy.

On Monday night, July 30, after a dinner at the McKechnie home, Bobby and Freda went out for a drive. Though the sun had set and a hard rain was falling, Freda—giddy with excitement over the impending nuptials—proposed that they go for a swim at Harvey's Lake. They arrived there shortly after nine o'clock. Parking at a spot called Sandy Beach, they changed into swimsuits and waded into the rain-pelted water.

When, about an hour later, the car drove away from the beach, Bobby was alone inside.

EARLY THE FOLLOWING morning, a local teenager, Irene Cohen, was strolling along the beach when she spotted a white rubber bathing cap bobbing at the shoreline. Looking up, she was startled to see a woman's body in an orange swimsuit floating facedown in the lake. Terrified, she alerted a lifeguard named George Jones, who ran into the water and pulled the lifeless body onto the sand.

Police were summoned, along with a local physician, Dr. H. H. Brown, who quickly determined that the woman had died not of drowning but from a savage blow to the back of her head with a blunt instrument. The murder weapon itself turned up shortly afterward when investigators, scouring the crime scene, came upon a leather-covered blackjack on the beach. By then, the victim had been identified as Freda McKechnie, whose parents had spent a sleepless night wondering why their daughter had never returned home from her drive with Bobby Edwards.

Within hours, Edwards was under arrest for suspicion of murder. At first he denied that he and Freda had been to the lake at all. After cruising around for a while—so he claimed—he had dropped Freda off in town, then gone to meet some friends whose names he could not remember. When his interrogators revealed that tire tracks found at the crime scene matched the tires on his car, he sheepishly admitted that he had been lying and offered to tell "what really happened."

He and Freda had, in fact, driven out to Sandy Beach and—despite the darkness, rain, and occasional flashes of lightning—had decided to go for a swim. After changing in the car, they "went into the water and waded to the float. I got a notion to dive. I dove. When I came up, my hand struck her under the chin. She fell backward and hit her head against the float." Stunned but still conscious, she had swum farther out into the water. A moment later, according to this wildly implausible account, Robert saw "her white bathing cap disappear. I went out for her but couldn't find her. I went back and got in my car and drove away."

On the morning after his arrest, following a visit to the crime scene, Bobby revised his story again. He admitted that he had struck Freda with the blackjack. He insisted, however, that she was already dead when he hit her.

According to this version, he and Freda had taken a rowboat out to the float. After swimming for a while, Freda had been overcome by the cold. As she stepped back into the rowboat to return to the shore, she suddenly collapsed. Bobby tried to revive her but was unable to detect a pulse or a heartbeat. Panicking, he swam back to shore and ran to his car. As he slid behind the wheel, he thought of the blackjack he carried in the glove compartment for self-protection.

"It occurred to me," he said, "that if there was some mark on Freda's body, it might make her death look like an accident and I would be left out of it. I knew Freda was pregnant. I knew she was not allowed to swim. When I returned to the boat, she was in the same position. She had not revived. I could do nothing. I put her head over my left arm and struck her on the back of the head with the blackjack. I didn't even realize what I had done, and I carried the body out to the water up to my chest and let it drop."

By this time, investigators knew that Bobby was in love with another woman and had a compelling motive to do away with Freda. When they confronted him with all the circumstantial evidence against him, he finally broke down. "I've prayed and read my Testament and my parents tell me to tell the truth. Here it is," he said. "Freda didn't faint, she didn't fall and hurt herself. I had been thinking of doing this ever since she told me she was to become a mother—because I wanted to marry Margaret Crain.

"We swam for a while," he continued. "We talked about her having a baby. The water was a little over four feet deep, and when she ducked down once, she came up with her back to me. I pulled out the blackjack quick and hit her on the back of the head. I hit her with the blackjack and then I left her in the water."

After tossing the murder weapon into the lake, Bobby had dressed and driven home, stopping along the way to buy a few chocolate bars for his mother at an all-night drugstore. Before going to bed, he had hung his swimsuit on the backyard line to dry. He slept perfectly soundly that night and went off to work the next morning as if nothing had happened.

No ONE KNOWS who first dubbed the case the "American Tragedy" murder. Ace newsmen from two Philadelphia papers, the *Record* and the *Bulletin*, both claimed to have invented the catchphrase, as did a writer for the United Press syndicate and a reporter for the *New York Times*. Very possibly all four thought of it at once, since the details of the tragedy were so strikingly similar to the plot of Theodore Dreiser's bestseller. Within days of Bobby Edwards' arrest, newspapers across the country were running front-page stories suggesting that the novel—or (as seemed more likely to many observers) the hit movie based on it—had provided the confessed killer with the blueprint for his crime.

As is the case with virtually every other work of literature or mass entertainment that has been blamed for inciting a murder, there turned out to be no truth to this accusation. By all accounts, Bobby Edwards had never read the book nor seen its cinematic adaptation. Still, the startling resemblance between the murder of Freda McKechnie and Dreiser's fictionalized version of the Chester Gillette–Grace Brown case turned the story into a nationwide sensation.

Dreiser himself saw the Edwards case as "an exact duplicate of the story which I had written" and wondered whether "my book had produced the crime." When the *New York Post* commissioned him to travel to Pennsylvania and cover the trial, he leapt at the chance. On opening day, October 1, 1934, the famed author was one of more than fifty reporters from all over the country who had flocked to the Luzerne County Courthouse in Wilkes-Barre. The scene, as he wrote, was "quite a spectacle":

> Two rooms ordinarily used for other purposes on the third floor had been closely packed with telegraph equipment and special wires. Newspapermen and women were thick as flies at the press table reserved for them. There was a shock brigade of photographers with cameras and flashlights. Over the courthouse and spinning around like wasps were moving picture and newspaper planes, with their cameras and observing photog-

raphers and reporters. Actually, the streets, the grounds, the courthouse halls, had somewhat the atmosphere of a gala event, like the entrance to a popular county fair or football game—even a Mexican bullfight.

The hundreds of sensation seekers who crammed into the courtroom hoping for a titillating show were not disappointed. The prurient high point came when the district attorney read a series of Bobby Edwards' steamy love letters to Freda McKechnie—writings so salacious that, according to one observer, they made John Cleland's pornographic classic *The Memoirs of Fanny Hill* "look like a toned-down version of *Little Women.*"

By then, Bobby Edwards—"the Playboy of the anthracite fields," as the papers now dubbed him—had recanted his confession and reverted to his claim that Freda died accidentally. His testimony failed to persuade the jury, which took less than twelve hours to convict him and sentence him to death. Still convinced that Bobby, like his predecessor Chester Gillette, was a victim of American social pressures, Theodore Dreiser wrote to the governor of Pennsylvania in an attempt to win a pardon for the condemned young man. His effort was in vain. Just after midnight on May 6, 1935—after spending his final hours reading the family Bible—Bobby Edwards, dressed in white shirt, black trousers, and black slippers, walked calmly to the electric chair at Rockview Penitentiary in Bellefonte, Pennsylvania. "He was murmuring a prayer," wrote one reporter, "as the black hood fell over his head."

[*Sources:* The most complete account of the Edwards-McKechnie case is Theodore Dreiser's "I Find the Real American Tragedy," a greatly expanded version of his *New York Post* dispatches that was published as a five-part series in the February–June 1935 issues of *Mystery Magazine.* Columnist and future TV personality Dorothy Kilgallen also wrote a fine piece on the murder, "Sex and the All-American Boy," reprinted in my book *True Crime: An American Anthology* (New York: Library of America, 2008).]

Erased   Reporting on the Edwards case for *Murder Mystery* magazine, Theodore Dreiser explained that as far back as 1892, during his days as a novice newspaperman in Chicago, he had "observed a certain type of crime in the United States"— one that "seemed to spring from the fact that almost every young person was possessed of an ingrowing ambition to be somebody financially and socially." This distinctively American brand of crime, explained Dreiser, involved "the young ambitious lover of some poorer girl who had been attractive enough to satisfy him" until "a more attractive girl with money or position appeared and he quickly discovered that he could no longer care for his first love. What produced this particular type of crime was the fact that it was not always possible to drop this first girl. What usually stood in the way was pregnancy."

To support his claim, Dreiser pointed to a half dozen such murders, including the 1894 case of Carlyle Harris, a young New York City medical student who "seduced a young girl poorer than he was," only to dispatch her with poison when he fell in love with "an attractive girl of much higher station than his own" (see p. 225); a 1900 case in Charleston, South Carolina, "wherein a girl was shot by her lover because he wanted to better his social position by marrying a Charleston society girl"; and, of course, the Gillette-Brown case of 1905, which served as the basis for *An American Tragedy*. Indeed, so common were such cases that, according to Dreiser, between 1895 and 1935 "there has scarcely been a year in which some part of the country has not been presented with a case of this type."

That murders of this kind continue to occur all too frequently in the United States is made alarmingly clear by Marilee Strong in her powerful 2008 book, *Erased: Missing Women, Murdered Wives*. An award-winning journalist who became obsessed with the 2002 case of Scott Peterson—the clean-cut, smooth-talking young fertilizer salesman who murdered his eight-months-pregnant wife, Laci, so that he could pursue his hedonistic life as a swinging single—Strong began investigating other, similar cases, dating back to the early twentieth century. Analyzing fifty such murders in her book, she presents a profile of a previously unrecognized type of criminal she labels the "eraser killer": the seemingly normal man and solid citizen who decides that he wants to rid himself of an "inconvenient" wife or girlfriend and coolly sets out to do away with her rather than put himself through the hassle of a breakup or divorce.

Strong is (justifiably) far less sympathetic to such men than Dreiser, who blamed their crimes on American society and its "craze for social and money success." In Strong's view, the "eraser killer" is not the pitiable victim of America's misguided values but a cold-blooded psychopath, motivated solely by a malign sense of "narcissistic entitlement"—a soulless being who cares about nothing but the gratification of his own desires.

ROBERT IRWIN,
"THE MAD SCULPTOR"

THOUGH REMEMBERED TODAY AS A MORAL CRUSADER WHOSE 1954 SCREED *The Seduction of the Innocent* called for the censorship of comic books, Fredric Wertham was no self-righteous bluenose but one of New York City's most enlightened and respected psychiatrists. German-born and educated in London, Munich, Paris, and Vienna (where he had a brief but memorable encounter with Freud), he immigrated to the United States in 1922, joining the Phipps Psychiatric Clinic at Johns Hopkins University. Ten years later he took up permanent residency in Manhattan, where—along with a myriad of other activities—he served as senior psychiatrist at Bellevue Mental Hygiene Clinic. It was in that capacity that he first encountered Robert Irwin.

Shortly before 2:30 a.m. on October 27, 1932, the twenty-nine-year-old Irwin—a "nice, well-spoken, frank-looking young man"—showed up at Bellevue's emergency room with his penis badly mutilated and a rubber band tightly wound around its base. Calmly explaining that he had tried to castrate himself with a razor, Irwin urged the intern to finish the job. Ignoring the demented plea, the young physician stitched the partly severed member back together and sent Irwin to the psychiatric clinic, where, on the following morning, he was first seen by Dr. Wertham.

Visiting Irwin on a nearly daily basis, Wertham soon garnered the central facts of his life. Like a surprising number of American psychopaths, he was raised by a fanatically devout mother, who christened him Fenelon Arroyo Seco Irwin—names, according to Irwin, with "special religious associations" ("Fenelon," for example, apparently referred to the seventeenth-century French theologian François Fénelon). His earliest memories, as Wertham later recorded, were of being dragged to frenzied tent meetings where "members of the church would speak in tongues which they had not heard before" and be "cured of all sorts of ailments by hysterical prayer."

Little Fenelon was only three when his father deserted

Robert Irwin, "The Mad Sculptor"
(*Courtesy of the New York* Daily News.)

the family, plunging them into a state of permanent hardship. Their home was a "shack with flour sacking neatly stretched over the unplastered walls." To support her abandoned brood—Fenelon, his two obstreperous brothers, and a little girl who would die at two of whooping cough—Mrs. Irwin worked at assorted menial jobs, from scrubwoman to sweatshop seamstress, rarely earning more than $3 a day. Meals consisted of "buttermilk and stale bread, with the bread obtained from bakeries by begging." Toys being an unaffordable luxury, Fenelon's only plaything was the bathroom soap. Molding it into various shapes, he discovered a gift for sculpting.

With three growing sons to raise on her own, Mrs. Irwin consulted whatever child-rearing manuals she could get her hands on. Having read "that children should not learn about sex in a smutty way and that parents should not treat sex as something mysterious," she made sure to bathe in front of her sons, naked from the waist up. When she wasn't displaying her breasts to young Fenelon, she was force-feeding him heavy servings of scripture, insisting that he "read three chapters of the Bible every day and learn a psalm by heart every Sunday." In reaction, he became a devotee of Robert Ingersoll—the noted nineteenth-century freethinker, regarded by Mrs. Irwin as "one of the devil's chief allies"—and changed his name to Robert in honor of his intellectual hero.

Unlike his delinquent brothers, who steadily progressed from reform schools to state penitentiaries, Bob managed to stay out of trouble throughout his adolescence. At eighteen, unemployed and an insupportable burden on his mother, he had himself voluntarily admitted to a juvenile home, where he befriended a sympathetic attendant who encouraged his artistic pursuits by providing him with modeling clay.

After fifteen months in the juvenile home, he embarked on a wandering life, working briefly in an art studio in Hollywood and studying with the eminent sculptor Lorado Taft in Chicago before ending up in New York City in 1930 at the age of twenty-three. Seeking any sort of job that related to sculpting, he found temporary employment as a clerk in an art supply shop, an assistant to the master sculptor Alexander Ettl, and a taxidermist's helper.

In early 1931, troubled with increasingly violent fantasies, he had himself committed to the psychiatric ward of Kings County Hospital in Brooklyn, explaining to the supervising physician, Dr. Samuel Feigin, that he was afraid he "would kill somebody so I would be hung." After a three-week incarceration, he was sent to the Burke Foundation, a convalescent home in White Plains. He remained there as a patient "for the period allotted by the providers of charity for the convalescence of poor people," then stayed on as a waiter.

He returned to Manhattan in the spring of 1932, but his dreams of finding art-related work were thwarted by the grim realities of the Depression. For a while he was reduced to sleeping on park benches and begging for food from restaurants. Eventually he found a job as a dishwasher at a restaurant called McFadden's on the city's East Side. A few days later, in October 1932, he rented a spare room in the Beekman Hill flat of a family named Gedeon.

Four members of the family inhabited the dreary fourth-floor walk-up on East Fiftieth Street: the fiftyish father, Joseph Gedeon, a Hungarian émigré who ran a little upholstery shop a few blocks downtown; his wife, Mary, a "once-gorgeous Magyar, still comely in her forties"; an older daughter named Ethel, a "placid brunette with impeccable morals"; and Ethel's younger, party-girl sister, Veronica. A stunning eighteen-year-old with one brief impulsive marriage already behind her, Ronnie, as she was known to the world, worked as an "artist's model," posing nude for the members of a seedy amateur camera club. She also modeled regularly for pulp detective magazines, appearing as the scantily clad, trussed-up victim of assorted sex fiends and lust killers in stories such as "Pretty but Cheap" and "I Was a Teenaged White Slave."

To supplement Joseph's meager earnings, the Gedeons regularly took in a boarder or two. Bob Irwin had been living in their overcrowded flat for only a couple of days when—"in order to bottle up his sexual energies for higher purposes" (as he later explained)—he locked himself in the bathroom, took a brand-new razor blade to his penis and tried to slice it off.

EVEN AFTER HIS admission to the Bellevue psychiatric ward, Irwin was intent on having his penis amputated, begging several of the surgical interns to perform the operation. Recognizing that the young man was "a potential threat to himself and society," Wertham arranged for him to remain in Bellevue for five months. At the end of that period, diagnosing his patient as "improved but not recovered," he persuaded Irwin to commit himself voluntarily to Rockland State Hospital. Irwin remained there until May 1934, when he returned to New York City and found work at various odd jobs—dishwasher, coatroom attendant, elevator operator. He also moved back in with the Gedeons. Within days, he had become fixated on the older daughter, the sweet-natured and virtuous Ethel.

At first she responded warmly to Irwin's friendly overtures. She enjoyed hearing him hold forth on art and happily accompanied him on visits to the city's museums. Eventually, however, she grew weary of him. Dejected by her growing indifference—and by his failure to find fulfilling work—Irwin sought out Wertham, who saw at once that Irwin was slipping back into a dangerously unstable state. In January 1935, at the psychiatrist's urging, Irwin had himself recommitted to Rockland.

Despite one bizarre outburst of violence—when he attacked a young doctor who had complimented him on a bust he was sculpting in the hospital's workshop—Irwin was discharged in September 1936 as "improved." At the suggestion of a sympathetic attendant, he applied for admission to the St. Lawrence Theological School in Canton, New York. He remained there six months. Along with the usual assortment of odd jobs—delivering newspapers, mowing lawns, and shoveling snow—he supported himself by teaching two sculpture classes, one for adults, one for children. By the spring of 1937, however, his behavior had become sufficiently erratic that he was expelled from the school. Taking a bus to New York City, he showed up at the Gedeons' flat on the morning of Good Friday, only to learn that there was no vacancy, the spare room having been rented to an Englishman named Frank Byrnes, a bartender at the tony Racquet and Tennis Club. Later that day, he found a furnished room a few blocks away, paying the landlady $1 for the night.

SEVERAL MONTHS EARLIER, Dr. Wertham had received an invitation from Johns Hopkins Hospital to deliver a paper at a conference celebrating the twenty-fifth anniversary of the Phipps Psychiatric Clinic. The topic he chose was the type of violent crime caused by an "aberration of reasoning under the impact of emotional complexes"— what Wertham called a "catathymic crisis." Among the examples he cited was that of Robert Irwin, whose "attempted self-emasculation" was a striking "case of violence turned against oneself." Wertham went on to predict that because Irwin had not fully recovered from his condition, he was certain to "break out again in some act of violence either against himself or others."

On March 28, 1937—Easter Sunday—his prediction came horribly true.

EMBROILED IN INCREASINGLY bitter arguments with his wife, Mary, over their younger daughter's untrammeled behavior, Joseph Gedeon had moved out of the family flat earlier that year, taking up residence in a cubbyhole room behind his upholstery store that he proceeded to stock with a large assortment of pulp girlie magazines. In a conciliatory gesture, Mary had invited him over for Easter dinner. They were to be joined by their older daughter, Ethel, now married and living with her husband, Joe Kudner, in the suburbs.

It was Joseph Gedeon who discovered the massacre. Arriving at noon with a bouquet of flowers for his estranged wife, he entered the unlocked flat and found Ronnie's nude and lifeless body sprawled on her mattress. Mary's corpse was stuffed beneath the bed. Their boarder, Frank Byrnes, lay dead in the next room, killed in his sleep from multiple stab wounds to the head. Paralyzed with shock, Joseph was standing dazed in the bedroom when Ethel and her husband showed up a few minutes later and—after taking in the appalling scene—notified the police. Autopsies conducted later that day by the city's chief medical examiner established that both women had been manually strangled, while Byrnes' face and skull had been punctured fifteen times with a pointed implement, evidently an icepick.

The irresistible mix of sensational elements—a triple murder on Easter Sunday featuring the nude corpse of a stunning young "artist's model"—made the case a tabloid editor's dream. "Police Hunt Beekman Hill Maniac!" screamed the headlines. By midweek, the *Daily News* was devoting no fewer than nine full pages—including its front and back pages and a double-page center spread—to the story, illustrated with sixteen photographs, nine of which featured Ronnie, "the Queen of the Crime Magazine," either seminude or in a negligee.

Suspicion initially fell on Joseph Gedeon, who "told detectives quite bluntly that he despised his wife and had nothing but contempt for his daughter Ronnie." Certainly he was strong enough to have choked the two women to death, his work as an upholsterer having left him with "unusually powerful hands." Evidence suggested, moreover, that the perpetrator was no stranger to the family. Though at least one tenant of the building had heard a sharp, quickly stifled scream emanate from the Gedeons' apartment on the night of the murder, no one had heard so much as a single yap from their Pekingese, Tonchi—a sign that the dog knew the killer.

Searching the upholsterer's squalid little room, police turned up "sexy photographs and erotic books," a discovery that the newspapers quickly trumpeted as evidence of his degenerate nature. Jealous rage was put forth as a motive after "neighbors repeated rumors that Mary Gedeon and roomer Frank Byrnes had a relationship that transcended the conventional one of landlady and boarder." Dragged from his bed after less than three hours of sleep and hauled down to the station house, Gedeon was grilled for thirty-three hours straight, while the tabloids rushed to announce that the cops had found their killer.

Even as Joe Gedeon was being tried and convicted on the front pages ("Eyes of a Killer!" blared one headline, accompanied by a close-up photograph of the scrawny little upholsterer's scowling face), detectives were focusing on a different lead. Soap carving, a hobby heavily promoted by Procter & Gamble, was a nationwide craze during the Great Depression. In their search of the murder scene, detectives had found a sculpted bar of castile soap on the bedroom floor, evidently carved by the killer as he patiently waited for his final victim to come home. Questioning Ethel about the family's boarders, the investigators first heard the name of the young sculptor Bobby Irwin. Their suspicions were heightened by several references to Irwin in Ronnie's diary. "I think he is out of his head," she had written in one entry. "I am afraid of B.," she confided in another. Several witnesses reported seeing Irwin in the neighborhood shortly before the crime.

Tracking his path back to Canton, detectives discovered Irwin's own diary, left in the rooming house where he had lived during his brief stint at the St. Lawrence Theological School. One entry in particular left little doubt that Irwin was the culprit:

> God, how I adore Ethel. Perfection. That's what she is. Absolute perfection...If only Ronnie and her mother hadn't interfered. It has made a shipwreck out of me.... Girl of my dreams. Can't you hear the still small voice in the night. Can't you hear me calling to you with words of adoration on my lips and a song in my heart. Sex? It means nothing now. How I hate Ronnie and her mother for what they have done to me.

It didn't take long for the tabloids to get wind of this latest development. "Scour City for Maniac!" screamed the headlines. "Hunt Artist in 8 States!" "Mad Sculptor Had Mania to Strangle!"

AMERICA'S MOST WANTED criminal would remain at large for three months. In late June, nineteen-year-old Henrietta Koscianski, a "buxom, black-eyed" pantry maid at Cleveland's Statler Hotel, was leafing through the latest issue of *Inside Detective* magazine when she happened on a story about the manhunt for the "Mad Sculptor," Robert Irwin. The article was accompanied by a photograph of the suspect, whose face bore a striking resemblance to a recent acquaintance of Henrietta's, a bar boy going by the name of Bob Murray who had been working at the hotel for about a month and a half. Encountering Bob later that day, Henrietta asked him if he "knew about Robert Irwin." "Never heard of him," said Bob. That evening he cleaned out his locker and skipped town.

The following day, June 26, 1937, a phone call came in to the newsroom of the Chicago *Herald and Examiner*, a Hearst-owned tabloid. Identifying himself as Robert Irwin, the caller offered to surrender himself to the paper for a suitable price. A deal was immediately struck. After signing a contract for $5,000, Irwin was spirited off to the Morrison Hotel, where for the next twenty-four hours he was kept incommunicado while he dictated a lengthy confession to city editor John Dienhart and a pair of reporters.

Having secured the biggest story of the year—"Irwin Surrenders! Confesses! Exclusive!" screamed the headline—Dienhart arranged for Irwin's surrender to the authorities. At around midnight on Sunday, June 27, Irwin was flown in a Hearst-chartered plane to New York City and hustled directly into the presence of Police Commissioner Lewis Valentine and District Attorney William C. Dodge. Suddenly clamming up—"You can beat the Jesus out of me, you won't make me talk," he told the DA—Irwin asked to see Dr. Wertham, who was roused from his sleep and rushed to headquarters by police car. Two hours later, at around 5:20 a.m. on June 28, Irwin finally opened up, spilling out a story that conformed in every detail to the confession he had made in Chicago.

After his arrival from Canton on Good Friday, Irwin had spent the following day in a futile search for a job. By evening, he had plunged into such a severe depression that he considered drowning himself in the East River. As he stood brooding on a pier, a new thought entered his deeply disordered mind: "I made up my mind to kill Ethel and go to the chair for it."

As he turned from the river, he "saw an ice pick lying in the gutter" and put it in his pocket. He then proceeded toward First Avenue. It was around 9:00 p.m. when he reached the Gedeons' apartment.

> No one was home. Finally Mrs. Gedeon came home. She was very tired. She asked me if I would take her dog out for a walk. I took him for a walk around the block and brought him back.
>
> I drew Mrs. Gedeon's picture to kill as much time as possible. Then in comes this little Englishman. She introduced him to me. He went to his room. . . .
>
> Then I said that I wanted to see Ethel. She said, "Bob, Ethel isn't here and it is very late." I said, "I am going to stay here until I see Ethel." All of a sudden she flew at me and yelled, "Get out of here or I'll call the Englishman."
>
> Well I hit her with everything I had. I choked her. I strangled her. All the time this damn Englishman was in the next room just ten feet away.

> She died right in front of that room . . . I had her by the throat and I never
> let loose of that throat for twenty minutes. She fell back on the floor with
> her legs back over her head and her dress over her head. She scratched
> my face like nobody's business. My face was scratched. My hands were
> full of blood. I smeared it on her, on her face, on her breast. I threw her
> in the bedroom under the bed.

When the Pekingese, Tonchi, crawled under the bed to cower beside his dead
mistress, Irwin thought briefly of killing it too, but "felt too much pity for the animal
to do it."

After washing the blood off his hands, Irwin turned off all the lights and sat down
to wait. It wasn't until close to 3:00 a.m. that Ronnie came home and went directly
into the bathroom. She stayed in there for nearly an hour, while Irwin improvised a
blackjack out of a soap bar and a rag. When Ronnie finally emerged,

> I let her have it. The soap went all over the floor. It didn't have the slight-
> est effect. I can very well believe that she was drunk because she didn't
> put up any fight at all. I grabbed her by the throat and took her in the
> room. I held her the longest time, just tight enough so that she could
> breathe. I didn't know what to do. . . . I asked her where Ethel was. She
> said she was married to that kid Kudner. I disguised my voice as well as I
> could, but it wasn't enough. Finally she said, "Bob, I know you. You are
> going to get in trouble if you do this." Then I strangled her. I ripped her
> clothes off. She didn't have much on, only a thin chemise . . . I only used
> my hands, nothing but the pressure of my hands. I held her a long time,
> at least an hour. I was holding her on the bed and strangling her. After-
> wards, I went right out because she immediately became the most repul-
> sive thing I had ever seen in my life when she was dead. It was like blue
> death just oozing out, a spiritual emanation just oozing out.

Though both murders occurred only feet from Frank Byrnes' bedroom, the
Englishman had never stirred, being almost completely deaf. He was still sound
asleep when Irwin, as he put it, "went in and fixed" him. "I just gave it to him in the
temple with the ice pick. I stuck him once and he kept on twitching." Irwin then pro-

ceeded to "put him out of his misery" with another dozen or so stab wounds to the head, one so deep that it penetrated the medulla.

The massacre completed, Irwin left the apartment, "as calm as I've been in my life." Still, he felt disappointed at the way things had turned out. "I never wanted to get any one of them except Ethel," he explained. "I wanted to kill Ethel because I loved her. If Ethel had come in first I would have killed her and nobody else."

Two DAYS AFTER being brought to New York City, Irwin was indicted on three counts of first-degree murder. By then he had managed to secure the services of famed attorney Samuel Leibowitz, best remembered for his defense of the Scottsboro Boys. Anticipating an insanity plea, the prosecution convinced the court to appoint a three-man "lunacy commission," which, without examining Irwin, concluded that he was legally sane. The tabloids, hungry for blood, applauded the finding, declaring that "the fiendish sculptor" was a "classic example of an insanity faker" and deriding any doctor who expressed sympathy for Irwin. A prime target was Wertham, whose diagnosis was satirized in a sneering tabloid limerick:

> He did not murder anyone
>   And such a charge not nice is:
> He's just a charming victim of
>   A "catathymic crisis."

Armed with the findings of his own team of experts—who had actually interviewed Irwin at length and pronounced him "both medically and legally insane"—Leibowitz was able to save his client from the chair by having him plead guilty to three counts of second-degree murder at his November 1938 trial. He was sentenced to life in Sing Sing, where (as Leibowitz expected) he was examined by prison psychiatrists, who promptly ruled that he was "very definitely insane." On December 10, 1938, he was transferred to Dannemora State Hospital. He remained institutionalized for the rest of his life, dying of cancer in 1975 in Matteawan State Hospital for the Criminally Insane.

The Easter Sunday Murders produced a legacy of outrage. "The whole case has exposed disgraceful conditions from start to finish," one writer thundered. "The incompetence of those state psychiatrists who released a dangerous psychopath three times; the crowded conditions of our inadequate state asylums which force the psychiatrists to release older inmates to make way for new; the shocking behavior of the police department in their treatment of Mr. Gedeon; the indecent behavior of the newspapers." Stung by criticism of his paper's over-the-top coverage, *Daily News* publisher Joseph Medill Patterson defended himself with an argument that was hard to deny. "Murder sells," he declared, "because we are all interested in murder."

[*Sources:* Alan Hynd, *Murder, Mayhem, and Mystery: An Album of American Crime* (New York: A. S. Barnes and Company, 1958); Jay Maeder, *Big Town, Big Time* (New York: Daily News Books, 1999); Jennifer Jane Marshall, "Clean Cuts: Procter & Gamble's Depression-Era Soap-Carving Contests," *Winterthur Portfolio*, Spring 2008, 51–76; Ellery Queen, "The Strange Case of the Mad Sculptor," *American Weekly*, March 10, 1957; Quentin Reynolds, *Courtroom: In the Criminal Courtroom with Samuel S. Leibowitz, Lawyer and Judge* (New York: Farrar, Straus and Company, 1950); Fredric Wertham, *The Show of Violence* (Garden City, NY: Doubleday & Co., 1949).]

VII

SOLDIER, SAILOR, SERIAL KILLER

1941–1961

EDDIE LEONSKI,
"THE BROWNOUT STRANGLER"

DESPITE THE FACT THAT HIS CRIMES TERRORIZED AN ENTIRE CITY AND NEARLY precipitated an international crisis, few Americans have ever heard of the mid-twentieth-century serial murderer Eddie Leonski. The explanation for this state of affairs seems obvious. Unique among U.S. psycho killers, Leonski perpetrated his murderous spree half a world away. Though his crimes were reported in the national press, they seemed too remote to resonate with the American public, particularly at a time when our country was preoccupied with much larger worries.

Surprisingly little is known about Leonski's early life, though the psychiatrists who eventually examined him were able to draw certain conclusions about the sources of homicidal mania. Born in 1917, he grew up in a tenement on the Upper East Side of New York City, one of six children of Polish-born parents, both confirmed alcoholics. He was seven when his father abandoned the family. Not long afterward, his mother, Amelia, took up with another drunkard. She herself suffered at least two mental breakdowns, severe enough to land her in Bellevue, where she was diagnosed with both manic-depression and incipient schizophrenia. From an early age, three of his brothers were chronic troublemakers, eventually racking up lengthy rap sheets. One of them ended up in a state psychiatric institution, where he lived out his life.

According to all accounts, Eddie was the apple of his unstable mother's eye. He, in turn, had the kind of deeply disturbing attachment to her found in other homicidal mama's boys. On the surface, he was slavishly devoted to her. Throughout his adolescence, he never had a girlfriend, declaring that—until some hypothetical future when

Serial killer Eddie Leonski
(© *Bettmann/Corbis. Used by permission.*)

he might decide to get married—his mother "alone would be the object of his affection." Beneath this adoration, however, there seethed a fierce subconscious hatred that would eventually vent itself in serial murder.

Typical of psychopathic personalities, there was a vast disparity between Eddie's dark, hidden self and the appealing mask he showed to the world. A shy, scrawny child, he took up weight lifting and developed into a powerfully built young man with a splendid physique—narrow waist, broad shoulders, and "thick muscular forearms." In contrast to his brothers, who rarely did an honest day's work, he undertook a three-year course in stenography following his high school graduation and tried his hand at various secretarial jobs before becoming a store

clerk at a branch of Gristede's, the venerable Manhattan supermarket chain. Always proud of his physical strength, he liked to impress his co-workers by performing impromptu weight-lifting stunts such as "snatching up a 100-lb. bag of sugar from the floor with one hand and holding it high over his head." With his bright blue eyes, sweetly innocent face, and million-dollar smile, he was a favorite of the female customers. A valued employee, he had just been transferred to the company's newest store when, on February 17, 1941, he was drafted into the U.S. Army.

After basic training in Fort Dix, New Jersey, Leonski was assigned to the Fifty-second Signal Battalion in Fort Sam Houston, a big army base in San Antonio, Texas. It was there that his erratic behavior first began to get him in trouble. Having grown up in a household of alcoholics, Eddie himself had taken up liquor at an early age. Now—perhaps because of the stress of separation from his mother—he began to hit the bottle more heavily than ever, favoring bizarre concoctions of whiskey or beer mixed with ketchup, mustard, hot peppers, and ice cream. Under the influence of drink, he would—according to the testimony of one superior—"act like a man out of his head": walking on his hands down the street, starting brawls, raving at the top of his lungs, or bursting into uncontrolled tears at the thought of his far-distant mommy. Though obedient and reliable when sober, with a boyish charm that was impossible to dislike, he was, as his commanding officer later put it, "perpetually in small trouble."

On one occasion, just a few weeks after his arrival in San Antonio, he found himself in trouble that was not so trivial. Cruising the red light district on the city's west side, he picked up a woman, got embroiled in a violent quarrel with her, and began to choke her on the street. Arrested and jailed, he escaped more serious consequences when the woman filed the relatively minor charge of simple assault. Surviving records do not reveal the upshot of the incident, though Leonski clearly incurred neither jail time nor a discharge. At the time, the United States was gearing up for war and the army needed every able-bodied man at its disposal. And so, on January 12, 1942, Eddie Leonski—who had wept so helplessly the night before his departure that his barrack mates had to pack his bags for him—departed for Australia along with forty-five hundred fellow soldiers.

By EARLY 1942, the Japanese—having embarked on what Franklin Delano Roosevelt called "their frenzied career of conquest"—had overrun Burma, Singapore, the Solomon Islands, New Guinea, Manila, and Kuala Lumpur. Having been forced to retreat from the Philippines, General Douglas MacArthur, recently appointed supreme commander of the Allied forces in the southwest Pacific Theater, retreated to Australia, which was to serve as America's base of operations in the Pacific for the duration of the war. Leonski and his comrades were part of the first wave of an estimated one million U.S. servicemen who would eventually pass through Australia.

The enormous influx of U.S. military personnel had a powerful impact on Australian society. While the exigencies of war made cooperation between the Allies a vital necessity, Australian troops quickly developed deep animosity toward their American counterparts, whose snazzy uniforms, superior pay, and general air of exotic glamour made them objects of desire for the local female population. "The Americans had the chocolates, the ice cream, the silk stockings and the dollars," one soldier commented. "They were able to show the girls a good time and the Australians became very resentful."

Thousands of young Australian women, intent on bagging an American boyfriend (or better yet, a husband) became branded with the label "Yank hunters." In Melbourne, where a nightly brownout was imposed to protect against a Japanese aerial bombardment, the dimmed streets and darkened windows seemed to encourage promiscuous behavior. For their part, the GIs, though seen as a bulwark against a Japanese invasion, were themselves widely viewed as "overpaid and oversexed" invaders, undermining the morals of Australian womanhood. Tensions between Australian and U.S. troops eventually culminated in a two-day eruption of violence known as the "Battle of Brisbane" that left one soldier dead and hundreds injured.

With thousands of GIs prowling for pickups, hitting the bars, and engaging in nightly brawls with resentful Aussie servicemen, Americans were bound to land in trouble with the local authorities. Exactly who would deal with U.S. soldiers charged with breaking Australian civil law became another bone of contention between the two countries. These highly charged issues—the perceived exploitation of Australian women by U.S. soldiers and the jurisdictional dispute over the trial and punishment of American lawbreakers—would be distilled in the sensational case of Eddie Leonski.

Upon his arrival at Camp Pell in Melbourne, Leonski, like the rest of his buddies, lost no time in hitting the town. With decent money in his pockets and plenty of free time between drills, he became a habitué of the barrooms, where he quickly gained a reputation both for his prodigious consumption of milk-and-ketchup-spiked whiskey and his trademark stunt of leaping onto the counter and walking along it on his hands. Out on the streets, he would drunkenly grab passing girls or sneak up behind them and shout "Boo!" That public behavior, however—boorish as it was—was benign compared to the secret crimes that Leonski had already begun to commit.

Sometime in early March, he shadowed a young woman to her home in suburban St. Kilda and, as she entered her apartment, shoved her inside, slammed the door shut, and attempted to rape her. Her screams roused some neighbors, who came to her aid just as Leonski slipped out a back door and vanished into the night. Not long afterward, he made a clumsy attempt to pick up a girl at an ice-skating rink. When she rebuffed his advances, he followed her to a streetcar stop and, leaning close, whispered, "I'm thinking of choking a dame, and it might as well be you." Before she could let out a scream, he grabbed her by the throat and throttled her into near-unconsciousness. Fortunately for her, a streetcar came along at just that moment and Leonski fled.

By the third week of March, less than a month after his arrival in Australia, Leonski's drinking was so out of control that, after being AWOL for six days on a monumental bender, he was thrown into the brig. No sooner was he released on April 20 than he embarked on another binge of nonstop drinking. Still determined to "choke a dame," he began to stalk women again. This time, his prey would not be as lucky as his first intended victims.

EDDIE LEONSKI SPENT most of Saturday, May 2, swilling booze with a buddy at the Bleak House Hotel, just across from Albert Park in Melbourne. At around 2:00 a.m., with the bar shutting down for the Sabbath, he decided to head back to camp. As he made his way up Victoria Street, he spotted a woman in the doorway of a dry cleaner's shop. Her name, as newspaper readers were soon to learn, was Mrs. Ivy Violet McLeod. A forty-year-old domestic, she had just left the apartment of a male friend and was waiting for a streetcar.

According to Leonski's later confession, Mrs. McLeod smiled at him as he strolled past. He paused and

> made some comment about her bag. I took it in my hands and then gave it back to her. The girl moved into the recess and I must have followed her. I had my arms around her neck. I grabbed her by the neck, the left side. I changed the position of my hands and grabbed her at the front of her throat. I squeezed and she fell rapidly. Her head hit the ground while I still had my hands on her throat. I started to rip and tear her clothes until I came to the belt. I just couldn't rip that belt. I ripped her clothes below the belt and came back to it. The belt made me mad. While I was still trying to rip her belt I heard footsteps. I picked up my hat which had fallen off; put it back on. I

turned to my right and walked up Victoria Street. I didn't look back. I don't remember what time or how I got back to camp.

A few hours later, a passerby discovered Mrs. McLeod's brutalized, seminude corpse in the doorway of the shop, her "legs wide apart and feet tucked up under her thighs, with genitals exposed." A postmortem revealed that her windpipe had been crushed by manual strangulation. Despite the obscene posture of her body, she had not been raped. A team of detectives was assigned to the case but—apart from the testimony of one witness who had seen an American soldier hurrying from the scene—there were no solid leads.

One week later, the serial murderer about to be known as "The Brownout Strangler" struck again.

WIFE OF A police constable and mother of two young children, Pauline Buchan Thompson, a pretty thirty-one-year-old brunette, juggled two jobs to help support her family: stenographer by day and radio station receptionist in the evenings. Blessed with a lovely singing voice, she also found time to contribute to the war effort by performing popular tunes for the troops at local concerts and dances.

On the evening of Friday, May 8, she was sitting by herself in a restaurant, waiting for her dinner to arrive, when a baby-faced American soldier came up to her table and asked if he could join her. The two traded pleasantries for a while before adjourning to the bar at the nearby Astoria Hotel, where they spent the next several hours chatting amiably while downing at least a half dozen gin squashes apiece.

It was nearing midnight when they left the bar. Mrs. Thompson's boardinghouse was only a few hundred yards away. As she and her escort, Eddie Leonski, walked along the deserted, drizzly street, she began to sing. "She had a nice voice," Leonski would recall in his confession. A few moments later they arrived at the front steps of the boardinghouse. Mrs. Thompson was still singing when he grabbed her around the neck.

> She stopped singing. I said, "Keep singing, keep singing." She fell down. I got mad and then tore at her, I tore her apart. There was someone coming across the street. I hid behind a stone wall. I was terrified. My heart was pounding a mile a minute. I couldn't bear to look at her. I saw her purse. I knew I had to get back and didn't have any money. I picked up her purse and put it be-

neath my coat. I knew I couldn't go far with such a big purse. I turned left and ran into an alley. I looked into her purse, there were lots of things in it. . . . I finally found the money. I dropped the purse. I went to a corner and took a taxi back to camp.

A few hours later, a night watchman named Henry McGowan stumbled upon the ransacked purse in the alleyway. After examining it for a clue to its owner, he continued on his rounds. He had gone just a short distance when he came upon Pauline Thompson's body, sprawled on the steps of her boardinghouse. Legs splayed, she was "naked down to the navel and up to the navel," he later testified. "There was just a little clothing across the center of her stomach." Like Ivy McLeod, she had been throttled to death by an assailant with unusually powerful hands. Also like McLeod, she had not been raped.

This second brutal murder set off the kind of panic that can easily seize a big city when a serial killer is at large: the kind that gripped Londoners during Jack the Ripper's savage spree, San Franciscans during the Zodiac Killer's reign of terror, New Yorkers when the Son of Sam was on the prowl. The "Brownout Strangler," writes journalist Ivan Chapman, "was feared more than the Japanese":

> Never before had a large Australian community been so utterly terrorized. People began putting out their milk cans long before dusk. Suburban doors were locked and bolted. Very few women dared come out after dark, and many offices and factories began allowing female staff to go home early. . . . Australian women in the armed forces were given leave after dark only in groups of six, preferably with male escorts whom they knew well. They had to specify their destinations and report in by telephone when they got there. Every servicewoman had to carry the police emergency number in her handbag. Hospitals in and around Melbourne stopped all-night leave for nurses, and female university students were strongly advised to stay away from evening lectures.

EVEN AS AUSTRALIAN detectives, assisted by American military authorities, intensified their hunt for the unknown killer, his identity had already been disclosed to one man, a soldier named Anthony Gallo.

On Saturday, May 9, the morning after the murder of Pauline Thompson, Leonski had awoken with a savage hangover. Desperate for a drink, he managed to find a bottle in a buddy's locker. It wasn't long before he had drunk himself into a state of blubbering self-pity. When Gallo, a friend since their basic training days, showed up at his tent in the early evening, a teary-eyed Leonski was perched on the edge of the bunk. When Gallo asked what was wrong, Leonski moaned, "I killed, Gallo, I killed."

At first Gallo dismissed the remark as nothing more than drunken babble. For the rest of the evening, however, and over the course of the following days, Leonski kept reverting to the subject, insisting that he was responsible not only for the murder of Pauline Thompson but for another recent killing as well. At one point he compared himself to Dr. Jekyll and Mr. Hyde. "I'm just like him," he exclaimed. "Two personalities." At another, he described himself as a "werewolf." He wondered aloud "why he had killed women older than himself," and seemed bewildered by his bizarre motive for strangling Pauline Thompson. "I wanted her to keep on singing. I choked her. How could she keep on singing when I choked her?"

Gallo didn't know what to make of these drunken confessions. At times he was terrified that Leonski was telling the truth; at others he was sure that his friend was simply "taunting him with some wild, sick joke." Gripped by a paralyzing mixture of fear, confusion, and doubt, he decided to do nothing. As a result, another woman would die.

On the evening of May 12, in separate incidents, an American soldier attacked two Australian women as they entered their homes. Both managed to break free and send the assailant fleeing. Two nights later, he forced his way into the home of another woman, who let out a cry of alarm. Running to her aid, her uncle, a Mr. Jackson, got a good look at the intruder before the soldier disappeared out the door.

Four more nights would pass before Leonski struck again—this time with fatal results. The victim was Miss Gladys Hosking, a forty-one-year-old secretary at Melbourne University. At around 7:00 p.m. on May 18—a cheerless, rainy Monday—she was walking home from work when Leonski materialized beside her and asked if he could share her umbrella. When they arrived at her house, Leonski—who had spent that afternoon in a bar imbibing an estimated thirty beers and seven whiskeys—urged her to "walk on with me and show me the way to camp." Like most women in Melbourne, Hosking—as she had made clear in a letter to her father—was keenly aware of the two recent murders and fearful of being out at night with the strangler at large. It is a testament to Leonski's boy-ishly innocent demeanor that she did not hesitate to accompany him along the lightless streets.

As with Pauline Thompson, it was Gladys Hosking's voice that seemed to trigger Leonski's madness. "We came to a very dark part of the street," he later confessed.

> She stopped and said, "There's the camp over there." She had a lovely voice. I wanted that voice. She was leaving to go to her home and I did not want her to go. I grabbed her by the throat. I choked her. She didn't even make a sound. She was so soft. I thought, "What have I done. I will have to get away from here." I then got her to a fence. I pushed her underneath it. I carried her a short distance and fell in the mud. She made funny noises, a sort of gurgling sound. I thought I must stop that sound, so I tried to pull her dress over her face. I became frightened and started to run away.

A few minutes later, he arrived at camp, slathered in yellow mud "from his tie down to his feet." Too fuddled and exhausted to clean himself, he stripped off his clothes and col-lapsed into bed. He was just waking up the next morning when, a short distance away, a butcher named Albert Whiteway discovered Gladys Hosking's obscenely exposed body sprawled facedown in a patch of yellow mud.

That distinctive mud—precisely matching the stains found on Leonski's uniform and inside his tent—would prove to be a key piece of evidence against him. So would the tes-timony of Mr. Jackson, the gentleman who had come to his niece's rescue a week earlier and who was able to identify Leonski in a lineup held at Camp Pell on the morning of May 20. It was Anthony Gallo, however, who would later claim most credit for Leonski's ar-rest. After two weeks of vacillation—an unconscionable delay that had cost Gladys Hosk-ing her life—he finally came forward with the story of his friend's chilling admissions. Taken into custody, Leonski quickly spilled out a full, highly detailed confession.

Despite the objections of powerful political figures who saw it as an affront to their national autonomy and dignity, the Australian government, after much heated internal debate, acceded to American demands. Though Leonski had violated Australian law, he would be tried by a U.S. military tribunal. At his five-day court-martial in June, his de-fense lawyer argued that Leonski was insane—a diagnosis seconded from afar by Dr. Fredric Wertham, the eminent New York psychiatrist whose patients had included Robert Irwin and Albert Fish. "Leonski was without doubt mentally deranged," Wertham declared.

> Eddie was completely dependent on his mother and was considered a mama's boy. The mother image dominated his whole life. He could not free himself from it. That his three victims were all women considerably older than he was is psychiatrically most significant. He unconsciously linked their voices with his mother. The whole psychological explosion occurred in a period of deprivation when he was away from home and separated from his mother—but not from her dominating image. The deeds constituted symbolic matricide.

Medical officers appointed to examine Leonski, however, concluded that though he was a psychopathic personality with a murderous mother complex, the prisoner was not psychotic. Found guilty, he was sentenced to die at Pentridge prison on November 9, 1942, his order of execution personally signed by General MacArthur. On the eve of his hanging, he was in a jovial mood, joking to a visitor: "If you've got any more dames you want choking, just bring 'em along and I'll fix 'em for you."

With his death, he earned a special distinction in the annals of infamy as the second American soldier to be executed in World War II (the first, army private James Rowe, convicted of murdering a fellow soldier at Fort Huachuca, Arizona, preceded him by three weeks, having gone to the gallows on October 17, 1942).

[*Sources:* Ivan Chapman, *Leonski: The Brownout Strangler* (Sydney: Hale & Iremonger, 1982); Fredric Wertham, *A Sign for Cain: An Exploration of Human Violence* (New York: Macmillan, 1966); Marilyn Lake, "The Desire for a Yank: Sexual Relations Between Australian Women and American Servicemen during World War II," *Journal of the History of Sexuality* 2, no. 4 (April 1992): 621–633; Max Haines, *True Crime Stories: 50 Headline-Grabbing Murders from Around the World* (New York: Barnes & Noble Books, 1987).]

No Rest for the Wicked

Like the familicide William Beadle (see p. 9), whose execrated corpse was repeatedly dug up and moved by his outraged neighbors, Eddie Leonski was not allowed to rest easy after death. Immediately after his hanging, he was buried in disgrace in a remote section of Melbourne's Springvale Cemetery that turned out to be reserved for Indonesians. On December 5, 1944, his remains were exhumed and transferred to another isolated site in the same cemetery. The following May, he was dug up again and moved to a cemetery in Ipswich, Queensland. He remained there for two and a half years. It was not until 1947 that he reached his final resting place: Honolulu, Hawaii, where, along with a half dozen other executed American servicemen, he was laid to rest in a segregated section of the Schofield Barracks military cemetery—a "shameful slice of American soil."

Other serial killers have had a hard time finding final resting places. In April 1895, two young San Francisco women, eighteen-year-old Blanche Lamont and twenty-one-year-old Minnie Williams, went missing. Not long afterward, their horribly mutilated corpses were discovered inside the Emanuel Baptist Church on Barrett Street, one shoved inside a storage room, the other stashed in the steeple. The perpetrator of these atrocities turned out to be a handsome young medical student, Theodore Durrant, quickly dubbed the "Demon of the Belfry." Despite his protestations of innocence, a jury took only five minutes to convict him at the end of a sensational three-week trial. Following his hanging in January 1898, his corpse was brought to the prison waiting room in an open coffin, where—in full view of their child's ghastly remains—his parents refreshed themselves with a hearty roast beef meal before taking his body away for burial. Such was the public's antipathy toward Durrant, however, that no cemetery in San Francisco would accept him. His parents were finally forced to transport the cadaver to Los Angeles for cremation.

Fearing that his own corpse might be exhumed after burial by either medical men eager to dissect it or ghoulish showmen hoping to put it on display, Durrant's contemporary Dr. H. H. Holmes—aka the "Chicago Bluebeard"—took precautions to ensure that his bones would remain undisturbed. Immediately after his execution at Moyamensing State Prison in May 1896, his body was placed in a cement-filled casket, which was then lowered into a jumbo-sized grave and blanketed with another layer of cement, two feet thick, before being covered with dirt.

Though rumors persist that the body of Ed Gein, the infamous "Butcher of Plainfield," was removed from its original resting place by indignant locals who did not want him defiling their cemetery and insisted that he be buried elsewhere, he does in fact reside in his family's plot in Plainfield Cemetery. His headstone, however, has never been left in peace. Because of the perverse admiration he inspires in horror fans—who, thanks to his role as the model for Norman Bates and Leatherface, see him as the "granddaddy of gore"—his grave has become a macabre pilgrimage site. Chunks of his original tombstone were chipped away by ghoulish relic hunters until the whole thing was stolen in 2001. Though subsequently recovered, it has been kept in storage ever since to keep it safe from collectors of serial killer souvenirs.

JULIAN HARVEY
AND THE *BLUEBELLE*'S LAST VOYAGE

TABLOID NEWSPAPERS HAVE ALWAYS THRIVED ON SENSATIONAL MURDERS. THEIR editorial credo is the cynical journalistic saying "If it bleeds, it leads." An early issue of *Mad* magazine perfectly captures the shamelessly lurid nature of such trashy publications in a mock tabloid called *The Daily Poop*, whose contents consist almost entirely of stories like "Man Carves up His Girlfriend," "Killer Admits Using Meat Grinder," "Girl Beaten," and "Most Nauseating Crime Ever." Tucked away on page five among classified ads for pimple medication, nose drops, and weight-loss pills is an item in microscopically small print about the outbreak of World War III.

The situation is very different with the staid *New York Times*, the "Gray Lady" of American journalism, which spurns any story that smacks of sensationalism. To make the front page of the "paper of record," a murder has to be exceptionally newsworthy. On November 21, 1961—along with articles about President Kennedy's meeting with Chancellor Adenauer of West Germany, a hunger strike by Algerian rebels, a United Nations proposal to assist the Congolese government, and a Supreme Court ruling exempting women from jury duty—an article appeared on page one of the *Times* headlined "Rescued Girl's Story Indicates Skipper Killed Others on Yacht." The skipper in question was a dashing sociopath named Julian Harvey. For all the attention his horrific crime generated at the time, however, he quickly faded into oblivion. Even the highly publicized reemergence of his only surviving victim, fifty years after the atrocity, failed to reignite interest in this strange all-American psycho.

BORN AND BRED in landlocked Wisconsin, Arthur Duperrault developed a love for tropical waters as a navy man in the South Pacific during World War II. In the years following his discharge, while building a reputation as one of Green Bay's leading optometrists, he harbored a dream to take his family on a lazy island-hopping cruise in the Bahamas. In 1961, determined not to delay any longer, he took an extended leave from his practice, made arrangements with his children's school, and headed down to Florida with his wife, Jean, and their three bright and vibrant kids: fourteen-year-old Brian, eleven-year-old Terry Jo, and seven-year-old René.

The initial plan was to buy a boat and spend the entire fall "vagabonding in southern waters." Unable to find a suitable vessel, they decided to charter one instead. At Fort Lauderdale's Bahia Mar yacht basin, they found what they were looking for: a sleek, sixty-foot, two-masted ketch called *Bluebelle*, skippered by a Hollywood-handsome forty-four-year-old named Julian Harvey who lived aboard with his wife of four months, a former TWA stewardess named Mary Dene.

Harvey was not only a former military man, like "Doc" Duperrault, but a bona fide war hero, a decorated bomber pilot in World War II and Korea. He was also a highly experienced sailor and former owner of a number of racing yachts. Everything about him inspired confidence. But as with most psychopaths, his inviting veneer concealed the dark, hidden truths of his life.

JULIAN HARVEY HAD the kind of improbable life story that could have been concocted by a studio screenwriter. He never knew his biological father, who left his mother—a beautiful Broadway chorus girl—when Julian was still an infant. A few years later, she married a vaudeville impresario who indulged the boy's every desire, reportedly buying him a sailboat for his tenth birthday, the beginning of his lifelong love of sailing. Though the Depression severely disrupted his home life, it didn't affect the level of affluence he enjoyed. When his mother's second marriage broke up in the aftermath of the 1929 crash, he was sent to live with a wealthy aunt and uncle who pampered him in the style he had grown accustomed to.

Scrawny as a child, he threw himself into bodybuilding, becoming a fitness fanatic decades before the workout craze took hold of America. By the time he reached adolescence, he had developed a splendid physique that he obsessively maintained throughout his life and never tired of flaunting. His face—ruggedly handsome and framed by golden curls—matched the beauty of his body. For a while, he worked as a male model for the famed John Roberts Powers Agency. A surviving publicity shot shows him posed in nothing but a skimpy swimsuit, aiming a drawn bow and arrow and looking like a combination of Tarzan and Cupid.

It was around this time that he first manifested a tendency that would remain a grimly recurrent feature of his life: a strange "affinity for accidents," as one journalist put it. He was behind the wheel of his first car, a Model A Ford convertible, when a wheel came off. He and his passenger, a male friend, managed to leap to safety as the car spun out of control and flipped over.

After a few aimless years at college, he enlisted in the Air Corps in 1941 and quickly distinguished himself with his wartime heroics. He flew more than thirty combat missions as a bomber pilot, surviving two crash landings. By the fall of 1944, he had won a chestful of medals including the Distinguished Flying Cross, risen from lieutenant to lieutenant colonel, and been chosen to pilot the plane in a death-defying test involving the deliberate ditching of a B-24 bomber in Virginia's James River—a feat that won him another major decoration, the Air Medal. No one doubted his coolness or courage, though there were some who looked askance at the glamour-boy look he affected: the "special-cut Eisenhower jacket, pearl-pink chino trousers, and yellow scarf" he loved to parade around in.

He was, of course, irresistible to women, though notably bad at holding on to them. He'd had five wives before Mary Dene. None of those marriages lasted very long, and one of them ended under deeply suspicious circumstances that would come to seem even more ominous in light of later events.

On the evening of April 21, 1949, Harvey, then residing at Eglin Air Force Base near Valparaiso, Florida, was driving home from the movies with his third wife, Joann, and his mother-in-law, Mrs. Myrtle Boylen. As they crossed an old wooden bridge over a bayou, the car went into a skid, crashed through the railing, and plunged into the murky waters. Both women drowned in the submerged car. Harvey escaped without a scratch.

He later told investigators that he had seen "the accident coming, and at the last minute I opened the door and was thrown free." The professional diver who went down to retrieve the bodies, however, found all four doors locked and the driver's window rolled down, suggesting a very different scenario: namely, that Harvey had gone down into the water along with Joann and her mother, then opened his window and escaped, leaving the two women to drown. Joann's father, convinced that Harvey's story was full of holes—and made deeply suspicious by his son-in-law's weirdly blasé reaction to Joann's death—demanded an official investigation. One military doctor who interviewed Harvey during this period concluded "that underneath his veneer of charm and sophistication was an amoral man with no real empathy for others, a man who could be dangerous." Still, authorities could find no hard evidence of any criminal action on Harvey's part, and the matter was dropped.

A few months later, after collecting on his wife's life insurance policy, Harvey was married again, this time to a young Texas businesswoman named Jitty. Though their marriage endured for three years, they saw virtually nothing of each other during that time. Just three months after their wedding, Harvey was sent to Korea, where he flew another 114 combat missions and added a bunch of decorations to his already impressive collection. When he returned to the states in 1953, he and Jitty were promptly divorced.

Within a year, he was married to his fifth wife, Georgianna. By then he had left the military and, fulfilling a long-cherished dream, had purchased a sixty-eight-foot yawl, the *Torbatross*. Less than a year later, with Harvey at the helm, the *Torbatross* sank in Chesapeake Bay after ramming into the submerged wreckage of an old World War I battleship, the USS *Texas*, that had been bombed in 1921 during a historic demonstration of military airpower. There were strong indications that the collision was no accident. The *Texas*, as one journalist reported, "was a notorious navigational hazard, marked by a buoy, and its exact location was known and visible." Several witnesses, moreover, testified that Harvey had "deliberately circled the wreck twice" before his boat ran into it. Despite the suspicious nature of the incident, however, Harvey eventually won a settlement of $14,258 (around $112,000 today) from the U.S. government.

He used the money to buy another boat, an eighty-one-foot luxury yawl, *Valiant*. In 1958—in the midst of an ugly alimony fight with Georgianna, who was suing him for divorce on the grounds of extreme mental cruelty—he was captaining the *Valiant* in the Gulf of Mexico when the boat mysteriously caught fire and sank. Once again, Harvey escaped unscathed. This time, he collected $40,000 on the insurance, a sum that conveniently saved him from his financial difficulties.

The doomed ketch *Bluebelle*

By 1961, he had taken to making his livelihood by skippering boats for charter parties. In the summer of that year he entered into an arrangement with a Hollywood, Florida, swimming pool contractor named Harold Pegg, owner of the *Bluebelle*. Harvey and his sixth wife, Mary Dene, whom he had just wed, would live aboard the boat and "crew it for chartered trips on salary."

Not long afterward, the *Bluebelle* was chartered by the Duperraults. On Wednesday morning, November 8, 1961, it set sail from Fort Lauderdale for a week's cruise in the Bahamas.

FIVE DAYS LATER, on Monday, November 13, a lookout on the *Gulf Lion*, an oil tanker bound for Puerto Rico, spotted a small wooden lifeboat drifting in the open sea. On board the dinghy were a "vigorous" Julian Harvey and the corpse of a little girl in an oversized life jacket, who turned out to be seven-year-old René Duperrault.

Rescued by the tanker, Harvey spilled out what *Time* magazine called "a tale of flaming horror." The previous night, so Harvey claimed, the *Bluebelle* had encountered a sudden tropical squall. At around 11:00 p.m., a powerful gust snapped the mainmast in two. A fifty-foot length came hurtling down, piercing the deck and rupturing the fuel lines, which burst into flame. While Harvey single-handedly fought the blaze with extinguishers, his wife and their five passengers retreated to the stern. By then, however, the ketch was going down. While the others leapt into the water, Harvey launched the dinghy, dove overboard, hauled himself into the lifeboat, and made a desperate effort to find Mary Dene and the Duperraults, shouting himself hoarse in the darkness. No one answered. At last he came upon the little girl, floating facedown in the water, her body buoyed by the life jacket. He hauled her onto the dinghy, but she was already dead. The others had vanished into the sea along with the *Bluebelle.*

Within forty-eight hours of his rescue, Harvey was back in Miami, where an official Coast Guard investigation was held on the morning of November 16. Spiffily dressed for the occasion in an expensive new sports jacket, matching slacks, and open-collared shirt, Harvey appeared remarkably chipper for a man who had just lost his bride in a tragic accident. Throughout the interrogation, he remained cool and composed, never deviating from his original story. Though there were some highly dubious details in his account (the lookout in a nearby lighthouse, for example, had seen no sign of a blazing ship, while experienced seamen scoffed at the notion that a broken mast could puncture a deck in the way he described), he parried the most pointed questions with aplomb. In the end, the investigators had no choice but to accept his version of events. There were, after all, no living witnesses to refute it. Or so Julian Harvey believed.

He had just concluded his testimony when—with the kind of improbable timing that would seem hopelessly contrived in a Hollywood thriller—a Coast Guard official burst into the hearing room with the startling news that a survivor had been plucked from the sea.

"Oh, my God," Harvey stammered. It took him a moment to regain his composure. "Why, that's wonderful," he said with a forced smile. Then, without another word, he rose from his chair and hurried from the room.

IT WAS A Greek freighter, the *Captain Theo,* that found her—a little girl perched on a cork life raft, floating alone in the vastness of the ocean. As the ship drew near, one of the crewmen snapped a photo of the remarkable sight. Published in *Life* magazine— which devoted a full ten pages to the story of the "death ship" and the miraculous rescue of its only surviving passenger—the picture briefly made her an international celebrity.

Hoisted aboard, she was carried into a cabin and gently placed in a bunk. That she had been through a desperate ordeal was clear from her condition. Emaciated, dull-eyed, dangerously dehydrated, and severely sunburned, she barely clung to consciousness as the captain plied her with questions. Finally she managed to rasp out a few words before sinking into a coma: the name of her doomed vessel, *Bluebelle*, and her own name, Terry Jo Duperrault.

A telegraph from the captain—"Picked up blonde girl, brown eyes, from a small white raft, suffering exposure and shock"—brought an immediate response from the Coast Guard. She was helicoptered to Miami's Mercy Hospital, where a throng of newsmen awaited the arrival of the "sea waif" (as the press quickly dubbed her).

For a child who had spent four days adrift without food or water after the annihilation of her entire family, she made a remarkable recovery. By Monday, November 20, five days after she was plucked barely alive from the water, she was strong enough to undergo a prolonged interrogation by Coast Guard officials. The story she related was radically

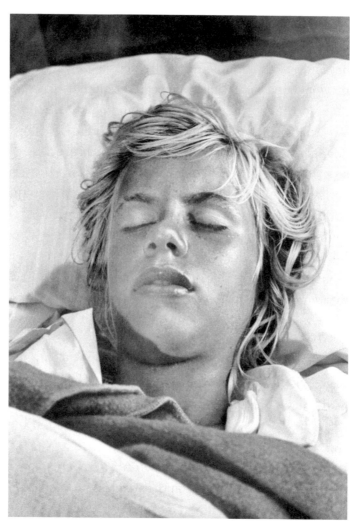

Terry Jo Duperrault lies in a hospital bed after her rescue. (*Photographer: Lynn Pelham/Time & Life Pictures/Getty Images. Used by permission.*)

different from the one they had heard from Julian Harvey.

On the night of the tragedy, Terry Jo explained, she had retired to her bunk at about nine o'clock. Some time later, she was jolted awake by "screaming and stamping." She thought it was her brother's voice, crying to their father for help. Creeping from her quarters, she saw her mother and brother lying motionless on the floor of the central cabin, blood pooling around their heads. Making her way up the companionway stairs to the main deck, she saw more blood near the cockpit. No one was in sight.

Suddenly, Harvey—his face contorted in fury—came rushing out of the darkness. "Get back there!" he roared, shoving her down the stairs. Stupefied with terror, she retreated to her bunk. She could hear water sloshing on the deck "and thought the captain might be washing off the blood."

Gradually she became aware that "oily-smelling" water was rising from the bilges and running into her room. All at once, Harvey—clutching what appeared to be a rifle—appeared in the doorway. For a long, terrifying moment, he looked at her without saying a word, then turned and headed up the stairway, leaving her in the darkness.

The water in her cabin continued to rise until it was lapping the top of her mattress. Realizing that the *Bluebelle* was going down, Terry Jo climbed back to the cockpit. She spotted Harvey and asked him if the ship was sinking. "Yes," he shouted. A moment later, he dove overboard and swam to the dinghy, which had been cast loose.

Abandoned on the foundering ship, Terry Jo suddenly remembered the flimsy raft of cork and canvas webbing, five feet long and thirty inches wide, lashed to the top of the main cabin. Undoing the knots, she managed to scramble onto the little float just as the *Bluebelle* went under. Why it sank she couldn't say. Contrary to what Harvey had claimed, the mast was intact and there was no sign of a fire. The sea, she testified, was calm.

Terry Jo's chilling account confirmed a belief already shared by most observers: that the *Bluebelle* disaster was no accident but—as one Coast Guard official put it—an act of "mass murder by a berserk man." Exactly what had precipitated the atrocity no one could say with certainty. By then, its perpetrator was already dead.

THREE DAYS EARLIER, after learning of Terry Jo's rescue, Julian Harvey had gone directly from the Coast Guard hearing room to the Sandman Hotel on Biscayne Boulevard and checked in under the name John Monroe. Sometime within the next twenty-four hours, he wrote a brief suicide note: "I'm a nervous wreck and just can't continue. I'm going out now. I guess I either don't like life or don't know what to do with it." After appending a final wish for burial at sea, he placed the letter on the center of the desk, pinned ten dollars to his pillow for the maid, and went into the bathroom, where, with a double-edged razor blade, he cut his left thigh down to the bone, daubed his own blood about the walls "like a child finger-painting," then slashed his ankles, wrists, forearms, and throat. So savage were the self-inflicted mutilations that police officers initially "wondered if he had been murdered and a clumsy attempt had been made to make it look like a suicide."

Struggling for an explanation, a few staunch friends insisted that he couldn't face life without his wife, Mary Dene. Virtually every investigator believed, however, that his suicide was prompted by Terry Jo's rescue and his realization that the jig was finally up—that the monstrous self he had concealed beneath his glamorous façade was about to be exposed to the world. That theory gained even more credence when detectives discovered that shortly before the *Bluebelle* set sail, Harvey had taken out a $20,000 insurance policy on Mary Dene's life. Moreover, Harold Pegg, owner of the *Bluebelle*, testified that he had noticed deep scratches on Harvey's right hand and arm when the latter got back to Miami. Harvey claimed that they were "wire cuts." But Pegg knew fingernail scratches when he saw them. He also knew that Mary Dene had exceptionally long fingernails. From all these facts, as *Life* magazine reported, "more than one investigator came to the same conclusion: that Harvey had set out to kill his wife, by sudden impulse or careful plan, had been surprised in the act by one of the Duperraults, and so decided to kill them all."

IN THE LAST week of November 1961, Terry Jo was released from the hospital and flown back home to Green Bay to be raised by relatives. In the misguided belief (typical of a certain repressive, midwestern ethos) that the best way to deal with disturbing emotions is to completely ignore them, her guardians erected a wall of silence around her traumatic experience. The *Bluebelle* tragedy was never mentioned at home, while friends, family members, neighbors, and teachers were instructed to avoid the subject. For Terry Jo (who eventually changed the spelling of her first name to Tere), this enforced denial resulted in years of emotional turmoil and a succession of marital crises. Thanks to her exceptional inner resources, however—the same strength of character that allowed her to survive the ordeal in the first place—she ultimately achieved a stable and fulfilling life.

She reemerged into the public eye in 2010 with the publication of a memoir, *Alone: Orphaned on the Ocean*, co-authored by psychologist Richard Logan. In this book, (which received nationwide media coverage), Terry Jo reveals that in 1999 she agreed to undergo a psychological interview while under the influence of the sedative sodium amytal. Her long-suppressed memories unlocked by this "truth serum," she recalled certain details of that nightmarish night—the pajamas her brother was wearing, for example, and a bloodied knife on the deck beside his body. Nothing she dredged up, however, shed further light on the events that precipitated the slaughter.

Along with Harvey's motivation, another unanswerable question remains, first raised by Erle Stanley Gardner, creator of the famous detective Perry Mason. In a widely syndicated newspaper article, "The Case of the *Bluebelle*'s Last Voyage," Gardner ponders what he calls "the mystery of the decade": "How did little Terry Jo Duperrault live through a murderous rampage? Why hadn't Julian Harvey shot her, bludgeoned her, or pushed her into the water without a life preserver? He had a perfect opportunity to destroy the last bit of evidence of his murderous acts. What stayed the killer's hand as he faced the only living witness to his crime?"

[*Sources:* Richard Logan and Tere Duperrault Fassbender, *Alone: Orphaned on the Ocean* (Green Bay, WI: Title Town Publishing, 2010); "The 'Bluebelle' Mystery," *Life*, December 1, 1961; Erle Stanley Gardner, "The Case of the Bluebelle's Last Voyage," *Sarasota Herald-Tribune*, March 25, 1962; Stuart B. McGiver, *Murder in the Tropics: The Florida Chronicles*, vol., 2 (Sarasota, FL: Pineapple Press, 1995).]

Antone Costa, the "Cape Cod Vampire"

At virtually the same time as Julian Harvey's murderous rampage, a crime occurred in the Boston suburb of Somerville, Massachusetts. However terrifying for the victim, it was a trivial affair compared to the carnage aboard the *Bluebelle,* hardly rating a mention in the local press. Only later did authorities recognize it for what it was: a harbinger of horrors to come, the inaugural crime of a serial killer who remains relatively obscure, despite the enormity of his deeds.

His name was Antone Costa. At around 4:00 a.m. on November 18, 1961, just days after horrific events aboard the *Bluebelle,* the sixteen-year-old Costa snuck into the second-floor apartment of a fourteen-year-old girl named Donna Welch. Awakened by his flashlight, she let out a scream that sent him fleeing. Three days later, Costa waylaid the girl after luring her to his building. Before he could drag her into the basement, several tenants of the building, alerted by her cries, came to her rescue. Convicted of "assault and battery and breaking and entering in the nighttime with intent to commit a felony," Costa was given a one-year suspended sentence with three years probation.

His behavior in the ensuing years was a textbook case of teenage sociopathy. In 1963, just shy of his eighteenth birthday, he married his underage girlfriend and promptly fathered three children. The marriage was a nightmare from the start, thanks largely to Costa's frighteningly erratic behavior, his fondness for drugs, and his predilection for asphyxiating his wife with a plastic bag while having sex with her.

In August 1967—after "accidentally" shooting a female friend with an arrow during a stroll in the woods—he decamped for San Francisco, where he threw himself into the drug- and sex-fueled scene of Haight-Ashbury, the epicenter of hippiedom. During his stay there, he acquired a girlfriend named Barbara Spaulding, who eventually vanished without a trace. On the very day of her disappearance, Costa headed back to Massachusetts.

Residing in Provincetown, on the northernmost tip of Cape Cod, Costa worked in construction when he wasn't tending to his marijuana crop or indulging in his new hobby, amateur taxidermy. Divorced from his wife, he took up with a girlfriend named Susan Perry, who vanished in September 1968, just a few months after the unexplained disappearance of eighteen-year-old Sydney Monzon, another Provincetown girl who had been spending much of her time in the company of Tony Costa.

In January 1969, a pair of twenty-three-year-old friends from Rhode Island, Patricia Walsh and Mary Anna Wysocki—one a teacher, the other a coed—took a weekend trip to Provincetown, where they struck up an acquaintance with Costa. A few days after their arrival, they checked out of their guesthouse and were never seen again.

Alerted by the young women's parents, local police undertook a search. Eventually the decomposed corpses of Walsh and Wysocki, along with those of Susan Perry and Sydney Monzon, were uncovered in a wooded area in the nearby town of Truro. All four had been killed with gunshots, then dismembered. Promptly arrested for the gruesome killings, Costa was transformed into a tabloid sensation—the "Cape Cod Vampire"—after the local DA announced (erroneously) that the victims' hearts had been cut from their bodies and that teeth marks were found on their flesh.

In May 1970 Costa was tried, convicted, and sentenced to life in Walpole prison. Exactly four years later, the twenty-nine-year-old serial killer hanged himself in his cell with his leather belt.

FINAL WORDS

I'M AN INVETERATE COLLECTOR OF QUOTES. FOR YEARS, I'VE FILLED A SERIES OF OLD-fashioned composition books with hundreds of thought-provoking lines, phrases, and entire passages garnered from newspapers, magazines, and books of every category: criminology, psychology, history, biography, poetry, fiction, and so on.

The quotes that grab my interest tend to be of two varieties: those that do a particularly good job of articulating insights I share—of putting my own thoughts into better words than I myself have managed to come up with—and those that light up my brain with new ideas.

Not all (or even most) of the quotes in my notebooks relate to murder, madness, and our deep-rooted attraction to the violent and horrible. But by validating my perceptions, crystallizing my thoughts, and giving me new ways to think about things, the ones that *do* deal with those subjects have had a big impact on my work in the field of true crime.

Here, then, culled from my collection, are a baker's dozen of quotes that, I hope, readers will find as meaningful and stimulating as I have.

"The virtuous man is content to dream what the wicked man really does."
—PLATO (360 B.C.E.)

"What, unknown or neglected by man, walks in the night through the labyrinth of the heart?" —JOHANN WOLFGANG VON GOETHE (1789)

"It is a general phenomenon of our nature that that which is sad, terrible, and even horrendous holds an irresistible attraction for us."
—FRIEDRICH SCHILLER, "On the Tragic in Art" (1792)

"Mr. Walker preached today on the government of the thoughts. Thought I, what thunders mutter in these commonplaces. Suppose he had rolled back the cloud of ceremony and decency and showed us how bad the smooth plausible people we meet everyday in society would be if they durst, nay how we should behave if we acted out our thoughts—not how devils would do, but how good people that hoped to be saved would do if they dared—I think it would shake us. These are the real terrors."
—RALPH WALDO EMERSON (1832)

"Men who have killed their wives, and committed other such everyday matters, have been condemned, executed, and are forgotten—but it takes a deed that has some of the sublime of horror about it to attract attention and set people crazy."
—JAMES GORDON BENNETT (1841)

"Madame Tussaud made the discovery that the effigies of a dead criminal would bring in thousands of shillings, while no one would expend a solitary sixpence to look upon the living image of Innocence herself." —JAMES RUSSELL LOWELL (1850)

"Ourself behind ourself concealed—
Should startle most—
Assassin hid in our Apartment
Be Horror's least."
—EMILY DICKINSON (1863)

"The average church-going Civilizee realizes, one may say, absolutely nothing of the deeper currents of human nature, or of the aboriginal capacity for murderous excitement which lies sleeping in his own bosom. Religion, custom, law and education have been piling their pressure upon him for centuries mainly with the one intent that his homicidal potentialities should be kept under. The result, achieved with infinite difficulty, is the public peace which until recently we have enjoyed, a regimen in which the usual man forgets that in the practical sense there is any bloodthirstiness about him, and deems it an exceptional passion, only to be read in newspapers and romances. . . . But the water-tight compartment in which the carnivore within us is confined is artificial and not organic. It will never be organic. The slightest diminution of external pressure, the slightest loophole of licensed exception, will make the whole system leaky, and murder will again grow rampant." —WILLIAM JAMES (1903)

"I and the public know,
What all schoolchildren learn,
Those to whom evil is done
Do evil in return."
—W. H. AUDEN (1939)

"The crime and punishment ritual is part of our lives . . . We need criminals to identify ourselves with, to envy secretly, and to punish stoutly. They do for us the forbidden, illegal things we wish to do and, like scapegoats of old, they bear the burdens of our displaced guilt and punishment." —KARL MENNINGER (1968)

"People are fascinated by representations of murder because, in the first place, they want to kill someone and, in the second, they won't. Surely one function of narrative is to allow in the imagination what we forbid in the flesh." —GEORGE STADE (1984)

"From at least the time of ancient Greeks, sex, disfigurement, and murder have sold . . . The 1890s are better remembered for Lizzie Borden whacking her parents than for, say, the Free Silver Movement." —*Newsweek*, January 2, 1995.

"We know how to make serial killers. You just take a Type A kid who's fairly bright and just beat the crap out of him day after day." —CORMAC MCCARTHY (2008)

ACKNOWLEDGMENTS

My gratitude to the following for their generous assistance:

Tracey Baker
Galin Colleen Brown
Sarah Burns
Stanley Burns
Damien Charles
Donna Eschenbrenner
Brian Fulton
Miyako Hannan
Anne Hays
Bruce Kirby
Lisa Rivera
Chris Stuart
Angela Troisi
Matthew Turi
Sarah Wilcox
Bob Wilkinson
Wayne Wright

INDEX

ABOUT THE AUTHOR

Harold Schechter is a professor of American literature and culture at Queens College, the City University of New York. He is widely celebrated for both fiction and true-crime writing, including *The Devil's Gentleman, The Tell-Tale Corpse*, and *The Serial Killer Files*. He lives in Brooklyn and Mattituck, Long Island, with his wife, the poet Kimiko Hahn.